I0815846

IN HONOREM PRINCIPIS·APOST PAVLVS·V·BVRGHESIVS·ROMANVS PONT·MAX·AN·MDCXII·PONT·VII

Praise for *American Pontiff*

"Dr. Paul Kengor's deep understanding of both Catholicism and America make him the right scholar to introduce Americans to a deeper understanding of the first American pontiff. As my wife Callista, who served as Ambassador to the Holy See, said, 'Pope Leo XIV is good for the Catholic Church and good for America.' Dr. Kengor has explained why she is right and why all of us should be excited that the conclave picked Pope Leo XIV."

—**HON. NEWT GINGRICH**, former Speaker of the U.S. House of Representatives

"Captures the drama that led to the election of the first American pope. Kengor is at his best in offering a biographical portrait of Leo; it gives us great insight into his thinking. His affection for Pope Leo XIII helps us to appreciate his mature understanding of social justice. This is more than a biography—Kengor knows how to tell a story. It is a story of a man whose holiness and humbleness was evident at a young age. While others sought to elevate themselves to the top, the man from Chicago never sought the limelight. We are fortunate that the world has now discovered him, and we are fortunate that Kengor illuminates his legacy with precision."

—**BILL DONOHUE, PhD**, president and CEO of the Catholic League for Religious and Civil Rights, and publisher of *Catalyst*

"If you have been wondering (like most of the rest of the world) who Robert Prevost—aka, Pope Leo XIV—is, you now have your answer, in a readable, intriguing, and balanced treatment by Dr. Paul Kengor, who himself knows a thing or two about popes and Americans. This book will be a reference point for every Vaticanista for years to come."

—**FATHER ROBERT SIRICO**, President Emeritus of The Acton Institute

"The election of American Robert Prevost as Pope Leo XIV shocked the world and raised many questions. Who is this man who now leads the Catholic Church? Why did the Cardinals choose him? What will be his agenda? How will he differ—or be the same as—his controversial predecessor Pope Francis? In *American Pontiff: Pope Leo XIV and His Plan to Heal the Church*, Dr. Paul Kengor ably addresses these questions and more. Avoiding easy or ideological answers, Kengor frankly accesses the current situation in the church with the eye of an expert historian and experienced church observer. Both Catholics and non-Catholics should care about the future of the Catholic Church, and Kengor helps the reader to better understand Pope Leo XIV and the challenges he faces."

—**ERIC SAMMONS**, editor-in-chief of *CRISIS Magazine* and author of *Holiness for Everyone*

"With his signature blend of intellectual rigor and compelling storytelling, *New York Times* bestselling author Paul Kengor charts the extraordinary ascent of Pope Leo XIV from the streets of Chicago to the seat of St. Peter. Drawing material from cardinals, theologians, and a long list of church insiders, Kengor's meticulous research unveils the drama and discernment behind the conclave that elevated Cardinal Robert Prevost to the papacy. In this compelling narrative, Kengor offers readers not only a glimpse into the making of a pope, but a hopeful vision for the church's future."

—**ANNE HENDERSHOTT, PhD**, director of the Veritas Center at Franciscan University of Steubenville, and author of *The Politics of Envy*

"No one knows politics and religion like Dr. Paul Kengor. This is the first DEFINITIVE biography of our new American Pope and I am sure it will be a bestseller because it is already a blockbuster."

—**CRAIG SHIRLEY**, presidential historian, Ronald Reagan biographer, and author of *UPHEAVAL*

"At a tumultuous period in Roman Catholicism and one in which the church has made an historic move in electing the first American Pope, Paul Kengor's biography of Pope Leo is 'must' reading for both Catholics and non-Catholics. His story of Leo's life and amazing rise from altar boy in Chicago to Supreme Pontiff of 1.4 billion Catholics worldwide offers clear clues on just how the new Pope will deal with issues ranging from his Church's relations with President Trump to the clash between traditional Catholics and those who see Vatican II as the wave of the future."

—**JOHN GIZZI**, NEWSMAX chief political correspondent

AMERICAN PONTIFF

POPE LEO XIV AND HIS PLAN TO HEAL THE CHURCH

PAUL KENGOR, PhD

Humanix Books
American Pontiff: Pope Leo XIV and His Plan to Heal the Church

Humanix Books, P.O. Box 20989, West Palm Beach, FL 33416, USA
www.humanixbooks.com | info@humanixbooks.com

Cover photo: Getty Images/Alessandra Benedetti-Corbis/Contributor
Cover design: Ben Davis

ISBN: 978-163006-331-3 (Hardcover)
ISBN: 978-163006-332-0 (E-book)

Printed in the United States of America
10 9 8 7 6 5 4 3 2 1

Contents

PREFACE

Habemus American

It was May 8, the Year of the Lord 2025. It was approximately 6:00 p.m. in Rome, with the sun beginning to lower on the horizon of the Eternal City, capping a picturesque day. A good day, it seemed, for a pope.

Across the Atlantic, it was roughly 1:00 p.m. Eastern Standard Time in the United States. Moving westward across the plains through the flat farm country of the Midwest—the nation's Heartland—it was nearing noon Central in Chicago, Illinois.

There was an electricity in the air at St. Peter's Square. Call it the Holy Spirit perhaps. And why not? The Holy Spirit had been invoked again and again by cardinal upon cardinal inside the conclave under the great Michelangelo's imposing fresco, *The Final Judgment*. The world anxiously awaited the cardinals' final judgment, their decision on the next leader of the world's largest group of Christians.

It was fair to say they waited patiently. After all, the experts had said that with the large diversity of *papabile* ("pope-able") cardinals this time, there was no consensus pick for pope. Pope Francis had been chosen in five rounds of balloting in 2013, Benedict XVI in four rounds in 2005, and the sainted John Paul II not until the eighth ballot in 1978.

This pope would not be chosen quickly. You could bet on it. Even the Vegas oddsmakers said that.

But now, lo and behold, there was smoke—white smoke bellowing from the Sistine Chapel chimney. This was a big surprise so early in the conclave of cardinal electors. A new pontiff by the mere fourth round of voting? It was expected that this conclave would run longer than usual, multiple ballots, easily pushed to the following week.

Those expectations were suddenly out the Vatican window, up in smoke. The conclave had spoken. The world had a pope. And very few would have predicted the man who had just been chosen.

In the world of cellphones, social media, and instantaneous technology, word spread out as quickly as the smoke. Citizens of Rome and tourists alike dashed for the ancient *piazza* where St. Peter himself—the first pope—had been scourged two millennia earlier. They were eager to learn who had been selected as the new heir to the Chair of St. Peter, the 267th pontiff of the Roman Catholic Church. Enthusiasm and excitement ran wild, as did the guesses.

Who had been chosen? Which cardinal? Who was he?

The odds-on favorites had been cardinals Pietro Parolin from Italy and Luis Antonio Tagle from the Philippines. Or was it Pierbattista Pizzaballa from Italy? Peter Erdő from Hungary? Robert Sarah from Africa? The only thing that everyone was certain about was this: whoever was picked certainly would not be an American. Not a chance.

An American pontiff? Preposterous. Not in the lifetimes of anybody watching. No way.

Approximately an hour after the white smoke appeared, the crowd erupted as the doors and curtain of St. Peter's Balcony finally drew open. As video footage attests, it is not an exaggeration to say that the shining sun had perched itself perfectly above the spot where the pope was about to be announced, seemingly beaming its approval, radiating warmth upon the multitude below, who audibly awed at the sight. The weather seemed tailor made. It was as if the Heavens approved.

Then came forth the official protodeacon, Cardinal Dominique Mamberti. He grabbed the microphone. The throng quieted, only to roar when Mamberti enthusiastically declared: "*Annuntio vobis gaudium magnum: HABEMUS PAPAM.*" Translation: "I announce to you a great joy: WE HAVE A POPE." Cardinal Mamberti let the crowd cheer and then settle as he announced the new pope with these words in Latin:

> *Eminentissimum ac reverendissimum Dominum Robertum Franciscum Sanctae Romane Ecclesiae Cardinalem Prevost qui sibi nomen imposuit Leonem Decimum Quartum.*

In English:

> The Most Eminent and Most Reverend Lord Robert Francis Cardinal of the Holy Roman Church Prevost who has taken the name Leo XIV.[1]

With that, there was a sudden hush in the stunned, confused crowd. This was not a name they knew. The raucous assemblage quieted as the faithful paused to try to figure out who Cardinal Mamberti had just named. They looked at their phones for information being rapidly posted. Who was this man?

He was 69-year-old Robert Francis Prevost, an American, a self-described "son of Augustine," more recently of Rome and Peru, but also a native of the Midwest, born in Chicago, and son of the late Mildred Agnes and Louis Marius Prevost of Dolton, Illinois.

Those were facts to be learned later. For now, the red curtain at last opened and the new Holy Father strode forth, as the gathering began to loudly cheer once again. The sense of mystery that at first led to bewilderment now seemed to fuel more excitement. What would this stranger say? Approximately an hour after the smoke had arisen, the next pontiff stepped out onto the Loggia, the central balcony on the facade of St. Peter's Basilica. He was quiet and did not say anything for a few moments, letting the moment sink in for himself and for all.[2]

The new pope's countenance betrayed a sense of surprise but also strength. He waited to speak, like he was absorbing the moment, taking it all in, trying to process it with humility, restraining his emotions, all the while knowing that he needed to show confidence. He was now officially the chief shepherd of a gigantic flock. He needed to be strong—*forza*, as the Italians put it. For that, he prayed, raising his hands and folding them prayerfully under his chin. He was slightly misty-eyed, a lump in the throat. He swallowed.

In that pensive moment of prayer, Robert Francis Prevost—now Leo XIV—composed himself to speak. He had prepared remarks, which he pulled out to read, though the first line he certainly knew from heart, saying in Italian: "*La pace sia con tutti voi!*" Translation: "Peace be with all of you!"

The mass gathering loudly cheered its approval. This was a good greeting. These were encouraging first words.

Lest there be any doubts, the new pope proceeded to explain the Scriptural meaning of those words. He followed: "Dear brothers and sisters, these are the first words spoken by the risen Christ, the Good Shepherd who laid down his life for God's flock. I would like this greeting of peace to resound in your hearts, in your families, among all people, wherever they may be, in every nation and throughout the world. Peace be with you!"[3]

As Jesus Christ had done with the disciples, Leo XIV twice repeated the greeting to the faithful, "Peace be with you." Overall, his opening statement, spoken mostly in Italian but also Latin and some Spanish, resounded the word "peace" no less than 10 times.

It was a word that would reign throughout the start of Leo XIV's pontificate, as would his repeated call for "unity" in a Church that under the previous pope had been racked and torn by chaos and confusion and disunity. Pope Francis had committed himself to (in his words) "make a mess of things." So many of the cardinals had hungered and ached for a pope who would clean up the mess and bring back unity, peace.

Now, a new pope pledged just that. His name was Robert Francis Prevost.

Habemus papam. We had a pope. The world had a pope. An American pope. *Habemus* American. Pope Leo XIV: the first American pontiff.

How he arrived at that moment at the Loggia overlooking St. Peter's Square on May 8, 2025, is quite the story. And where he and his Church go from here could be quite the journey.

ONE

Where Peter Is

There is no history like the history of the papacy. What happened in Rome on May 8, 2025, has extraordinary roots dating back to the first century *Anno Domini*. It is a history that has rarely been easy for the faithful. It has been a history of 2,000-plus years of trials and travails.

The Christian flock has always been tested and suffered for the faith, as did Christ himself. As did the first pope.

"YOU ARE PETER"

In the dark of the night on July 18 in the year 64 AD, a hellacious fire broke out in the world's most powerful city, ultimately known as the Eternal City.

The blaze started in the merchant shops around Rome's packed, boisterous Circus Maximus, a massive public entertainment complex near where the Colosseum stands today. The conflagration raged for over a week, destroying much of the great city that was the home of the planet's mightiest empire. Romans were horrified by the destruction and at who would be blamed.

The emperor was none other than Nero, one of history's worst scoundrels. He was only in his late twenties, having assumed the throne in 54 AD at age 17. He was a debauched, perverse, and all-around terrible human being, so rotten that he even had his own mother murdered. Nero's life was one of death, death, and death. Fittingly, he responded to the fire's mass casualties with a prescription of still more death. What he created was not what a later great pope, John Paul II, would have dubbed a "culture of life."

Some believed that Nero himself had a hand in the fire, which perhaps he had initiated to clear the ground for a coveted palace of gold that he characteristically planned for himself. He relished a typically decadent structure adorned by lakes and statues, including a 120-foot-tall statue of his person. To deflect accusations that he was responsible for the fire, Nero seized the moment to blame the catastrophe on his despised group of enemies: Christians. It was said that Nero had fiddled while Rome burned, but he did not fiddle around when his sights were set on Christians. He now focused keenly on persecuting them.

The historian Tacitus records that "an immense multitude" of Christians were subsequently rounded up. They were treated brutally, not just executed but also humiliated. "Covered with the skins of beasts," wrote Tacitus, "they were torn by dogs and perished, or nailed to crosses, or were doomed to the flames and burnt, to serve as a nightly illumination, when daylight had expired."[1] Flaming bodies were converted into human torches that pierced the night sky.

Among the Christians that Nero fingered for blame was an aging Galilean fisherman who had become the leader of Christ's people: Peter. It was Simon Peter who Christ had identified as the rock for building His church. "You are Peter," proclaimed Christ, "and on this rock I will build my church, and the gates of Hell will not prevail against it." (Matthew 16:18)

To the early Christians, Peter was the head of their Church. To Christians ever since, into the time of Martin Luther and his Reformation and to Catholics and non-Catholics still today, this made Peter the first pope—the first in a long line of 267 pontiffs stretching from the first century AD to our current day.

The first pope was about to become a martyr, like the Church's founder Himself.

Christ had signaled as much. He had told his apostles and disciples and followers of all stripes that if they truly wanted to follow Him, they needed to pick up their cross and carry it. Suffering would be part of the Christian life. He told them they would be persecuted because of Him.

As for Peter specifically, Jesus had forewarned him after the Resurrection: "Very truly I tell you, when you were younger you dressed yourself and went where you wanted; but when you are old you will stretch out your hands, and someone else will dress you and lead you where you do not want to go." According to John's Gospel (21:15–19), "Jesus said this to indicate the kind of death by which Peter would glorify God. And when He had said this, He said to him, 'Follow me.'"

Nero ensured just that in Peter's case. There are dramatic accounts of what followed, some more reliable than others.

One apocryphal account from the Christian tradition, namely, the *Acts of Peter*, states that a frightened Peter was fleeing persecution from Rome and encountered Christ Himself during a vision as he was traveling along the Appian Way. The astonished Peter asked Jesus, "Domine, quo vadis?" which translates to "Lord, where are you going?" Christ replied that He was going to Rome to be crucified for a second time—the assumption being that Peter was failing in his duty to carry his cross. Christ wanted Peter to understand that his fleeing from Nero represented a cowardly failure of his Christian duty. He should go back to Rome and stretch out his hands and be willing to go where he did not want to go.[2]

Again, that specific report is considered apocryphal, though we do know for certain that Nero had a special hatred for Peter and his Christian brothers and sisters. He had a special plan for Peter's execution.

Like Christ, Peter was flogged and scourged. Though historians do not know every detail of his final days and hours, he very likely would have carried upon his shoulders the crossbeam to which he would be nailed. Wearing a loin cloth, spectators would have been able to see the torn, bleeding flesh on his bare back, ripped up by the multi-tailed whip embedded with metal or jagged bits of bone specially designed to tear up the victim's flesh.[3] Badly beaten, he was then led to a site across the Tiber River known as Vatican Hill.

It was there that Peter was crucified, like Christ but also distinctly unlike Christ in one very visible way: it is said that Peter asked his executioners to crucify him upside down, as he deemed himself unworthy to die in the same manner as his Lord and Savior.[4]

That was how and where Peter perished. He had followed Jesus to the cross. He picked up his cross and carried it, unto death.

Early Church father Tertullian (160–240 AD) had said that "the blood of the martyrs is the seed of the Church." Christ had thrice told Peter to "feed my sheep" just before informing him of the kind of death he would experience with hands stretched out. Now, the sheep hastened to tend to their fallen shepherd, the first bishop of Rome.

Mourning Christians rushed to Peter's corpse and buried it, awaiting better days with an emperor more kind to them and their cause (namely, Constantine in the early fourth century).

Peter's body is still in Rome to this day. The first pope physically remains in Rome, as have the hundreds who have followed in his footsteps.

"WHO GOD MEANT YOU TO BE"

Thus resides the so-called Chair of St. Peter. Rome was where the pope needed to be. He was not to leave nor flee, even under threat of persecution and martyrdom. And yet, staying in Rome has not always been an easy charge for the occupant of the chair.

To that end, picture two scenes, two dates, many centuries later. One of them in the year 1377 and the other nearly six centuries after that, in 1939. Both were periods of tumult for the world and for the long, majestic history of the papacy.

The first involves a diminutive but formidable Italian woman named Catherine of Siena, destined to become a saint and one of the few female doctors of the Roman Catholic Church.

Born in the venerable medieval city of Siena on March 25, 1347, Caterina Benincasa was the 24th child of Lapa and her husband, Giacomo. From early on, she possessed wisdom and holiness well beyond her years. At roughly age 16, Catherine joined a group of penitent Third Order Dominican laywomen who called themselves the *Mantellate*, which translates into "cloak" or "cape." The word refers to their distinctive form of dress: a black mantle or cape over a white habit.

Catherine engaged in severe acts of penance and mortification on behalf of her suffering mother Church, the *Chiesa* of her beloved Jesus, the bride of Christ. Like Jesus, she would live to only age 33, succumbing perhaps in part to the constant deprivation she put her body through as a "living sacrifice" (in the words of St. Paul) for sinners.[5]

Catherine's striking spiritual works and displays of piety were witnessed by thousands. Like Saint Francis two centuries earlier, no one doubted her authenticity. Here was a girl who walked the walk. So much so that she soon had the attention of popes. The clergy of her era, as well as laypeople, believed Caterina Benincasa when she said that God the Father was speaking to her (words ultimately transcribed into her most famous written work, *The Dialogue*). Priests and bishops believed her. Cardinals believed her.

The pope believed her.

At that time, the pope was located outside of Rome. Catherine was born into a Church where the papacy was in exile in Avignon, France, from 1309–77.[6] No fewer than seven successive popes reigned from France in those decades, a period that some described as the "Babylonian captivity of the papacy." According to Catherine, God did not like this. She said she was told by Him to tell the popes to move their cowardly carcasses back to Rome.

That was not what the popes wanted to hear. Rome had become a dangerous place for them. In Avignon, they were safe and comfortable, fat and happy.

But of course, the heirs to the Chair of St. Peter were never called to be comfortable. They were always to be ready for martyrdom, to give up their lives, to suffer, as did Jesus and Peter. Catherine reminded them of this, urging them to grow a spine, have some backbone, to man up—to go back to Rome. This tough little *ragazza* put the fear of God into them, truly. To not do what God called of them and the papacy was a sin unbefitting an heir to the Chair of St. Peter.

"Most Holy Father," Catherine urged one pope of her day, "it is time to detest sin in yourself, in your subjects, and in the ministers of holy Church."[7]

Ultimately, one of these popes, Gregory XI, listened to the repeated impassioned pleas of the young woman from Siena, though still with fear for his safety. She told him to man up, literally: "I beg of you, on behalf of Christ crucified, that you be not a timorous child but manly," admonished Catherine in one of her many letters to the pontiff. "Open your mouth and swallow down the bitter for the sweet." She pushed: "I have prayed, and shall pray, sweet and good Jesus that He free you from all servile fear, and that holy fear alone remain. May ardor of charity be in you, in such ways as shall prevent you from hearing the voice of incarnate demons, and heeding the counsel of perverse counselors, settled in self-love, who, as I understand, want to alarm you, so as to prevent your return, saying, 'You will die.' Up, father, like a man! For I tell you that you have no need to fear."[8]

Gregory was the seventh of the Avignon popes. In the seventh year of his papacy, in January 1377, he returned the papal court to Rome after 70 years in Avignon. He moved his court back to the Eternal City. The papacy was back in Rome, with Peter, where it belonged.

And just to show the pope that she was unafraid, St. Catherine moved there as well, and died there, on April 29, 1380. Like her Savior at age 33, she succumbed after a period of intense suffering, which she offered up for the world's sins. Her message to the popes and the world was fearless: "Be who God meant you to be and you will set the world on fire."

PETER IS WITHIN

Fast-forward nearly six centuries to the year 1939. The pope has long since been back in Rome, thanks in no small part to Catherine of Siena. In fact, this pope, Pius XII, would show his and the Church's gratitude by declaring Catherine the co-patron of Italy (along with another legendary mystic, Saint Francis of Assisi).

It is the first year of a 19-year-long papacy for Pius XII (1939–58), and it could not be a more challenging one, with the eruption of World War II. In the course of world history, few years have been as infamous as 1939, the year that history's deadliest war broke out. But amid it all, buried beneath the rubble, lay signs of hope.

One day in 1939, during a routine excavation while reconstructing the grottoes below St. Peter's Basilica at the Vatican, a workman's shovel struck not the expected clang of rock or thud of dirt but open air. The excavator had come upon something thoroughly unexpected. What was underneath? As he and fellow workmen peered through the small hole they made in the roof of the mausoleum, they looked with intense curiosity at the prospects of what might lie below. They informed the pope, and Pius XII secretly authorized an investigation. He intuitively suspected what it might hold. The Holy Father and the excavators considered a tantalizing possibility: Were they approaching the bones of St. Peter himself?

Could it be? Could this be the literal Peter of St. Peter's Basilica? "What lay beneath?" asked historian Thomas Craughwell in recounting their thinking in his gripping book, *St. Peter's Bones*. "The answer and the adventure await."[9]

Of course, what made St. Peter's Basilica so special is that it is actually the basilica of St. Peter himself, built above him. Think about how profoundly and utterly unique that is: For every church in the world named after St. Peter, including those in Pope Leo XIV's home country, those parish buildings are merely that, namely, they are named after St. Peter. But at the Vatican, the possessive in *St. Peter's* Basilica is distinctively accurate. That particular church is built over the bones of St. Peter. It is Peter's church.

Recall that Jesus Christ had said to his apostle: "You are Peter, and on this rock I will build my church, and the gates of Hell will not prevail against it." Catholics have taken that literally as well as figuratively, with Peter being physical as well as spiritual. Although Jesus Christ never got to Rome in His earthly trek, Peter did. Another such tangible reminder is the obelisk that to this day stands in the middle of St. Peter's Square; it was the pillar at which Peter was scourged two thousand years ago.

Vatican officials long accepted the traditional belief that the incredible, ornate basilica that exists there today was erected over Peter's corpse. The central altar in the basilica today, where popes such as Francis—266th heir to the Chair of St. Peter—have presided, is situated above those bones. Visitors can descend the steps to the left of the altar and venture into the crypt and view the encasement (behind a glass wall) that contains the actual bones. Many onlookers stand in awe at what rests before them. And yet, those bones were rediscovered only recently, nearly 1,900 years later, by excavators under the cautious, watchful eye of Pope Pius XII.

"With the permission of Pope Pius XII," wrote Thomas Craughwell, "a team of archaeologists began a full-scale dig that eventually led them to a modest little mausoleum beneath the high altar. Considering the splendid mausolea they had found, there was nothing remarkable about his little tomb, except for a Greek inscription scratched on one of its walls." That inscription read: "PETR ENI," or "PETER IS WITHIN."[10]

The excavators were ecstatic. One of the archaeologists, who was also a priest, first touched a bone—gripping a bone about five inches long. Shining his flashlight further within, he spied other bones inside. They were human remains. He squeezed himself backward out of the hole and breathlessly informed his colleagues. One of the archaeologists quickly ran to inform the pope, who was thrilled by the news, but also had to exercise the utmost caution given that Hitler's Nazi troops were at the gates.[11]

It was an exciting discovery. Sure, it was long assumed that the bones were there. History and tradition had said so. But Peter's bones were laid to rest so very long ago. No, there was no reason to think they would be anywhere else, given the care with which they had been overseen by the early Christians of the first century, by emperors like Constantine in 325 AD, and by popes and Vatican officials ever since. But still, to dig below the altar and sift through the dirt and work through ancient walls to at last find those bones was extraordinary.

Peter was there, and he still is today, in spirit and in bones—and in the ongoing spirit and bones of the heirs of St. Peter: the popes.

These dramatic incidents in the life of the papacy, from Peter the fisherman and Nero the emperor to St. Catherine of Siena and Pope Gregory XI, and then onward through Pope Pius XII and the rediscovered bones of St. Peter, say much about the remarkable life, continuity, and majesty of the papacy. No matter what has been thrown at the figure of the pope since the first century, the gates of Hell have not managed to destroy the Roman Catholic Church instituted by Jesus Christ when He told Peter that he was the rock upon which Christ would build His one, holy, catholic and apostolic Church.

There is a famous anecdote in which the egotistical little dictator Napoleon Bonaparte (1769–1821) confronted the pope with a threat to destroy the Church, to which the reigning Pius VII (1742–1823) responded, "Oh my little man, you think you're going to succeed in accomplishing what centuries of priests and bishops have tried and failed to do?"[12]

Napoleon conquered much of Europe, as did Adolf Hitler, but neither man could take down the Holy See. At one point, the pope went so far as to excommunicate Napoleon, who in turn arrested the pope. The pope of Hitler's day, Pius XII, knew he faced a man consumed by evil and dedicated to the devil's work. Pius took part in at least three active plots to take out Hitler.[13] The Nazis, in turn, plotted to kidnap the pontiff.[14] But a stoic Pius was undeterred. He would not leave Rome, even if the Nazi beast was at the gates and licking its chops.

"This is where Christ told Peter the Church should be built," Pius XII affirmed defiantly. "And here is where the Pope will remain."[15]

When the Nazis of the era were not plotting against Pius XII, Joseph Stalin and the Soviets were.[16] As militant Marxist atheists, the Soviets detested the papacy. It was enemy number 1. So much so that on May 13, 1981, communists from Bulgaria working for

Moscow tried to assassinate Pope John Paul II in St. Peter's Square, right by that ancient obelisk where Peter was scourged, and they very nearly succeeded.[17]

From Napoleon to Hitler to various Soviet despots, these men were menaces, enormously destructive to their worlds and their times, but the jaws of Hell would not prevail against the Roman Catholic Church then or in the 2,000 years since it was instituted.

The fact that that Church remains standing, despite so many bad priests and bishops and—yes—even some bad popes, has long suggested to many observers, Catholic and non-Catholic, that maybe this Roman Catholic Church indeed was established by a divine hand with divine protection. Think of all the other institutions that have come and gone over the centuries and millennia, from countries to empires, including the vast Roman Empire itself. Martin Luther led a Reformation over 500 years ago that inadvertently succeeded in launching countless thousands of splinter churches and denominations and even non-denominational independent churches that today constitute their own denominations in and of themselves, with every pastor of such church serving as a one-man sort of College of Cardinals/Magisterium/pope himself. So many a small-*c* "church" have come and gone, but the Roman Catholic Church built on Peter somehow remains.

Even the worst bishops, cardinals, and popes—and a horrific, downright diabolical sexual-abuse scandal involving priests in the 20th century (particularly in Pope Leo XIV's home country)—have not managed to destroy the papacy. And yes, for those Catholics concerned about the tumult, chaos, and confusion in the Church under the most recent former pope from 2013–25—Pope Francis—it has still managed to survive.

TWO

"I Want a Mess": The Francis Papacy

On the night of March 13, 2013, 30 days after lightning twice struck the Vatican after Pope Benedict XVI stunned the world by announcing that he was resigning as pope,[1] Cardinal Jorge Mario Bergoglio stepped onto the Loggia of St. Peter's Balcony. The Argentinian Jesuit was announced as the new pontiff of the Roman Catholic Church, calling himself Pope Francis. Very few people knew who he was. When his death was announced to the world the morning of April 21, 2025, very few people still knew who he was. That is, who he *really* was.

Perhaps one of the most revealing testimonies came from Pope Francis's most high level, vocal, and harshest critic, a man controversial to Francis fans and foes alike: Archbishop Carlo Maria Vigano. Vigano's litany of charges against Francis, before and after the pontiff excommunicated the archbishop, were nothing short of astonishing. The formal apostolic nuncio to America from 2011–16 dubbed Francis everything from a heretic to an apostate, a "false prophet," and charged him with serving Satan.[2] Vigano went so far as to publicly declare that Francis was an illegitimate pope, placing the title "Pope" in quotes when referring to him.

Thus, perhaps it was equally astonishing that when Vigano gave his first assessment of Francis shortly after the pontiff's death, he said this: "No one ever knew what was going through his head, or whether what he said corresponded to what he really thought."[3]

To be sure, Vigano in that statement accused Francis of the usual bad behaviors he directed at the pontiff: duplicity, deception, corruption, not having any moral scruples, and "raging with unheard of malice" at his opponents, some of whom (many agree) the pope indeed seemed to view as enemies to be punished.[4] Those words from Vigano were expected toward Francis, though less expected was his acknowledgment that no one ever really seemed to know what was truly going on in Francis's head or what he really thought. That assessment from Vigano was less a statement of charity than clarity.

Personally, I can relate. And here I will use first-person references because my own experience illustrates the confusion and frustration, which I hope will lead readers to trust me more as I proceed to be critical of Francis in the pages ahead. As a Francis watcher and public defender for most of his papacy, earning the label "popesplainer," a term effectively nonexistent until the Francis papacy, I found myself countless times trying to figure out how much of what Francis did was his own volition or the doing of others around him pushing his buttons or tugging his strings or nudging him. The American conservative Catholic pundit Michael Knowles would often say of Francis that "personnel is policy," an axiom accurately applied to American presidents. In other words, the personnel that the chief executive surrounds himself with shapes his policies. That seemed especially true for this particular pope.

Across the spectrum, Francis's statements and actions often left observers confounded. Whether critics or advocates, from the right or left or in between, from social justice warriors to rad-trads, from those wanting same-sex "marriage" and female priests to SSPXers and Sedevacantists, from the most left-wing German cardinal to the most conservative African bishop, from Fr. James Martin fans to TLM proponents that Francis suppressed, pretty much everyone after 12 years of the Francis papacy came away unsatisfied and unclear about what the man really wanted and where he desired to take the Church on so many fundamental matters.

Did any of these individuals or factions, including progressives who often wanted to claim Francis, really get what they wanted?

Even liberals, secular or religious, could not have been happy with what they ultimately got—or did not get. Did Francis give them same-sex "marriage" and women priests and deacons? No. He dashed the hopes that they felt he had given them. Though he thrilled them with the statement, "Who am I to judge?" regarding homosexuals, which when unpacked probably never meant what they projected it to mean, he also flung derogatory slurs, more than once using antiquated invectives like "faggotry" and several times demanding of homosexuals: "Keep them out of the seminaries!" In one instance in June 2024, Francis told priests at the Salesian Pontifical University in Rome: "*In Vaticano c'è aria di frociaggine.*" Translation: "In the Vatican, there is an air of faggotry." Francis cautioned that gay men can be "good boys," but yet again insisted that they must be banished from seminaries.[5]

Personally, in March 2019, the halfway mark of his papacy, I wrote an extraordinarily lengthy piece for *Crisis Magazine* chronicling such Francis remarks. It required an editor's note justifying the unusual length. Titled, "The Politically Incorrect Francis—14 Shocking Statements," it laid out over a dozen categories of Francis statements on everything from same-sex "marriage" and parenting to transgenderism and even what Francis dubbed "adolescent progressivism."[6] Those Francis views should have infuriated liberals and thrilled conservatives.[7]

Here are merely a few examples:

Francis denounced gender theory as equivalent to "the educational policies of Hitler."[8] And to the work of Lucifer. "Gender ideology is demonic!" he thundered in the summer of 2015. In the fall of 2017, he remonstrated: "Behind all this we find gender ideology.

In books, kids learn that it's possible to change one's sex. Could gender, to be a woman or to be a man, be an option and not a fact of nature? This leads to . . . error."[9]

Francis consistently torched gender ideology and transgenderism in the harshest terms.[10]

As for homosexuality, Francis ordered Italian bishops in May 2018 to ensure that no gay men walk through the door of a seminary: "If there's a doubt about homosexuality, it's better not to have them enter the seminary. If you think that the guy is homosexual, don't put him in the seminary."[11] Francis actually said this repeatedly.[12] Despite perceptions to the contrary, he was very critical of homosexuality, a reality somehow unknown or forgotten or oddly forgiven by liberals because of his mere one statement about not wanting to "judge" homosexuals.[13]

As for homosexuals marrying one another, Francis firmly rejected the idea. On October 25, 2014, before an audience of 7,500 at Pope Paul VI Hall, Francis snapped: "What they are proposing is not marriage, it is an association, but it is not marriage! It is necessary to say things very clearly and we must say this!"

He had long blasted the ideas of same-sex couples marrying and parenting. When he was a cardinal in Argentina, Jorge Mario Bergoglio declared same-sex "marriage" a diabolical effort of "the Father of Lies" to "destroy God's plan . . . and deceive the children of God." He said that such marital arrangements target "the lives of many children who will be discriminated against in advance, and deprived of their human development given by a father and a mother and willed by God. At stake is the total rejection of God's law engraved in our hearts."[14]

As for abortion, in June 2018 Francis horrified his liberal "pro-choice" admirers when he equated abortion with Nazi eugenics and "doctors" who do abortions to Nazis with "white gloves." What Francis said was widely reported in the mainstream media: CNN,

Fox News, *USA Today*, the *Wall Street Journal*, the *Los Angeles Times*, the Associated Press, *Newsweek*.[15] "It pains me to say this," said Francis. "In the last century the entire world was scandalized over what the Nazis were doing to maintain the purity of the race. Today we do the same thing, but with white gloves." Pro-choicers winced each time their perceived "progressive" pope on numerous occasions compared a woman getting an abortion to "hiring a hitman!"

I laid out numerous remarks like these from Francis in my widely read March 2019 *Crisis Magazine* article. Even as I did so, I conceded the chaos and confusion between some of his words and actions, especially in appointing the most progressive bishops, cardinals, and Vatican officials. I concluded that article by asking of such Francis statements: "What are we to make of this? As for traditional Catholics who don't like Francis, what do you do with this? As for liberals who love Francis, surely you're asking the same question for different reasons. . . . What does this say about Francis and the mess going on around him?" I further added in that March 2019 piece: "These past six years of his papacy have constituted a period of great turmoil . . . and it seems to be only getting worse."

I finished with this: "This has been an unsettling, challenging time. Five more years of Benedict XVI would have been preferable at least to spare us the vast confusion under Francis. Above all, it's difficult to trust Pope Francis right now, whether this is his fault or not, and if his fault, then whether fully or not."

And that turned out to be only the halfway point of Francis's reign. Things would get far more confusing for everyone, whether Francis's fans or foes.

Personally, my public defenses of the man would soon end, especially by the early 2020s and the COVID period when Francis outrageously, unconscionably undermined the moral objections of Catholics who pleaded not to be forced to take experimental COVID "vaccines" for religious or medical reasons, and he did so against the established guidelines published by his own Vatican.[16] Overall, so many things unfolded and unraveled under Francis that I did not know how to interpret, react to, or assimilate much of what was happening. No one did. The Francis papacy became inexplicable, baffling. As someone who had been a Francis "pope-splainer," defending him countless times in articles, public lectures, on podcasts, TV, radio, and every format when asked to comment on his latest bewildering action, I became overwhelmed and exhausted and just stopped.

So many felt that way.

Surely liberals must have felt badly misled, teased, duped. They placed great hopes in the various Francis synods, but in the end, no doctrine was changed whatsoever. Zilch. Everything seemed to be questioned, but nothing seemed to be changed.

As for Church traditionalists, they certainly felt no more satisfied. Every synod and unnerving Francis statement from 2013–25 gave them the sweats, put them on the rack, and at times nearly drove them barking mad.

By 2025, many if not all sides were fed up with the decade-plus reign of chaos and confusion. Or to borrow from a Francis phrase that became infamous: the "mess of things."

"MAKE A MESS OF THINGS"

Let us go back to 2013, the start of the papacy of Jorge Mario Bergoglio. In retrospect, a dubious slogan for the Francis papacy was bequeathed that first year by the man himself.

In July 2013, the opening months of his papacy, Francis urged a group of young Catholics to "make a mess of things." He had said that with a smile to a group of Argentine pilgrims going to World Youth Day in Rio de Janeiro: "I want to tell you something," said

Francis with an impish grin. "What is it that I expect as a consequence of World Youth Day? I want a mess. We knew that in Rio there would be great disorder, but I want trouble in the dioceses!"[17]

Francis spoke off the cuff, which was always an unsettling practice that held the potential to be a dangerous prospect each time it occurred during his pontificate. He proceeded to partly explain what he meant by saying that he wanted to "get rid of clericalism, the mundane, this closing ourselves off within ourselves, in our parishes, schools or structures. Because these need to get out!"

Whatever he meant by it, the phrase turned out to be mordantly prophetic. Still more revealing, it was hardly the only time that Francis would prescribe this.[18] Each time he did, the mess he was making was getting worse. Surely he noticed the turmoil.

Indeed, when Francis midway through his pontificate in a 2019 Christmas Eve message at midnight Mass stated that God loves even those who make "a complete mess of things," one had to wonder if the pope was offering a public self-confession.[19]

But alas, such speculation would have been wrong, given that Francis continued to push for a mess and averred that God Himself wanted a mess.

As late as September 2024, while he was still traveling and before he got sick and went into the hospital and was sidelined for much of the remainder of his papacy, the pontiff implored yet another group to "make a mess." Speaking that September 11 in East Timor, Francis urged another group of Catholic young people to "wreak havoc, make a mess." His parting advice to them was to "never forget" to "wreak havoc" for God.[20]

A metaphor for his papacy.

Francis may have shared this odd advice with a chuckle, and yet again without clarity to a bemused world wondering what he intended, but a decade into his papacy, few were amused. This wasn't funny.

The chaos was so bad that arguably the single best summation of the papacy had been offered by embattled Australian Cardinal George Pell in a memo published just after his death in January 2023. "[T]his pontificate is a disaster in many or most respects," said Pell, "a catastrophe." Pell called it a "toxic nightmare."[21]

Pell in that memo had effectively forecast what the vast majority of cardinal electors two years later would be seeking in Francis's successor in the Chair of St. Peter: "The first tasks of the new pope will be to restore normality, restore doctrinal clarity in faith and morals, restore a proper respect for the law and ensure that the first criterion for the nomination of bishops is acceptance of the apostolic tradition."

The discontent sown by the Francis papacy underscored precisely what a papacy should never be. The entire world looks to the Bishop of Rome for normality, clarity, stability.

For many people, their frustration over the Francis chaos eventually turned to anger and then ultimately—and sadly—to indifference. Near the end of the Francis papacy, many of the faithful had become almost dead to whatever the pope was saying, whether (seemingly) good or bad.

WHAT CONSERVATIVES DIDN'T LIKE

What has been presented in this chapter thus far seem like things that conservative Catholics would have liked about Francis, and thus overall might have been pleased with his papacy. But of course, that was not the case. There was much more they disliked, that seemed to contradict his words, that often downright mystified in their incongruity, and that overall frustrated them terribly.

Detailing all such matters would require a separate book on Pope Francis alone. We will see plenty of examples in the pages ahead. For now, what follows are three items of significance worth underscoring as this narrative on Francis's successor moves ahead. They will surface throughout the book and very much affected the selection of the next pope as well as heralded his future challenges.

FRANCIS AND COMMUNIST CHINA

The worst foreign-policy fiasco of Francis's tenure was his scandalous agreement with communist China, even as he made noble, laudable overtures in other parts of the world, such as trying to mediate peace with Russia amid Vladimir Putin's war on Ukraine. This chapter cannot do full justice to what transpired in China under Francis. The whole mess began erupting in early 2018. Much could be said about that catastrophe, but one source to highlight for the outrage was Bishop Marcelo Sanchez Sorondo, Francis's man for Beijing, and one of many disastrous Francis appointments throughout his papacy.[22]

Astonishingly, Francis had appointed his fellow Argentinian as chancellor of the Pontifical Academy of Sciences and the Pontifical Academy of Social Sciences, a position beyond Sorondo's credentials and depth. Sorondo proceeded to make that clear when he made an astounding statement about communist China, a notoriously abusive nation responsible for more deaths than any other country in world over the past 100 years (at least 70 million deaths under Mao Zedong and countless tens to hundreds of millions more from the one-child, forced-abortion policy). In a breathtaking statement, Sorondo gushed that communist China is the planet's one nation to "best realize the social doctrine of the Church."[23]

Yes, Sorondo really did say that.

In an interview with *Vatican Insider*, Francis's right-hand man on China explained that he had recently visited the communist nation, where he found that "they [the Chinese] seek the common good, subordinate things to the general good." And although no country in history had killed as many children in the womb as China, forcing countless millions of women to have abortions against their will and be forcibly sterilized, Sorondo insisted that the People's Republic of China "has defended the dignity of the human person." Perhaps like Pope Francis, he was most impressed with China in the area of climate change, where Sorondo insisted that the dictatorship was "assuming a moral leadership that others have abandoned."[24]

Human-rights advocates worldwide, from the left to the right, were speechless at such stunning statements and the overall Beijing actions and agreement by Francis's Holy See. They had repeatedly begged the pontiff and his team for explanations and mere undisclosed details regarding their scandalous China policy and for a desperate course correction. But much like the original "dubia" bishops who submitted questions to Francis following one of his first encyclicals, they never got answers, despite Francis's constant claims of being a pope of "dialogue."[25]

We will see more on this issue in the pages ahead, including how it very likely sandbagged the papal candidacy of Vatican Secretary of State Cardinal Pietro Parolin. Indeed, this was a Francis action that directly affected the choice of his successor by almost certainly ruining the chances of Cardinal Parolin.

TARGETING TRADITIONALISTS: FRANCIS'S *TRADITIONIS CUSTODES*

It is hard to choose the single most divisive document issued by Francis during his papacy. But a leading candidate would be his apostolic letter *Traditionis custodes*.

Released July 16, 2021, *Traditionis custodes* is an official *motu proprio*, meaning a papal document issued in order to address a matter of special concern to the reigning pope. This particular document sought to establish and enforce specific guidelines on the liturgy of the Catholic Mass, which Pope Francis strangely felt was being threatened not by radical "liturgy reformers," but by traditionalists seeking to preserve the integrity of the Roman Catholic Mass as it had been practiced for millennia and had been recently reinforced by Pope Benedict XVI in one of the signature actions of his papacy. Some traditionalists sought a return to the so-called "TLM," or Traditional Latin Mass (Tridentine Rite). Francis seemed to harbor a unique dislike for these individuals, and *Traditionis custodes* became his weapon against them.[26]

The opening words of *Traditionis custodes* stated that Francis was doing this "In order to promote the concord and unity of the Church, with paternal solicitude towards those who in any region adhere to liturgical forms antecedent to the reform willed by the Vatican Council II, my Venerable Predecessors, Saint John Paul II and Benedict XVI, granted and regulated the faculty to use the Roman Missal edited by John XXIII in 1962."

The guidelines that followed in the document were very technical. A reader would need a nuanced understanding of what had been changed or preserved in the Mass under Vatican II (1962–65) and under Popes Paul VI (1963–78), John Paul II (1978–2005), and Benedict XVI (2005–13). Navigating through *Traditionis custodes* was no easy task, almost as exasperating as trying to decipher Francis's later document on same-sex blessings. When Pope Francis had said with a grin that he wanted to "make a mess of things" with his pontificate, *Traditionis custodes* was a perfect case in point.

The great irony of *Traditionis custodes* is that those two words translate to "guardians of Tradition," whereas the document in truth had sought anything but that. Its target was the most traditional members of the Roman Catholic Church. Tellingly, when one Googles "Traditionis custodes," the first definition that pops up, courtesy of Wikipedia, accurately states that the document "restricts the celebration of the Tridentine Mass of the Roman Rite, sometimes colloquially called the 'Latin Mass' or the 'Traditional Latin Mass.'"[27]

That was very much a universal interpretation of Francis's goal with the document. Others put it more pointedly, especially those genuinely interested in preserving tradition. As Catholic scholar Larry Chapp observed, *Traditionis custodes* quickly became notorious for "imposing severe restrictions on the celebration of the Mass in Latin." As Chapp noted, it was seen as a "punitive" measure to "suppress" the Latin Mass. It became a tool to restrict if not indeed repress the traditionalists whom Pope Francis not only disliked but seemed to despise.[28]

Pope Francis constantly talked of "mercy," but he was plainly merciless toward traditionalists, and at the least highly uncharitable. He portrayed them as modern Pharisees guilty of what he condemned as "Pharisaism."[29]

Francis's attacks on traditionalists escalated as his papacy went on. A striking example was a homily that he gave at Casa Santa Marta in October 2018 that can only be described as cruel. His stridency was alarming, as he spoke heartlessly in ways that popes do not speak of their flock. In that homily, Francis blasted "rigid" Catholics as akin to the "Pharisees and doctors of the Law." He borrowed from the words of Jesus Christ in denouncing them as "evil." Appropriating Christ's words directed at the Pharisees of His day, Francis lambasted these modern Catholics as akin to "whitened sepulchres," shiny and clean on the outside but "wicked" on the inside.[30]

This was shockingly abrasive language from a pope.

Moreover, it came from a pope who had famously said of homosexuals, "Who am I to judge?" But here, he did not hesitate to judge. With contempt in his voice, Francis called out these "rigid" Catholics as, "Beautiful on the outside, all perfect . . . all perfect . . . but within, full of rottenness, therefore of greed, of wickedness. . . . These lords are 'doctors of appearances': always perfect, always. But within, what is there?"

In Francis's assessment, these Catholics were rotten, greedy, evil. They might view themselves as "perfect," but they were "wicked," according to their shepherd. Francis warned fellow members of his flock to "Be careful around those who are rigid. Be careful around Christians—be they laity, priests, bishops—who present themselves as so 'perfect,' rigid. Be careful."

Francis again judged them, asserting: "There's no Spirit of God there."

The words of the Holy Father were startling. Traditionalists worldwide, who hardly viewed themselves as "perfect," were shaken at the apparent charge against them. If anything, these excessive adherents of "the law" might be judged as overly "scrupulous," excessively going to Mass and Confession because they believed they were far from perfect; contrary to Francis's view of them, they personally viewed themselves as utterly imperfect, racked with sin. Was the pope talking about *them*?

More such harsh words flowed from Francis. When this pope got a hold of a microphone during an airplane press conference, the faithful shuddered at what remark might issue forth that would explode in the press and ignite weeks of debate and discussion over whether certain Church doctrines or teachings were being challenged or changed. Well, in June 2019, traditionalists got a mouthful of it, applied to them.

From 40,000 feet in the air above southern Europe, Francis tore into Catholic "fundamentalists." He described them as individuals with a "nostalgia" for "returning to the ashes." Here he made clear that he was speaking of traditionalists, namely, the upholders of "tradition" who sought not to preserve the best of the past but who wanted to "safeguard the ashes." "Tradition," lectured Francis, "is . . . not the container of the ashes."[31]

Ultimately, Francis did more than talk. He took concrete action.

Judging these people as a major threat to the universal Church, Francis in July 2021 issued a special papal document to spare the Roman Catholic Church from these perceived cretins. He discerned a need to step in and "guard tradition" from these modern Pharisees. *Traditionis custodes* was that document, which above all sought to restrict the Traditional Latin Mass that was thriving in many churches in the West, and especially in the United States.

In turn, the worshippers at these TLM parishes were shell-shocked and hurt. As they should have been.

Indeed, this was terribly odd and ironic—and indeed hurtful to these worshippers—because they tended to be the more serious Catholics, highly reverent and desirous of the transcendent. Not only did they never miss Mass, but each Sunday (if not on week-days), they dressed up in their best suits and ties and dresses and veils (not in shorts and t-shirts, as in many other parishes), packed their large families in 12-passenger vans, and headed for worship services that often exceeded two hours, even four or five hours on occasions like the annual Easter Vigil service that sometimes kept them in the pews well after midnight. The typical TLM types gave birth to large families that were so serious about their faith that they were producing religious vocations: priests and nuns. They stood out for that. In almost every diocese in America, the Church is starving for vocations, with the priesthood drying up and parishes closing and consolidating. These TLM families were one of the few supply chains that seemed to have the potential to save the Church from a lethal crisis of vocations. Where would the Western churches get new priests? Answer: the traditionalists.

And yet, these people were now suddenly reeling, and wondered: Did the pope hate them? Did he see really them as Pharisees? Why was he restricting them?

They were particularly baffled at being targeted knowing that the obvious problem at most parishes in America and the West was not the orthodox but the heterodox; not those committed to tradition but those engaging in widespread abuses and disrespectful of established liturgical norms. Liturgical abuses by progressive priests and deacons and even music directors and choirs had chased traditionalists out of the *Novus Ordo* churches. (*Novus Ordo* is Latin for the "New Order" of the Mass promulgated after Vatican II by Pope Paul VI; it is the "Ordinary Form" most commonly celebrated today.) Throughout America and the West, liberal clergy and Baby Boomer choirs frequently turn the sacred liturgy into a clown show.[32] At any given parish on a Sunday, choirs—in violation of Vatican II no less—ring out with maracas and tambourines and electric guitars and loud drums by individuals who seem more intent on making the Mass a place for them to perform than for solemn reflection. Rather than fight these priests and parish officials, thus creating confrontation and division, traditionally minded parishioners simply left, seeking safe haven among kindred spirits in more traditional parishes, oftentimes at the cost of long drives from their hometown churches.

One wonders if Pope Francis—an Argentinian who had never been to America prior to his papacy—knew of these abuses in American and Western European churches. Ironically, his Masses at the Vatican were reverent, sacred, holy, beautiful, and yes, traditional, teeming with Latin, chant, the music of Palestrina, incense, candles, the heavenly Vatican choir, kneeling, and veiling. Did Francis not know where the real problem was with parishes? And yet, instead, the Holy Father spearheaded a crackdown aimed at the very people who sought a return to reverence. *Traditionis custodes* targeted them. Those traditionalists feared that the *motu propio* and their pope intended to destroy tradition.

The Francis effect with *Traditionis custodes* was to send TLM worshippers fleeing yet again. It narrowed in every diocese the number of parishes where the old Mass could be celebrated. Depending on the bishop (the bishops unevenly enforced the *motu proprio*), this could be so restrictive that many TLM communities ended up congregating not in the beautiful old church buildings that had been closing their doors in many major cities, or even in the ugly 1970s-built structures that looked more like Protestant churches or post-modern architectural monstrosities, but in gyms and social halls. Even then, the nearest such venue might be an hourlong drive or more. Nonetheless, these worshippers were willing to make the sacrifice. So were their TLM priests and newly ordained priests who wanted to learn the ancient rite but were forbidden without Vatican approval—an approval they feared was unlikely.

It was hardly surprisingly that Catholic progressives, including liberal priests and bishops, seized on the pope's *Traditionis custodes* to undermine traditionalists. It would not be a stretch to say that some of them weaponized the *motu proprio*, slinging it against an enemy they shared with Francis. It was like manna from heaven for them. They no doubt savored with an impish smile the title affixed to the document, "Guardians of Tradition," which seemed to almost mock the traditionalists they opposed. In the height of irony, the radical reformers used a document purported to "guard" tradition against the very folks in the Church who cared the most about the traditions that the liberals wanted to undermine. *Traditionis custodes* became their battle plan to martial against their "rigid" foes. It was not unlike political-cultural liberals in America who deploy words like "tolerance" and "inclusion" for the contrary purpose of intolerance and exclusion of conservative Christians.

Francis's advocates at liberal Catholic newspapers and websites cheered on these new restrictions on the TLM and against the so-called "rad trads." Church liberals were invigorated. Liberal Catholic reporters on Sunday mornings trekked quietly into traditional parishes with phones and notepads hoping to expose these modern practitioners of "Pharisaism." These "wicked" "whitened sepulchres."

And alas, to the most enthusiastic Francis advocates, *Traditionis custodes* was used to do just that. In the concluding chapter of this book, we will look at a shocking case that erupted in the opening days of Pope Leo XIV's pontificate, courtesy of liberal Bishop Michael Martin of Charlotte, North Carolina (among others). As we shall see, it presents one of the first major challenges of Leo's young papacy and could say much about his pontificate moving forward. Moreover, we will learn of a major press leak under Leo of an alarming Francis document revealing that the late pope did not accurately represent what his Vatican had learned from a survey commissioned to study these traditional worshippers. The survey was misrepresented by the pope.

This has developed into a hot issue in the Roman Catholic Church. Pope Leo knows it and must deal with it.

IDEOLOGIZING AMERICAN CARDINALS

Traditionalists tend to be conservatives, of course—although they would hasten to caution that they are simply trying to be faithful Catholics. Political conservatism plays a distant second to their faithful Catholicism. Nonetheless, yes, they tend to be (broadly speaking) conservatives, spiritually, culturally, politically, ideologically.[33]

Something else that bothered conservatives about Francis, prompting them and others to view Francis as a progressive even as he did things that liberals should despise (including denouncing "adolescent progressivism"), were his highly ideological cardinal appointments in much of the West, especially in America.

In the opening months of his papacy, Francis on June 23, 2013, told his papal nuncio to America, Archbishop Carlo Maria Vigano, that "the bishops in the United States must not be ideologized." Pointing to Archbishop Charles Chaput of Philadelphia, who happened to be a longtime registered Democrat, Francis insisted: "They must not be right-wing, like the archbishop of Philadelphia."[34] Conversely, said Francis, bishops also must not be left-wing, "and when I say left-wing, I mean homosexual."

These were provocative comments, widely published, including by the *New York Times*.[35] Neither American conservatives nor liberals liked or knew what quite to think of them. Liberals found it confusing and not amusing that Francis defined "left wing" as "homosexual." Though no one at that time was exactly sure what to make of the comments, by the end of Francis's 12 years, this much was clear: Francis wanted left-wingers for his top American clergy, not right-wingers. By left-wingers, that would mean politically and ideologically liberal bishops. The pope spent 12 years doing the precise opposite of what he reportedly said to Vigano in June 2013. He ideologized the bishops.

Once again, the lingering, baffling question with Francis was whether he had thus proceeded under his own knowledge or via the careful guidance if not manipulation of certain close lieutenants, whoever those long unclear mystery men might be. (Many American right-wingers asserted that men like disgraced American Cardinal Theodore McCarrick were influencing Francis, though such was pure speculation.) Nonetheless, what was clear was that Francis from 2013–25 in America—more so than any other country in the world—operated in a highly ideological manner, elevating from bishops to cardinals mainly left-wingers rather than any "right-wingers."

Worse, what got someone defined as "right wing" was not necessarily right wing at all. The "right-wing" sin of Archbishop Chaput was that he became a fierce defender of the First Amendment freedoms and conscience rights of American Catholics and Christians generally during the onslaught of the abortion and LGBTQ lobbies, especially after the 2015 *Obergefell* decision legalizing same-sex "marriage." Only two decades earlier, the entire US Congress, Republicans and Democrats alike, as well as Democrat President Bill Clinton and First Lady Hillary Rodham Clinton (and Senator Joe Biden), supported the Defense of Marriage Act defining marriage in America as the sole province of one man and one woman. Suddenly by 2015, holding such a position—the position of all humanity for multiple millennia and the Catholic Church's unflagging teaching since the first century—could get the person, even a Roman Catholic archbishop, labeled a "right winger."

When Archbishop Charles Chaput turned 75 years old in September 2019, he offered his resignation to the pope in accordance with standard Church age-retirement rules. The pope has the option of refusing or accepting these resignations. Chaput, sharp and healthy and vigorous and productive (and popular and influential), would have happily continued his role as archbishop, and years earlier surely expected to have been elevated to cardinal by that point. But neither was about to happen under Pope Francis. The pontiff sent the bishop out to pasture, immediately accepting the resignation offer of his dread "right-wing . . . archbishop of Philadelphia."

American liberals, fighting fiercely for everything from government-funded abortion to transgenderism to fining, firing, and jailing Christian bakers, florists, wedding planners, and county marriage clerks who disagreed with their redefinition of marriage, joyously celebrated Francis's decision with Chaput. American left-wing publications like the *New York Times* and *National Catholic Reporter* derided Chaput as a "conservative" fomenting a "culture war" because he dared to defend the conscience and First Amendment rights of Christians.[36] When Francis accepted Chaput's resignation, the American LGBTQ lobby jubilantly danced on the archbishop's grave. The gay-rights flagship publication, *The Advocate*, extolled the end of the "homophobic" Chaput, blaring the celebratory headline, "Anti-LGBTQ Archbishop Charles Chaput Fired in Philadelphia."[37]

Francis, they crowed, had "fired" Chaput.

Many American Catholics, from the left to the right, had long expected Chaput to become a cardinal, following the trajectory of bishop brothers like Timothy Dolan and Sean O'Malley, but that would not happen under the Francis regime. Instead, the Argentinian Jesuit stacked the American cardinalate with left-wing prelates like Robert McElroy, Kevin Farrell, Joseph William Tobin, Wilton Gregory, and Francis's American point man, Blase Cupich.

Similar to Chaput's fate, other veteran, respected American archbishops, like Jose Gomez in Los Angeles and Salvatore Cordileone in San Francisco, had long been expected to be promoted to the level of cardinal, but instead spent years in an effective exile under Francis. Francis (or again, at least those influencing and guiding him) apparently judged the likes of Gomez and Cordileone to be "right-wingers." Cordileone evidently earned such a tag for his battles with his most famous/infamous flock member, the staunchly pro-abortion Catholic Speaker of the House Nancy Pelosi. The two prominent California archbishops were kept in their place with no promotion under Francis. Meanwhile, Francis leapfrogged over them the most left-wing bishops, some of them staunch ideologues, which was precisely what Francis suggested he was against.

The most shocking of all such Francis's elevations was Robert McElroy, the farthest left of all of them. In a jaw-dropping move nearing the end of his pontificate, Francis promoted McElroy to Washington, DC, to replace Cardinal Wilton Gregory. When Francis had made Gregory archbishop in the nation's capital in 2019, he had once again sought a left-winger, though Gregory did a commendable job of behaving in a seemingly largely nonpartisan way in the world's most political city. One wonders if that displeased Francis (or those around the pope). When Gregory offered his resignation, Francis tapped as his replacement the most ideologically liberal bishop in America: McElroy.

Francis made this appointment in January 2025, just before Donald Trump's inauguration and return to the presidency for a second term. Typically, a pope would appoint a more neutral, calming voice to the position of archbishop of Washington, DC, especially with Donald Trump returning to the Oval Office. But Francis, a master of division and disunity, did just the opposite.

Who recommended this highly ill-advised shift by Francis? It was widely rumored that his move to appoint Robert McElroy was opposed by the two previous occupants of the Washington office—both Cardinals Gregory and Donald Wuerl—as well as by the papal nuncio to the United States and several figures in Rome. But Francis (or his unnamed "mystery men" advisers) went for McElroy against all such advice.[38]

Francis's appointment in Washington was bound to make a mess.

Finally, when it came to ideologizing the Church, it must be noted that another American churchman that Francis favored was the LGBTQ activist Jesuit Fr. James Martin. Francis met with, approved of, and seemed to be inspired and influenced by Martin's LGBTQ activism. Martin described one of his private meetings with Francis as "amazing," saying, "He was incredibly supportive of me."[39]

No one doubted that, even as Francis referred to homosexuality as "faggotry" to other priests in private.

Notably, there were fears that with the coming resignation offer by Cardinal Timothy Dolan in New York when Dolan turned 75 in February 2025, Francis might make the extraordinary, breathtaking move of leaping Fr. Martin into that position. Impossible? Unthinkable? By 2025 under Jorge Mario Bergoglio, truly anything seemed possible.

Would such a move have been a wild mess? Yes. But remember, Francis wanted a mess.

Francis instead grew very sick at that time and thus never detonated such a bombshell. Dolan, who had been appointed by Pope Benedict XVI in his final year as pope, would be there at the conclave in May 2025 to help elect Francis's successor. More than that, as we shall see, Dolan would reportedly champion the candidacy of Robert Francis Prevost as the new Holy Father.

It is fascinating how that sequence played out.

WHAT ABOUT FRANCIS APPOINTING CARDINAL PREVOST?

A favorite Francis phrase was his denunciation of what he termed "ideological colonizations" and generally the "ideologizing" of things spiritual. And yet, the Argentinian Jesuit ideologized American cardinals. At no time in the history of the American Catholic Church were appointments done with such ideological fervor as they were under Pope Francis. The appointments were so one-sided that conservative Catholics could be forgiven for thinking that Francis and his team had an ideological litmus test for American cardinals.

With all of that said, an important closing thought on this subject—if not the elephant in the living room—is the matter of Robert Francis Prevost, that is, Pope Leo XIV. It must be remembered that Prevost, after all, was an American made cardinal under

Pope Francis in September 2023. Is Prevost an exception to the rule among Francis's choices of uniformly left-wing American cardinals?

When Prevost was elected by the conclave as Pope Francis's successor in May 2025, many conservative American Catholics were suspicious and concerned, given that Francis's picks of American cardinals had been so ideologically slanted to the left. Surely then, Prevost must also be a left-winger, and a Chicago left-winger at that, in the mold of Francis chief lieutenant Blase Cupich.

However, as the pages ahead will show, Prevost in many ways stood out as different from the other American cardinals. He was said to be the "least American" among the American cardinals. In fact, this American as a bishop was not even a bishop in America, but in Peru, more like a Latin American. He was never known to be an ideologue or a left-winger. Unlike Bishop McElroy, Bishop Prevost had no track record of left-wing statements and sentiments. McElroy was an ideological lighting rod, whereas Prevost seemed an ideological unknown.

In fact, so many cardinal-electors in the conclave chose the Francis-elevated Cardinal Prevost as pope in part because he was not a known ideologue. As we will see in the pages ahead, the Prevost pick was hailed by American prelates as diverse as liberal Fr. James Martin and conservative Cardinal Raymond Burke (appointed before the reign of Francis). Perhaps in the greatest of ironies if not strokes of divine providence, a Francis-appointed American cardinal is succeeding him as pope, and that American cardinal, Prevost, appears to be the one Francis-picked American cardinal who was not a notorious left-winger, and in fact has a reputation as neither left-wing nor right-wing.

In the strangest of ironies, Pope Francis's June 2013 statement that American bishops "must not be right-wing [and] they also must not be left wing," might find its best and most surprise fulfillment in the person of Pope Leo XIV.

We shall discuss that and more in the pages ahead.

Finally, a few closing thoughts on the Francis papacy, the good and the bad as well as the ugly.

Pope Francis did so many things that left people alternately angry or happy or mystified. Among the good, he reached out to the so-called "periphery" and appointed cardinals from countries and regions that never before had had a cardinal. He wanted to minister to those areas. He envisioned the Church as a "field hospital" to nurse a suffering world in need of healing. That included the poor but also the old and forgotten. He lamented the selfish, consumeristic, materialistic "throwaway culture" that ignored so many people who need love, care, attention, and affection. He did not hesitate to call out advanced industrial countries like the United Kingdom that touted the world's most compassionate healthcare system and yet let children like Indi Gregory, Charlie Gard, and Alfie Evans die against their parents' wishes. In dramatic overtures, his Vatican and Italy's Prime Minister Giorgia Meloni intervened and sent airplanes to London to try to save these kids.

Francis was superb on the scourge of human trafficking, prostitution,[40] child labor, and modern forms of slavery. He saw these things as evil and said so. He constantly warned of the presence of evil, the devil, and demons in this realm. He made a vigorous push for the training of a new generation of exorcists. He called for at least one exorcist in every diocese in the world.

Francis was strong on issues of basic human dignity. Sometimes he showed that personally. Among the most touching images of the Francis papacy are the photos and video showing him reaching out to severely disabled children and embracing and kissing them.

Also touching was his frequent plea to his audiences: "I shall pray for you and please pray for me."

But alas, with the good, there was no denying the bad and the ugly and the confusion and mess of things. When Pope Francis passed to the next world on April 21, 2025, there was a widespread consensus among the cardinals that the next pope needed to be a man who would bring clarity and unity to a Church that Francis had rent asunder.

Who would that man be?

THREE

I Papabili (The Pope-ables)

With the death of Pope Francis on April 21, 2025, preparations for the next conclave pushed ahead with haste, though the reality was that plans for a conclave had actually begun months earlier, if not years earlier.

Way back in December 2021, veteran journalist John Gizzi broke a remarkable report in *Newsmax* that the Vatican was prepping for a conclave because, in the words of one unnamed source, "the pope is dying."[1] In retrospect, one is tempted to borrow from Mark Twain: claims of the pope's imminent death were greatly exaggerated.

The reality, however, is that Pope Francis was in poor health for years. When he was chosen in March 2013 he was not in good health. Among other ailments, he had serious lung issues going back many decades. He was 76 years old when selected in March 2013, and few expected a 12-year papacy. He outlived expectations. He was a survivor. Even after his long, grave hospitalization early in 2025, it looked like the ailing pope might turn the corner. That was so much so that news of his death the Monday morning after Easter Sunday came as somewhat of a surprise, given that he had been out in public again in recent days (including that Sunday) and seemed to be perhaps on the mend.

But alas, he was not. The time on this earth for Jorge Mario Bergoglio (1936–2025) had finished. And now a conclave awaited.

THE GENERAL CONGREGATIONS

Part of the conclave process was a period of general congregations, a dozen meetings held in the Vatican's Synod Hall between April 22 and May 6, right after the death of the pope and just prior to the start of the conclave to elect a new one. The meetings were attended by both cardinal electors under the age of 80 and the nonelector cardinals over 80. All were encouraged to join in discussions.

These meetings allowed cardinals to get together to discuss their thoughts about the Church and its needs going forward and to better get to know other cardinals they had never met before. Many of the current mass of 135 cardinal electors simply had not become acquainted with one another since the time they had been given the red hat. Some of them, like Cardinal Robert Francis Prevost, had been selected just two years earlier.

The general congregations also afforded cardinal electors the time to get to Rome from their posts scattered throughout the world. Even in the modern era, this was not as easy as it might seem. Because of their varying places, ages, and health conditions, not every cardinal could pick up and travel on a dime. And in fact, among the 135 cardinal electors, two would not be able to make the conclave.

What quickly emerged from the pre-conclave meetings is that a substantial, if not large, majority of cardinals wanted someone who was not like Francis, who could clean up his desired "mess of things." That included many of those appointed by Francis himself.

Of course, Francis did have his advocates, diminishing as they were. And their discontent with the prevailing anti-Francis atmosphere at the general congregations was noted by liberal Catholic publications in America, such as the Jesuit *America* magazine and *National Catholic Reporter*, to which progressive cardinals leaked information about the pre-conclave discussions.[2]

"We have listened to many complaints against Francis's papacy in these days," complained one anonymous cardinal to *America* magazine about the general congregations. The unnamed prelate pointed to a speech by Italian Cardinal Beniamino Stella as an example of "the worst." Stella had expressed the widespread objection to Pope Francis's appointment of laypeople in the governance of the Church. Though the general congregations and Francis himself all stressed "diversity" and "dialogue," this kind of dissent by Cardinal Stella was not welcomed by Francis-philes. The anonymous cardinal bitterly told *America* that he felt Stella had "openly attacked Pope Francis."[3]

Such dissent was apparently deemed unacceptable by the so-called "Bergoglians." As in the days of Francis, you did not deviate from this pope. It was not kindly tolerated.

Another cardinal who dared to voice his disagreement at the general congregations was 93-year-old Joseph Zen of Hong Kong, who had suffered under the Francis papacy because of the dreadful China policy. More than just about any other cardinal, Zen had earned a right to express concerns. And yet here again, an anonymous cardinal complained to *America* magazine that Zen was one of several cardinals who had spoken too long in the general congregations; he did not "respect the time limit" on speeches. Making things worse for this Francis loyalist, Cardinal Zen had dared to criticize Francis's odd "Synod on Synodality," a curious cornerstone of his papacy—and which, strange as it might have been, was supposed to encourage dialogue and diversity of thought.

Zen, too, was learning that Bergoglian "diversity" had its limits.

But despite the displeasure among Francis acolytes, there was a clear consensus in the pre-conclave discussions that things had gone awry under the prior pope. The ship needed a new captain to steer the Barque of St. Peter back in the right direction, be it a more centrist course or simply some form of stability—a steady hand—to keep the boat from rocking like it had the previous 12 years.

One of the remaining Bergoglians who was so deeply offended by this consensus that he bolted Rome in anger was Cardinal Óscar Rodríguez Maradiaga. The Honduran cardinal had helped elect Francis at the 2013 conclave, but by 2025 was no longer a cardinal elector because he had surpassed the under-80 age requirement to cast ballots. Once hopeful for a "Francis II," Maradiaga's hopes were dashed as he watched the pro-Francis alliance coming apart at the seams at the congregations. He vented that even many of the cardinals who had been appointed by Francis were "betraying" the late pontiff.

Maradiaga's bitterness was captured in a May 4 headline titled, "Conclave, the tear of the Bergoglian," in the Italian daily newspaper *Il Fatto Quotidiano*, which reported that the cardinal had "already left Rome with a sense of bitterness and disillusionment, 12 years after he contributed decisively to the election of Pope Francis." The Central American cardinal lamented that many erstwhile supporters of Francis had become "turncoats." Maradiaga headed back to Honduras, reportedly "leaving behind a Conclave where stabs at Bergoglio's pontificate come from those who were chosen by him."[4]

Distraught as he was, Cardinal Óscar Rodríguez Maradiaga should not have directed his anger at the Francis-appointed cardinals. They, too, were tired of the mess. Whether liberals or conservative or in between, none preferred more chaos. That was the fault not of them but of Francis, the man who Cardinal Maradiaga had helped elect. The time to solidify a pro-Francis alliance had been the years 2013–25, when Francis was alive and could have brought people together rather than fracture and frustrate them—including those he himself had appointed.

FRANCIS HAD STACKED THE CONCLAVE

This implosion of the Bergoglian bloc was fascinating to watch.

It was said and feared by Church conservatives that the next conclave after the death of Francis would elect "another Francis," given that Jorge Mario Bergoglio had appointed the vast majority of cardinal electors and had actually expanded and "stacked" the conclave with advocates and allies who were like him. Indeed, Francis had blown by the recommended number of cardinal electors to the conclave, which had been 120.

This was another striking unilateral action by the Argentinian Jesuit.

The original maximum of 120 cardinal electors was not some whim or fancy generated by some committee of faceless Vatican bureaucrats. It had been firmly established in 1996 by Pope John Paul II in his Apostolic Constitution *Universi Dominici Gregis*. The pope and future saint had there decreed: "the universality of the Church is sufficiently expressed by the College of one hundred and twenty electors, made up of Cardinals coming from all parts of the world and from very different cultures. I therefore confirm that this is to be the maximum number of Cardinal electors."[5]

Everyone was satisfied with that number, except for Francis. He changed it.

Francis proceeded to increase the number of cardinal electors by 12 percent in 12 years, subtly but craftily inching it up 1 percent per year, ultimately from the cap of 120 to 135, and no doubt with intentions to keep it rising. In doing so, Francis could reshape the conclave according to his own preferences, as he had done with the American cardinalate. Moves like this prompted critics to label Francis an autocrat and "the dictator pope."[6] Some compared him to the Argentinian authoritarian of his upbringing, Juan Peron. (A friend of mine from Argentina informed me that some in Francis's home country referred to him as "JP2." Not John Paul II, of course, but Juan Peron II.)

Many outsiders unfamiliar with this stacking scheme had scratched their heads at how Francis in merely 12 years had managed to pick over 80 percent of cardinal electors, specifically, 108 of 135. They puzzled: *Surely this is impossible*? After all, the previous two popes, John Paul II and Benedict XVI, had been appointing cardinals over the previous 35 years (1978–2013). How could Francis so quickly tilt the entire body in his direction? The answer is that he was able to pack the conclave with his own picks in only 12 years because he unilaterally decided to expand the conclave. In the United States, some presidents and political parties (namely, Franklin Roosevelt and the Democrats), in the past and still today have wanted to likewise "pack" the Supreme Court, but they have been halted by legislators from both sides of the aisle who agreed that it would not be fair politics. But Francis, Peron-like, acted on his own and sought to pack the conclave.

Thus, it was presumed, the next pope would be effectively "Francis II." And yet, to repeat, those who said and feared that would soon learn that even many of the Francis appointees were exhausted by the Francis mess of things. They wanted someone else, not another Francis but an un-Francis.

The result was that there was no consensus for a "liberal" or "conservative" pontiff but for someone closer to the center.

"There's a sense amongst most of the cardinals who will vote that the pendulum needs to get back to the middle," said Bill Donohue of the Catholic League.[7] That was indeed the feeling going into the conclave.

Above all, the cardinals were looking for a man who was less a personality than simply a pope. Someone, to borrow from G. K. Chesterton, who, like the Catholic Church he represented, would not be captive to his age—a child of his age. "The Catholic Church," said

Chesterton, "is the only thing which saves a man from the degrading slavery of being a child of his age."

The pope is not a successor of the secular world or of his predecessor but of St. Peter. German Cardinal Gerhard Ludwig Müller put it this way in an interview after the death of Francis with the Italian newspaper *la Repubblica*: "Every pope must serve the mission of St. Peter: he is *servus servorum Dei*. The future pope is not a successor of his predecessor but a successor of Peter." Moreover, said Müller, the pope is not "a symbol of secularized religion," and thus within the Church, "We cannot accept that atheistic Communists, enemies of humanity, write our catechism books." Müller's advice to the College of Cardinals: "Everyone needs to remember that we are the mystical body of Christ, and not an international humanitarian and social organization. This pleases a lot of secularized people, the elite, the oligarchs, who would like the Pope as a symbol of their religion—but the Pope is not a symbol of secularized religion."[8]

And so, who would be this man? Who were the leading contenders? Who among them were the most "pope-able"—*papabile*? Who were the pope-ables—*i papabili*?

THE CONTENDERS

Names of prominent, pope-able cardinals began popping up immediately after the passing of Francis. In short order, there were betting odds on the next pope. Las Vegas lit up with numbers.

Bookies listed Italy's Cardinal Pietro Parolin as the favorite, with odds ranging from +225 to 15/8, or roughly 30 to 35 percent. Trailing close behind him was Cardinal Luis Antonio Tagle of the Philippines, at around 21 to 25 percent. Right behind them were cardinals Pierbattista Pizzaballa of Italy, Matteo Zuppi of Italy, Peter

Turkson of Ghana, and Peter Erdő of Hungary. As those names suggest, the Italian people were particularly excited about their odds—with Italy boasting three of the four top favorites going into the conclave, though Italians feared that their *fratelli* could split votes in a way to clear the path for a non-Italian.[9]

A long shot who barely registered among the oddsmakers was a largely unknown American cardinal who had been a longtime bishop outside the United States, namely in Peru, Robert Francis Prevost. The Chicago native was considered a 66/1 outsider, with remote odds of less than 1 percent.[10]

In assessing the top *papabile*, Vegas oddsmakers, pundits, press people, and papal watchers worldwide were well informed by the good research of Catholic journalists Edward Pentin and Diane Montagna, who produced an impressive and widely clicked *College of Cardinals Report*, a go-to guide for many. Pentin and Montagna, the project's executive director, brought together an international team of Catholic journalists and researchers who worked in association with Sophia Institute Press and *Cardinalis Magazine*. Their report was released in December 2024. It profiled 40 leading cardinals, including 22 thought to be *papabile*.[11]

Pentin himself was on top of this subject because five years earlier, in 2020, he had written a book called *The Next Pope*. He was already a well-established *Vaticanista* based on his work as Vatican correspondent for the *National Catholic Register* and EWTN television. His full-book treatment on the topic of the next pope gave him special expertise as the conclave approached.

Pentin published in the *National Catholic Register* a list of "10 Papal Contenders You Should Know."[12] That list included many of the predictable names: Erdő, Parolin, Zuppi, Pizzaballa, plus a few notables being given chances by the oddsmakers, such as Dutch Cardinal Willem Eijk, Malta Cardinal Mario Grech, Portuguese Cardinal José Tolentino Calaça de Mendonça (at 59 years old, the youngest *papabile* cardinal on Pentin's list of 10), American Cardinal Raymond Burke, and Guinean Cardinal Robert Sarah.

Among them, Cardinal Sarah was a highly accomplished theologian and former prefect of the Dicastery for Divine Liturgy and the Discipline of the Sacraments. He was known for being theologically orthodox. And though the Francis papacy was a tough time for the orthodox, Cardinal Sarah always managed to show respect for Francis and in turn received the pontiff's respect. The African cardinal exhibited a deference and grace while at the same time not wavering in his commitment to insist on firm theological doctrine. The only reason that Cardinal Sarah was not one of the top favorites for the papacy in May 2025 was his age. He was nearly 80. Had this conclave occurred 10 years earlier, or even four or five years earlier, perhaps even three, he would have been a front-runner.

"Despite having lost his status in the Church with his retirement in 2021," noted Pentin, "Cardinal Sarah has gained recognition as a steadfast defender of the faith. If he were to be elected pope, which would appear unlikely given the makeup of the electorate, he would be the first African Successor of Peter since Pope Gelasius I in the fifth century."

Yes, the first African and black pope in some 1,500 years, if he were not turning 80 years old that June. But with his age, on the heels of a frail pope hobbled by ailments in his final years, Cardinal Sarah by May 2025 really did not have much of a chance. His time had passed, a cruel, unavoidable condition of his advanced age.

As for Cardinal Burke, he was still more of a long shot. Like Cardinal Sarah, the 76-year-old Burke's moment of opportunity had dissipated with age. Nonetheless, Pentin shared some key insights on this Sarah ally and favorite of conservatives—and chosen enemy of Pope Francis.

Pentin's appraisal: "Widely respected but considered an outlier partly due to his impassioned but respectful criticisms of Pope

Francis is American Cardinal Raymond Burke." As Pentin noted, Burke was one of the Roman Catholic Church's foremost canon lawyers known for his orthodox views and willingness to uphold the Church's Magisterium. He had done so faithfully as prefect of the Apostolic Signatura, the Church's high court on canon law. He was a leading voice on Church discipline, moral teachings, and liturgy. He was a stalwart defender of the Magisterium, especially against those dissenting from the Church's central teaching body and endeavoring to change or reverse it.

Burke was targeted and damaged by Francis. He was persecuted by the Jesuit pope. Burke had questioned whether divorced and civilly remarried Catholics and pro-abortion Catholic politicians should receive Holy Communion. He infuriated Francis by defending the Traditional Latin Mass. When Francis talked of traditionalists as "rigid" "Pharisees," it was widely assumed that he was talking about the likes of Cardinal Burke.

Francis also seemed to be alluding to Burke when the pontiff criticized bishops who opposed the COVID jabs and had almost died from the virus. The pope said, "There were even a few anti-vaxxers among the bishops: some came close to death." This charge prompted a rejoinder by Eric Sammons, editor of *Crisis Magazine*, titled, "Have you no decency, Holy Father?" Sammons said that this was the second time Francis had taken such a shot at Cardinal Burke as an "anti-vaxxer," even though Burke was not against vaccines. Sammons called it a "veiled and disgraceful" jab at Burke.[13] Francis, of course, was a COVID vax absolutist who said that every Catholic had a "moral obligation" to get the shot.[14]

Pope Francis did not like Cardinal Raymond Leo Burke.

For this faithfulness to Church teachings, and for daring to submit *dubia* (Latin for "doubts") questions to Pope Francis in November 2016 over the pope's confusing *Amoris Laetitia*, Burke was persecuted by the pope who preached mercy. Shortly into

Francis's papacy, he stripped Burke of his position as prefect of the Apostolic Signatura. He pastured him to the position of patron of the Order of Malta, largely a ceremonial role that Francis and his allies celebrated as a due demotion. That punishment came several days after Burke had said the Church under Francis was becoming "like a ship without a rudder." The pope of "dialogue" and "synodality" tolerated no such dissent. Burke was moved out immediately. And worse was yet to come.

In a crude move that struck nearly everyone by its meanness, Francis in November 2023 punished Burke by cutting his salary and health insurance and dramatically increasing the rental price on his Vatican apartment by lifting the long-standing Vatican subsidy of his residence. A wounded Burke, already smarting from Francis's previous punitive measures, did his best to keep his mouth shut, learning acutely that this was not a pope that one dared to criticize. Why had Francis done this to Burke? The usually loquacious pontiff was mum, as he was when Burke asked him for clarification with *dubia* questions. A Vatican official, however, quoted the pope as privately complaining that Burke was "working against the Church and against the papacy" and that he had sown "disunity" in the Church.

In the mind of Francis, the widening Church fissures under his papacy were the fault not of the pope but of traditionalists—those "whitened sepulchres"—like Cardinal Burke.

Still, Francis was not yet finished with Cardinal Raymond Leo Burke.

In another extraordinary moment during this Bergoglian persecution, the Argentinian Jesuit summoned Burke to his office for a dressing down in late December 2023. For seven years, Francis had refused to meet with Burke and respond to any of his questions for clarification. Burke's last private audience granted by the pontiff was November 10, 2016. But apparently, Francis's anger had boiled to the point where he wanted to confront Burke one on one.

And so on Friday, December 29, 2023, four days after Christmas, Francis called in Burke for a confrontation. This was a month after the pope said he was stripping the elderly cardinal of some of his Vatican privileges.[15]

What was said in this Francis interrogation of Burke the first week of Christmas 2023? Here again, the usually talkative Francis would not say, and neither would his Vatican. For his part, Burke likewise shared no details, doing his best to remain silently obedient to the Holy Father. However, he was stopped by a Reuters reporter as he shuffled back to his rent-hiked apartment after the Francis slap-down. "Wearing a floor-length black overcoat and black hat and with rosary beads in his left hand, he [Burke] walked away on a street near the Vatican," reported Reuters. "Asked . . . outside his residence in Rome if the meeting had gone well, Burke responded: 'Well, I'm still alive.'"[16]

Yes, he was still alive. The cardinal from Wisconsin would manage to outlive his Argentinian tormentor.

By the time of the May 2025 conclave, Burke's callous treatment at the hands of a seemingly authoritarian pope—as well as the wide respect for him as a canon lawyer—might have garnered him some votes in the first round of balloting if not for his age and for the fact that Francis had stacked the conclave with anti-Burkes. His *papabile* status was also hurt by the fact that he was an American, which was widely considered a disqualifying factor for a pope.

And hence, Edward Pentin summed up Burke's chances: "His chances of being elected pope are considered slim." Pentin did note, however, that a lengthy, protracted conclave could possibly increase Burke's chances, though a more likely role for the Wisconsin cardinal would be that of an "influential kingmaker" in helping to push to the top a preferred candidate.

Finally, nearly last, but most certainly (in retrospect) not least, was one more notable name on Pentin's top 10 to watch for. Near the bottom of Pentin's list was an obscure American cardinal who no one seemed to know anything about: Robert Francis Prevost.

"Cardinal Prevost is being promoted as a possible compromise candidate if leading candidates are unable to obtain enough votes," noted Pentin. "His lengthy missionary service in Peru, first as a priest and later as a bishop over a total of 22 years, allows him to be seen more as an international candidate than an American one, which mitigates choosing a pope from a superpower in his case. However, he might be considered too young and too recently made a cardinal (2023) to be seriously considered *papabile* with any significant chance of being elected."

Yes, he might. Or he might not.

OTHER *PAPABILE* NAMES

Those were by and large the favorites. But as the saying goes, "The cardinal who goes into the conclave a pope, comes out a cardinal."

One never knows.

Still, a betting person would have placed odds on Parolin, Tagle, Pizzaballa, Erdő.

The *College of Cardinals Report* had profiled 22 leading candidates, highlighting a smaller list of the top 12 among them. In order of their appearance on the website, the 12 were cardinals Erdő, Zuppi, Sarah, Tagle, Malcolm Ranjith of Sri Lanka, Parolin, Pizzaballa, Cardinal Fridolin Ambongo Besungu of Congo, Eijk, Anders Arborelius of Sweden, Charles Bo of Myanmar, and Jean-Marc Aveline of France.[17]

Looking back at the 12, salient for his absence was Cardinal Robert Francis Prevost. He was not entirely neglected, however. Prevost was among the top 22, but not in the top 12.[18]

Much, of course, could be said about all these cardinals. Many were subjected to intense press coverage that they had theretofore never experienced at any point in their lives as clergy. Some of the coverage was positive. But in many cases, these men of the cloth faced unfriendly scrutiny that was new, jarring, and unsettling.

Cardinal Parolin faced both positive and negative treatment. He was portrayed by unfriendly sources as selfishly fixated on getting the job, as lobbying for it in an unseemly way not befitting a prince of the Church, as something of a schemer. One Italian newspaper dubbed Parolin "the great manipulator who wants to pope." The high-ranking cardinal was accused of personally manipulating the general congregations in order to smooth a path for himself at the conclave.[19]

Fair or unfair, Parolin endured some rather cynical and unsympathetic portrayals, which often happens to the front-runner, in sports and politics as well as, apparently, the papacy.

Some of the underdog cardinals benefited from friendlier press, as underdogs often do. Two of the perceived conservative candidates who got a lot of press were Sweden's Anders Arborelius and Hungary's Peter Erdő, with Arborelius very much an underdog. Predictably, both were framed along ideological lines by newspapers either aligned with them or pitted against their views.[20]

A most-intriguing candidate who surged in popularity and received largely excellent press coverage was Cardinal Pierbattista Pizzaballa, the Latin Patriarch of Jerusalem. He had garnered headlines for bravely offering himself in exchange for Jewish civilians taken hostage by Hamas after the terrorist group's assault on Israel in October 2023. He was commended for his stoicism, his thoughtfulness, and for the undeniable fact that the man plainly looked and comported himself like a pope. He had a certain aura about him. Reporter Ellie Gardey Holmes of *The American Spectator* had it right when she noted that "all the cardinals are talking about Pizzaballa."[21]

So was a lot of the media. As the conclave approached, Pizzaballa had surged in the papal "polls." Sports analysts talk of a team's "momentum" going into the playoffs. Pizzaballa had momentum. He would have been a smart bet.

In fact, it felt as if Pizzaballa was catching if not surpassing Cardinal Tagle. The friendly 67-year-old Filipino cardinal was sometimes referred to as the "Asian Francis." *Newsweek* at one point in the pre-conclave runup had crowned Tagle "the new favorite."[22]

There were also names floated who had no business being mentioned as *papabile* but nonetheless were pushed by ideologues. The left-wing *National Catholic Reporter* one day out of the blue declared the obviously non-*papabile* American Cardinal Joseph Tobin a "contender." He was not. This was an absurd invention out of thin air. Only the liberal *National Catholic Reporter* had this liberal American from Newark, New Jersey, listed, because of shared sexual views.

Appointed by Pope Francis in November 2016, American liberals fell in love with Tobin when he welcomed a "pilgrimage" of LGBTQ Catholics to the archdiocese's cathedral in 2017. A close ally of LGBTQ activist priest Fr. James Martin, Tobin's language about "welcoming" LGBTQ people appealed to the likes of the *National Catholic Reporter* and the *New York Times*. Of course, the Church believes that everyone is welcome, but it also says that homosexuality is wrong, with the *Catechism* defining it as "intrinsically disordered." Nonetheless, Tobin, like Fr. James Martin, rejected this language. He openly repudiated it, saying, "Well, I don't call them 'intrinsically disordered.' . . . It's very unfortunate language."[23]

Such statements in direct opposition to official Church teaching immediately brought Tobin gushing, swooning media coverage by liberal reporters in the United States.[24] It even prompted the erroneous claim that he was a leading candidate for the papacy. In a transparent attempt to campaign for Tobin, the *National Catholic*

Reporter ran a headline that unbelievably asserted, "Once on the outs, American Cardinal Tobin now a contender."[25]

The *NCR* was notorious for this sort of "reporting" slanted by ideological biases. In July 2020, the newspaper's executive editor had called radical New York congresswoman Alexandria Ocasio-Cortez "the future of the Catholic Church," an astonishing declaration for a secular self-identified "democratic socialist" of whom it was not even known if she attended Mass or happened to be a practicing Catholic.[26]

And now, the liberal Catholic newspaper had its "contender" for pope: Cardinal Joseph Tobin. The *National Catholic Reporter* alone viewed Cardinal Tobin as *papabile* (if it really did).

Ultimately, it would turn out that there was only one American cardinal who was legitimately pope-able: Robert Francis Prevost.

HEADING INTO THE SISTINE CHAPEL

Amid all this buzz over the future of the Chair of St. Peter, the cardinal electors tried to keep their heads level and focus on the profound task of deciding the next pontiff. They would earnestly pray and seek the guidance of the Holy Spirit.

Taking a lead in that respect was, fittingly, Cardinal Burke, the prelate targeted by Pope Francis. As he had often done during the previous 12 years, the Wisconsin native felt that his best recourse was the only one that the Argentinian Jesuit had left him as an option: prayer. Burke started a Novena for the next pope.[27]

Despite being persecuted by Francis, Cardinal Burke was quite gracious to the Argentinian after his death, immediately releasing a public statement issuing a universal call for "prayer for the eternal rest of Pope Francis." Mere days after the death of Francis, Burke launched a "Solemn Novena of Hope to Our Lady of Good

Counsel." His specific prayer intentions were for the universal Church, the world, and the eternal rest of his persecutor. The nine-day prayer would commence on May 1, day one of the month of Mary, and would finish on May 9.

Anticipating the month of Mary ahead, Burke had already planned a novena before Pope Francis's death on April 21. With the passing of the pontiff, however, Burke now added Francis to the novena intentions, as well as the coming conclave. "Asking the intercession of Our Lady of Good Counsel is especially important," said Burke, "given the critical decisions which will be made during the coming days and weeks for the good of the Church and of the whole world."

Many Catholics worldwide joined Cardinal Raymond Leo Burke in that plea—for Francis and for the conclave that was ready to begin.

FOUR

Conclave

At last, on May 7, 2025, after much fanfare and amid a worldwide whirl of excitement and expectation among Catholics and non-Catholics alike, the conclave opened at the Vatican. The whole globe watched as this ancient Roman Catholic ritual commenced, attracting and seeming to fascinate all, regardless of religious affiliation. Catholic or not, folks everywhere were intrigued. The international press coverage was nonstop. All eyes turned to Rome to see who the College of Cardinals would choose as the 267th heir to Saint Peter, the rock upon whom Christ built His Church.

It was the 4:00 hour Rome time, five hours ahead of US Eastern Standard Time. Bedecked in red, 133 cardinal electors (of 252 cardinals worldwide) sauntered toward the Sistine Chapel. There existed 135 cardinal electors in total at that moment in the Roman Catholic Church, but two of them because of health issues could not make the trip to St. Peter's Basilica. A vote of 89 ballots would be needed to decide the new head of the Holy See.

The cardinal electors came from all parts of the earth. The largest region represented was Europe, which hosted 39 percent of the electors, a proportion that was down notably from the 51 percent European majority that had comprised the 2013 conclave. This change in composition was a direct, intended result of Pope Francis seeking out more cardinals from "the periphery." Among the 52 voting cardinals from Europe, a third (17) were Italians, with Italy hosting more cardinals than any other country. About 18 percent were from the Asia-Pacific region, another 18 percent hailed from Latin America and the Caribbean, 12 percent came from Sub-Saharan Africa, 10 percent from North America, and a small portion of 3 percent came from the Middle East and North Africa. Among these were 10 cardinal electors from the United States (second only to Italy): Blase Cupich, Wilton Gregory, Timothy Dolan, Joseph Tobin, Raymond Burke, Kevin Farrell, Robert McElroy, Daniel DiNardo, James Harvey, and Robert Francis Prevost.[1]

For these unique individuals who made up one of the globe's most exclusive clubs, the atmosphere was special, even unworldly. How could it not be? Sure, since the time they had been little boys—altar boys—they were accustomed to candles, incense, chant, and all the so-called "bells and smells" that no entity does as powerfully as the Roman Catholic Church. But the ambience here was certainly altogether different. Many of the electors knew that they might do this only once in their lifetimes, especially given that by age 80 they are disqualified as voting cardinals. This was quite a moment.

From the instant the conclave formally started, the feeling was ethereal. The pageantry yet solemnity of the ceremony was impossible to put into words, with the angelic sounds of the Vatican choir initiating the procession of cardinals by intoning a lengthy Litany of the Saints and then slowly, almost methodically, chanting the *Veni Creator Spiritus*. An ancient Latin hymn over 1,100 years old, it implores the Holy Spirit to come and be with the cardinals to guide them in this time of singular need: "*Veni, Creator Spiritus, mentes tuorum visita, imple superna gratia quae tu creasti pectora.*" Translation: "Come, Holy Spirit, Creator blest, and in our souls take up Thy rest."

Now the cardinals were ready. In the 5:00 hour, the most senior-ranking cardinal and leader of the process, Pietro Parolin, read the oath and swore all the cardinals to follow the 1996 conclave rules set forth by Pope John Paul II. The process is delineated in the Apostolic Constitution *Universi Dominici Gregis*. (The same set of guidelines that had capped the number of voting cardinals at 120, which Pope Francis had changed.) The oath goes as follows:

> We, the Cardinal electors present in this election of the Supreme Pontiff, promise, pledge, and swear, as individuals and as a group, to observe faithfully and scrupulously the prescriptions contained in the Apostolic Constitution of the Supreme Pontiff John Paul II, *Universi Dominici Gregis*, published on 22 February 1996.
>
> We likewise promise, pledge, and swear that whichever of us by divine disposition is elected Roman Pontiff will commit himself faithfully to carrying out the *munus Petrinum* of Pastor of the Universal Church and will not fail to affirm and defend strenuously the spiritual and temporal rights and the liberty of the Holy See.
>
> In a particular way, we promise and swear to observe with the greatest fidelity and with all persons, clerical or lay, secrecy regarding everything that in any way relates to the election of the Roman Pontiff and regarding what occurs in the place of the election, directly or indirectly related to the results of the voting; we promise and swear not to break this secret in any way, either during or after the election of the new Pontiff, unless explicit authorization is granted by the same Pontiff; and never to lend support or favor to any interference, opposition, or any other form of intervention, whereby secular authorities of whatever order and degree or any group of people or individuals might wish to intervene in the election of the Roman Pontiff.

Each cardinal then took the oath individually, stating: "And I, [name], do so promise, pledge, and swear." While placing his hand on the Gospels, the cardinal added: "So help me God and these Holy Gospels which I touch with my hand."

Yes, to make doubly clear: each cardinal swore an oath on the Gospel itself. This was serious business. No man of God could fail to understand the gravity of his charge at hand.

Cardinal Pietro Parolin himself went first, followed by each cardinal who was named and identified by position. They moved along in order of rank. Following Parolin, appropriately, was the other odds-on favorite for the papacy: Filipino Cardinal Tagle. One by one they followed, with other *papabile* candidates among the early names, from Cardinal Prevost to Cardinal Sarah to the 133rd and final prelate.

They made their way inside the Sistine Chapel.

Once the voting was about to commence, all nonelectors, including the Master of Papal Liturgical Celebrations, the secretary of the College of Cardinals, and any ceremonial officers, had to exit the Sistine Chapel. The thick double doors were closed and the Latin words "*extra omnes*" were pronounced, meaning "everyone out." This meant the expulsion of all media and anyone other than the cardinals required to be there.

With that, only the electors remained. There inside, under Michelangelo's *Last Judgment*, they vowed to God the Almighty not to divulge what happened in that room. What transpired over the coming hours and days was supposed to remain the exclusive knowledge and shared secret of the 133 cardinal electors. The senior-most cardinal deacon then closed the doors.

The room was locked.

The voting began. Each cardinal, in order of rank, wrote the name of his chosen candidate on a rectangular ballot. Printed on the top half of each ballot were the words, *"Eligo in Summum*

Pontificem" ("I elect as Supreme Pontiff"). The bottom half of the ballot was left blank for each cardinal to write down the name of his chosen candidate. The cardinal then folded the ballot in half and carried it to the altar. As he did so, he held up the ballot so that it was visible. There on the altar of the Lord rested a plate where the cardinal placed the ballot. He then used the plate to slide his vote into a chalice where the ballot was then covered. At that point, each cardinal elector stated in Italian: "*Chiamo a testimone Cristo Signore, il quale mi giudicherà, che il mio voto è dato a colui che, secondo Dio, ritengo debba essere eletto.*" ("I call as my witness Christ the Lord, who will be my judge, that my vote is given to the one whom I believe should be elected according to God.") The cardinal then bowed to the altar and returned to his seat.[2]

Among the cardinals, a senior member presided as an appointed formal deacon who supervised the process of drawing lots to appoint three so-called scrutineers to count the votes, another group of three *infirmarii* to collect votes from aged or sick cardinals too weak to walk to the altar, and three additional cardinals to verify the count.

From these secret ballots, a two-thirds majority was required for the election of a new pontiff. After each round of submissions, ballots were read aloud and then burned in a cast-iron stove. It was these ashes and subsequent smoke that served to inform onlookers in St. Peter's Square whether a pope had been chosen.

The process prompted an insightful observation from Bishop Robert Barron, who was doing live commentary on the conclave for EWTN television. Barron was inspired to quote his late mentor, Cardinal Francis George, who had waxed spiritual and historical during an earlier conclave. The Chicago-based cardinal had observed as he watched the process that the Emperor Nero had tried to wipe out Peter, and yet, here they were, two millennia later, and Nero was dust but the spirit of Peter was very much alive, long outliving Nero.[3]

The vote was scheduled for 7:00 p.m. Rome time, Wednesday, May 7.

It would be the first of several expected ballots before the white smoke would emanate from the chimney atop the Sistine Chapel and it could be declared *habemus papam*!

THE DECISIVE BALLOT

The big day would turn out to be Thursday, May 8. It was day two for the conclave. Here was the planned schedule for the conclave that day, as posted by *Vatican News*:

- **7:45 a.m. Vatican time (2:45 a.m. ET).** The cardinals leave Santa Marta (where they stayed during the conclave) for the Apostolic Palace (the pope's official residence).
- **8:15 a.m. Vatican time.** The day starts with Mass in the Pauline Chapel.
- **9:15 a.m. Vatican time.** Midmorning prayer in the Sistine Chapel.
- **10:30 a.m. to 12:30 p.m. Vatican time.** Two votes permitted in the morning.
- **12:30 p.m. Vatican time.** The cardinals return to Santa Marta for lunch.
- **3:45 p.m. Vatican time.** The cardinals return to the Apostolic Palace.
- **4:30 p.m. Vatican time.** Voting resumes in the Sistine Chapel.
- **5:30 p.m. to 7:00 p.m. Vatican time**. If white smoke appears, it is expected after 5:30 p.m. local time.
- **7:30 p.m. Vatican time.** Voting is concluded. If no pope is chosen, then the cardinal electors return to Santa Marta.

That was the plan for Thursday, May 8, the day that lay ahead. Of course, if at any time during that day a certain cardinal got the minimum of 89 votes, the conclave would need not proceed any further into the late afternoon or evening.

Few outsiders were projecting an early day. The consensus from Vatican insiders to Vegas oddsmakers was that a new pope would not be elected among this diverse, divided group until a minimum of Friday, May 9. Pope Francis's election required five rounds. Pope John Paul II, succeeding a pope who had reigned only 33 days, needed eight rounds. Surely, this one would go at least five rounds.

How long might this one go? Technically, it could take days, even weeks.

According to the formal rules, each day voting would occur twice in the morning and twice in the afternoon—four times in total per day. If no candidate was chosen after three days, the voting would be paused for one day of prayer and reflection before starting again. If no candidate was chosen after another seven additional rounds, another pause would follow.

If there was no success after 21 rounds of ballots, there would be a final pause for prayer and reflection and also dialogue, but this time with a significant twist in the rules: the cardinals could choose between only the two candidates who received the most votes in the prior round. The field would be forcibly narrowed to two cardinals, neither of whom would be permitted to vote. However, the winner would not be decided by a mere majority. Once again, a two-thirds majority was still required.

The world would have been surprised by something lengthy along the lines of a 21-ballot contest, but there would have been equal surprise with a decision rendered within three or four ballots. And so, by midday Thursday, May 8, the world anticipated more rounds of voting ahead.

But God's ways are not the ways of the world. Heaven had other plans.

The scheduled 3:45 p.m. return by the cardinals to the Apostolic Palace to vote once again, for a fifth ballot, was called off. By the fourth ballot, we had a pope.

FIVE

Pope of Surprises: The Unexpected Prevost

Pope Francis coined the phrase "the God of surprises."[1] It was a popular expression sometimes turned against him, as Francis became notorious for sloppily saying something off-the-cuff to journalists on an airplane or in an interview with an infamous atheist that seemed to instantly question two millennia of Church teaching. Such exasperating if not infuriating moments prompted detractors to derisively refer to Francis as "the pope of surprises."

And yet, a final big surprise from Francis came posthumously when the cardinals assembled to choose his successor. The prevailing wisdom was that because Francis had expanded and stacked the conclave with his preferred appointments, his successor would be just like him. But we should not have been so sure. Remember the sage aphorism: *He who enters the conclave as a pope emerges as a cardinal.* Or to borrow from the good-natured Italians, "Hey, you get a fat pope, then you get a skinny pope."

You never know. Only God knows. Perhaps the Holy Spirit had a surprise in store.

The reality of papal history should have taught the world to expect the unexpected. The history of the papacy since the early 20th century has been quite revealing. The two so-called "liberal" popes, Francis and John XXIII, were picked by conclaves created by a succession of "conservative" popes (flawed as these labels are for popes). John XXIII was the Vatican II pope, whose short papacy went from 1958–63. Many traditionalists feel that Vatican II derailed the Church, allowing radical reformers to remake it in their own image. Nonetheless, the John XXIII conclave had been composed of cardinals appointed by a long string of traditional popes: Pius X (1903–14), Benedict XV (1914–22), Pius XI (1922–39), and Pius XII (1939–58). As for Pope Francis, he was preceded by Pope John Paul II (1978–2005) and Pope Benedict XVI (2005–13). The conclave filled by those two "conservative" popes selected the "liberal" Francis.[2]

But here was a notable fact regarding the Francis appointees, which made them less predictable along "liberal" versus "conservative" lines: of the 108 cardinal electors that Francis had appointed by 2025, many were from what he called "the periphery." Though most of his appointments were from the West, they comprised a smaller portion than in previous conclaves. Of Francis's 108 appointees, 38 percent were from Europe, 19 percent from the Asia-Pacific, 19 percent from the Caribbean and Central/South America, 12 percent from sub-Saharan Africa, 7 percent from North America, and 4 percent from North Africa and the Middle East region. In other words, 62 percent were non-European, and 55 percent were outside Europe and North America. Francis appointed cardinals from 25 countries that had never had a cardinal before.[3]

It was the Francis picks from Western Europe and North America who had been the more liberal ones, particularly in America. The Francis "periphery" picks from Asia and Africa were not focused on the "culture war" issues plaguing the West—gender, marriage, sexuality. Those periphery cardinals were not known to be especially liberal, as those cultural issues were not hot-button topics in their homelands.

Moreover, in recent conclaves there had been other forces at work to make the expected unexpected.

A key factor in Jorge Mario Bergoglio getting picked by the 2013 conclave filled by John Paul II and Benedict XVI was the scheming of a group of rebel left-wing cardinals known as the St. Gallen Mafia, of which articles and books have been written.[4] That cabal plotted in a premeditated way that John Paul II had forewarned about and tried to create rules to avert. In 2025, certain cardinal members of the new conclave were on the alert to ensure such scheming would not happen again, precisely because of the conniving of the St. Gallen Mafia.[5] Such maneuvering was a theme of the 2024 movie by the very name *Conclave*.

Hence, in May 2025, perhaps it was time to be surprised. Perhaps the pope who spoke of surprises might exit the world with a big surprise in store for his successor.

Well, indeed, now came a pope of surprise. A huge surprise.

HABEMUS PAPAM!

On May 8, 2025, at roughly 6:00 p.m. Rome time, white smoke billowed from the Sistine Chapel chimney. That itself was a surprise, as everyone figured this conclave would run into multiple ballots through at least Friday, and likely later. But a bigger surprise was yet to come, especially to those watching from their screens in America.

The embers in the oven at the Sistine Chapel stoked excitement at St. Peter's Square. Many Romans were ending their workday at the office. Tourists had queued up at espresso bars and gelato stands and around the bountiful gorgeous old churches that perched from every few blocks. With the roar that greeted the white smoke, all stopped what they were doing and dashed toward the ancient *piazza*. They and the world had a pope. Yes, already—on merely the fourth ballot.

As the mass gathering outside waited in anticipation at which cardinal had been chosen, the electors inside huddled with the new leader of their universal Church. They knew what the outside world did not, namely, that the vote had been decisive, even overwhelming. But the chosen cardinal still had to give his consent. God had given His creatures free will. That included the chief shepherd of the Church. The final call was his.

And so, the would-be top shepherd was asked the big question.

"Do you accept your canonical election as Supreme Pontiff?" asked the conclave's senior-most cardinal inside the chapel. That cardinal just happened to be Pietro Parolin, who just days before had been widely considered the favorite to be in that position. Parolin had previously imagined that question being asked to him. But instead, he was the one asking the question—to Cardinal Robert Francis Prevost.

"*Accepto*," replied the 69-year-old cardinal.

As fellow cardinals clapped cheerfully, Parolin was not bitter. The good sport would later say of the moment: "I don't believe I'm revealing any secrets when I write that a very long and warm round of applause followed the 'I accept' that made [Robert Prevost] the 267th pope of the Catholic Church." At that moment and later at the Loggia, Parolin said of Prevost: "What struck me most about him was the serenity that emanated from his face in such intense and, in a certain sense, 'dramatic' moments, because they completely change a man's life. He never lost his slight smile, even though I imagine he was very aware of the many and not-so-simple problems facing the Church today."[6]

Upon providing his consent, the newly elected pontiff was then asked by Cardinal Parolin: "By what name do you wish to be called?"[7]

Robert Francis Prevost, the unassuming cardinal from Chicago—never considered one of the top *papabile*—shared his choice of name: Leo XIV.

No doubt, his fellow cardinals awed at the choice. Leo XIII had been a pope that everyone liked, including those so-called "liberals" and "conservatives" alike. It was a name to unify. And already, by name alone, this pope was different than the previous one. No recent pope over the last hundred-plus years carried a name with the unifying power of Leo XIII. This was quite the choice.

The new Holy Father then returned to the Sistine Chapel, where the heir to the Chair of St. Peter took his seat on a specially designated chair. Here, a brief but powerful ceremony began, led by the senior cardinal of the Order of Bishops. It was that cardinal's prerogative to select one of two very appropriate passages from the Gospels at that moment, either "You are Peter, and on this rock I will build my Church" or "Feed my sheep."

Such is the standard protocol for every newly elected pope in whatever century. And yet, those words of the Gospel were especially fitting for this particular conclave. May 8, 2025, was a Friday, and it happened to fall between two Sundays in which the Gospel reading in the Mass Lectionary could not have been more appropriate. The Sunday, May 4, reading (it was the Third Sunday of Easter) was John 21:1–19. This is the long narrative in which a frustrated Simon Peter tells the other disciples that he is going fishing, only to end up empty-handed until an unexpected Jesus shows up shoreside and tells them to cast their net over the right side of the boat, yielding a magnificent catch. The Gospel reading finishes with Jesus asking Peter to "feed my sheep." Likewise fitting, the Sunday that followed May 8—that is May 11, the Fourth Sunday of Easter—is the day that the Roman Catholic Church marks as Good Shepherd Sunday. This time, the reading was from John 10:27–30, which opens with Jesus saying that "My sheep hear my voice, I know them, and they follow me."

How perfect it was then that the conclave chose the Church's new chief shepherd between those two Sundays. Had the ballots run later, as projected, the conclave would have been halted over the weekend and postponed until Monday, with a decision coming the following week, with different readings not as ideally fitting.

How appropriate it was that the newly elected pontiff was asked there in the Sistine Chapel if he consented to be pope and was exhorted to "feed my sheep." He agreed to feed the sheep.

At this point in the brief ceremony inside the Sistine Chapel, with the world eagerly awaiting at the massive square outside, the Protodeacon—French Cardinal Dominique Mamberti—offered a prayer for the new Holy Father, and then each cardinal elector, in order of precedence, came forward to greet the new pontiff and pledge his obedience one by one.

The ceremony finished with the newly elected pope leading all the cardinals in the singing of the *Te Deum*, an ancient Latin hymn composed likely in the fifth century by Saint Augustine or his mentor Saint Ambrose. This, too, was fitting, given the Augustinian roots of the new pontiff. The words of the Latin hymn sung inside the Sistine Chapel were wrought with spiritual significance. They begin with praise not of the Holy Father but of God the Father that he serves: "*Te Deum laudamus: te Dominum confitemur. Te aeternum Patrem omnis terra veneratur.*" Translation: "O God, we praise Thee, and acknowledge Thee to be the supreme Lord. Everlasting Father, all the earth worships Thee."

The *Te Deum* makes clear that though the moment at hand is about the new pope, the focus is really about—always—the everlasting Lord.

With the finishing of the hymn, the cardinals and their new shepherd made their exit from Michelangelo's grand frescoes toward the crowd reveling below. A fresh breeze blew through as the cardinals flanked the balconies. The 132 (133 minus one) took their spots now as spectators to watch the reaction to the emergence of the brother cardinal they had chosen.

The throng watched carefully for movement in the central balcony. Emerging from the Loggia was Protodeacon Mamberti. Here we go! The assemblage went wild when Cardinal Mamberti declared those two words that everyone wanted, "*Habemus papam*!" Then, in the language of the Church, Latin, he announced the new pope: "*Robertum Franciscum . . . Cardinalem Prevost.*" And he disclosed that the new Holy Father had taken the name Leo XIV.[8]

With that, something odd happened, though only momentarily. The once raucous crowd went strangely silent. The flock was confused. And why wouldn't it be? This was not Cardinal Parolin or Cardinal Tagle or Cardinal Pizzaballa. Who in the world was Robert Francis Prevost?

No one expected this man to have been picked—this unknown American more recently of the backwoods of Peru. Over the prior minutes, the crowd had been loud, jubilant, ecstatic. At the naming of Prevost, it went quiet out of confusion, befuddlement. The faithful had no idea who this person was. When Cardinal Mamberti had started with the name "*Robertum*," many figured it was Cardinal Robert Sarah. It was not.

It was Cardinal Robert Francis Prevost.

And yet, when the red curtain opened and he emerged, bedecked with his traditional vestments and pectoral cross, this man looked like a pope. He did not look out of place. It was striking to see that he already, immediately, bore the countenance of a pope. He had somehow quickly assumed the role. He appeared slightly nervous, perhaps felt a bit overwhelmed, and yet still somehow seemed comfortable, prayerful, confident, though not in any way arrogant.

That was how he looked. What would he now say?

"PEACE BE WITH YOU"

Leo XIV's first words at that moment were profoundly important, packed with deep spiritual meeting for the man inheriting the Chair of St. Peter. He lifted his head, opened his hands and lips, and stated to the world in Italian, the tongue of the Bishop of Rome: "*La pace sia con tutti voi.*" Translation: "Peace be with all of you."

It is hard to imagine a better choice of words for that occasion. They were the words of Christ, though not just any words. Consider:

Jesus Christ's relationship with Peter is central to Roman Catholicism. It is also generally one of the more fascinating themes of the New Testament. Peter at one point tells Christ that he will defend Him anywhere and at any time, even if everyone else deserts Him. Peter is crestfallen when Jesus disappointingly replies that Peter that very night will deny Him—not once or twice but three times, and amid Christ's greatest moment of abandonment and need: His path to Calvary.

But with the sadness of the crucifixion comes the hope and joy of the resurrection, and thus another major incident in the interaction between Christ and Peter. And that next encounter—and the words of Jesus to Peter and to all of His most intimate followers—speak to the first words out of the mouth of the newly chosen heir to the Chair of St. Peter, Pope Leo XIV, from the Loggia that Thursday, May 8, 2025.

After the expiration of Christ on the cross, the Apostles had fled and hid, and were shuddering in fear. The man they had come to view as their Lord had been ignominiously executed. Their hopes were crushed. Surely, they were next. Jesus had told them and anyone who wanted to follow Him that doing so meant a willingness to carry their own cross. Well, that appeared to be a likely scenario, sooner than they imagined. But then came the most incredible turn of events in what has been called "The Greatest Story Ever Told." John's Gospel put it this way: "On the evening of that first day of the week [after the crucifixion], when the doors were locked, where the disciples were, for fear of the Jews, Jesus came and stood in their midst and said to them, 'Peace be with you.'" (John 20:19–25).

This group of Jews, led by a Jewish fisherman named Simon Peter, feared the Jewish religious officials who sought the death of Christ. That was one component of their fear. But consider what the New Testament does not say in that passage: they were also filled with fear because a dead man had just walked into their room through a locked door. Have you ever seen a ghost? Such would be rather alarming. Of course, this ghost was actually a physical, real person in the flesh, who had once foretold them that one day He would be crucified, would die, but would rise again. Now, here He was in the flesh.

"When He [Jesus] said this," John's Gospel continues, "He showed them His hands and His side. The disciples rejoiced when they saw the Lord."

In other words, He showed them the marks of his crucifixion, a dead-ringer sign that this really was Jesus among them. Another apostle, St. Thomas, the skeptic, who was not there in the Upper Room, would later say that unless he saw and felt the holes in Christ's hands, he would not believe. "Unless I see the mark of the nails in his hands and put my finger into the nail marks and put my hand into his side, I will not believe."

But Thomas saw, he touched, and he believed.

With this amazing news, John's Gospel continues, the disciples rejoiced. Here was nothing less than life after death, resurrected from the depths of despair.

And yet, there was probably still trepidation at that instant of jubilation, especially from Peter, who Jesus had last seen publicly denying Him. Would Christ now rebuke Peter in front of His group of closest followers? Not at all. John's Gospel records Jesus's next words, which are the same as His first: "Peace be with you," He repeats.

Jesus then tells them, "As the Father has sent me, so I send you." He then breathed on them, saying, "Receive the Holy Spirit. Whose sins you forgive are forgiven them, and whose sins you retain are retained." The Church really began at that moment, with these men commissioned *in persona Christi* and given the ability to forgive sins in Christ's name.

But note above all the words that Christ repeated: "Peace be with you."

That brings us back to Pope Leo XIV and his first words to his flock from the balcony overlooking St. Peter's Square.

Catholics everywhere in every Mass hear the priest during the liturgy before consecrating the Eucharist say to the faithful, "Peace be with you." The faithful respond, "And with your spirit" (prior to the recent changes under Pope Benedict XVI, they had said, "And also with you"), prompting the priest to respond, "Let us offer each other the sign of peace." Every Mass is a message of universal peace.

Thus, the theological significance of those opening words from Leo XIV were profound, not only for the words of Christ noted here, but as a departure from Pope Francis. Francis spoke constantly of peace, but during his 12-year papacy, the chaos was highly unsettling, leaving many with distressing feelings of unease. There was most distinctly a lack of peace. Traditionalist Catholics certainly felt like Francis was warring against them. Throughout the Francis years factions and forces within the Church were at one another's throats.

Surely the new pope was offering the hope of something better.

SIGNS OF STABILITY

Immediately, the new Holy Father showed signs of stability, order, of quelling the chaos. He conveyed this not only through his demeanor but his dress. He wore a white cassock, a white zucchetto, a red mozzetta, a red-and-gold stole, and a shiny pectoral cross with five relics of major figures in the life of his Augustinian order, including a bone relic of Saint Augustine himself.

The red cape is the sign of the Church's and pope's universal authority. It was that and that traditional ceremonial dress that Francis had ditched when he walked out onto the balcony 12 years prior. When Francis had stepped onto the Loggia on March 13, 2013, he had a deer-in-the-headlights look, nervous, lacking confidence, like a man unsure what to say, which indeed he was. His first words were, "*Fratelli e sorelle, buonasera.*" Translation: "Brothers and sisters, good evening." Given Leo's words, it is fascinating to see in retrospect that the word "peace" was never uttered once by Francis in his short opening statement. Francis had given a very brief statement (only about 320 words, half the length of Leo XIV's remarks) lacking any theological depth, and that concluded with a mere "Good night and sleep well!"[9]

The stark contrast was remarked upon by Dr. John Rao at the website OnePeterFive, who in March 2013 had been standing in the *piazza* when Cardinal Bergoglio was announced as the next pope. He found the contrast to Leo "very, very stark indeed." As with Cardinal Prevost, Rao noted that neither he nor his companions had likewise known anything whatsoever about Cardinal Bergoglio in 2013. "Nevertheless," wrote Rao, "his ghostly appearance on the *loggia*, the tense minute-long silence that followed, and then his replacement of the mention of Christ with a lugubrious '*buona sera*' created a deep spiritual chill enhanced by the unpleasant evening weather." He added: "We kept expecting something—anything—that sounded Catholic." They evacuated the square with a feeling of gloom and doom.[10]

As for Rao's feeling when Prevost stepped onto the Loggia, it "was quite different. Yes, it is true that my knowledge of Cardinal Prevost was almost as sketchy as that of Bergoglio, with just a few negative judgements expressed by some of my Vatican journalist friends vaguely bubbling up in my head. But as events unfolded, it was clear that at least my first impressions were not going to be anything comparable to 2013."

Rao noted how he even the weather seemed to agree: "The threatening morning weather had disappeared, the Satanic clouds replaced with a triumphant Catholic sun. . . . Then Leo XIV appeared. Properly dressed. . . . Greeting us with Christ's words after His Resurrection. Telling us repeatedly that Christ was our bridge to eternity. Evoking the Blessed Mother. Actually giving us a blessing, accompanied by a Plenary Indulgence."

Leo XIV in May 2025, unlike Francis in March 2013, looked notably prepared, humbled, surely likewise nervous, but composed. So much so that he had thought carefully and prewritten what he wanted to say. It was "peace be with you all."

For many Catholics, that was a reassuring statement after the "catastrophe" (the apt words of Cardinal George Pell) of the Francis papacy. There was much anxiety at the moment of the announcement of Francis's successor. And given that virtually no one seemed to know anything about Cardinal Robert Francis Prevost, there remained much apprehension as his name was announced to an ecstatic audience in St. Peter's that suddenly went dead silent at the revealing of this unknown American cardinal whose diocese was in Peru.

Was the chaos and confusion going to continue?

Pope Leo XIV hopefully was telling everyone that things would now be better. He prayed for peace in the world and for "a Church that always seeks peace."

UNIFYING WORDS OF AUGUSTINE

In addition to that specific message, Leo XIV had more to say.

There had been much talk of the need for unity since the death of Francis. This new pope sought it immediately, not only wishing everyone peace, but thanking Pope Francis and making overtures to the previous pope. As he showed visible signs of returning to tradition by his mere dress alone, he made outright positive statements about Francis and his "synodality." Leo used the phrase "synodal Church" and three times used the word "dialogue." That transition from speaking of peace to respecting Francis was evident in his next series of statements from the Loggia:

> It is the peace of the risen Christ. A peace that is unarmed and disarming, humble and persevering. A peace that comes from God, the God who loves us all, unconditionally.
>
> We can still hear the faint yet ever courageous voice of Pope Francis as he blessed Rome, the Pope who blessed Rome, who gave his blessing to the world, the whole world, on the morning of Easter. Allow me to extend that same blessing: God loves us, God loves you all, and evil will not prevail! All of us are in God's hands. So, let us move forward, without fear, together, hand in hand with God and with one another other! We are followers of Christ. Christ goes before us. The world needs his light. Humanity needs him as the bridge that can lead us to God and his love. Help us, one and all, to build bridges through dialogue and encounter, joining together as one people, always at peace. Thank you, Pope Francis!

The new Holy Father then thanked his fellow "brother Cardinals, who have chosen me to be the Successor of Peter and to walk together with you as a Church, united, ever pursuing peace and justice." He also spoke of charity, a word he used twice.

Next came an important statement, a pivot back in time and to the religious order that formed Robert Francis Prevost. The statement reflected who Leo was theologically: "I am an Augustinian, a son of Saint Augustine," declared Leo to applause.

From the balcony, Leo did not elaborate on Augustine, but soon after his opening remarks, it was divulged that when Robert Francis Prevost had been consecrated a bishop, he had chosen as his episcopal motto a slogan from St. Augustine: "*In Illo uno unum*." That Latin motto translates to, "In the one Christ we are one." The words are taken from St. Augustine's sermon on Psalm 127. In that commentary, Augustine said that though Jesus Christ speaks to many, "these many are one in Christ." Augustine wrote: "When I speak of Christians in the plural, I understand one in the One Christ. You are therefore many, and you are one; we are many, and we are one."[11]

It is the perfect message for a pope, whose global flock is vastly diverse, from all parts of the earth and every ethnic background, and yet they are one—united together—in Christ.

Once again, the message was unity. That message applied to any pope at any time, but especially to this one now after 12 years of Francis fracturing the flock.

The new pope then quoted this from Augustine to the faithful: "With you I am a Christian, and for you I am a bishop." That was a particularly apt quote from Augustine, given that Robert Francis Prevost was no longer just an Augustinian but the bishop of these people in Rome to whom he was now speaking. Indeed, he next said enthusiastically: "A special greeting to the Church of Rome!"

Then followed a special greeting from this bishop to his flock back in Peru, to whom he spoke in Spanish: "And if you also allow me a brief word, a greeting to everyone and in particular to my beloved Diocese of Chiclayo, in Peru, where a faithful people has accompanied its Bishop, shared its faith and given so much, so much, to continue being a faithful Church of Jesus Christ."

Returning to Italian, he ended his opening remarks by noting that that particular day was the day of the Prayer of Supplication to Our Lady of Pompeii, a figure of special veneration to the people of Italy. "Our Mother Mary always wants to walk at our side, to remain close to us, to help us with her intercession and her love," said Leo. "So I would like to pray together with you. Let us pray together for this new mission, for the whole Church, for peace in the world, and let us ask Mary, our Mother, for this special grace." He then led the faithful in the "Hail Mary" in Italian.

Tellingly, Prevost spoke no English at all from the Loggia. He had started with Italian and also spoke Latin and some Spanish. That was appropriate, given how much of his priestly life has been in Latin America.

Some American Catholics might have taken offense at their pope—the first American pope—speaking no English nor extending a greeting to his native land.[12] But such should not have been a surprise (heaped atop a surprise), given that this first American pope who had done most of his priestly work abroad and especially in Peru wanted to show the universal Church that he was universal. Of course, speaking English might have normally accentuated that point, but on the other hand, there was likely another factor at work, namely: it was long believed by papal watchers that there would "never" be an American pope, at least not in their lifetimes. They rightly suspected a fear factor among non-American Catholics—a concern that America was already the world's political-military colossus. No country dominated the global stage like the United States. The best-known temporal leader in the world was always the American president, and especially so under Donald Trump. To have the only other world leader who rivaled the American president in influence—not temporal but spiritual—was too much for much of the world. So perhaps choosing not to speak English was Prevost's strategy to allay those anxieties. It was a diplomatic overture.

One might also add that in the overwhelmingness of the moment—having spent an arduous two days at the conclave, seeing his name pick up votes upon votes, trying to come to grips with the awesome knowledge and feeling that he had been named to an exalted position that he surely never theretofore imagined, and then going into the Room of Tears to try to process it emotionally as well as intellectually and spiritually, Prevost might not have given extended thought to whether he should speak English. As for the Room of Tears, the antechamber inside the Sistine Chapel where the newly elected pope for the first time dons his papal cassock, it bears that name not because of tears of joy but because of the tears of reckoning over the weight and burden of the office he must now bear until his life's end—his last breaths. Prevost might have simply gone on autopilot with perfunctory Latin, with the proper first-language choice as Rome's bishop to speak Italian, and then to pick up with a few remarks made in the Spanish tongue in which he had toiled for the last nearly three decades. The thought of speaking English maybe never crossed his mind.

And so, he spoke mainly Italian and Latin, with a little Spanish, with the Spanish more a shout-out to his diocese in Peru. In this sense, importantly, he spoke in the tongue of his people as a bishop in Peru and now as Bishop of Rome.

LEO XIV'S FIRST BENEDICTION

With that, Leo XIV ended his first greeting to the universal Church. He finished with an official blessing from the Loggia, which, formally, is called the Loggia of the Blessings. The pope starts from that balcony in part because he starts his papacy with a blessing.

As is the traditional custom of the Roman Catholic Church, he closed with the special *Urbi et Orbi* Apostolic Blessing, one of the most meaningful and solemn expressions of prayer in the Catholic Church and provided by the papacy, most uniquely and distinctive to the Bishop of Rome. The Latin phrase *Urbi et Orbi* translates as "to the City and to the World," and is meant specifically to be delivered to both the city of Rome and the world. It reflects the pontiff's dual role and shepherdship as Bishop of Rome and leader of the worldwide Catholic Church. It has historical roots in the ancient Roman Empire, where it was used in official proclamations by the emperor that were targeted at the city of Rome and to the larger empire beyond.

The *Urbi et Orbi* prayer can be given on only three occasions: Christmas Day, Easter Sunday, and after the election of a new pope, instituting his first public act from the central balcony of St. Peter's Basilica before the faithful gathered below. All those who hear it, in person or (in today's world) by broadcast, receive a plenary indulgence for the remission of the temporal punishment of sin.

Here is the prayer in Latin:

> "*Sancti Apostoli Petrus et Paulus, de quorum potestate et auctoritate confidimus, ipsi intercedant pro nobis ad Dominum. Precibus et meritis beatæ Mariæ semper Virginis, beati Michaelis Archangeli, beati Ioannis Baptistæ, et sanctorum Apostolorum Petri et Pauli et omnium Sanctorum, misereatur vestri omnipotens Deus; et dimissis omnibus peccatis vestris, perducat vos Iesus Christus ad vitam æternam. Amen.*"

Here is the English translation:

> "May the Holy Apostles Peter and Paul, in whose power and authority we trust, intercede for us before the Lord. Through the prayers and merits of the Blessed Mary ever Virgin, of Blessed Michael the Archangel, of Blessed John the Baptist, and of the Holy Apostles Peter and Paul, and of all the Saints, may Almighty God have mercy on you,

> forgive you all your sins, and bring you to everlasting life through Jesus Christ. Amen."[13]

Fittingly for this particular new pope as a successor to Leo XIII, the prayer invokes St. Michael the Archangel. It was Leo XIII who composed the St. Michael the Archangel Prayer (more on that later in this book). That prayer calls for protection against the devil and evil spirits who "prowl about the world seeking the ruin of souls."

This new pope would need that protection.

Leo XIV then offered his benediction in Latin. The crowd clapped and the bells of the blessed basilica clanged.

SIX

A Surprised World Reacts

No sooner had the new pope wished the world peace before hell's bells clanged and the world's destroyers of peace pounced into action. Frantic online searches commenced among media mavens and verbal bomb throwers on the internet digging for dirt on the new Holy Father.

There was a problem for these maniacal searchers, however. Robert Francis Prevost was a veritable clean slate. No one knew anything about the man, and there was almost nothing about him online.[1] Perhaps the cardinals, like millions of Catholic laity they represent, were exhausted by the spectacle of a pope recklessly spouting off personal opinions and tossing the Church into a tizzy. Maybe Prevost's absence of provocative statements was precisely what the cardinal electors had been aiming for.

A blank slate with no track record of controversial statements? How refreshing!

But even then, few individuals in today's world lack some semblance of a paper trail, especially a cardinal. And so the internet erupted with rabble rousers seizing upon the smallest Prevost post to claim him as a liberal or conservative.

THE CARDINAL VS. THE VICE PRESIDENT

Liberal Americans reveled in an X post from Cardinal Prevost three months prior, in February 2025, which had referred to a comment by Donald Trump's Catholic vice president, JD Vance, on the subject of love, family, and immigration. On February 3, Prevost on his theretofore largely unread X account had reposted a February 1 article from the left-wing *National Catholic Reporter* reacting negatively to a Vance statement during a January 29 Fox News Channel interview. Vance had said:

> "There's this old school—and I think it's a very Christian concept by the way—that you love your family and then you love your neighbor, and then you love your community, and then you love your fellow citizens in your own country, and then after that, you can focus and prioritize the rest of the world. A lot of the far left has completely inverted that. . . . They seem to hate the citizens of their own country and care more about people outside their own borders. That is no way to run a society."

Interestingly, Cardinal Prevost had reacted to that.

Prevost's X account had reposted not the original Fox News link with Vance's statement but an article by writer Kat Armas of the *National Catholic Reporter* (which had referred to the original Fox News report) claiming that Vance's statement "echoes a medieval concept known as *ordo amoris*—the order of charity" which "feeds the myth that some people are more deserving of our care than others." (It is claimed that JD Vance himself first used the phrase *ordo amoris*, but the paper trail on that is not clear.[2]) That *NCR* headline was boldly titled: "JD Vance is wrong: Jesus doesn't ask us to rank our love for others."[3]

This Prevost post exploded just after his announcement as the 267th pope. It was immediately claimed by Vance critics that Cardinal Prevost himself had said that "JD Vance is wrong." That is not accurate. Prevost's account had posted the article that carried that title. To be sure, Prevost may have indeed agreed that Vance was wrong, but Prevost himself did not use those words. Notably, *ordo amoris* is a Thomistic concept built upon the work of Augustine, and thus very much something that Prevost, with a doctorate in canon law from the Angelicum and a proud Augustinian, would know something about and would be prompted to weigh in on.[4]

Befitting his more taciturn, prudent nature, Prevost had never been a wild Trump-like tweeter. The Vance item was one of the very few comments on his X page that had a grand total of 674 followers when Prevost stepped onto the Loggia as the next Holy Father, but was now suddenly exploding with millions of curious clickers.[5] In fact, Prevost had been so inactive and mild-mannered on his X page that even CNN was careful to characterize the Prevost posts on his X page—including the JD Vance item—as not necessarily posted by the person of Prevost himself (they could have been posted by someone on the cardinal's staff). CNN cautiously put it this way in its report on the Prevost posts: "An X account listed under Prevost's name did not appear to personally write any of the critical posts, but reposted articles and headlines from others. CNN has reached out to the Vatican, X and friends of Prevost, but has not been able to independently confirm the X account is connected to the newly elected Pope Leo XIV."[6]

Nonetheless, progressive Americans relished the post that pushed back against Vance, gleefully weaponizing it in the hope they had a progressive pontiff who was anti-Vance, anti-Trump, and anti-Republican. The Prevost page would be quickly taken down (presumably by the Vatican) once the cardinal became pope, but in the initial hours and days after his selection by the conclave, liberals were off and running with this dart to throw at Vance and the Trump administration. Screenshots of the post went viral, along with innumerable social-media posts claiming that the new pope "said that JD Vance is wrong." Left-wing publications like the *Daily Beast* smoked off gleeful headlines with hyperbolic titles like, "New Pope Leo XIV bashed Trump and JD Vance on Twitter just weeks ago."[7]

This became one of the first salvos fired in the political-cultural war by those who care more about ideology than theology, more about polemics than the sacraments, more about hackery than holiness.

As for Vance and President Trump, they were hardly bothered by the reported Prevost post. In fact, both men thrilled over the selection of an American pope: "Congratulations to Leo XIV, the first American Pope, on his election!" Vance posted immediately on X. "I'm sure millions of American Catholics and other Christians will pray for his successful work leading the Church. May God bless him!"[8]

Trump, the ultimate America firster, was ecstatic at the news of the first American pontiff: "Congratulations to Cardinal Robert Francis Prevost, who was just named Pope," the president immediately posted. "It is such an honor to realize that he is the first American Pope. What excitement, and what a Great Honor for our Country. I look forward to meeting Pope Leo XIV. It will be a very meaningful moment!"[9]

In short order, President Trump invited the new pope's older brother Lou to the White House. A self-identified "MAGA" Trump Republican, Lou had been active on social media with posts highly critical of and often insulting toward liberal Democrats. His posts were quickly mined and reposted and became an immediate sensation, especially his derogatory comments about 2024 Democratic Party presidential nominee Kamala Harris and former Democrat Speaker of the House (and Catholic) Nancy Pelosi. Lou scurried to remove or cover for these posts to spare his little brother—the new pope—from embarrassment.[10] Nonetheless, they were noticed, including by President Trump.

An appreciative Trump invited Lou and his wife Deborah to the Oval Office on May 20. They were photographed with the president and vice president. "I like the pope and I like the pope's brother," Trump told reporters with a smile. He said of Leo: "I look forward to getting him to the White House. I want to shake his hand. I want to give him a big hug."[11]

ACCUSATIONS OF COVERING UP SEX ABUSE

Unfortunately, not all the reception for Pope Leo was so euphoric. Material immediately began circulating claiming that Prevost had covered up clerical sex abuse in Chicago and in Peru.[12]

One of the most-clicked reports came from a post at Edward Pentin's Substack newsletter. Pentin is a serious, respected reporter, and his *College of Cardinals Report* was a go-to source on the backgrounds of the *papabili*. Thus, what his May 5 post had reported just three days earlier was indeed troubling.[13]

The post was an article not by Pentin but by Spanish reporter Jaime Gurpegui in the independent Spanish-language newspaper *InfoVaticana*, founded in 2013 by Gabriel Ariza and Fernando Beltrán.[14] Titled, "A chance encounter with Fr Martin and Austen Ivereigh reveals their papal candidate," it reported on the author, Gurpegui, strolling around *Borgo Pio* in Rome during the days just before the conclave and running into LGBTQ activist-Jesuit Fr. James Martin and British biographer of Pope Francis, Austen Ivereigh, both Francis enthusiasts. Gurpegui wrote:

> Upon seeing them, my friend and travel companion wanted to say hello, so we introduced ourselves: "We're from *InfoVaticana*." The reaction was immediate and, frankly, revealing. James Martin, author of *"Building a Bridge,"* that book that claims to build bridges between the Church and those on the margins, turned his back on us without saying a word. No dialogue, no bridge, not even a greeting. . . .
>
> Austen Ivereigh, on the other hand, did speak to us . . . though perhaps he wishes he hadn't.

Gurpegui described Ivereigh as "visibly upset—and increasingly so as the conversation went on." He said that Ivereigh "strongly reproached us for the 'campaign' he believes we're running against Cardinal Robert Prevost." Gurpegui replied, "No, not against Prevost; against the culture of cover-up in the Church—are you now in favor of that?" In this case, a cover-up that also involved Cardinal Prevost allegedly hiding sex abuse in Peru. Gurpegui said that Ivereigh's "discomfort was palpable." When Gurpegui and his colleague explained that "there are many cases, all documented," Ivereigh was displeased. Said Gurpegui: "His reaction left no doubt: Prevost was their man, the candidate in whom they had placed all their hopes. The scene could not have been more telling. Just hours before the Conclave begins, the insiders are nervous. Not because anyone is slandering Prevost, but because the truth is coming to light."

According to Gurpegui, "the documents, the testimonies, and the omissions [against Prevost] are there—documented and published. And more are on the way." As for the reactions of Ivereigh and Martin, Gurpegui concluded: "It's revealing: the same circle that calls for synodality, transparency, and bridges of dialogue cannot stand it when the dark corners of their allies are illuminated.

For some, the culture of cover-up isn't a past to overcome—it's still a strategy they're trying to maintain."

Were these claims accurate?

Valid or not, Edward Pentin's same-day post of the May 5 Gurpegui article at *InfoVaticana* went viral upon the announcement of Prevost being named the next Holy Father. Personally, I received it from a Vatican insider as a text message at 1:31 p.m. EST that Thursday, May 8, immediately after Leo was first announced at the Loggia. The texter was furious, especially at the likes of Fr. Martin and Ivereigh for pushing for a pope that this Vatican insider believed was compromised and felt certain that more would later come out on these allegations, embarrassing the Church as a whole. "This is a TRIUMPH of James Martin and the Left," texted the insider.

The report was initially favored and picked up by right-wing sources, who feared that the conclave had selected another pontiff in the mold of Pope Francis. The extraordinarily influential and controversial right-wing talk-show host Alex Jones ran with it. I began receiving other texts. One friend wrote, "The Catholic Church is toast. This is going to explode."

Soon, other articles surfaced from the previous couple of days, including a May 4 piece (which preceded the *InfoVaticana* article) from a publication called *Globe Banner* and a May 6, 2025, article from an Italian Catholic publication. Here, too, both featured shocking allegations.[15]

How soon before this scandal exploded into the mainstream media? The answer: not long. The morning after Prevost had become pope, CNN.com dropped a bombshell headline: "Victims' group alleges Pope Leo XIV mishandled sexual abuse cases involving priests in Chicago and Peru."[16] The article focused on alleged Prevost cover-ups in Chicago and in Peru. It opened with this:

> Six weeks before American Cardinal Robert Prevost became Pope Leo XIV, the activist group Survivors Network of those Abused by Priests (SNAP) filed a complaint against him, along with other church leaders, to the Vatican's Secretary of State, Cardinal Pietro Parolin.
>
> The group alleged Prevost "harmed the vulnerable and caused scandal" by mishandling two situations—in Chicago in 2000, and in Peru in 2022—involving priests accused of sexual abuse.

According to CNN, the group charged that Prevost, as "provincial supervisor" in Chicago for the Augustinian order in 2000, had allowed a priest accused of abusing at least 13 minors to live at the Augustinian order's St. John Stone Friary in Hyde Park, which was only half a block from St. Thomas the Apostle Elementary School. The priest, Fr. James Ray, had been barred for nearly a decade from any parish work or from being alone with minors. According to the group's complaint, these were restrictions that the Archdiocese of Chicago had noted when it asked Prevost to allow Ray to live at the friary. And yet, claimed the group's spokeswoman, "The school was never notified."

According to CNN, in 2002, "after the US Conference of Catholic Bishops tightened their policies, Ray was moved from the priory and removed from public ministry. He was removed from the priesthood in 2012." The report did not say if Prevost had been the person in 2002 who removed Ray.

The article had more such details, including an allegation from Peru.

These were certainly not friendly reports on the new pope, who, for the record, did have defenders who rushed to his side.

Regarding the allegations in Peru, the current bishop of Chiclayo, Edinson Farfán—who was Prevost's successor in that position—came to his defense. Responding to a question at a press conference regarding the allegation that Prevost had covered up sex abuse in the diocese, Farfán stated: "That's a lie. He has listened, he has respected the processes, and this process is still ongoing . . . believe me, I am the most interested person in justice being served and, above all, in being able to help the victims."[17]

A particularly forceful defense came from Bill Donohue's Catholic League. It blasted the new pope's accusers as "smear merchants." Donohue wrote: "Having written a book on this subject, *The Truth about Clergy Sexual Abuse: Clarifying the Facts and the Causes,* I can say with confidence that the accusations of a cover-up by Cardinal Prevost are false. If anything, Pope Leo XIV acted fairly and with dispatch."[18]

The Catholic League distributed that statement twice, on May 14 and again a few weeks later on July 2 when the story resurfaced. Given that this story likely will not go away, the Catholic League will surely stay on it in the years ahead. We can expect re-releases of that statement.

"NEGATIVE REMARKS" ABOUT GAYS: "AT ODDS" WITH FRANCIS

The knives were out. But soon enough, the attackers were conflicted.

Liberal journalists who initially delighted in Prevost's post against JD Vance grimaced upon hearing reports that the new pope is a Republican. Among the first sources to dig up that information was conservative activist Charlie Kirk, whose Turning Point USA has a huge following, as well as Bill Donohue's Catholic League, which included that information in a May 9 e-newsletter.[19]

That Republican revelation no doubt frosted the liberal American media. Liberal journalists went to work, digging for dirt on the new pope. At 3:00 EST the day after Leo's selection came another report that really made progressives fume: a piece by the left-wing British newspaper *The Guardian*. It went viral among liberals.

Darkly titled, "Unearthed comments from new pope alarm LGBTQ+ Catholics," it included the subhead, "Previous negative remarks by Pope Leo XIV about 'homosexual lifestyle' at odds with papacy of Pope Francis."[20] *The Guardian* article opened with an outrageously inaccurate statement of comparison: "After years of sympathetic and inclusive comments from Pope Francis, LGBTQ+ Catholics expressed concern on Thursday about hostile remarks made more than a decade ago by Father Robert Prevost, the new Pope Leo XIV, in which he condemned what he called the 'homosexual lifestyle' and 'the redefinition of marriage' as 'at odds with the Gospel.'"

In truth, as this book has shown, Francis for years as pope (and prior as a cardinal) made harsh, if not incendiary, comments about homosexuality and same-sex "marriage." Only uninformed liberals, who knew of only the single "Who am I to judge?" comment from Francis, could be so ignorant of his many other remarks, including referring to homosexual activity as "faggotry." As for Cardinal Prevost's one unearthed remark on homosexuals, it was remarkably mild by comparison. (That October 2012 statement by Prevost will be examined in the pages ahead.) Prevost had quite innocuously stated that the "Western mass media is extraordinarily effective in fostering within the general public enormous sympathy for beliefs and practices that are at odds with the Gospel—for example abortion, homosexual lifestyle, euthanasia."

The Guardian piece was widely clicked and distributed and quickly became the basis for belligerent social-media accusations among progressives that the new pope was "homophobic," "intolerant," "divisive," and "hates" gay people.

FR. JAMES MARTIN AND CARDINALS BURKE AND SARAH UNITE

As usual, much of the media and sparring politicos behaved like scoundrels, looking to take the Catholic Church and world right back into the Francis days of division, seeking to pit people against one another. But from inside the Church, there were immediate displays of unity, even among American Church officials who came from firmly opposite sides.

Despite the suggestions that the new pope did not like "gay" people, he had LGBTQ activist Jesuit priest Fr. James Martin firmly on his side.

Martin was very pleased with the selection of Robert Francis Prevost and did not hesitate to heap praise on the new pope. He was ebullient in his thrill over the choice, so much so that his gushing statements of support struck fear into Church traditionalists that the Prevost pick was something ominous that they should greatly fear.

The first statement from Martin came immediately with the naming of Prevost, signaling that he had been ready for the post if Prevost turned out to be the choice. Martin posted on his X account at 1:49 p.m. EST on May 8: "I know Pope Leo XIV to be a kind, open, humble, modest, decisive, hard-working, straightforward, trustworthy, and down-to-earth man. A brilliant choice. May God bless him."[21]

It was fascinating to see followers of Fr. Martin pounce on the priest, seeing his endorsement as a menacing omen regarding the new Holy Father. "Well then, that settles it. Another non-Christian Pope," said the first response. Another reply: "Hopefully he defrocks you." Yet another denounced Martin in harsh terms: "Hopefully, you'll regret this, you disgusting heretic."

More charitable to Martin, but also symptomatic of the blowback to the Jesuit's endorsement, was this reply from Deacon Keith

Fournier: "your reassurance does not help Father. You reject the unchangeable teaching of the Catholic Church on marriage as solely possible between one man and one woman and the intrinsic evil of homosexual acts. Reaffirm the teaching of the scripture, the Magisterium, and the natural law."

Clearly, many of Fr. James Martin's X followers are not fans.

Martin could not contain his excitement over Prevost. He fired off multiple posts and statements and videos of himself raving about the new pontiff. The next day, May 9, he posted one of several videos, stating of the new pontiff: "He's committed to continuing this process (of Synodality) of Pope Francis to make the Church more listening, more welcoming, and more inclusive." The video highlighted every element of Prevost that Martin saw as progressive or social-justice oriented, making Leo XIV sound more like a man of the political left.[22]

Once again, Martin's followers pounced on this video, which just three days later already had over 278,000 views. The first three comments were all negative if not vitriolic toward Martin. "So he's [Leo] a globalist socialist . . . gotcha," read the first post. The next one wished for Martin: "Hoping that you repent and become Catholic, publicly denouncing homosexuality and deeming it a mortal sin, warning people of its dangers." And the third reply: "When is this guy going to finally be defrocked?"

Again, Martin's followers did not seem to be Martin fans. And his words that had sought to reassure the world of this new pope had merely unsettled those who did not like the LGBTQ Jesuit priest.

And what really rattled Martin's opponents was the aforementioned May 5 Substack piece by Edward Pentin from *InfoVaticana* that went viral, which had reported that Fr. Martin and Austen Ivereigh were campaigning for Prevost: "Prevost was their man, the candidate in whom they had placed all their hopes."[23]

That reality quickly dashed hopes of many conservatives concerning the new pope. Fr. James Martin's endorsement and encomiums upset conservative Catholics who suspected that Robert Francis Prevost was a Manchurian candidate slid through the conclave by a leftist cabal.

However, there was a key problem with that theory, as will be evident in the pages ahead:

To soar through that conclave in only four ballots, at a time of a half dozen to a dozen legitimate *papabili* candidates, Prevost must have had backers from the left, the right, and in between. Did the likes of conservative Cardinals Burke, Sarah, and Erdő vote for him or at last eventually fall behind him in subsequent ballots?

Indeed, here was a big twist for conservative Catholics disheartened by Fr. Martin's excitement for Prevost: both Cardinals Raymond Burke and Robert Sarah, like Fr. James Martin, quickly came forward with strong words of support for Leo XIV. No, their words were nothing like the effusive praise heaped by Fr. James Martin, but they were positive nonetheless.

Burke immediately posted an online statement that May 8:

> Please join me in thanking Our Lord for the election of Pope Leo XIV, Successor of Saint Peter, as the Shepherd of the Church throughout the world. The Shrine of Our Lady of Guadalupe at La Crosse has a particularly strong bond with the Roman Pontiff, especially through its affiliation with the Papal Basilica of Saint Mary Major.
>
> I urge all pilgrims and friends of the Shrine to pray fervently for Pope Leo XIV that Our Lord, through the intercession of Our Lady of Guadalupe, Saint Peter Apostle, and Pope Saint Leo the Great, will grant him abundant wisdom, strength, and courage to do all that Our Lord is asking of Him in these tumultuous

> times. May God bless Pope Leo and grant him many years. *Viva il Papa!*[24]

The Cardinal Burke statement might be dismissed by some as a general statement that could be given for any new pope, with a cardinal offering perfunctory prayers and seeking those of others, including heavenly intercessors. On the other hand, the statement was quite positive, suggesting enthusiasm and gratitude. The very first words in the statement are especially significant: "Please join me in thanking Our Lord for the election of Pope Leo XIV."

Raymond Leo Burke is a highly educated and nuanced Church theologian, a careful canon lawyer who served as no less than prefect of the Supreme Tribunal of the Apostolic Signatura under Pope Benedict XVI. For him to credit the Lord Himself for election of Pope Leo XIV was no small thing.

The same applies to close Burke friend, colleague, and fellow cardinal Robert Sarah. Sarah likewise issued a strong statement of support for Leo XIV, which he posted on his X account the next day.[25]

"God cares for us, God loves all of us, and evil will not prevail!" declared Cardinal Sarah. "We are all in God's hands. Therefore, without fear, united hand in hand with God and among ourselves, let us move forward." Sarah shared several quotations from Leo XIV's opening remarks from the Loggia. He concluded quite positively: "Great joy! May God abundantly bless Pope Leo XIV! We pray fervently!"

As with Burke's statement, Sarah's appraisal could be viewed as a general, perfunctory show of support for the new head of the Roman Catholic Church. And yet, the highly positive nature was undeniable.

It is difficult to find other areas of such shared ground among Robert Sarah, Raymond Leo Burke, and James Martin.

To be sure, Sarah and Burke issued just one initial statement—which would be expected—but Fr. James Martin went wild with many posts and statements, which is expected of Martin and the social media beast that he is. We will see, however, that Burke would issue another strong statement on Leo XIV's behalf in the weeks ahead.

PRAISE FROM MORE CARDINALS

In the days and weeks ahead, many Church officials stepped forward to hail Prevost as the right man at the right time, as Spirit-led and divinely inspired. And again, they came from across the spectrum.

Among them, Singapore Cardinal William Goh called Prevost a "gift of God." He predicted of Leo: "I believe that there will be greater collaboration and greater dialogue so that we can truly bring about a greater unity in the Church." Like Pope Francis, Cardinal Goh touts the idea of "synodality," but clarifies: "I keep on emphasizing that we cannot talk about synodality without unity in doctrines, without unity in faith."[26]

Goh said that the Church and larger world had been craving a pope "who can unite" rather than divide with ambiguity. He said: "I believe Leo XIV is the right man for the job." Goh gave a sense of how he voted when he said in an interview roughly two weeks after the conclave: "I don't vote based on continent or culture. I want to vote for a pope who is truly inspired by the Holy Spirit."[27]

The Asian cardinal also sees a distinct advantage in Prevost speaking English as his first language, particularly for fellow Asian clergy. "The good thing about Pope Leo is that he speaks English, because very often many of the Asian cardinals don't speak Italian so well," said Goh. "So we want to communicate and to share our views with the Holy Father but it's a bit difficult because of the language."

Cardinal Gerhard Müller, another traditionalist in the camp of Burke and Sarah, credited the Prevost selection to the hand of the

Holy Spirit. "Despite the predicted partisan fights, it all happened in 24 hours," he said of the conclave's surprisingly quick decision. "That shows that there was a great deal of unanimity, that it was not possible to push a candidate, but that someone who was relatively unknown to the public was elected so quickly." Cardinal Müller concluded: "You can only really understand this if you are a Christian believer and believe in the Holy Spirit, i.e., in the work of grace."[28]

Müller further stated: "After all, the [College of Cardinals] was set up so heterogeneously by the will of Pope Francis that all nations and languages—some of them couldn't speak Italian or even English—were represented, so you have to wonder why this decision was able to emerge so quickly from such a heterogeneous college."

Müller confidently predicted that Pope Leo "will certainly contribute to greater unity and reduce unnecessary conflicts."

High praise also came from Swedish Cardinal Anders Arborelius. "The Conclave was a wonderful experience of unity in the Church and openness to the voice of the Spirit," said Arborelius. "It was really an experience of God's grace to see a cardinal who suddenly became the vicar of Christ, and I could feel that he was the right person, chosen by God." The first-ever Scandinavian cardinal said he was "struck" by Pope Leo's "humility and simplicity." He viewed Leo as "a person eager to establish dialogue on so many levels."

Cardinal Arborelius summed up, "I am very grateful for Pope Leo."[29]

Many readers here know that most of these cardinals are considered conservatives. And when it came to Leo XIV, they stood with Fr. James Martin. There was unified praise among voices from across the divide.

And such was precisely what the new pope and his Church had been seeking in Francis's successor.

SEVEN

The Vote at the Vatican: A Prevost Consensus

The pick of Cardinal Robert Francis Prevost as the next head of the Roman Catholic Church had been a stunner. Nonetheless, after trying to process the initial shock of the pick that Thursday afternoon, May 8, one began to slowly suspect that Cardinal Prevost must have been some sort of consensus candidate given that he was chosen by merely the fourth ballot. Most observers had figured that the consensus guy would be someone like Cardinal Parolin or Cardinal Pizzaballa. Surely Prevost received support from both so-called liberals and conservatives alike, as well as those in between. After all, he needed 89 votes. He got them, and much sooner than anyone would have guessed.

Speculation ran wild.

As for the conservatives, one source estimated:

> Well, when Francis appoints 80+ percent of the eligible Cardinals, we never had a chance of getting a true traditionalist. Francis appointed 108 voting eligible cardinals . . . no need for consensus when you stack the deck. My only hope is Leo is to even slightly to the right of Francis and we can slowly build towards the good old days.[1]

Liberals, too, seemed perplexed. They were banking on several potential candidates, none of them named Prevost.

Adding to the mystery about the man chosen is that Prevost did not have a long public track record. The lack of a paper trail spoke volumes, suggesting that Prevost was not one inclined to shoot off his mouth. Indeed, maybe that taciturn nature—call it prudence, i.e., a virtue—was one of the reasons he was selected by his fellow cardinals. He might be more silent, thoughtful, and thus offering less chaos.

That thoughtfulness would be just what the doctor ordered, or cardinals ordered.

Still more mysterious, though an American, Prevost had done most of his priestly mission work outside the United States and specifically in Peru. He had become a naturalized citizen of Peru—a dual citizen of two Americas, both North and South America. The day after Leo XIV's announcement, the Italians were saying that Leo was the "least American" of the American cardinals, which was not meant as an insult but as a statement of fact. One might also say that he was the most universal of the American cardinals. Unlike all the other American cardinals, this one did not have an American diocese. Indeed, because of Prevost's universality, American papal watcher and longtime Catholic Church journalist John Allen had said that if there would be an American pope it would be Prevost.

Such was the early thinking, rife with speculation and uncertainties about how this historical quirk had happened.

PREVOST OVER PAROLIN

In short order, more information began emerging on how the cardinals voted and how rapidly a consensus had built up for Prevost. Evolving information appeared in the Italian press the next day.

The multi-line headline in the Italian newspaper, *Il Giornale*, said much about Italian feelings regarding the new pope and about the nonselection of Cardinal Pietro Parolin: "The Italian disappointment. The favorite Parolin remained without the votes from Africa and Asia. Decisive pre-Conclave and [Cardinal Timothy] Dolan's 'direction.'" That lengthy title was followed by this subhead: "The Secretary of State [Parolin] entered with a package of 40–50 consensus, but half the world looked elsewhere. The conservative American cardinal [Dolan] is a true kingmaker."[2]

For the record, how reporters were able to get any of this information is itself an intriguing if not disturbing question, given that the cardinal electors were sworn to silence regarding what happens behind the locked door of the Sistine Chapel. Recall the oath that the cardinal electors had taken just two days earlier at 5:00 Rome time on May 7 before walking into the chapel, which included this specific vow of confidentiality:

> In a particular way, we promise and swear to observe with the greatest fidelity and with all persons, clerical or lay, secrecy regarding everything that in any way relates to the election of the Roman Pontiff and regarding what occurs in the place of the election, directly or indirectly related to the results of the voting; we promise and swear not to break this secret in any way, either during or after the election of the new Pontiff.

Clearly, that oath was violated by certain unnamed cardinals who talked about what had occurred in the place of the election. Then again, such divulging of secrets and explicit oath-breaking has become standard fare for papal elections. Some cardinals apparently cannot zip their lips and take their oath more seriously. Pope John Paul II had tried to stop this, and by May 9 was (yet again) rolling over in his grave.

Regardless, the world was more than happy (and hungry) for any details regarding how Robert Francis Prevost had been chosen. Here was what was subsequently reported:

The *Il Giornale* piece was written by reporter Stefano Zurlo. *Il Giornale* is an Italian newspaper with Italian sympathies. Its take on what had just happened showed a special favoring of the Italian Secretary of State Cardinal Parolin, who undoubtedly had been the worldwide projected favorite for the papal post. "The whole world looked to the Secretary of State," said Stefano Zurlo. "And to the party of Italian cardinals." That was true, given other leading Italian candidates such as Matteo Zuppi and Pierbattista Pizzaballa. Sure, conceded Zurlo, the name of Robert Prevost had surfaced in recent days "but always in the background" (at best) and in front of him always "until last night there was always him: Pietro Parolin."

Yes, until the last night. As they say in sports, the game isn't over until it's over. There may be a heavy favorite, but that's why you play the game.

Alas, regretted Zurlo, "It didn't go that way. Parolin is the big loser, even if it is difficult to say how the turning point that few expected has matured."

Zurlo noted that some observers had in retrospect speculated that Prevost had already surged to the fore during the general congregations, the pre-conclave meetings among the cardinals following Francis's funeral. Zurlo acknowledged that such analysis had elements of truth: "After all, the pre-Conclave always has great importance. Even more so in this session, with many cardinals who barely knew the names of their colleagues."

But here was where the *Il Giornale* piece brought in some provocative new information. Stefano Zurlo said that "decisive" was the "activism of the archbishop of New York Timothy Dolan who played as a kingmaker." Dolan was presumed to have made the case for Prevost, this "atypical figure" who stood "at the crossroads of different cultures: a father with French and Italian origins, a Spanish mother. And then the missionary dimension, but without losing its roots in the United States." Zurlo portrayed Cardinal Dolan as pushing for Prevost and attracting cardinal voters from North and South America, from the English-speaking world, including "the old British Empire," and even from South Africa, India, and the Tonga Islands.

As for Parolin, Zurlo claimed that the Italian secretary of state had entered the conclave with "a certain package of votes, it is said between forty and fifty," but not enough to "reach the quorum." For Parolin, "The problem is that at the first vote it was discovered that another candidate, Prevost, had captured a lot of consensus in the shadows." As for "the Bergoglians"—those cardinals hoping for "Francis II"—they had divided themselves "into different groups and were unable to propose an alternative: for example, the French, also highly rated, Jean-Marc Aveline, or the Maltese Mario Grech."

As for another Italian *papabile* of considerable respect and standing, Pierbattista Pizzaballa carried some unanticipated baggage. Ironically, his wartime experience in Jerusalem was not considered a strength but a liability. Being that he was "coming from Jerusalem, one of the most overheated areas of the earth, [he was] therefore fatally judged too political."

As much as Zurlo appeared to know with this news report, he conceded that it was still "impossible to know" exactly what happened in the Sistine Chapel, though he conceded that, "After the first vote, something must have clicked among the cardinals, particularly those from Africa and Asia. They must have seen in Prevost, who is also highly esteemed in Rome, not the leading exponent of the world's leading power, but the best expression of a West that does not wallow in the mirror but is able to launch itself beyond its limits."

In his nuanced analysis, Zurlo returned once again to the subject of Pietro Parolin, who had walked into the conclave as the top dog and left defeated, carrying the same rank in the Curia as when he entered. Zurlo repeated what others were reporting and speculating, namely, "that the secret and controversial agreement reached with the Beijing government weighed on Parolin."

That was no doubt true. By May 2025, there remained the still mystifying, inexplicable, embarrassing if not humiliating, ignorant if not inane, naïve if not duplicitous, and above all bafflingly unclear, Vatican–Beijing agreement negotiated by Francis and his crony, Argentinian Bishop Marcelo Sanchez Sorondo. Recall that Sorondo was Francis's right-hand man on China, who in February 2018 had doted on the deadly communist leadership in Beijing. He claimed that more than any other country in the world, the communist Chinese "best realize the social doctrine of the Church" and had "defended the dignity of the human person." The dictatorship, said Sorondo, was "assuming a moral leadership that others have abandoned."

This scandal unavoidably circled back to the person of Pietro Parolin. Parolin was secretary of state all 12 years of Francis's papacy. As the Holy See's top foreign official, Parolin took much blame for the China fiasco, whether he personally deserved it or not. How much did Parolin know and do? Again, as with so much that unfolded under Francis, no one ever got answers. Was this disaster the pontiff's doing or his personnel? The pope, an adviser, or the secretary of state? It was certainly fair to assign responsibility to some extent to the secretary of state who served the entirety of Francis's 12 years. The Beijing debacle became an albatross around the neck of Francis's once-respected chief diplomat. That one issue alone may have cost Pietro Parolin the papacy.

Consequently, said Stefano Zurlo, such factors meant that something had changed on the way into the conclave, and the most eligible cardinal, Parolin, was out, leaving "according to tradition, from the Conclave exactly as he had entered."

Whichever cardinal enters the conclave as "pope," leaves as a cardinal.

Instead, averred Zurlo, in a very much unforeseen turn of events, Robert Prevost became the first pope of the First World, backed by cardinals of the Third World. "A political masterpiece," marveled Zurlo, "but also a sign of the extraordinary unpredictability of the Spirit that blows where it wills. Disrupting all predictions."

The *Il Giornale* report summed up with a distinctly Italian lament: "the dream of bringing an Italian—Parolin, or perhaps Pizzaballa or Zuppi—back to St. Peter's" was dead once again. It was not unlike what had happened in 2013, when the time that had seemed tailor made for Italian Cardinal Angelo Scola instead crowned Jorge Mario Bergoglio. In 2013, the time was ripe for a South American with Italian ethnic roots; in 2025, it was a cardinal from a South American diocese with North American ethnic roots.

Much more could be said about Parolin, though the focus of this book is Prevost. We shall close with this, which offers another telling insight into the failure of the top candidate for the papacy to get the job, and further illustrates how remarkable it was that Prevost in just four rounds of balloting blew past the Vatican secretary of state.

Another Italian publication, *La Nuova Bussola Quotidiana* (*The New Daily Compass*), had reported on May 3 that Pietro Parolin was lobbying hard for the job (unlike Prevost). And though the secretary of state was "currently in the lead, personally hunting for the missing votes to secure the papacy," reporter Riccardo Cascioli foresaw too many obstacles for Cardinal Parolin—liabilities and casualties from having been such a high-ranking official in the Francis regime. These included matters ranging from the China fiasco to the scandalous case of Italian Cardinal Giovanni Angelo Becciu (another unpleasant topic altogether).

Yes, once again, the China issue.

In a rather fascinating display, *La Nuova Bussola Quotidiana* noted that the China albatross reappeared in full flight those days before the conclave by the presence of the brave Cardinal Joseph Zen in Rome for the Francis funeral, who apparently had been permitted the travel by the Chinese communist leadership. The 93-year-old Zen was a hero, what the late Bishop Fulton Sheen might have called a "dry martyr," sacrificed by the Francis regime's "social doctrine" champions. He was ignored if not mistreated by the Bergoglians, akin to how the "dry martyr" Hungarian Cardinal Mindszenty had been sacrificed by Pope Paul VI and his group of Soviet accommodationists in the 1970s.[3]

When Zen showed up in Rome for the pre-conclave meetings, it was like a ghost hovering around Francis's casket, reminding everyone of his dry martyrdom the last several years by the previous pope and his lieutenants. The specter of this still surviving symbol of human rights haunted anyone associated with Francis who hoped to be pope. Though Zen was too old to be an elector in the conclave, his presence cast a shadow, if not effectively a vote or two or many more.

What was Parolin going to do with that specter? If he was lobbying to be pope, Zen and China were not helpful to the cause. Still, the crafty diplomat reportedly got to work.

The May 3 article in *La Nuova Bussola Quotidiana* was tellingly titled, "Parolin, the great manipulator who wants to be the Pope." It claimed that Parolin, not wanting those serious weaknesses from 2013–25 to come to light during the pre-conclave general congregations, was carefully controlling and even "manipulating" the meetings, steering them toward a preconceived purpose, all the while claiming to want "dialogue," which had been very much the Francis way at the pope's synods. However, a dozen years of such manipulations had tired and angered cardinals who were sick of being promised "dialogue" while feeling all along that meetings were staged rather than functioning as real forums for debate and discussion. According to *La Nuova Bussola Quotidiana*, the pre-conclave meetings organized by Parolin and Camerlengo Kevin Farrell—Prefect of the Dicastery for Laity, Family, and Life, and a liberal American cardinal appointed by Francis—had aimed "to suppress and direct as much as possible the debate on the most important issues for the Church."[4]

The degree to which Parolin allegedly wanted to be pope was eye-opening, requiring his best diplomatic and political skills. According to *La Nuova Bussola Quotidiana*, the secretary of state was attempting quite a balancing act, "showing himself on the one hand to be close to Pope Francis and his successor, but at the same time giving the impression of marking the distance that would reassure those who have suffered the confusion (to use a euphemism) of the pontificate that has just ended." This reportedly prompted a fascinating overture by Parolin.

La Nuova Bussola Quotidiana reporter Riccardo Cascioli claimed from his sources (unnamed) that "it is Cardinal Parolin himself who has approached some of his fellow cardinals, promising to cancel *Traditionis custodes* (the witch-hunt against the ancient rite) and *Fiducia supplicans* (the blessing of same-sex couples) in exchange for their votes." If accurate, such an overture by Parolin would have been plainly remarkable, and yet not entirely surprising given the mess created by those two Francis documents. As Cascioli predicted, such a move by Parolin might have satisfied and won over some of the cardinals, "but it remains to be seen whether it will be enough to reach a quorum" (i.e., the 89-vote threshold).

It turned out that it would not be enough. Cardinal Parolin did not make the threshold. It was Cardinal Prevost who did. Blame it on China.

THREE-WAY RACE FROM THE START

As the hours, days, and weeks proceeded, yet more tantalizing details emerged on the conclave balloting.

Another Italian newspaper, *Corriere Della Sera*, likewise provided some very interesting numbers the day after the vote unfolded. According to Vatican reporter Alberto Melloni, by the third ballot, Parolin and Prevost had become the two leaders, with Parolin at 49 votes and Prevost at 38, while a third of remaining cardinals were split up among preferred others. That 49, however, seemed to be Parolin's ceiling. By the afternoon, said Melloni, "the votes shifted to the American cardinal, exceeding the figure of 89."[5] Perhaps Prevost's strong second-place posting had suggested to the cardinals not supporting Parolin that they had their man in Prevost.

These electors, said *Corriere Della Serra*, felt the need for an "anti-Bergoglian reversal [to keep] the barque of Peter sailing in the stormy sea of history." The ship "must continue to sail."

As time moves on, still more inside information may emerge on how the conclave vote had proceeded, despite the vows of silence taken by cardinal electors.

To that end, about a month after the vote, another intriguing report appeared in *La Nuova Bussola Quotidiana*, claiming that the papal vote had been a "three-way race" from the outset, with Prevost one of the three, along with Cardinal Parolin and the conservative favorite, Cardinal Peter Erdő of Hungary. According to the newspaper's sources, the first ballot ended with 25 votes for Erdő, 25 for Prevost, and 24 for Parolin.[6]

In other words, Prevost had never been an underdog.

La Nuova Bussola Quotidiana reporter Nico Spuntoni related that a salient fact that emerged on day one of the conclave was the unity of the conservatives. Though aware that they were in the minority within the conclave, they "were determined to make their presence felt nonetheless." Apparently, their 25 votes for Erdő was a strong signal of that.

What about the other two front runners, Parolin and Prevost?

According to Spuntoni, another significant factor that emerged in the first round of voting was that Parolin's name "was considered as weak as Prevost's." That weakness spoke unfavorably of Parolin's candidacy (given that he had been the perceived front-runner) but favorably for Prevost.

Moreover, the favorable emergence of Prevost "came as only a partial surprise, as the Augustinian had already attracted attention during the general congregations, being named as the first choice by several Latin American cardinals and as the second or third choice by other influential cardinals." Prevost's history as a missionary in Peru served as a strengthening "counterbalance" to his American nationality. But even then, said Spuntoni, the "not too American" cardinal was seen as someone who could "revitalize the relationship with Catholicism in the United States, which had deteriorated during Bergoglio's twelve-year pontificate, and as a counterweight to Donald Trump's cumbersome presidency."

This was a crucial, keen insight by Spuntoni.

Francis's ideological colonization of the American cardinalate had taken a toll on the American Church, where Catholicism had thrived under Popes John Paul II and Benedict XVI. Francis had blown a hole in it. Perhaps an American pope could help heal the rift.

And thus, reported Spuntoni, by the evening of May 7, the "Augustinian from Chicago" must have returned to Santa Marta "feeling something like Angelo Roncalli" did at the start of the 1958 conclave, when the would-be Pope John XXIII felt like "the water was boiling" for him. Moreover, there were no salient or overwhelming objections to Prevost, as there were for Parolin. Plus, Prevost was also perceived as perhaps "the only one of Bergoglio's prefects" who was "appreciated by conservatives."

And thus, assessed Spuntoni, what transpired is what has often happened in the long history of papal conclaves: "the first consideration was who not to elect, and the choice of who to elect then became almost natural." The convergence of conservative votes that had once gone to Erdő realized that the Hungarian cardinal would not get the three-quarters needed and "most likely" went to Prevost, including the votes of fellow countrymen such as cardinals Raymond Leo Burke and Timothy Dolan.

As for Parolin's bid, Spuntoni reported that after round one, it was inevitable that Parolin and "his people" would step aside. By day two, "the conditions were in place for the momentum that led Prevost to secure over 100 votes in the fourth ballot. . . . The Sacred College emerged from the Sistine Chapel more united than expected." Here Spuntoni added that Leo XIV's initial actions from the Loggia confirmed to the electors that they had made the right choice.

Spuntoni wrapped up by saying that, "After twelve difficult years, the conservatives made a flattering impression in the Conclave by converging on an 'outsider' candidate who was unassailable."

Looking forward, Spuntoni speculated that perhaps Leo XIV will "recognize" the group of conservatives who backed him by bringing Erdő into the Curia. Moreover, he averred that it "would also not be surprising" if the new pope continued on with Parolin as secretary of state "for at least the first year of the pontificate."

In sum, according to this analysis, Robert Francis Prevost had never been the underdog that Vatican watchers had forecast him to be. He had been a front-runner from the outset.

PREVOST'S OVERWHELMING MARGIN OF VICTORY

Overall, these articles in the Italian press contained some revelatory early information, as did some reports by English-speaking journalists. The data was extraordinary in the unanticipated degree to which it showed an overwhelming margin of victory for Robert Francis Prevost.

On May 12, the first Monday after the vote, veteran Vatican journalists Edward Pentin of the *National Catholic Register* and *Inside the Vatican*'s Robert Moynihan both reported the scoop circulating among Vaticanistas in Rome, namely, that Prevost by the fourth ballot had reached not only 89 votes but soared to over 100.[7] Yes, 100 plus. It was a landslide for the Chicago native and now head of the Holy See.

The Pentin piece was particularly revealing, breaking important material on the voting patterns at the conclave. It was interesting that Pentin's piece opened with a quote from an encounter with Cardinal Parolin, which showed the secretary of state not to be a sore loser.

"You must be very happy that an American was elected," said a smiling Parolin to Pentin as he strolled along the Via della Conciliazione toward the Vatican on a sunny Sunday afternoon. He generously told Pentin that with the election of Prevost the Church will be "at peace," as it once had been "at the time of the apostles, under the guidance of the Holy Spirit."

That was truly high praise. It signaled the immediate widespread feeling of a positive, marked departure from the previous pontificate.

Pentin reported that Parolin's sentiments echoed a palpable sense of "hope, optimism, and peace" that seemed to suddenly be pervading Rome on the heels of Leo's election. Pentin provided an array of quotes from Church liberals and conservatives alike reflective of that sunny optimism that Sunday.

Pentin next quoted one of the most radical of the German cardinals, Walter Kasper, who along with his Bavarian confreres had sowed much division in the Church during Francis's 12-year pontificate. At 92 years old, Kasper could not vote in the conclave, but he remained president emeritus of the Dicastery for Promoting Christian Unity, an ironic title for a man whose rebellious left-wing ideas became so disunifying that even Francis had to push back against him and his cohorts. But on this day, Kasper conveyed to Pentin that he similarly saw Leo XIV as a man of peace who listens, a conciliatory figure "not too far to the left or to the right," who "wants continuity with Pope Francis." Kasper remarked that both attributes are "very important."

Other such assessments followed in Pentin's piece. Swiss Cardinal Kurt Koch, who was Kasper's successor as head of the Vatican's ecumenical dicastery, welcomed Leo as a "man of dialogue" who he hoped would "bring harmony" to the Church. Pentin also quoted Fr. Rok Pogančnik, a traditional Slovenian priest, who already liked what he saw from Leo XIV and hoped that "he will bring much needed peace to the Church."

Likewise, Archbishop Georg Gänswein, the longtime personal secretary to Pope Benedict who was effectively exiled by Pope Francis, said optimistically of Leo XIV: "Now a new phase begins. I sense a certain widespread relief. The season of arbitrariness is over." He added: "We can begin to count on a papacy capable of guaranteeing stability and relying on existing structures, without overturning or disrupting them." He said: "Pope Prevost gives me great hope."[8]

Also pleased was Gänswein friend and ally German Cardinal Gerhard Ludwig Müller, the former doctrinal chief of the Vatican, who was not one of the radical left-wing German cardinals. He said of the conclave attitude toward Robert Francis Prevost: "I think it was a good impression of him to everybody, and in the end it was a great concordia, a great harmony. There was no polemics, no fractionizing." Asked by a reporter if he had voted for Prevost to be pope, Müller said, "Oh, I cannot say. But I am content, no?"[9]

Among the assessments, the message seemed unanimous, regardless of whether the prelate was a progressive or conservative, a modernist or traditionalist, a foe or fan of a pope like Benedict XVI: Pope Francis had disrupted if not overturned the peace in the Church. The unending arbitrariness and lack of stability had divided everyone. All hoped and prayed to God that Leo XIV would first and foremost bring peace. There now seemed to be a sense of widespread relief.

Particularly illuminating in Pentin's analysis was his information on how the voting had proceeded inside the conclave.

Pentin confirmed that Cardinal Parolin had been the leading contender during the early voting, especially among Pope Francis's staunchest supporters, and had the backing of a substantial voting bloc of about 40 to 50 cardinals. However, he was unable to move beyond that and obtain broader support. Other leading candidates, such as cardinals Luis Tagle, Matteo Zuppi, Mario Grech, Pablo Virgilio David, and Jean-Marc Aveline, found their votes split up and spread thin, especially among the Italians but also the Asians and some Africans. Likewise, they hit a low ceiling and could not gain any momentum. As for the "conservative" vote, it was balkanized among cardinals Robert Sarah, Peter Erdő, Pierbattista Pizzaballa, and Malcolm Ranjith. As with the liberal vote, it was divided in a way that kept not a single cardinal from pulling away from the rest of the pack.

All of which cleared a path for someone closer to the middle and without baggage—like Robert Francis Prevost.

"Once all these candidates were effectively eliminated," reported Pentin, "the stage was then set for Cardinal Prevost to emerge. Already considered a possible compromise candidate by many cardinals going into the Conclave, he began picking up votes in the third vote, including among conservative voters."

As had been reported by the Italian press, Pentin confirmed that Prevost was helped considerably by New York Cardinal Timothy Dolan "lending his weight to Cardinal Prevost's candidacy." The conservatives must have figured that this was their best chance of avoiding a progressive pope, while also accepting the reality that they did not have the votes to elect one of their own. The liberals must have felt likewise regarding their preferred progressive; they, too, looked for a reasonable compromise candidate.

Thus, all eyes turned toward Cardinal Prevost. And to say "all" is not much of an exaggeration. By the fourth ballot, said Pentin, Prevost had secured more than 100 ballots. He soared well beyond the two-thirds majority—89 votes—required to be elected.

And unlike Parolin, Prevost had not promoted himself. As Edward Pentin noted, victory came "without any pre-Conclave lobbying on Cardinal Prevost's part." Notably, there had been reports in the Italian media that Prevost had visited with Cardinal Raymond Burke in Burke's apartment (presumably the apartment that Francis coldly tried to strip from Burke as punishment for his dissent) during the period of the general congregations, but Pentin said that he and the *National Catholic Register* were able to confirm that these reports were not accurate. (Likewise, Vatican reporter Diane Montagna said that a Burke–Prevost apartment summit did not take place. Montagna personally knows Burke and the other key sources. She said that she knows for certain that such a meeting "never happened."[10])

As for how the cardinals generally were feeling the weekend after the vote, Pentin reported an impressive consensus: "Overall, cardinals who were Francis's closest supporters are pleased with the result, and so too are those who were critics of the previous pontificate, even if Cardinal Prevost was never their first choice." In Pentin's words, all tended to view Leo XIV as "bringing a necessary period of calm and peace to the papacy after the divisions of the Francis pontificate."

Pentin reported that that lack of calm and peace had been the prevailing issue raised throughout the 12 general congregations that had preceded the conclave. Those discussions were collegial and "very frank," with both criticism as well as praise for the previous pontificate.

Significantly, the criticism included the unhappiness with the "loose adherence to Church law during the past 12 years." The hope was that Prevost, possessing a doctorate in canon law, could help right the ship that the Francis crew had wrecked along the Tiber.

Overall, summed up Pentin, those concerns, coupled with Pope Leo's attitude of one genuinely willing to listen, to dialogue, and to build bridges (not mere rhetoric in his case), had "instilled considerable hope and confidence in Rome and beyond."

The conclave consensus that had picked Robert Francis Prevost had blossomed into a consensus of optimism that peace and unity could once again come back to the Roman Catholic Church. Here was a pope—it was hoped—who would not just talk that talk but walk the walk.

WORD FROM THE AMERICAN CARDINALS

Though likewise vowed to secrecy, and careful about what they could and could not say about the conclave, the American cardinals—in a very American way (given how media-obsessed America is)—held a press conference after the conclave, sharing a few thoughts and insights regarding what had transpired.[11]

The conference was held at the Pontifical North American College in Rome, a hilltop seminary a short walk from the Vatican. The cardinals sat on a stage in front of an American flag and a Vatican flag. The organizers did not conceal how proud they were to suddenly have an American pope. The speakers blasted American songs, including Bruce Springsteen's "Born in the U.S.A." and Don McLean's "American Pie."[12]

There were seven cardinals altogether, including six American cardinal electors and Cardinal Christophe Pierre, the Apostolic Nuncio to the United States. They included Cardinal Daniel DiNardo, Archbishop Emeritus of Galveston–Houston; Cardinal Timothy Dolan of New York; Cardinal Joseph Tobin of Newark; Cardinal Blase Cupich of Chicago; Cardinal Wilton Gregory, Archbishop Emeritus of Washington, DC; and Cardinal Robert McElroy of Washington, DC.

DiNardo went first. Both he and Dolan said right off that although Robert Francis Prevost is indeed a citizen of the United States, he is really a "citizen of the world," noting his work in South America, specifically in Peru, in Rome, and as the former head of his Augustinian religious order. "Yes, he is an American," said DiNardo, "but yes, he also represents the big, big picture of the Church." Added Dolan: "He's a citizen of the world and he reminds us that we all have our true citizenship in heaven, as St. Paul taught us, and that is his role as universal pastor. Where he comes from is sort of now a thing of the past." Dolan said dramatically: "Robert Francis Prevost is no longer around; it's now Pope Leo."

Here again, as with varying cardinals around the world (including the Germans), the so-called conservatives and liberals among the American cardinals were united around Prevost.

"When he [Prevost] accepted it [the papacy], it was like he was made for it," said Cardinal Tobin. "All of whatever anguish was resolved by the feeling that . . . this wasn't simply his saying yes to a proposal, but God had made something clear, and he agreed with it."

Tobin shared the most moving image of the press conference. Referring to Robert Prevost as "Bob," Tobin said: "I took a look at Bob . . . and he had his head in his hands and I was praying for him, because I couldn't imagine what happens to a human being when you're facing something like that."

Cardinal Cupich agreed that Prevost was the unifying candidate: "We were over 130 people with different languages, cultures, backgrounds from more than 70 countries and within 24 hours we were able to come to unity. . . . I hope that's a signal to the world that we have the opportunity to reconcile and have peace."

That was quite an admission from Cardinal Cupich. He had been Francis's top dog in the United States, including as the pope's designated Rottweiler on COVID vax enforcement. When Francis needed someone to crack the whip against Catholics who dared to appeal to their conscience to not be forcibly vaxxed against their will, Cupich was his man.[13] But Cupich, too, seemed tired of the lack of peace in the Church of Francis. The COVID attack-dog likewise hungered for unity.

For Cardinal Gregory, the election of Leo was a sign of hope for which he, too, gave thanks. "I could not be more grateful that it happened in the Holy Year of Hope," said Gregory. "We are Pilgrims of Hope. . . . I felt comfortable saying to Pope Leo, 'From one Southsider of Chicago to another, I promise you my respect, my fidelity, and my love.'"

The most liberal among the group, Cardinal McElroy, likewise showed his hearty approval of Leo. "I always thought it would be impossible to have an American pope in my lifetime," said McElroy. "We were looking for the soul who has the capacity at this moment of time to really be a witness to Christ." McElroy spoke to how there was a big push toward Prevost by the second day of balloting: "There was a great movement on the second day, a great movement within the body that was there, and it could be nothing other than the grace of God moving us toward this consensus, which I thought would have taken a lot more time to get to."

Everyone thought so, inside and outside the conclave. And yet, by day two, a Prevost consensus prevailed.

Cardinal Pierre spoke of feeling the presence of the Holy Spirit at the conclave. He spoke mystically of how a process that began with a political feeling movingly gave way to the spiritual: "What I experience is that everything begins in politics and finishes mystic. This is what we lived. We started in this kind of confusion: the confusion of the languages, the confusion of the persons, the uncertainty because nobody told us where to go."

Pierre said that although the process began with claims of dialogue and listening, it was unavoidable that cardinals entered the conclave with certain preconceived prejudices: "At the beginning, let's be honest, we have difficulty to listen to one another because you project your prejudice, you see the person as you think he is or she is. But at the end of it, things became the process of discernment. I think the Conclave is a moment of discernment."

That eventually led to the discernment of Prevost as their preferred choice.

Crucial to that discernment, according to the American cardinals, were the general congregation meetings prior to the conclave after the death of Pope Francis. That was where dialogue and discernment did in fact take place. "I think if the Conclave was limited simply to the Conclave, then it would have been an even greater struggle," said Cardinal Tobin. "However, there were these two weeks following the funeral of Pope Francis where there was a daily and intentional getting to know you and we listened to each other for the better part of that time. . . . They had heard each other talk about what we thought was important."

When asked if there was one thing that Cardinal Prevost had said at the general congregations that made him stand out, Cardinal Gregory stated: "I don't remember any particular intervention that then-Cardinal Prevost offered to the General Congregation. But I do believe he engaged quite effectively in the smaller group conversations. . . . It wasn't that he got up and made this overwhelmingly convincing speech that just wowed the body."

Prevost was also effective in showing himself as someone who was less an American cardinal than a cardinal of the universal Church. The American cardinals were asked if his election was an attempt to counterweight the global impact of President Donald Trump. The cardinals did not feel that way.

"I think the impact of him being an American was almost negligible in the deliberations," said Cardinal McElroy.

Dolan agreed: "I would back up what Cardinal McElroy said. I don't think the fact that Cardinal Prevost was from the United States had much weight." Dolan spoke of Pope Leo as a potential "bridge builder," asserting: "That's what the Latin word 'pontiff' means. He's a bridge builder. Will he want to build bridges to Donald Trump? I suppose, but he would want to build bridges with the leader of every nation."

To that, Cardinal Gregory, who had represented Washington, DC, during the Trump and Biden years, added that the cardinals did not see the conclave as "a continuation of the American political election." Rather, they were concerned about "who among us can bring us together; who among us can strengthen the faith."

And finally, what of Pope Leo and Pope Francis? Were some of these cardinals looking for another Francis in Leo? Cardinal McElroy, the most liberal of Francis's American appointees, demurred: "It was said many times in the general sessions leading up to the Conclave—but I think I could say this much without giving anything away—that we're looking for someone following the pathway of Francis but we're not looking for a photocopy. And I believe Pope Leo will not be a photocopy of Pope Francis."

As an addendum to this very positive press conference on the new pope, the next day Cardinal Dolan—crowned the "kingmaker" by the Italian press—published a piece in the *New York Post* offering his insights on Prevost. They were again positive, though not suggestive of someone who had championed and prodded Prevost over the finish line. He had not known Prevost well enough to be his kingmaker.[14]

Referring to the general congregations, Dolan said he was often asked about this long-shot *papabile* from America: "During those many hours of meetings, at coffee breaks, or over lunch or dinner, I was often asked by other cardinals, 'Tell me about Cardinal Prevost. What kind of man is he?'"

Dolan's answer: "I had to reply that, in all honesty, I did not know him."

Of course, Dolan said that he "knew of" Prevost, "and what I had heard had impressed me greatly." He found Prevost "somewhat shy" but "a good listener; someone who spoke several languages; a priest with broad experience in Latin America; a former leader of his religious order; and, finally, someone who had spent the last few years in Rome, familiar with the workings of the bureaucracy that is the Roman Curia." He quoted other cardinals saying of Prevost, "He runs a good meeting," and "he hears everyone out, but is able to make a decision when one is needed." Still another said, "he has a deep love for the poor."

Dolan did say that he had breakfast with Prevost one morning prior to the vote that elected him pope. "He was open and engaging, and we swapped some stories about my hometown of St. Louis, where he had lived during his novitiate with the Augustinian order," said Dolan. "I came away impressed."

Impressed enough, surely, to vote for his fellow Midwesterner.

And what of that Midwesterner? This American pontiff?

He is an American all right, but he is actually a little something of everything—the American Midwest, but also the American

South, even Creole, and yet also some sprinkling of Europe, from France to Italy.

And though it was being said in Italy that this was the least American of the American cardinals, the reality is that Robert Francis Prevost's ethnicity is remarkably diverse. It may well be the most diverse of any pope ever.

So, who is this man? Where does he come from? Let us look at the roots of Robert Francis Prevost.

EIGHT

The Roots of Robert Francis Prevost

The reaction to the surprising papal election of Robert Francis Prevost by his fellow American cardinals, Church officials, leaders, and opinion makers around the world were remarkable for their praise, unity, and optimism. But surely the most moving and endearing reactions came from the family of Robert Francis Prevost—his remaining family—his older brothers, Louis and John.

Lou had turned on his TV to watch the papal coverage on *Newsmax*. He was not feeling well that day, so he had called off work and was resting in bed. But soon, he was sitting up—jumping up.[1]

"The cardinal came out to announce to the crowd that we have a new pope," Lou Prevost told *Newsmax* anchor Ed Henry. "I'm waiting, and he starts to say the name 'Roberto.' And as soon as he started, [my] mind started blowing because I think there was only one other cardinal with the name Robert. And when he said 'Francisco,' that sealed it because there's no Robert Francis [other] than Robert Francis Prevost."

When Lou heard that, he sprung "up out of bed in a shot, got dressed, ran to the other room, put it on the big TV and sat there in awe." He could not put into words his "feelings of joy and exuberance." He told *Newsmax*: "Imagine it's your little brother. He's the pope. Yes, it's an indescribable feeling. I'm super proud of him."

Lou shared a moment of levity. He said that while watching his brother switch easily from Italian to Spanish from the Loggia, he quipped at the TV: "Okay, quit showing off, you little jerk."

But more seriously, he was reflective, musing at memories distant past, with his mind flashing back to the three brothers growing up together in the 1950s and 1960s. He pondered: "Remember that time way back when, when we used to tease him about being the pope? And he's the pope."

Yes, the pope. Little brother "Rob" was now the Holy Father.

Lou recalled of his kid brother: "He just had this calling, I believe, since birth. You could just see the way he acted, behaved, was around our parents and other kids. There was something different."

Brother John had similar thoughts when trying to absorb the stunning news. The new pope's other brother said "there are no words" to describe how proud he was of the family's baby brother when he heard the announcement. "It's overwhelming pride," shared John, "but it's also an overwhelming responsibility, being the first American pope from Chicago—and a relative. Frightening."[2]

Like his brother Lou, John's mind raced back to his little brother's boyhood as a precocious, pious Catholic who wanted to be a priest. John said that everyone foresaw him as a priest, but some saw something even greater. Much greater.

"The interesting thing is way back when he was in kindergarten or first grade, there was a parent, a mom, across the street—one across the street that way and another down the street," gestured John Prevost from his home in New Lenox, Illinois. "Both of them said he would be the first American pope, at that age."[3]

This was not just some flight of fancy by sentimental church ladies down the block. Lou Prevost himself harbored similar intimations regarding his brother. Many folks did.

"We used to tease him all the time—you're going to be the pope one day," Lou told ABC News shortly after the May 8 election. "Neighbors said the same thing. Sixty-some years later, here we are."[4]

Those feelings constituted quite the prophecy. And from more than one person. It says something extraordinarily revealing about the young Robert Francis Prevost. Few to no papal observers and Vatican experts predicted an American pope one day, but friends and family of Robert Francis Prevost long ago had foreseen something altogether uniquely possible.

So how did that happen? What was this boy like? How was such a kid raised? What of those roots of Robert Francis Prevost?

A POPE WHO'S AMERICAN—AND EVERYTHING ELSE

On the evening of May 8, 2025, the Italian people were disappointed to learn that the Chair of St. Peter had not returned to one of their native sons. For so many centuries and millennia, the pope had been Italian. When the first Slavic pope was elected in October 1978, with Karol Wojtyla taking the name John Paul II, the Polish pontiff had succeeded an Italian whose papacy had lasted only 33 days. Albino Luciani's untimely death at age 65 had shocked the world. By that point, Italians had occupied the Chair of St. Peter for 455 consecutive years.

Though the Italians had high hopes with cardinals like Parolin, Pizzaballa, and Zuppi among the *papabili*, they nonetheless failed to get the seat back in May 2025. Robert Francis Prevost was now the fourth consecutive non-Italian pope.

Well, sort of. The reality is a bit more complicated.

It is often forgotten that Pope Francis (that is, Jorge Mario Bergoglio) was ethnically Italian. He was born in Buenos Aires, Argentina, in December 1936 to Italian immigrant Mario José Bergoglio, an accountant from the Piemonte region in northwest Italy, and Regina María Sívori, a housewife born in Buenos Aires to a family of northern Italian origin. When Bergoglio walked out onto the Loggia on March 13, 2013, he spoke fluent Italian, befitting his family's native ethnic tongue, and he thrilled the largely Italian gathering at St. Peter's Square by being the first ever pontiff to choose for his papal name the beloved male patron of Italy: the revered St. Francis of Assisi. As his papal name was announced, the name "Francesco! Francesco!" jubilantly echoed through the crowd.

So it was not as if Italian lineage had left the papacy without a trace starting with the election of Karol Wojtyla on October 16, 1978. And indeed, the same can be said, for a smaller, albeit *diluted* degree for the new Pope Leo XIV.

Born September 14, 1955, Robert Francis Prevost is a typical American. He is what many of us native-born Americans jokingly refer to ourselves as: a "mutt."[5] Prevost is a prototypical product of the American melting pot, with possibly more varied ethnic DNA than the last five centuries of popes combined. Both his parents were Chicago natives, which as most people who know Chicago realize, does not suggest homogeneity. Chicago is one of America's and hence the world's most mixed melting pots, and Prevost's parents were no exception.

Robert Francis Prevost's mother, Mildred Agnes Prevost (1911–90), was born Mildred Agnes Martinez, a common Latino surname. She hailed from a mixed-race family of Hispanic and Black Creole origin in New Orleans, Louisiana. Her parents were variously described in U.S. Census documents as black, mulatto, and white, a convoluted diversity that was not uncommon for the period. Documents list her father as born in Haiti and the Dominican Republic.[6] The complex backgrounds of Prevost's mother and maternal grandparents quickly prompted some black Americans to claim in Leo XIV a black pope.[7] No doubt, the new Holy Father on his mother's side seems to have black ancestry in the family tree.

This also prompted some observers to claim in Leo "the *first* black pope." But in fact, the Catholic Church had black popes in the past (or at least men of darker skin complexion), with several popes from northern Africa in the first centuries of the Church. The ethnic identification of every pope is uncertain, as it is with many early notable saints, including Saint Augustine (354–430 AD), who had northern African lineage and was possibly partly black. In that sense, it is interesting that in his opening remarks on the Loggia, the Augustinian Robert Francis Prevost proudly referred to himself as "a son of Augustine."

Europeans reading this should know that modern "woke" Americans—fixated on acronyms like "DEI" and "CRT"[8]—are unfortunately obsessed with skin color, and thus there was immediately much focus in the American media on Leo XIV's familial background. Moreover, fine distinctions are not always made among the race-obsessed over what is considered "black" complexion or a "person of color" versus roots from Africa or another country in which the natives have darker skin.[9] But that said, Prevost inarguably has roots on his mother's side that would be typically considered black among most black Americans.

And so, in sum, it is both true and an undeniably cool thing that the first American pope does have some black ancestry.

Equally intriguing, Prevost's complex roots on his mother's side would suggest a high possibility of slavery in the bloodline. The slaves could have come from the American south or from Haiti and the Dominican Republic.[10] Genealogists immediately went digging into that specific element of his roots.

And yet, it must be said that Leo XIV certainly would not be the first pope with slavery in his background. The Catholic Church has had popes who were slaves, not to mention numerous famous saints (black and white) who had been slaves (a prominent example is St. Patrick, who was white).[11] There are two particularly inspiring black American slaves who are currently on a path to sainthood, Pierre Toussaint (1766–1853) and Augustus Tolton (1854–97), the latter of whom was a priest near Prevost's home environs.

This rich record of race hails merely from Pope Leo XIV's mother's side, which is anchored largely in the Western Hemisphere. Going to his father's side takes us across the Atlantic.

Robert Francis Prevost's father was Louis Marius Prevost (1920–97). His background was less mixed than his wife's, though still diverse. Whereas Prevost's mother's family hailed from the New World, his father's family came from Europe, i.e., the Old World.

Louis was of Italian and French descent. His father was Salvatore Giovanni Gaetano Riggitano (1876–1960), a Sicilian immigrant from the village of Milazzo near the city of Messina who immigrated to the United States in 1903. Giovanni became a teacher of Romance languages, namely, Italian, French, and Spanish.[12] The complex circumstances of his relationship with and subsequent marriage to Suzanne Fontaine, a Frenchwoman from Le Havre, France, are unclear and became somewhat of a local scandal in their day.[13] Whatever those details, Giovanni and Suzanne (who eventually changed their last name to Prevost) became the parents of Louis Marius Prevost, Pope Leo's father.[14]

But note Giovanni's roots in southern Italy. Thus, his grandson, Robert Francis Prevost, is an American who has Italian in his blood.

Notably, when Leo XIV nearly a month into his papacy addressed in Rome the National Italian American Foundation and said, "As you well know, tens of millions of Americans proudly claim their Italian heritage, even if their ancestors arrived in the United States of America generations ago," he could well have been talking about his own ancestors, or at least his paternal grandfather.[15]

That is not the only Italian connection for the American pope.

Think of the middle name: Robert *Francis* Prevost. Whereas Jorge Mario Bergoglio *chose* the papal name "Francis," Robert Francis Prevost was assigned and blessed with the name at birth. The name Francis—again, for the revered Italian St. Francis of

Assisi—was bestowed on him by his parents. He could claim the name longer than Pope Francis could.

Like Jorge Mario Bergoglio, Robert Francis Prevost's ethnic roots and place of birth mean that he has a foot in both the old world and new worlds, in Europe and in America. And of course, it must be said that America (as every Italian proudly knows) was discovered by the great Italian explorer from Genoa, Cristoforo Colombo—or Christopher Columbus, as it is anglicized in America—and named for his contemporary, Amerigo Vespucci, the great Italian explorer from Florence.

Thus, in truth, the new American pope, Robert Francis Prevost, is closer to the Italians than they initially thought. Do not lament, dear Italians! No, they did not get a full-blooded Italian pope, but they got a pope with some Italian in his bloodline.

It should be further emphasized that Prevost's footprint in both the old and new worlds applies not only to his familial background but also to his spiritual-professional background as a priest, bishop, and cardinal. Because of his time as a priest and bishop in Peru, he is a dual citizen of Peru and America. The new pontiff maintains three passports: one from Peru, one from the United States, and one from Vatican City. He has now also become a citizen of Italy in his capacity as Bishop of Rome.

In all, in personal ethnicity and priestly service, Robert Francis Prevost genuinely blends—and himself is a blend—of the old and new worlds, of Europe and the Americas.

Going forward, yet more will likely be learned about his ancestry. For instance, a study conducted by a team of experts led by Harvard historian Henry Louis Gates Jr., host of the PBS documentary program *Finding Your Roots*, traced the pope's lineage back 15 generations into the 16th century, where researchers identified over 100 forebears for Leo. They hailed from France (40 forebears), Italy (24), the United States (22), Spain (21), Cuba (10), Canada (6), Haiti (1), and even the remote southern Caribbean island of Guadeloupe (1). And notably, those forebears include both African slaves as well as slaveholders. Professor Gates called the new Holy Father's multicultural background "one of the most diverse family trees we have ever created."[16]

What the whole world (Italians included) should celebrate with this first American pope is the striking reality of the most ethnically diverse pope ever—a fitting pedigree for the universal Church. The word "catholic" means "universal." In his sheer ethnic catholicity, Robert Francis Prevost is surely the most genuinely universal Holy Father in the history of the Roman Catholic Church.

THE PREVOST FAMILY FROM CHICAGO

If readers find these details difficult to follow, well, welcome to the world of American ancestry. So many modern Americans have similarly complex family trees. Oftentimes, fully sketching out these familial lines requires a giant chalkboard.

Let us return more simply to Robert Francis Prevost's mom and dad, moving beyond the aforementioned discussion of ethnic/racial backgrounds and toward the simpler, modest little home and parish in which the current pope was raised.

Robert Francis Prevost was born September 14, 1955. That day is a special day on the Roman Catholic liturgical calendar. Every September 14 is the Feast of the Exaltation of the Holy Cross. For over 1,300 years, the day has commemorated the recovery of the holy cross—said to be the True Cross—on which Jesus Christ was crucified. The cross had been found by St. Helena (246/248–330), mother of the Emperor Constantine (272–337), in Jerusalem in the fourth century. Unlike Good Friday, which is dedicated to Christ's passion and crucifixion, the Exaltation of the Holy Cross venerates the Cross itself as the sign and symbol of Christian salvation and of Christ's mercy—of Mercy Himself.

Robert Francis was born that day *at* Mercy: He was born at Mercy Hospital at 25th Street and Prairie Avenue in the Bronzeville neighborhood of the South Side of Chicago. He was the third and final child of Mildred Agnes and Louis Marius. Preceding him were two older brothers, Louis Martin and John Joseph.

Mildred was older than Louis Marius. At the time of the birth of baby Rob (as the family called him), she was 43 years old and Louis was 35. They were living in a tiny box of a brick house on 212 E. 141st Place in Dolton, not even 1,000-square-foot in size.[17] They got a bank loan to purchase the newly built structure in 1949. Their mortgage was $42 per month.[18]

Mildred was raised by a devoutly Catholic family in Chicago. She had five sisters, two of which became nuns. One of them, Sr. Mary Amarita, joined the Sisters of Charity and took her first vows in August 1928. Born in 1906, she died before the age of 40, passing away prematurely in 1945. The other sister became Sr. Mary Sulpice, and had a life of remarkable longevity, serving with the Sisters of Mercy for 77 years until her death in 1999.[19]

Mildred chose married life, though likewise she always faithfully served the Church. She graduated from Immaculata High School for girls in June 1929. In addition to being a good student, she was a good singer—a contralto soloist who performed and competed in music festivals.[20]

At a time when not as many young women went to college, Mildred steadfastly sought higher ed possibilities. She attended DePaul University in Chicago, founded in 1898 by the Vincentians and named for the 17th-century French priest Saint Vincent de Paul (1581–1660), highly regarded for his service to the poor. There she earned a bachelor's degree in library science in 1947. Two years later, in 1949, she picked up a master's degree in education at DePaul.[21]

Mildred became an educator and librarian. Her positions included a job as an educator at Mendel Catholic High School, a college preparatory high school for boys in the Roseland neighborhood of Chicago. It was named for the famed Austrian scientist Gregor Mendel (1822–1884), the eminent biologist, botanist, and mathematician, who was also an Augustinian friar. The school was operated by the Order of Saint Augustine, the later order of the little school's most famous alumnus, Pope Leo XIV.

As for the pope's father, he was likewise an educator.

Louis Marius grew up in Chicago's Hyde Park area. When his country went to war, the 5-foot-5, 140-pound son of Italian and French immigrants saluted the flag and did his duty. In 1942, he applied to the US Navy's V-7 accelerated training program. This would allow him to enter the Navy as an officer upon graduation the following year. He received a letter of recommendation from his pastor at St. Thomas Apostle Church in Chicago, who described him as "a good Catholic and a young man of good character and steady habits." He was accepted and received his commission on November 24, 1943.[22]

Louis Marius distinguished himself by serving on an infantry landing craft during the Normandy landings in southern France on June 6, 1944: D-Day. Small of physical stature but not of heart, the 23-year-old Prevost served aboard the LST-286, which was tasked with delivering and landing the 5th Special Engineer Brigade and the 16th Infantry of the 1st Infantry Division at the hellacious Omaha Beach invasion. Prevost survived the brutal operation and went on to command a Landing Craft Infantry vessel operating in the Mediterranean.[23]

After the war, he remained an officer in the Naval Reserve until 1956.

The war had interrupted Louis Marius' education. In June 1940, he received a degree from Woodrow Wilson Junior College.[24]

After the war, he attended the same master's program in education that Mildred had enrolled in at DePaul. In 1949, he, too, received his master's degree from that program.[25]

Like his wife, Louis became an educator, and relatively high ranking. He served as superintendent of the south suburban schools in District 169 and as superintendent of Brookwood School District 167 in Glenwood, Illinois. He later became the principal of Mount Carmel High School, a Catholic school in Chicago Heights.[26]

Mildred and Louis raised their family in that little house in Dolton, Illinois, and at their home parish. That church was St. Mary of the Assumption in nearby Riverdale. It sat at the far southern edge of Chicago, straddling the line dividing the Windy City from the village of Dolton at South Leyden Avenue and East 137th Street.

The parish was like a second home to the family, especially to Mildred and her youngest son Rob. The family did not miss Mass. It was always the top priority. The family awoke each morning and attended daily Mass at 9:15 a.m.[27] The pope would later recall to a group of young people: "starting from when I was around 6 years old, I was also an altar boy in the parish. And so before going to school—it was a parochial school—there was Mass at 6:30 a.m. And Mom would wake us up and say 'We're going to Mass!' Because serving Mass was something we liked because starting from when I was young, they taught us that Jesus was always close to us."[28]

The entire family was involved at the parish, serving as lectors and singing in the choir, with the boys serving as altar boys, and the family generally acting as volunteers and steady participants in the parish life.

The mother and father were quite the duo at the parish. Both at different times served as president of the Altar and Rosary Society. They put their varied talents to work in a multitude of ways, including their library skills. The two organized a library in the basement of the parish. For her part, Mildred also helped organize libraries at Holy Name Cathedral and other nearby parishes and schools.[29]

Mildred became known to St. Mary's parishioners as sweet "Millie," a constant presence who helped keep the place running. "She was one of the ladies that we called church ladies," recalled Marianne Angarola, who was in the same graduating class as the future pope. Angarola says of the Prevost family: "They went to Mass on a daily basis. They cleaned the altars, the church, the sacristy. She was involved in everything, including the fundraising activities. I don't ever remember seeing her wear pants."[30]

Another member of the parish, Betty Lyons-Geary, recalls how Louis was very supportive of his wife's efforts: "Lou was just very staunch. He was always there for Millie. But he stayed in the background because she was always doing things at the parish."[31]

Obviously, this rubbed off on the children of Mildred and Louis.

The boys developed a strong faith, nurtured by their parents at home as well as at church. They did not leave their faith at the parish door. The family prayed grace before meals and the Rosary every night after dinner.[32]

As for Rob, he felt the call of the priesthood from an early age. During play time, the future pope always wanted to play being a priest. Even as young as age five or six, said his brother Lou, "while me and my friends are out playing with cap pistols and BB guns, and Rob wants to play priest, and we used to tease him to no end about that. Come on, come on, let's do something!"[33]

What Rob wanted to do was be a priest.

For his education, Rob attended the parish school at St. Mary of the Assumption. He and fellow students started their day with Mass, which was said in Latin. Young Rob took it all in. It seemed like there was nothing about the life of the parish and Church that he did not like. He enjoyed reading and memorizing his *Catechism* and preparing for the sacraments of Reconciliation and Holy Communion.

Some youngsters tired of these routines and requirements, or slacked off, but not the young Prevost. "Robert Prevost never complained," recalled classmate Marianne Angarola. "We used to pray with our hands, you know, our fingers pointing to heaven, and, after a while, you get tired of doing that, and you just want to fold them over. Robert Prevost never folded his hands over. He was just godly. Not in an in-your-face way. It was part of his aura, like he was hand-selected, and he embraced it. And he wasn't weird. He was nice."[34]

The piety of the boy made an impression on his classmates. They actually referred to him as "holy," so much so that it became a nickname for him. "We even called him 'Holy,'" said classmate John Doughney. "His brothers even referred to him as 'Holy,' and he really was."[35]

And yet, holy as he was, Rob's classmates saw no arrogance in him. They saw him as humble and kind, even as he seemed to be not only the holiest student in the class but the smartest. They described him as "kind, compassionate and humble."[36]

"He was always kind," said Doughney. "Never saw him have [hostile] words with anybody else. And certainly no kind of physical altercations, which was a common occurrence in the south side of Chicago."[37]

Rob was very much other-directed. He had set his sights higher.

"I do believe that he knew what his path was [ultimately] going to be," adds Doughney. "I don't know that he knew his path would take him to the papacy, but he knew his path was into the Catholic church as a priest and then as a missionary. And very few 13-year-olds are that steadfast in knowing, 'this is the path I'm taking and this is what I'm going to do for the rest of my life.'"[38]

Rob's classmates unambiguously saw in him the makings of a future priest. "It was pretty apparent back then that [the priesthood] was going to be his route," said Doughney. "Some of us had considered it. It was kind of a fantasy for most young men. For him, I think it was a true calling. And, even as a young teenager, he knew what he wanted to do and where he wanted to go."[39]

In that respect, the young boy had awed not only his classmates but his teachers and the nuns and priests. He was described as "the pride and joy of every priest and nun" in the building.[40]

Clearly, there was a shared sense that this student had something quite different going on. There was an understanding that for this youngster something special lay ahead.

EMBRACING THE AUGUSTINIAN

There was no mistaking the signs of the youngest Prevost boy's interest in the priesthood. John recalls how his little brother was so serious about his call that he was ready to go straight into seminary after eighth grade. "The only thing that was in question until eighth grade was, would it be an order priest, or would it be a diocesan priest?" says brother John. "That was his decision to make."[41]

Rob considered his options. In those days, when there were far more priests and young men considering the priesthood, boys of Robert Francis Prevost's seriousness would get visited and recruited by seminary vocation directors. The seminary would consider whether the young man was a good fit, and vice versa. "I remember sitting around a table each time someone was coming, and they would come, and then everyone would ask questions," says John Prevost.[42]

In the case of Rob, he was visited and persuaded to join an Augustinian seminary through Fr. L. Dudley Day, described in a July 2025 *Time* magazine article as "a Catholic of the old school, whose views were conservative enough that he later parted ways with his local church over a disagreement about modernization."[43]

Born in 1927 in Chicago, Fr. Day spent most of his life at St. Rita Church. He was baptized and received First Communion and Confirmation there. He also attended St. Rita School. (Later, in 1981, Fr. Day became pastor of his home parish, and in 1987 was assigned to his home school, St. Rita High School.) After attending several Augustinian schools and seminaries, including the Augustinian Novitiate in New Hamburg, New York, and Villanova University, Dudley Day was ordained a priest in June 1953. He returned to the Chicago area in 1954 as a priest assigned to Mendel Catholic High School, where he worked with Mildred Prevost as a fellow educator. From 1961–76, he became the regional vocation director for the Province of the Order of Saint Augustine. In that capacity, he organized Seminary Weeks at St. Augustine Seminary, in Holland, Michigan.[44]

It was likely one of those Seminary Weeks that attracted Rob Prevost to the Holland seminary. And as for Fr. Day, he must have been close to the Prevost family and was likely a mentor or at least keen influence on Rob, who proceeded to follow some of the same steps to the priesthood that Day had tread. Starting with the seminary in Holland, Michigan.

St. Augustine Seminary High School was a minor seminary located in Holland, a lovely little town in western Michigan, situated on Lake Macatawa, near the shores of Lake Michigan. It is a short drive from Grand Rapids, in a community historically known more for Calvinism than Catholicism. One was much more likely to meet a Christian of the Dutch Reformed persuasion than Roman Catholic. The town was more Presbyterian than Augustinian.

The minor seminary had opened in 1949 on 550 acres and a mansion purchased from the estate of Chicago inventor and industrialist Dorr Felt. From Dolton, it was about 140 miles, a two-and-a-half-hour drive (on a good traffic day) from I-94 to Rt. 196. The long drive was made more pleasant by the picturesque route along the eastern side of Lake Michigan much of the way.

The fact that Rob Prevost would choose to go this far away from home when there were many closer options in Chicago says a lot. It was clearly the draw of an Augustinian seminary for the budding "son of Augustine." He could have chosen any number of other minor seminaries in the Windy City. Rather than go the route of, say, the Jesuits, he looked to the Augustinians.

Rob Prevost attended the school from 1969 to 1973, though it would be more accurate to here refer to him as "Bob," the name he would be called by friends as he grew older and left Dolton. He was very active at the school. He was editor in chief of the yearbook, served on the student council and speech and debate team, and participated in a few sports, mainly tennis and bowling. He was head of the speech and debate team and captain of the bowling team.

The minor seminary was a boarding school for the roughly 50 to 100 boys who attended in the 1960s and 1970s from Michigan and the nearby states of Indiana, Illinois, Ohio, and Wisconsin, with the majority coming from the Chicago metro area (no doubt a recruiting impact of Fr. Dudley Day). The boys were introduced to the discipline of priestly life. They awoke every day at 6 a.m., attended Mass, and had their schedule filled with classes, prayer services, and various activities until about 8:30 p.m., with only a few hours of free time before sleep.[45]

In a rigorous academic environment, Prevost stood out among his peers for his intelligence and performance, earning distinctions as a member of the National Honor Society and co-valedictorian of his class. He also helped other students as a tutor when they struggled academically.

Bob Schick, a classmate, recalls how Prevost reached out to students who needed help, whether academically or personally, whether struggling with the books or with missing their homes and families. "Bob was one of the students who took people under his wing," said Schick.[46]

He was quiet, pensive, humble, and liked and respected. He was also disciplined and committed. The class of boys that he had entered with in 1969 had included several dozen students (about 50), but ultimately, he was one of only 13 students in his class to graduate.

And here as well, as in grade school, his fellow students were struck by his kindness, decency, and attentiveness.

His seminary schoolmate, Thomas Becket A. Franks, who today is a Benedictine monk at St. Procopius Abbey, in Lisle, Illinois, referred to Prevost as "the smartest person" and yet "probably the most humble person I've ever met and yet at the same time, the most helpful person." Fr. Becket recalled how they both were "away from family, away from neighborhood friends. Bob, as I still refer to him, was quiet but involved in everything."[47]

Bob was known for quietly listening to everything you had to say. "When you spoke with him or talked to him, he listened intently," says Fr. Becket. "He would look right at you, and listen intently. What he was doing was formulating a response, or how to respond to you. It was never flippant, nothing really quick. He was never 'off the cuff.' Even in discussions you knew what he was saying he had been thinking about for a while."[48] Prevost got not only an education but learned things like "dealing with people and learning patience and how to behave."[49]

It is worth pausing here to note the marked contrast with Pope Francis. Some of Francis's worst papal moments came via off-the-cuff responses quickly, flippantly made to reporters, without a carefully formulated response. Prevost, conversely, has long displayed the opposite temperament.

What Fr. Becket saw over a half century ago in the young Prevost gives him great optimism for what the world may now see in Pope Leo XIV: "I look back now 50-some years on and I see the beginnings of holiness and great maturity," says Fr. Becket. "A great thinker and a great gift to the world. I think he learned the way of holiness. I think we're going to encounter an extremely holy person, and every time I look at him now, I'm thinking I can see the beginnings of a saint way back in high school."[50]

In all, says Fr. Becket, "Everything that we went through at St. Augustine Seminary High School prepared Robert Prevost for his position" today as pope.[51]

A MATH MIND AT VILLANOVA

During those four years in Holland, Michigan, Prevost was not home much. Likewise for his college years to follow. "The whole high school years, college years," recalled his brother John, "we didn't really know him other than the summer vacation."[52]

His final summer vacation after high school had him focused on the next level of schooling: college. He wasted little time enrolling at Villanova University, located about 35 miles outside of Philadelphia.

Here again, the major attraction to Prevost was that Villanova is an Augustinian institution, one of only two such colleges in America.[53] The university is named after Saint Thomas of Villanova, a 16th-century Spanish Augustinian monk and archbishop, a relic of whom Pope Leo XIV today carries in his pectoral cross. The college was founded by the Order of Saint Augustine in 1842. It is the oldest Catholic university in Pennsylvania and the oldest Augustinian Catholic university in the nation. Among the many Catholic institutions of higher learning in America, Prevost based his decision on Augustine.

It is also interesting and revealing that for his major at Villanova, Prevost chose mathematics. Yes, math.

The math focus is not something to glide over in Prevost's background. Before he was a trained theologian, he was a mathematician. And that was very much his choice.

In 1972, a major change had occurred with candidates for the priesthood in the Order of St. Augustine in the Villanova Province. Previously, they were required to major in philosophy. That requirement was changed. Students could major in something else, as long as they took at least 30 credits of philosophy. Prevost took those credits, plus elective courses in Latin and Hebrew, befitting his interests and intentions with the Church going forward.[54] Still, he took advantage of the change in policy to major in math.

The fact that Pope Leo XIV is a mathematician says something about his mind—his very orderly mind. This is something that math majors and aficionados quickly remarked upon when learning that the new pope was a mathematician.[55] Catholic reporter Matthew McDonald was struck by it and interviewed several mathematicians who took to numbers to interpret Pope Leo XIV.[56]

McDonald quoted Martin Nowak, a professor of mathematics and biology at Harvard University and a Catholic. "I'm not surprised that the pope has studied mathematics, because I'm convinced that God is a mathematician," said Nowak. "It makes a lot of sense that his pastor on Earth is a student of mathematics."

McDonald also quoted mathematician and Catholic Brad Jolly, who stated: "Often, the kind of person who wants to become a priest is the kind of person who sees order and beauty and truth and the transcendentals of nature in the world, and the people who see these things are naturally attracted to mathematics." Jolly added: "Having a Pope with a mathematical background at a time like today is just such a blessing. My hope is that he would take this ability to think about things in an abstract way that addresses many problems at once and offer ways to solve problems that give us principles."

Mathematicians operate within a system of absolutes. McDonald also quoted James Franklin, retired professor in the School of Mathematics and Statistics at the University of New South Wales in Australia. "The basic idea is that study of mathematics attunes you to a certain kind of eternal realities," notes Franklin. "With mathematical proof, you understand not only that Pythagoras's theorem (say) is true but why it must be true, in all possible worlds. That gives you an anchor, a firm intellectual position from which you can be skeptical about the ebb and flow of opinion in the humanities, politics, etc."

Franklin continued: "Especially in these postmodernist days, an education restricted to the humanities, law, politics, etc. can leave you with the historicist view that all 'truths' are up for grabs and can change with time. Someone with a mathematics degree won't be tempted to believe that." In turn, observes Franklin, this should leave such a person "more confident of being able to reach permanent truths in spiritual and ethical topics, which is where you need to start to be a confident priest."

And indeed, the conclave that chose Robert Francis Prevost was hoping for a more confident chief shepherd, firmly grounded in reality, laws, and truths rather than relativism.

Prevost inherited a Francis papacy that confused the faithful with its disorder. Math, on the other hand, seeks to bring order out of chaos. Mathematicians are problem solvers. They can take a lot of information scattered about and carefully discern how to put the pieces together. They also understand that there are rules, absolutes, truths. Applying rules to arrive at these absolute truths involves rigor and discipline.

Such will be the task of Leo XIV, pope and mathematician. He will want to tidy up the Francis "mess of things" that frustrated all. And beyond Francis, he deals with the wider mess in Western culture generally, generated by what Pope Benedict XVI had called the "dictatorship of relativism."

Speaking of which, the Villanova University that Prevost chose in the early 1970s is not the college it once was. The Villanova that Prevost graduated from is today steeped in postmodernism. In recent decades it has been rapidly abandoning its Catholic commitment by embracing secularism, radical abortion feminism, LGBTQ activism, and leftist ideology, particularly among dominant heterodox faculty not committed to the teachings of the Church. It has become a bastion of wokeism and of what Pope Francis himself denounced as "toxic" gender ideology. It has become a place of secular American liberalism more than faithful Roman Catholicism.

In Prevost's day, however, there were still remnants of the more faithful past at Villanova, and he himself was a student who seemed to do his part in trying to stay true to the university's original identity. Professor Anne Hendershott of Franciscan University in Steubenville writes: "Villanova had historically been an ardent defender of the faith and zealous protector of the social and moral teachings of the Catholic Church." Author of the book, *A Lamp in the Darkness: How Faithful Catholic Colleges Are Helping to Save the Church*, Hendershott agrees that "the faithful Villanova University of the 1970s—the years when Pope Leo XIV attended—is very different from the more secularized Villanova of today."

As for Prevost's life at the university, Hendershott notes that Robert Francis Prevost as a student helped start a pro-life group on campus called Villanovans for Life, which still exists today, nearly 50 years later. Even then, those pro-life students face an uphill battle against campus and faculty leftists and "pro-choice" Catholics. Hendershott notes that "there remain several feminist faculty members on the Villanova campus who have been trying to convince students that access to abortion is not only permissible but necessary."

It is Hendershott's hope that Prevost today, some 50 years later, can once again have a positive impact for the cause of unborn human life on the campus, this time as pope rather than student.

She hopes that Leo XIV can help Villanova and other colleges recover the Catholic identity that the pontiff himself experienced when he attended the once faithful school.

"That would be the best gift Pope Leo can give to the university that nurtured his vocation," says Hendershott.[57]

NOVITIATE, SOLEMN VOWS, AND THE ANGELICUM

Prevost graduated from Villanova with a bachelor's degree in mathematics in 1977. When he returned to Chicago, he taught math part-time at Mendel College Prep High School, where his mother worked, and occasionally substituted as a physics teacher at St. Rita High School. He needed to earn some money. Back at Villanova, in addition to his studies, Prevost had worked part-time at a cemetery as a groundskeeper at Saint Denis Roman Catholic Church in nearby Havertown, Pennsylvania.[58]

But now, Prevost above all set his sights on the novitiate—on taking the steps to become a priest.

On September 1, 1977, shortly after graduating from Villanova, he entered the novitiate of the Order of Saint Augustine in Saint Louis, in the Province of Our Lady of Good Counsel of Chicago. He would make his first profession of vows on September 2, 1978. Three years later, on August 29, 1981, he made his solemn vows to become an official member of the Order of Saint Augustine.[59]

He also sought more education. He next went to Catholic Theological Union (CTU) in the Hyde Park section of Chicago, where he earned a Master of Divinity degree in 1982. The mathematician was now also a theologian.

At the time of the writing of this book, little is known about Prevost's time at CTU, nor whether the institution was or remains theologically liberal or closer to mainstream Catholicism. A lengthy feature piece on Prevost in *Time* magazine suggests a more liberal atmosphere, one that Prevost graduated from and soon thereafter left for less liberal environs at the Angelicum in Rome. The *Time* profile includes this assessment from the reporter and a Prevost contemporary, Fr. Paul Galetto:

> After he graduated from CTU and took his solemn vows in 1981, [Prevost] was invited to study canon law in Rome. "Americans had stopped going to study in Rome," says Galetto, who was one of the first to return. "We thought American theology was better, more modern. It wasn't based on patristics, but more on psychology and sociology." When [Prevost] arrived with Robert Dodaro, his co-valedictorian from way back at high school, neither speaking Italian, Galetto was their guide. John Paul II, now St. John Paul II, had just been elected. . . . "There was this electric feel," says Galetto. "Large crowds were coming to the audiences."
>
> While Prevost was studying a historic and doctrinaire subject, essentially the legal framework for the Catholic Church's operations, at the Angelicum, a 440-year-old school where John Paul II had also studied, he was surrounded by the excitement of a new era. The Augustinian house was across St. Peter's Square from the Vatican.[60]

One wonders if this suggests that Prevost left a more theologically liberal place at CTU in Chicago in hopes of attending a more theologically traditional, orthodox institution at the Angelicum in Rome. It is not clear.

What is clear is that at CTU he had impressed his peers and teachers, who all envisioned bigger steps for him ahead. Indeed, a big one was about to commence when in 1982 he went to Rome to study canon law at the Pontifical University of Saint Thomas Aquinas, also known as the Angelicum.

The storied Angelicum is one of the most impressive theological institutions on the planet. And for a priest that everyone felt had still higher horizons, it was in so many ways the right place to be. (More on the Angelicum in the next chapter.)

By his late 20s, Robert Francis Prevost was living quite an American story. He had sojourned from the modest home of his parents in Dolton, Illinois, to his minor seminary in Holland, Michigan, to Villanova University outside Philadelphia, to CTU in Hyde Park, and now the majestic Angelicum in Rome.

Many years later, non-Americans—the Italians, the cardinals, and so many at St. Peter's Square in Rome that extraordinary day of May 8, 2025—would dub Prevost "the least American American," which was certainly true among the American cardinals at the conclave. But as this chapter has shown, as genuinely universal as he would become, Robert Francis Prevost—Leo XIV—is also a very American American. And he is now the biggest American name in the history of the universal Roman Catholic Church.

But of course, that was much later to come—several decades later.

For now, circa 1982, at this point in his trajectory, Prevost still had much that lay head, including his ordination to the priesthood. Such would be his first big step from Chicago toward a much wider, universal world.

NINE

From Priest to Bishop (1990s to 2010s)

On June 19, 1982, 26-year-old Robert Francis Prevost was ordained a priest in the Order of Saint Augustine. He was ordained in Rome by Archbishop Jean Jadot of Belgium, then Pro-President of the Secretariat for Non-Christians, who had previously served as apostolic delegate and pro-nuncio in Asia, Africa, and the United States. The ceremony took place at the Cappella di Santa Monica degli Agostiniani—the Augustinian Chapel of Saint Monica, named after the mother of Saint Augustine. That chapel in central Rome is located mere steps from the Vatican and from Piazza del Sant'Uffizio, where Pope Leo XIV today resides.[1]

The commemorative holy card that Prevost ordered for the occasion bore an image from a 15th-century Russian icon of the Last Supper as well as a quote from Saint Augustine: "For me to feed all of you with ordinary bread is something I cannot do. Yet this Word is your portion. I feed you from the same table which nourishes me. I am your servant." Expressed by Saint Augustine in his Sermon 339, the words spoke of the Word of God as well as servanthood (a common theme in the writings of Augustine),[2] to which the new priest was making a commitment. He was also committing to providing the extraordinary Bread of Life to the faithful *in persona Christi*.[3]

The new priest left the Cappella di Santa Monica refreshed, inspired, and at long last officially imbued with that priestly mission he had long sought since the time he was a boy in Dolton,

Illinois. He would no longer merely play priest. He was now an actual priest, formally, by the Church's sacred rite, a successor to the first Apostles nearly two millennia ago. He was ready for the call by his order to find out where he would be sent.

TO THE PERIPHERY—PERU

During this time, Prevost continued his education. He would first earn a licentiate (1984) and then a doctorate (1987) in canon law from the Angelicum.[4] But in between, there was work to do; servanthood beckoned. His Church called him elsewhere. And Prevost obeyed the call.

In 1985, while preparing his doctoral thesis, Rob from Dolton was sent far away, to a place he likely never imagined, a remote area that the later Pope Francis would have identified as "the periphery." He was tasked to an Augustinian mission in Peru, specifically, the city of Chulucanas in the Piura district of the country, where he would stay through 1986.

The outsider might have been dismissed as a "gringo" by some not pleased to see an American. They would soon learn, however, that Prevost came from quite the mixed ethnic background, including a mother with a Latino last name and a grandfather (on his father's side) who had taught Romance languages, including Spanish. It was a language he would one day speak from the Loggia to the world as its next pope—to these same people of Chulucanas.

Prevost lived modestly. He had hardly been assigned to some glorious basilica surrounded by espresso bars and high-end restaurants. He would be lucky to get air-conditioning. He lived at St. Joseph the Worker Parish, where he slept in a small room.[5]

Prevost from the outset made an impact, a lasting one. A witness to that is the account of Héctor Camacho, a teenager who served as an altar boy for Prevost at the cathedral in Chulucanas. "He always instilled in us the importance of believing in God, having faith, being respectful, polite, and trying to excel in life," said Camacho 40 years later after learning in awe that the young priest he met in 1985 had just been named the world's Holy Father.[6]

Prevost back then was a young priest with charm and charisma, who attracted young and old alike. "He had this aura that spoke to people," remembered Camacho. "People flocked to him."[7]

Camacho experienced just that as he and Prevost together walked from place to place. The altar boy traveled with the priest as they rose early in the morning, often barely sunrise, to do Mass at the various adobe mud-brick churches with dirt floors that were scattered throughout the countryside. They went by foot or sometimes on horseback, carrying with them the priest's liturgical bag with crucifixes, wine, and the Eucharistic bread.

Camacho recalled that Prevost came up with ideas to keep the impoverished boys out of trouble and away from crime and gangs. He hired and brought in coaches and instructors for swimming, basketball, and karate. "He came here when he was really young," said Camacho, "but we thank that young man who walked with us, played basketball in the arena and would take us to the beach for the weekend."[8]

Prevost spent two years in Chulucanas, and he would return again. For a time, however, he went back to Rome. He had to defend his dissertation, which in those pre-internet days, and in a third-world country lacking high tech, he had somehow managed to continue to work on from his little room at St. Joseph the Worker Parish in Peru. This young priest, very much the Augustinian intellectual, had continued to tend to his flock while he also tended to his doctoral thesis.

A DOCTORAL THESIS ON . . . THE ORDER OF AUGUSTINE

At this point in the narrative of the life of Robert Francis Prevost, it would not surprise readers one bit to know that he did his dissertation on something Augustinian. In 1987, he defended his doctoral thesis, titled, "The Role of the Local Prior in the Order of Saint Augustine."

Prevost earned his doctorate in canon law from Rome's Pontifical University of St. Thomas Aquinas, also known as the Angelicum, a storied placed of great intellects and theological scholarship, befitting its namesake, the so-called "Angelic Doctor," with St. Thomas Aquinas (1225–74) being one of only 38 doctors (or teachers) of the Church.[9] In earning his doctorate there, Prevost stands in good company not only among past Church figures but recent ones, including a fellow pontiff: Pope John Paul II also did his doctoral work at the Angelicum, specifically on the writings of the 16th century Spanish mystic St. John of the Cross.

Not only had Karol Wojtyla (the future John Paul II) studied there (in the late 1940s), but the faculty at the time that Prevost attended had helped the Polish pope in the 1980s when he was spearheading an intellectual resurgence in the Roman Catholic Church. Dominican Father Thomas Joseph White calls this period at the Angelicum a "golden age of our canon law faculty." He says that the college's canon law professors assisted Pope John Paul II in preparing and editing the 1983 Code of Canon Law that remains in effect today under Pope Leo XIV.[10]

Fr. White has read Prevost's dissertation and describes it as "a really mature work of a 30-year-old who's extremely learned, very well read, and deeply thoughtful and spiritual." White says that the thesis reflects "on obedience and authority in the Catholic Church and the communal nature of shared life, or communion of persons, the respect of conscience, the respect of the human persons, gifts, the talents of the brethren, and also the limitations or sufferings of the brethren." White says that Prevost's work reflects on how the prior is "supposed to refer himself to Christ and to the rule, and cultivate a selfless way of life for the service of the common good of all."[11]

In a very practical sense applied to the head of a religious order, as well as perhaps a pope, White says that Prevost's work underscores how the superior must respect the consciences of members of the order, honoring their freedom but also ensuring that final decisions accord to "the communion and unity of the group."[12]

This means that members of the order are to be granted freedom, but they must also submit to the obedience that priests are pledged to honor. So must the superiors themselves. All are called to obedience. That obedience is itself an act of freedom—of the free will—for the benefit of the unity of the community. Religious communities generally operate under the "rule" of their order. That rule must be respected. As Prevost noted, this is a delicate balancing act between the individual and his larger group, but it is nonetheless something that must always be balanced.

"Obedience is something exerted through the life of the mind," says Fr. White, "and the will is to consent freely by understanding a shared truth the community wants to live together." White calls it "his [Prevost's] Dominican vision of obedience," though it is a vision common to the traditional religious orders, whether Dominicans, Benedictines, Franciscans.[13] (The Dominicans actually follow the Rule of St. Augustine.)

Beyond that, the larger picture of how this would later apply to the priestly life of Robert Francis Prevost is significant, given that two decades after writing this dissertation he himself would become head of the Augustinian order, and some four decades later he would become head of the Roman Catholic Church. What does it thus portend for his style as pope?

In all likelihood, this would suggest that Pope Leo XIV will seek to honor the freedom of bishops worldwide, while at the same time calling them to obedience to the rules and teachings of their mother Church. The best exercise of their freedom and free-will decision making will be in accordance with the peace and unity of the Church as a whole.

BACK TO PERU (1988–99)

That same year (1987) that he defended his doctoral thesis, Prevost was briefly sent back home to the Midwest, as he was appointed vocations director and missions director of the Augustinian Province of "Mother of Good Counsel" in Olympia Fields, Illinois.[14]

He was not home for long, however. He was sent packing once again to Peru. This would be yet another extension of his long stints of service abroad that one day would have members of the Italian press referring to the *papabile* cardinal as the "least American American." Or at least *North* American. He was hopping on a plane again for South America.

In 1988, Prevost was sent by the Augustinians to a different part of Peru. He was tasked to Trujillo, a coastal city in the northwestern part of the country, and its third most populous city. There in Trujillo, Prevost served as director of the joint formation project for Augustinian candidates from the vicariates of Apurímac, Chulucanas, and Iquitos.[15]

His positions there were so varied and almost technical at times that the list compiled by *Vatican News* reads like bullet points on a job résumé:

From 1988–98, he served in Peru in a variety of capacities for his religious order, initially as prior of the Augustinian community (1988–92), then as instructor for professed members (1992–98), and also as formation director (1988–98). These positions overlapped, with Prevost always wearing two or more hats. Indeed, add a fourth: From 1989–98, he acted as judicial vicar for the Archdiocese of Trujillo. Still more, the canon law expert spent time in the classroom, following in the steps of his parents as a teacher. He served as professor of canon law, patristics, and moral theology at the Major Seminary "San Carlos y San Marcelo."[16] There, at the Augustinian diocesan seminary in Trujillo, he taught canon law for nearly a decade.

Many of those positions were administrative roles for the order, but he also served the faithful as a priest with his own parish. The shepherd maintained a flock. From 1988–99, he was the pastor of Saint Rita parish in an impoverished part of Trujillo. He also acted as the parish administrator at another church, Our Lady of Monserrat, during this same time (1992–99).[17]

Prevost held so many positions that his head must have been spinning at times. Were he to recite them to his parents and brothers back home, the family would probably sigh at the task of trying to keep track of them. He was one busy son of Augustine.

RESISTING MAOIST TERRORISTS IN PERU

Much of this rings like common work for a clergyman in a religious order or diocese. There was lots of paperwork but also meaningful parish life for an overseas priest who formed touching relationships with members of his churches. But Prevost's time in Peru could not have been all peace and bliss. The geopolitical reality is that this was a scary, threatening time for a foreign priest to be sent to Latin America.

The 1980s was a period when communist movements were rife in the region. They formed guerrilla groups and roaming bands of violent revolutionaries. There were Marxist terrorists and outright killers on the loose in several Latin American countries, with Peru home to one of the most venomous of them: *Sendero Luminoso*, also known as "Shining Path."

Latin America had become a cauldron of toxic liberation theology and violent Marxism exported and sponsored throughout the region by Fidel Castro's Cuba and the Soviet Union. The United States became intimately involved. The Reagan administration in October 1983 ordered a US invasion of the Caribbean island of Grenada to prevent a Soviet-backed takeover.[18] The United States also supported the anti-communist Contra rebels against the Sandinista Marxist regime in Nicaragua as well as the anti-communist authoritarian government in El Salvador, which was threatened by a Marxist movement called the FMLN (Farabundo Martí National Liberation Front). El Salvador was stuck in a nasty spot between the far right and far left, with few good choices.

Many nations in Central America and South America were under constant threat and dominated international headlines. There were dramatic albeit under-the-radar operations such as the Reagan administration's remarkable clandestine move in the spring of 1983 to stop a communist coup in the nation of Suriname, located at the northern tip of South America. There, too, Reagan officials feared the prospect of "another Cuba," one with a Soviet base acting as a crucial proxy of the USSR with 386 kilometers of coastline along the strategic Atlantic.[19]

Each of these countries presented a tense, precarious situation. The Marxist movements within tore these nations apart and pushed them to the brink of civil war. They also drew in the two superpowers, the United States and USSR. Much of the Western world got involved, with huge protest movements and rallies held against US policy from New York City and Washington to London and Paris. For the Reagan administration, the Nicaragua fiasco led to the worst scandal of President Ronald Reagan's eight years, the Iran-Contra affair, which threatened the very popular president with impeachment.

Keeping these developments closer to the focus of this book, in many of these countries, churches were repressed, and priests and bishops were killed and martyred, from the likes of Bishop Oscar Romero (ultimately canonized as a saint), to Blessed Stanley Rother, to nuns who were assassinated in El Salvador, to the infamous case of three priests martyred in Peru in 1991 (more on that in a moment).[20]

As for Peru, its Marxist faction was especially bloody. The Shining Path insurgency was founded by a notorious professor-turned-revolutionary, Abimael Guzmán (1934–2021). Guzmán was a dead ringer for Fidel Castro. He admired the Cuban caudillo. He especially admired China's Mao Zedong, a man responsible for the deaths of over 60 million Chinese people between 1957 and 1969. Like his role model Chairman Mao, Abimael Guzmán called himself "Chairman Gonzalo." Novelist Mario Vargas Llosa said that Guzmán's model was "that of the Russia of Stalin, the [Chinese] Cultural Revolution of the Gang of Four, and the Pol Pot regime of Cambodia."[21] In other words, he was inspired by the three biggest killers of the 20th century, if not all of history: Josef Stalin, Mao, and Pol Pot.[22]

Guzmán had been a founder of the country's Communist Party before going underground in the 1970s to organize *Sendero Luminoso*. The group's name was inspired by a 1920s Latin American Marxist axiom that "Marxism-Leninism will open the shining path toward the revolution."[23]

Guzmán's criminal past made him ideal for launching Shining Path. In June 1969, he took part in the kidnapping of a prefect in Huerta, in the Ayacucho Province of Peru. For this, he was sent to jail but was soon released and went into hiding to plan for the revolution. The armed struggle commenced in the spring of 1980, with the guerrilla group's first armed actions in the cities of Chuschi and Lima. In short order, there were assassinations, kidnappings, executions, killings (by bullets, axes, knives, hanging), tortures, mutilations, and countless explosions. The targets were the numerous people—from political officials to teachers to peasants—who were declared "traitors" to the Marxist vision. In 1984 alone, Shining Path carried out more than 2,600 acts of violence. Chillingly, Guzmán predicted that "the triumph of the revolution will cost a million lives" (out of a population of less than 20 million).[24]

Naturally, the very peasants that the merciless Shining Path claimed as its championed *proletariat* attempted to flee this brutality. Those who resisted were captured, enslaved, and thrust into Maoist labor camps, where they were subjected to forced indoctrination, coerced into reading the writings of Chairman Gonzalo and other revolutionaries. Shining Path set up in the jungle what was known as the "Peruvian gulag."[25]

Guzmán and other revolutionaries had been influenced by another damaging Peruvian Marxist, Fr. Gustavo Gutierrez (1928–2024), a core founder of liberation theology. Gutierrez was infamous for his 1971 screed, *A Theology of Liberation*.

Radical, heretical, liberation theology priests peddled their Marxist nostrums in the name of "social justice" for the poor. But most of the world knew better, including the Polish pope who had suffered under communism in his native land behind the Iron Curtain, and who directly admonished Central American bishops to stay far astray of this collectivist ideology that his Church had long ago declared "evil" and "Satanic."[26]

Liberation theology had become a tool for leftists inside and outside the Church to undermine anti-communist governments that stood in the way of their ardor for Marxist-Leninist and Maoist rule. The militantly atheist Soviet Union itself pushed the "theology" for such purposes. In fact, Lt. Gen. Ion Mihai Pacepa, the leading Romanian spy chief who defected to the West in the late 1970s, claimed that liberation theology was created by the KGB. "The movement was born in the KGB," stated Pacepa unequivocally, "and it had a KGB-invented name: Liberation Theology."[27]

Pacepa, who had been a very high-level Communist Bloc intelligence official, gave specific details about that process, stating that, "The birth of Liberation Theology was the intent of a 1960 super-secret 'Party-State Dezinformatsiya [Disinformation] Program' approved by Aleksandr Shelepin, the chairman of the KGB, and by Politburo member Aleksey Kirichenko, who coordinated the Communist Party's international policies." Pacepa literally wrote the book *Disinformation.*[28] According to Pacepa, this Soviet disinformation program "demanded that the KGB take secret control of the World Council of Churches (WCC), based in Geneva, Switzerland, and use it as cover for converting Liberation Theology into a South American revolutionary tool."[29]

That was precisely how Peruvians Guzman and Fr. Gutierrez and the Shining Path used liberation theology in their South American nation.

Peru suffered terribly from these pernicious ideological influences. Among Latin America's Marxists, the Shining Path Maoist guerrillas were among the most brutal. Their massive insurrection sent Peru into the throes of a civil war that cost the impoverished nation at least $20 billion. Tens of thousands of people died. The seminal Harvard University Press book, *The Black Blook of Communism*, credits Shining Path with 25,000–30,000 deaths, whereas other sources have much higher numbers.[30] The deaths included many children. The destruction of families in the war zones left some 50,000 children abandoned or orphaned.[31]

TARGETING PRIESTS IN PERU

Here it must be said, as we circle back to Fr. Robert Francis Prevost, that Shining Path targeted priests as well. And viciously so. The rebels steamrolled anyone standing in the way of their Marxist "social justice" revolution, including clergy, and especially foreign priests.

On two separate occasions in August 1991, the group murdered three priests after Mass. *Sendero Luminoso* killed two young Polish Franciscan Friars, Michał Tomaszek and Zbigniew Strzałkowski, and an Italian diocesan priest, Alessandro Dordi. After executing the two Polish friars, the Shining Path terrorists hung signs around the priests' necks declaring them "imperialist lackeys."[32]

Even priests were not safe, nor spared.

Into this Marxist madhouse stepped an innocent humble priest from Dolton, Illinois. And indeed, one day in Peru, Robert Francis Prevost himself was almost a victim.

Upon his arrival in Chulucanas in 1985, Prevost would have been well briefed on the brutality of the Shining Path. Soon, he got a personal lesson when a bomb was detonated on the church steps of one of the parishes where he was present. A witness was Fidel Alvarado, who today is a priest in the Chulucanas diocese, but at the time was a 20-year-old student in the Augustinian seminary.

Alvarado said that the bomb destroyed the church door and that "grave threats" were issued to the priests inside, including to Prevost. Prevost and the other North American priests were told to leave within 24 hours or they would be killed. They decided not to leave. Prevost and the others stayed with their flock. "What convinced them to stay was the people," said Alvarado, "they had traveled around and felt the love of the people."[33]

Ultimately, Prevost and his confreres were unharmed, but the dangers always remained.

This was surely not the only occasion when Prevost faced Marxist rebels during his many years in Peru that precisely coincided with the height of *Sendero Luminoso*'s reign of terror. We know of this particular incident only because of recent reporting by two Reuters reporters who traveled to Chulucanas and interviewed Alvarado and others shortly after Leo's election, and even then learned few specific details. What Prevost has stated about the incident is not known at this point. The quiet priest was quiet about it.

The hope is that in time we will learn more about this incident and other surely traumatic threats to Robert Francis Prevost during his challenging period in Peru when Maoist thugs terrorized the population and murdered priests.

In all, a takeaway from this moving forward into the papacy of Pope Leo XIV is that the world once again has a Holy Father who understands communism not only because he knows what his Church teaches about the evils of Marxism but because of personal experience,[34] akin to what John Paul II had dealt with in Poland. It is telling that Leo XIV's pectoral cross includes a relic of a priest martyred during the Spanish Civil War—that is to say, killed by communists—which he began wearing as a bishop. Moreover, mere weeks into his papacy, on June 20, 2025, Leo XIV took the profound step of recognizing a large group of 124 martyrs killed out of hatred for their Christian faith by communists during the Spanish Civil War.[35]

No doubt, his run-ins with Marxists in Peru enlightened him.

1990–97: ROB LOSES HIS MOM AND DAD

In the meantime, Prevost dealt with death back home.

It was in this decade of the 1990s, as Prevost spread his spiritual wings and dealt with tumult (and joy) in Peru, that he lost the beloved, faithful parents who had raised him. His mother, Mildred

Agnes Martinez, passed first. She died on June 18, 1990, at age 78. His father, Louis Marius Prevost, who was younger than his wife, outlived her by seven years. He died on November 8, 1997, and was buried next to his dear wife in Assumption Catholic Cemetery in Glenwood, Illinois.[36]

The death of Mildred offers a touching story exemplifying the close personal relationships that Robert Francis Prevost had formed with his people in Peru. Recall Héctor Camacho, the altar boy noted earlier in this chapter.

As a moving testimony to how Prevost impacted him and others, Camacho recalls the young priest resolving to stay in touch after he had first left Chulucanas in 1986. As Camacho grew up and later married and had a daughter, he gave her the name "Mildred," after Prevost's mother.

That came about a decade later, when Camacho had relocated to the large Peruvian city of Trujillo to study, which was where Prevost happened to be sent next by his order. It was June 1990, and Prevost had informed his young friend of the death of his mother and that he would be leaving for a few weeks to travel to the United States for her funeral.

"One day I found him packing his clothes and he said he was going back to the United States because his mother had died," recalled Camacho. "I felt an immense pain, I cried for him, but he had this calmness. He was very prepared, like his mother was in the hands of God, who would receive her."[37]

A moved Camacho asked Prevost's permission to name his newborn daughter after Prevost's mother. He went still further, asking the young priest to be his daughter's godfather. Prevost said yes.[38]

That goddaughter, Mildred, is today 29 years old and marvels that her godfather is now the world's Holy Father. Like her father, she stayed in touch with Prevost in the years ahead. In fact, she has kept in touch with him all the way through his appointments as bishop, cardinal, and into the Vatican. "He sent me letters, he sent me mail, he told me about his trips, missions," she says. "His phrase was always, keep me in your prayers as I have you present in mine."[39]

She adds: "What he always told me was: 'Live with joy, live happily.'" In May 2025, Mildred said of her papal godfather: "He always told us that faith isn't just about going to Mass but about living with charity, loving one's neighbor, and being a light for others. He always inspired me to have hope and not give up in the face of difficulties."[40]

It is spiritual children like these who have become a part of Prevost's close-knit family.

With his parents now gone, Leo remains as close as ever to his brothers, talking to them by phone or by FaceTime "almost every day."[41] The three boys remain the dear sons of Mildred and Louis. With no sons of his own, the pope remains in touch with his brothers constantly. They continue to be a tight family.

1999–2013: BACK TO CHICAGO AND BECOMING PRIOR GENERAL OF OSA

After all of this, Prevost once again left Peru for Chicago, where, in 1999, he was elected provincial prior of the Augustinian Province of "Mother of Good Counsel." This began a steady rise to some prominent posts for Prevost.

On September 14, 2001—his 46th birthday—Robert Francis Prevost was selected to the significant position of prior general (also known as Superior General) of the ordinary General Chapter of the Order of Saint Augustine (OSA). Based in Rome, he was now head of all Augustinians—that is, of the roughly 2,800 friars around the world. He would serve a six-year term in that post until 2007, when he was once again selected for a second and final term (the position has a two-term limit), finishing in September 2013.[42]

This position put Prevost on the Church radar in a way he had not experienced before in his priesthood. To oversee the entire global Order of Saint Augustine was a big deal. He would now get special calls to Rome to participate in key conferences on the life of the Church.

One such example was a major synod of the Church held in Rome in October 2012. What Prevost said there really only emerged—going nearly viral—once he was elected pope in May 2025. These statements are worth our attention because they tell us much about the views of this otherwise quiet priest of whom little was known.

OCTOBER 2012: PREVOST ON ABORTION, MARRIAGE, SEXUALITY, SECULARIZATION

The occasion of these statements from Prevost was the October 7–28, 2012, synod on the New Evangelization. The pope was Benedict XVI, and the focus of the synod was the challenge of maintaining the faith amid the West's rapidly secularizing and de-Christianizing societies—what Cardinal Ratzinger prior to his election as pontiff in April 2005 had dubbed "the dictatorship of relativism."

That synod under Pope Benedict felt very different from those under Pope Francis, which became anxiety-ridden, seemingly pre-arranged, staged forums, in which it felt like many Church beliefs might be thrown into question. Also unlike Francis, who claimed that he wanted "dialogue" at these synods but instead heavily restricted and manipulated them, this synod of Benedict XVI was open, and the speeches that were given by participants in the closed-door sessions were made available to the press.

In total, the Vatican press office released summaries of 11 statements—so-called "interventions"—by various Church officials of different rank, from priests to bishops to cardinals. The text of Fr. Robert Prevost, the prior general of the Order of St. Augustine, was impressive enough that it was posted first among the 11 by the Holy See Press Office.[43]

Prevost's synod statement caught the attention of the Catholic News Service's Rome bureau chief, Francis X. Rocca. Rocca remembered it as "one of the most quotable and provocative talks."[44] Prevost had lamented how the secular Western mass media was promoting "anti-Christian lifestyle choices," including (as he named them) "abortion, homosexual lifestyle, euthanasia" as well as the "redefinition of marriage" and "alternative families comprised of same-sex partners and their adopted children." Prevost had stated:

> Western mass media is extraordinarily effective in fostering within the general public enormous sympathy for beliefs and practices that are at odds with the Gospel. For example, abortion, the homosexual lifestyle, euthanasia.
>
> Religion is at best tolerated by mass media as tame and quaint when it does not actively oppose positions on ethical issues that the media have embraced as their own. However, when religious voices are raised in opposition to these positions, mass media can target religion, labeling it as ideological and insensitive in regard to the so-called vital needs of people in the contemporary world.
>
> The sympathy for anti-Christian lifestyle choices that mass media fosters is so brilliantly and artfully ingrained in the viewing public, that when people hear the Christian message, it often inevitably seems ideological and emotionally cruel, by contrast to the ostensible humaneness of the anti-Christian perspective. Catholic pastors who preach against the legalization of abortion or the redefinition of marriage are portrayed as being ideologically driven, severe, and uncaring, not because of anything they say or do, but because their audiences

> contrast their message with the sympathetic, caring tones of media-produced images of human beings who, because they are caught in morally complex life situations, opt for choices that are made to appear as healthful and good.
>
> Note, for example, how alternative families comprised of same-sex partners and their adopted children are so benignly and sympathetically portrayed in television programs and cinema today.

Impressed by Prevost's eloquent, candid, and bold insights, Rocca followed up by contacting Prevost's order to request an interview. According to Rocca, Prevost "promptly said yes." Thus, Rocca and his CNS colleague Robert Duncan went to Prevost's office just a few yards from St. Peter's Square. They brought their pens, notebooks, and cameras.

Rocca recalled that he encountered a future pope who was "gracious though a bit reserved . . . but grew animated when discussing the great saint whose works are the foundation of his religious order." He and Duncan interviewed Prevost on camera, which became a 34-minute-long video in which the Augustinian expanded upon his synod remarks.[45] (See endnote for a link to watch the interview.) Rocca and Duncan also created a second and much shorter two-part video, whereby they interspersed audio of Prevost himself reading the original text of his synod statement along with media footage. The footage included images that illustrated with examples the Western media culture that Prevost was criticizing.[46] (See endnote for a link to watch the video.)

The longer 34-minute video contains some revealing insights from Prevost on secularization and evangelization. It needs to be watched to be fully appreciated. Here are a few highlights:

It was telling that it took Prevost no longer than a minute and 30 seconds into the interview to quote St. Augustine. What prompted his response was a question from his interlocutors on the relationship between personal experience and faith. "In terms of experience," said Prevost, "again I'll come back to St. Augustine." He noted that one of the reasons that Augustine's *The Confessions* continues to be one of the most widely read books in the history of the world is "precisely because of Augustine's insight into human experience. And he does a magnificent job of communicating both his own experience and what he lived, and how that experience can, indeed, be a window, if you will, an opening into discovering a personal experience of God in human life."

Prevost said of St. Augustine: "Human experience, he says, is precisely where you *can* find God. And the humanity of Augustine is not something which leads into a kind of personalized egoistic 'it's all about me, and only me' world. . . . So often today, in the highly individualistic society that people are growing up in, people think that 'my experience is the criteria of am I happy or not happy.' . . . 'If I feel okay, that's all that matters.'" Prevost asserted: "Augustine gives some insight into helping people understand that having an experience of God brings you far beyond yourself, and includes that dimension of what I would call human solidarity. . . . It's not just about me and my experience."

Prevost further stated: "Augustine, in *The Confessions*, talks about friendship, talks about family, talks about the importance of his mother, talks about his father, talks about human ambition. He talks about so many aspects of human life . . . of what humanity is about, what human life is about, and, therefore, what the encounter with God is about."

To repeat, these Prevost remarks—articulated in his characteristically smooth, calm, soothing manner—were recorded on video by Francis Rocca and Robert Duncan for Catholic News Service. The longer video interview accompanied the shorter two-part video that the two CNS journalists produced. When Rocca sent these finished products to Prevost, the future Holy Father was pleased, writing to

Rocca: "Many thanks! I enjoyed seeing the video presentations, and have sent the links out to different places."

Prevost shared the links. He was happy with the results.

Rocca noted that he did not see Fr. Prevost again for more than 10 years after their interaction. Interestingly, Rocca was surprised when Pope Francis in 2023 appointed Prevost to head the Dicastery for Bishops, "making him his top advisor in choosing Church leaders around the world." Presumably, given Prevost's views in 2012, Rocca figured they would have disqualified him from being later elevated by Francis. When Rocca encountered Prevost at a reception held by the US embassy to the Holy See, he reminded him of their meeting in October 2012. "A lot of water under the bridge since then," said Prevost in a manner that Rocca described as pleasant but brief and somewhat enigmatic.

Rocca's colleague Robert Duncan got a lengthier response. Duncan actually talked directly to Prevost about the October 2012 interview on the very day of the September 2023 consistory where he became Cardinal Prevost. When Duncan asked Prevost if his views had changed since his 2012 synod speech, the future pope responded: "Pope Francis has made it very clear that he doesn't want people to be excluded simply on the basis of choices that they make, whether it be lifestyle, work, way to dress, or whatever. Doctrine hasn't changed, and people haven't said yet, you know, we're looking for that kind of change. But we are looking to be more welcoming and more open, and to say all people are welcome in the church."[47] (See endnote for a link to watch the video.)

Doctrine had not changed, even under Francis, but the tone had. Cardinal Prevost in that sense was trying to be respectful of the pope's wishes.

Predictably, when Francis Rocca wrote up this material for a May 10, 2025, piece for *National Catholic Register* just two days after Prevost's election as pope, the videos went viral. Even more predictable, secular leftists roared that the new pope was "homophobic," "intolerant," and a "hater."

From them, it was the usual hate. Their response said more about them than it did him.

But regardless of the uproar, Prevost had made clear his position on these issues, which were very much the long-held positions of his Church. They were also not in conflict with the views of Pope Francis, who had never supported abortion, euthanasia, the redefinition of marriage, and same-sex parenting, and who (despite claims of his welcoming tone) before and during his papacy condemned such things far more stridently and provocatively than the language that Prevost had used in October 2012.

Prevost had actually been more diplomatic in tone than Francis.

THE POPE IS A REPUBLICAN: VOTING RECORD IN THE 2010s

Many observers will want to assess these remarks from Prevost during this period along American political-ideological lines, and will assert that he is a conservative Republican.

To be sure, these specific cultural-social-sexual views of Prevost absolutely accord with American conservative Republicans and stand in direct contrast with American liberal Democrats, especially in the 2010s, when Democrats shifted to the far left on such issues under President Barack Obama and congressional leaders like Rep. Nancy Pelosi (D-CA), particularly on abortion and marriage. The Obama years saw the Democrats take a hard left turn on matters from taxpayer funding of abortion to redefining marriage, codified by the June 2015 *Obergefell* decision, which the Obama administration celebrated by jarringly illuminating the White House in the colors of the LGBTQ Pride Month rainbow flag.

Robert Francis Prevost's aforementioned positions represent a complete contrast to those liberal Democrat positions. Indeed, as Prevost's brother Lou has said, the pope is not "woke."[48]

It thus should surprise no one to learn that voting records from this period show that Robert Francis Prevost voted in the Illinois Republican primaries in 2012, 2014, and 2016. More specifically, he voted in the general elections in 2012, 2014, 2018, and 2024 (apparently skipping the 2020 election). He voted in the 2024 presidential election via absentee ballot.[49] To repeat, when he voted in primaries, he voted not in the Democratic primaries, but Republican.[50]

So yes, the pope appears to be a Republican.[51] And yet, it needs to be understood that on these hot-button cultural-social-sexual issues, noted in this section and elsewhere in this book, what Robert Francis Prevost really is first and foremost is a Roman Catholic.

Yes, the world might have a pope who is a Republican, but what it really has is a pope who is a Catholic.

PERU: 2015–24

During that October 2012 synod interview, Robert Francis Prevost was not yet a bishop. That big promotion as well as an elevation to cardinal remained ahead, and in short order.

Prevost continued to maintain high-profile positions in his Augustinian Province in Chicago until Pope Francis directed him back to Peru. He was first made a bishop by Francis in 2014, appointed to the titular see of Sufar. A year later came a major promotion in the life of Prevost when the pope on September 26, 2015, appointed him bishop of Chiclayo, Peru.[52]

During this time, Prevost became involved in a number of initiatives seeking to halt the secular liberal push for gender ideology and abortion.

As bishop of Chiclayo, he spoke out against a government initiative to promote the teaching of gender ideology in schools. "The promotion of gender ideology is confusing, because it seeks to create genders that don't exist," Prevost told the local news media. He also advocated for the pro-life movement. In 2015, Prevost posted on his social media accounts a photograph from the March for Life rally in Chiclayo, exhorting his followers: "Let's defend human life at all times!"[53] In a 2019 homily at Chiclayo, he stated: "We cannot build a just society if we discard the weakest—whether the child in the womb or the elderly in their frailty—for they are both gifts from God."[54]

Those statements and actions from Prevost were fully consistent with Pope Francis's likewise strong condemnations of abortion and gender ideology, the latter of which Francis had vividly dubbed an "ugly ideology of our time."[55]

Here again in Peru, Prevost impressed the flock with his temperament and leadership. The assessments of the new bishop by parishioners echoed what had been said about him as a priest when he first came onto the scene in Peru 30 years earlier.

Among them, Jesus Leon Angeles, the coordinator of a Catholic group in Chiclayo who first met Prevost 2018, describes him as a "very simple" person who went out of his way to help others but above all listened to others. Leon Angeles said that Prevost was a man who exhibited notable leadership skills "but, at the same time, he knows how to listen. He has that virtue." He always had "the courtesy to ask for an opinion, even if it's from the simplest or most humble person. He knows how to listen to everyone."[56]

Again, a common appraisal. And traits that continued to serve him well. These skills were being noticed in the highest places outside of Peru, including at the Vatican.

Soon thereafter, Pope Francis elevated the 65-year-old Prevost to several other key appointments, including making him a member of the Congregation for Bishops on November 21, 2020.[57]

Robert Francis Prevost, that humble man from Dolton, Illinois, was suddenly not far from being a cardinal.

In sum, what was evident in the life of Robert Francis Prevost in this long period, from being a new priest in Peru in the 1980s, to becoming head of his Augustinian order in the early 2000s, to returning to Peru in the 2010s as a bishop, was a unique prelate who was both a missionary and an intellectual. Here was someone who could both mingle with the flock and study canon law. His first stint in Chulucanas in 1985–86 had been emblematic of his career ahead, as he toiled on his dissertation while getting his feet and hands dusty at dirt-floor parishes, leaving the village only to defend his thesis at the Angelicum in Rome before returning again to be with the people of his parishes.

Thus, in May 2025, the world would receive a pope who is both missionary and theologian, who both traveled to country parishes by foot and horseback in the fields of Peru and studied canon law at a top college in Rome. For the first time in a long time, the Catholic Church has a missionary pope.[58]

And yet, should there be any other type of pope? Jesus Christ called His disciples to engage in a Great Commission. The whole world, to the universal Church and to its chief shepherd, is a vast mission field. People are hurting and have needs everywhere, from the dirt paths of Chulucanas to the paved streets of Chicago's Magnificent Mile shopping district, from impoverished shacks in Trujillo to the espresso bars of Rome. Whether poor or wealthy, they all need mercy, salvation, and God.

In Robert Francis Prevost, they have an American pope who has seen much.

TEN

The Rapid Rise of Cardinal Prevost (2023–25)

The year 2023 represented the pinnacle of Robert Francis Prevost's professional-clerical achievements, or at least thus far.

A major step in his ecclesiastical life came on April 12, 2023, when he was installed as prefect of the Dicastery for Bishops, replacing Canadian Cardinal Marc Ouellet, who had been in the position since named by Pope Benedict XVI in 2010. Ouellet had been an influential figure, once considered *papabile* himself. Prevost had assumed leadership of an important position.

That same day, Prevost was also installed as president of the Pontifical Commission for Latin America, an appointment by Francis that was quite the testimony to the North American's life and priestly service in South America. Seven months later, on September 30, 2023, he was granted the red hat by the Holy Father, officially elevated to the position of a cardinal in the Roman Catholic Church, rarified ground for any Catholic clergyman.[1]

It is quite interesting and yet another contradiction of Pope Francis that Robert Francis Prevost was the only American that the Jesuit pontiff elevated to the level of cardinal who was not a vocal liberal or an ideologue. As noted, despite Francis's denunciations of "ideological colonizations," he had ideologically colonized the American cardinalate with liberals. Prevost, on the other hand, had no signs in his past of being an ideological progressive. Quite the contrary. He was, however, discreet. If Prevost was conservative, he was not a big mouth about his views. What no doubt resonated with Francis was the American's unique missionary work in the periphery, in Peru, in Francis's own native Latin America, as well as his measured, thoughtful serenity as he quietly did his job.

PREVOST ON FRANCIS: "WE WEREN'T ALWAYS IN AGREEMENT"

It now seems significant that Prevost himself would say after his appointment of bishop that he and Pope Francis certainly did not always agree, including when they first met and talked one on one.

Prevost shared a rather notable statement about he and Francis prior to the pope elevating him to cardinal. The date was March 14, 2023, and the bishops of Peru had granted the Chicago native one of their highest commendations, awarding him the Gold Medal of St. Toribio de Mogrovejo for his exceptional pastoral work in the country and for him being named prefect of the Dicastery for Bishops by Pope Francis. During that ceremony, Prevost recalled how he had met Cardinal Jorge Mario Bergoglio several times during the years he served as prior general of the Augustinians. "I won't tell you the reason, but let's just say that when Cardinal Bergoglio and I met, we weren't always in agreement," Prevost said with a smile.[2]

Typical of Prevost, he was tight-lipped and did not share their specific areas of divergence. Nonetheless, their split must have been substantial, because Prevost said that when Bergoglio was elected pope in March 2013, he "said to some of my brothers: 'Well, that's very good, and thank God I'll never be a bishop.'"

One wonders what the disagreement was about. Had Francis ripped the Latin Mass, praised liberation theology, judged someone in the room a "rigid" "Pharisee?" Prevost did not say.

And yet, that Jorge Mario Bergoglio one day ahead as Pope Francis would make Prevost a bishop and a cardinal. Why?

The question deserves pondering. Despite his claims of dialogue and synodality, Pope Francis did not tend to appoint people he disagreed with. He often refused to respond to them, demoted them, plainly did not like them, and in some cases persecuted and cruelly judged them—especially traditionalists who he judged "whitened sepulchres." Prevost himself likes tradition, which became evident from the opening weeks of his papacy as Leo XIV. He likely got by Francis because if he was both traditional and conservative, he was not brashly outspoken in a way that got him get red-flagged by the Argentinian Jesuit and his cronies.

Any perceived demerits against Prevost would have been far overshadowed by what Francis would have seen as his admirable missionary work in "the periphery." Francis often crudely said that he wanted his shepherds to "smell like the flock," that is, to get close to the flock (who he presumably felt carried a bad odor). Robert Francis Prevost was the one American cardinal who uniquely did that. Francis himself never once returned to his native Argentina as pope—to smell like the flock—but Prevost was a Chicagoan who returned again and again to Peru. Francis must have been highly impressed by this priest who walked the walk.

Surely for these reasons, Francis liked him.

Moreover, it should be noted that Prevost was installed as a cardinal by Francis late in 2023. By that time and through 2024, Francis's growing sicknesses got worse and worse. He went on a steady decline. His final 18 months were a time of poor health leading to his long hospitalization and death. He likely did not have the time or occasion or energy to initiate a clash with Prevost.[3]

"A SURPRISE TO ME"

And so it happened that on the morning of September 30, 2023, at St. Peter's Square, 68-year-old Robert Francis Prevost was among 19 bishops and two presbyters who were created cardinals of the Roman Catholic Church by Pope Francis. The kid from St. Mary the Assumption parish in Dolton, Illinois, had come a long way. The former altar boy was now a prince of the Church.

The previous day, despite a hectic schedule, Prevost took the time to sit for an interview with a writer from the Vatican's General Curia office. It was a revealing interview that was posted at the official website of the Augustinian order.[4]

Prevost was first asked about the moment in January 2023 when he learned that Pope Francis was appointing him as prefect of the Dicastery for Bishops. Prevost conceded that, "The fact that Pope Francis asked me to accept this mission came as a surprise to me." He said that when Francis had first broached the possibility of the appointment to him years earlier, Prevost told the pope, "You know that I am very happy in Peru. Whether you decide to appoint me or to leave me where I am, I will be happy; but if you ask me to take on a new role in the Church, I will accept."[5]

No doubt, the fact that Prevost was happy in Peru pleased Francis. The pontiff must have figured it made Prevost worthy of higher things as a bishop and eventually a cardinal.

"To be a good shepherd means to be able to walk side-by-side with the People of God and to live close to them, not to be isolated," said Prevost. "Pope Francis has made this very clear on numerous occasions." Prevost said of the pontiff: "He does not want bishops who live in palaces. He wants bishops who live in relationship with God, with their brother bishops, with priests and especially with the People of God in a way that reflects the compassion and love of Christ, creating community."

That was particularly true of Prevost's priestly service. In Peru, he walked side-by-side with his people, sometimes by foot to adobe mud-brick churches, living certainly not in palaces but in community.

At the close of that September 2023 interview, the new cardinal was asked what advice he would give to seminarians. Here he chose a favorite phrase of Pope John Paul II, taken from the Gospel: "I suppose the first thing I would say are the words that Christ repeated so many times in the Gospel: 'Do not be afraid.' The Lord calls—and His call is true. Do not be afraid to say Yes." That yes included accepting the call to higher places in the hierarchy of the Church, even if the priest happened to like where he was. "Do not be afraid to open your heart to the possibility that the Lord is calling you to religious life," said Prevost, "or to Augustinian life, or to the priesthood, or to other forms of service in the Church."

And now for Robert Francis Prevost, that call was cardinal.

ON BLESSINGS FOR SAME-SEX COUPLES, FEMALE DEACONS/ PRIESTS, AND ABORTION

During this period as cardinal, Prevost found himself often called to Rome for various conferences and tasks. This also brought him more frequently into the presence of cameras and journalists and microphones, more than what he had faced in Peru. He could be asked questions on key issues and controversies the Church was dealing with, especially messy ones under Pope Francis.

To that end, more information inevitably emerged on Prevost's position on certain timely issues, including some of the cultural-moral matters noted in the previous chapter. One hot-button controversy he could not escape was Pope Francis's messy guidelines on the blessing of same-sex couples, which had everyone confused and many people in the Church, the pews, and the culture at one another's throats.

On that, Prevost did not say much, but when asked, he did not hesitate to try to reach common ground with the vocal dissenting African bishops who did not want to obey Francis's new declaration. And in fact, one wonders if Prevost's reasonable take on the matter may have been one of the opinions that pushed Francis himself to seek an accommodation with the Africans. "The bishops in the episcopal conferences of Africa were basically saying that here in Africa our whole cultural reality is very different," said Prevost on October 23, 2023. "It wasn't rejecting the teaching authority of Rome, it was saying that our cultural situation is such that the application of this document is just not going to work." He added: "You have to remember there are still places in Africa that apply the death penalty, for example, for people who are living in a homosexual relationship. . . . So, we're in very different worlds."[6]

The world of Africa, as well as Asia and the periphery that Prevost had served for decades, was most assuredly not the Western world consumed by the dictatorship of relativism. New Yorkers, Californians, and the people of Boston and Portland might be clamoring for "gay blessings" and "transgender" rights and attending pride parades, but such things were nowhere on the radar, moral universe, or mental wherewithal of Ugandans and Malaysians. Prevost, an American native who spent most of his recent years in rural areas in Chulucanas, understood that.

San Francisco was not Sri Lanka.

It seemed reasonable to assume that Francis's initial framing of concepts like synodality and localism ought to allow some flexibility on such a delicate matter among differing bishops scattered among vastly different areas of the world.

Cardinal Prevost also weighed in on the matter of ordaining women as deacons or priests at an October 25, 2023, synod press conference. "Something that needs to be said also is that ordaining women—and there's been some women that have said this interestingly enough—'clericalizing women' doesn't necessarily solve a problem, it might make a new problem," Prevost told journalists. "And perhaps we need to look at a new understanding or different understanding of both leadership, power, authority, and service . . . brought to the life of the Church by women and men." He clarified: "the apostolic tradition is something that has been spelled out very clearly, especially if you want to talk about the question of women's ordination to the priesthood."[7]

Cardinal Prevost underscored that the Catholic Church is not supposed to be like the world. It "needs to be different." He noted that the Church had its long tradition with a male priesthood, and "It isn't as simple as saying that, 'You know, at this stage we're going to change the tradition of the Church after 2,000 years on any one of those points.'" At the same time, he certainly was supportive of the roles that women have in the Church: "I think there will be a continuing recognition of the fact that women can add a great deal to the life of the Church on many different levels." But those roles for women did not extend to the diaconate and priesthood.[8]

These positions by Prevost were the same as Pope Francis's stance on women as deacons and priests. Mere months into his papacy, namely, on his flight to Rio for World Youth Day on July 28, 2013, Francis had said this of women being priests: "As far as women's ordination is concerned, the Church has spoken and said: 'No.' John Paul II said it, but with a definitive formulation. That door is closed." Francis's position was unchanged throughout the 12 years of his papacy, even as he allowed for the divisive issue to be debated, angering not only conservatives but also liberals by once again giving progressives false hopes that were never realized.

Prevost also continued to make pro-life statements during this time as cardinal. At the October 2023 synod, he stated: "The Church must walk with all people, especially the most vulnerable, ensuring their dignity is upheld from the womb to the end of life, as this is the heart of Christ's mission." And in his 2023 address to the Dicastery for Bishops, he said: "Bishops are called to be shepherds who defend the sanctity of life, ensuring no one—neither the unborn nor the aging—is left without the Church's love and protection."[9]

To be sure, Cardinal Prevost was not chasing down reporters and begging to be interviewed. In fact, when he was announced as the next pope on May 8, remarks like these were searched out on Google by interested parties. To most people outside and even many inside the Church, he was a blank slate.

And yet, throughout late 2023 and into early 2025, Cardinal Prevost was quietly making himself a steady presence at the Vatican, especially within the Curia.

CARDINAL PREVOST'S REMARKABLE RÉSUMÉ AT THE CURIA

While the election of Cardinal Robert Francis Prevost as pope was a shock to the general public, it was not to his fellow cardinals who gave him over 100 votes by the fourth ballot at the conclave. He might have been unknown to the masses, but he was widely known among the cardinals, among bishops, and with the Roman Curia. The extent to which that is true is striking.

A very revealing study of Prevost's rapid rise through the Curia was published five days after his election, by Professor Giovanni Sadewo of Divine Mercy University.[10]

The Roman Curia is the central governing body of the Roman Catholic Church. Its officials assist the pope in managing and governing the Church. This includes matters of administration and finance. Unfortunately, the Curia has long been plagued by waste and corruption. With the appointment of every new pope, there are desperate cries for reform of the Curia, and each and every pope seems to fall short if not fail in that regard—no matter how effective the Holy Father might be on matters of faith and morals. The pope is not only a spiritual leader but also effectively the CEO of the Church. There was hope that Francis would reform the Curia and its tangled web of bureaucracy and mismanagement. He did not.

All of which is important background to the choice of Robert Francis Prevost. As only the cardinals knew, he happened to have acquired broad, diverse, and exceptional experience within the Curia in a very short time, unusually so—as shown by Professor Sadewo's analysis of data gathered from the *Annuario Pontificio* for the years 2020 through 2024.

The *Annuario Pontificio* (Italian) is the official *Pontifical Yearbook* that serves as the annual directory of the Vatican, listing all officials who serve in the various departments of the Roman Curia. It also lists every bishop and cardinal and their dioceses, all priests with and above the rank of monsignor, plus much more.

Prevost began his service in the Roman Curia in 2019 as a member of the Congregation for the Clergy. That service apparently went so well that by the end of 2020 he got a second appointment as a member of the Congregation for Bishops. He served in both capacities through 2022.

According to Professor Sadewo, by the end of 2021, Prevost already had "shared curial membership" with 34 cardinals, rising to 36 by the end of 2022. And yet, there was a swift "increase in his network" when he was appointed prefect of the Dicastery for Bishops in 2023. At that point, everything changed. His trajectory took off. By the end of that year, Cardinal Prevost held positions in at least 11 different curial bodies, including:

- Dicastery for Evangelization
- Dicastery for the Doctrine of the Faith

- Dicastery for Oriental Churches
- Dicastery for Bishops
- Pontifical Commission for Latin America
- Dicastery for the Clergy
- Dicastery for Institutes of Consecrated Life and Societies of Apostolic Life
- Dicastery for Culture and Education
- Dicastery for Legislative Texts
- Pontifical Commission for Vatican City State
- Several Permanent Interdicasterial Commissions

According to Sadewo, this extraordinary breadth of work made Prevost the cardinal with the "broadest familiarity and network within the Roman Curia," with shared membership alongside 103 other cardinals serving in the Curia. How high of a percentage was that among the 130-plus cardinal-electors in the Church? It was the highest in the entire Curia. Among all cardinals, Prevost had quickly and quietly risen dramatically from being ranked 60th "in terms of curial familiarity" to number one. No cardinal had gone higher, and especially so rapidly.

Those numbers are still more revealing when considering who Prevost had surpassed. According to Sadewo's analysis, Prevost blew past long-time Curia members such as Cardinal Luis Antonio Tagle, who had been part of the Roman Curia since 2012 and had consistently ranked among the top five most-networked cardinals. When Prevost hit number one in 2023, it was Tagle who he supplanted in that top spot. Keep in mind that it was cardinals Tagle and Parolin who were two odds-on favorites to be elected pope after the death of Francis. Prevost replaced both men as the most-networked cardinal in the Curia in 2023.

Notably, Sadewo reports that the only other cardinal who experienced a similarly steep rise in that period was Francis's right-hand man, Cardinal Victor Manuel "Tucho" Fernández. A few words on

Fernández, given his influence in Francis's Curia and in fostering key controversies that Leo XIV must now deal with:

A progressive Latin American theologian who had ghostwritten several of Pope Francis's most controversial documents—and whose prior most-noted published work was *Heal Me with Your Mouth: The Art of Kissing*—Francis in late 2023 had placed his fellow Argentinian in the position of prefect of the Dicastery for the Doctrine of the Faith, a prestigious and influential Vatican position for which Fernández had neither the academic training nor intellectual chops. He was immediately over his head. For both him and his pope, the explosive modern moral-cultural issues they had to deal with were highly challenging and required men with the theological and intellectual heft of predecessors like Cardinal Joseph Ratzinger/Pope Benedict XVI.

Fernández's role in the Francis regime speedily and predictably became disastrous, especially with the outrageously convoluted mishandling of the same-sex blessings fiasco, expressed in the Christmas 2023 document *Fiducia supplicans* (examined in a chapter ahead). The document created confusion and chaos. It was among the messiest of the messy things that Francis did. And fellow Jesuit Fernández was its chief architect.

The left-wing Jesuit *America Magazine*—which certainly cheered *Fiducia supplicans*—had inadvertently veered into the truth when it jubilantly reported in January 2024 that, "In just three months at the helm of the Dicastery (formerly Congregation) for the Doctrine of the Faith, Argentine Cardinal Victor Manuel 'Tucho' Fernández has rapidly changed what was once the Vatican's most formidable department."[11] He had indeed. He rapidly made it unformidable, turning it into a laughingstock, a tragic shell of its former self. Given Fernández's troubling background, few were surprised by this. At the time of his appointment, the Spanish publication *La Esperanza* had run the headline, "Tucho Fernández, the perfect prefect for the *demolition* of the Faith."[12]

Fernández's work had become so messy that no one in the Curia, from left to right, wanted him anywhere near a list of *papabili* to replace Francis in May 2025. Among all the lists, the name of Fernández was a salient no-show. The cardinal-electors were looking for someone like a Prevost, Tagle, or Parolin, Pizzaballa, or Erdő, or anyone but Fernández.

Returning to the point of Professor Sadewo's analysis of the Curia during this time, the only cardinals who approached Prevost's quiet and unassuming depth of Curia experience were Francis's right-hand man Fernández and his potential *papabile* successor, Tagle. That really revealed something significant about Robert Francis Prevost, who had not even been made a cardinal until September 2023!

This was something that only those Vaticanistas in-the-know realized. By the end of 2023, Prevost already had a higher percentage of experience in shared curial bodies than any other Church official, including all of the leading *papabili* favored to replace Francis in May 2025. Just as Prevost hopped over all of them in curial experience, he soon also hopped them in the conclave.

So by the time of the conclave balloting in May 2025, the cardinals knew Prevost, even as the public did not. They knew him as a peer.

And with their choice, the whole Church and world were about to get to know Robert Francis Prevost: that is, Leo XIV.

ELEVEN

What's in a Name? The Leo Legacy

When a new pope is first selected inside the conclave, he is asked two questions: first, whether he accepts the call to the Chair of St. Peter, then second, the papal name he has chosen. After giving his consent, Robert Francis Prevost in Latin voiced the name Leonem Decimum Quartum, Leo XIV.

When Prevost uttered those words, they surely elicited oohs, aahs, and applause inside the Sistine Chapel, as they did when the name was first shared with the world from the Loggia on May 8, 2025.

His invoking of the papacy of Leo XIII was a brilliant, inspired choice. Prevost would immediately call for peace—his first word spoken from the Loggia—and for unity. And indeed, as far as popes go, the world needs to go that far back—that is, to the pontificate of Leo XIII from 1878–1903—to find a pontiff that virtually everybody inside the Catholic Church (and outside) universally liked and praised. He was a unifying force. Many would have winced if Prevost had called himself Francis II, Benedict XVII, or even John Paul III, Pope Paul VII, John XXIV, or Pius XIII. Of all popes going back the last two centuries, Leo XIII is the one nearly everyone seems to approve of. Pope Francis had opted for the name of the great Saint Francis, another figure who everybody loves, but Francis as pope managed to make himself extremely divisive. So much so that many Catholics would have wailed and gnashed their teeth if Prevost had invoked the name of the wonderful saint from Assisi by going with Francis II.

And so, for a new pope striving for unity, Robert Francis Prevost could scarcely do better than to pick up the mantle of Leo XIII.

THE NAME OF LEO

He was now the new bishop of Rome, Pope Leo XIV, formerly known as Robert Francis Prevost. We might say formerly because, as with Jesus Christ telling Simon Bar-Jonah, "you are *Petras* [Peter], and on this rock I will build my Church," Robert Francis Prevost is forever changed. He will now always be known as Pope Leo XIV. Or as Cardinal Timothy Dolan had put it, "Robert Francis Prevost is no longer around; it's now Pope Leo."

The Leonine line is most venerable. It dates back nearly 1,600 years, all the way to the fifth century with its namesake, the first Leo, also known as Leo the Great (391–461). Prevost himself might here interject to note that the first Leo was a contemporary of St. Augustine (354–430). It was a century of many esteemed Church figures.

Leo the Great occupied the papal throne from 440 to 461. He oversaw the Council of Chalcedon (451 AD), which was one of the crucial early Christological councils that (on the heels of the Council of Nicaea, among others) affirmed and defined the very nature of Jesus Christ (one person, both fully human and fully divine) as well as the doctrine of the Holy Trinity. That was just one of several things the first Leo did that earned him the title of "great."

The first Pope Leo would be declared a saint, as would several that followed him. Remarkably, the first four Leos were all canonized. Also later sainted was Pope Leo IX, who occupied the Chair of St. Peter for a short but significant five-year stint from 1049 to 1054. This was the time of the Great Schism.

Similarly, a millennium after the reign of Leo the Great was another historic figure in the Leonine line who dealt with a major split: Pope Leo X. This Leo ruled from 1513 to 1521 and was dealt the enormous historical-spiritual blow of Martin Luther and his revolt that forever disunified the Church. While Leo XIV today wants unity, it can be said with confidence that few popes craved unity like Leo X. The rupture he faced was unprecedented in the history of Christianity.

But above all, when Robert Francis Prevost invoked the Leonine line, he was thinking of the most recent papal Leo: Leo XIII.

WHO WAS LEO XIII?

The beloved figure known as Pope Leo XIII was born Vincenzo Gioacchino Raffaele Luigi Pecci on March 2, 1810, in Carpineto Romano. He was the sixth of seven sons born to Anna Prosperi-Buzi and Count Lodovico Pecci. His parents were devout people keen on raising their boys in the faith. When Vincenzo turned eight years old, Anna and Lodovico sent him and his ten-year-old brother, Giuseppe, north of Rome to the medieval city of Viterbo to study at a new Jesuit school. Vincenzo quickly impressed his teachers, excelling in everything from theology to law to mastering Latin.

Vincenzo's teachers pushed him to continue his studies at a deeper level, which he did with enthusiasm. By the age of 22, he had already earned a doctorate in theology. Astonishing as that was, perhaps it was not surprising for a man who one day would compose some of the richest writings in the history of the Church.

Vincenzo's mind and piety struck Church officials. He pursued the priesthood with the same rigor he had dug into his studies. He was ordained in 1837. Sixteen years later, in 1853, he became a cardinal, in his mere early forties. From there, he continued to rise up the ranks of the Church hierarchy.

Throughout his years as cardinal, Vincenzo had served the longest reigning pontiff since St. Peter. Pope Pius IX had been elected in 1846. In 1877, his 31st year as pope, he tapped his underling, Vincenzo, for the influential position of Vatican camerlengo. It was as if Vincenzo was being prepared to succeed Pius IX. And precisely that happened with the death of Pius IX in February 1878.

When the conclave chose him as the next heir to the Chair of St. Peter, Vincenzo Pecci took the name Pope Leo XIII, invoking a long, Leonine line of venerable pontiffs. Like his predecessor, he would preside over a lengthy pontificate. He would serve longer than any pope besides Pius IX and St. Peter, holding the seat until his death in July 1903. At age 93, he was the longest surviving pope.

That 25-year-long pontificate began on February 20, 1878. It was a historic papacy known for numerous profound statements, including *Quod Apostolici Muneris* (1878), *Aeterni Patris* (1879), *Arcanum divinae* (1880), *Immortale Dei* (1885), *Humanum genus* (1884), *Libertas* (1888), *Rerum Novarum* (1891), and *Providentissimus Deus* (1893), among others. Most to all of these stand out for their potential significance for the papacy of Pope Leo XIV, from *Arcanum divinae* on the subject of Christian marriage to *Libertas* on the matter of human freedom.

Here are some highlights from a few of these statements.

ON SOCIALISM AND COMMUNISM

In the first year of his papacy, and just three days after Christmas 1878, Leo XIII issued *Quod Apostolici Muneris*, a major statement on the socialist ideology that was infecting much of Europe. It was a crucial statement that today is too forgotten among "social justice" warriors who would like to claim that popes like Leo XIII condemned communism but not socialism. Of course, as Leo and the popes before and after him knew, Marx and Engels taught (both men were still alive and active at the time) that socialism was the finally transitionary step to communism; the two "isms" were not to be separated.[1]

Consider what Leo XIII's predecessor had said of that. In his December 1849 encyclical, *Nostis Et Nobiscum*, Pius IX denounced both socialism and communism as "wicked theories" and "pernicious fictions." Pius IX's most impactful statement on this subject was his November 1846 *Qui pluribus*, which stated that communism is "absolutely contrary to the natural law itself" and if implemented would "utterly destroy the rights, property, and possessions of all men, and even society itself." *Qui pluribus* denounced communism as a "dark design" of "men in the clothing of sheep, while inwardly ravening wolves." It also prophetically stated of communists: "After taking their captives gently, they mildly bind them, and then kill them in secret. They make men fly in terror from all practice of religion, and they cut down and dismember the sheep of the Lord." Pius IX said the writings of communists constituted a "filthy medley of errors" that teach "sinning" and spread "widespread disgusting infection."

Leo XIII's statements echoed these teachings from his predecessor. His December 28, 1878, *Quod Apostolici Muneris* was only the second encyclical of his pontificate. It described communism as "the fatal plague which insinuates itself into the very marrow of human society only to bring about its ruin." And it likewise blasted the stepsister of communism: socialism. "We speak of that sect of men who, under various and almost barbarous names, are called socialists, communists, or nihilists," wrote Leo XIII, "and who, spread over all the world, and bound together by a wicked confederacy, no longer seek the shelter of secret meetings, but, openly and boldly marching forth in the light of day, strive to bring what they have long been planning—the overthrow of all civil society."

As Leo XIII put it, these socialists, communists, and nihilists "leave nothing untouched." They even go so far as to "debase the natural union of man and woman, held sacred even among barbarous peoples; and its bond, by which the family is chiefly held together . . . . Doctrines of socialism strive almost completely to dissolve this union."

This cannot and should not be ignored today, especially given that in the quiet background of today's Leo XIV there were some scary battles against communism in countries like Peru, one of which involved a direct threat to his life. He also has a special appreciation for Spanish martyrs killed by communists during the Spanish Civil War. Notably, the most scathing indictment of communism in the history of the Catholic Church was Pius XII's March 1937 encyclical *Divini Redemptoris*, which described the ideology as a "Satanic scourge" orchestrated by the "sons of darkness," and was released (in part) as a response to the evils being perpetuated by Marxists during the 1936–39 Spanish Civil War (among other parts of the world).

Unfortunately, these inspired, vociferous condemnations of communism, which continued into the papacies of John Paul II and Benedict XVI, were not reinforced in Pope Francis's writings and statements. To be sure, Francis did say (in December 2013) that "the Marxist ideology is wrong," but he said very little beyond that. Critics could be forgiven for thinking that Francis was hardly a vocal critic of socialism and communism.[2]

Will Leo XIV speak out more forcefully, especially in places of communist persecution of Christianity like China, Nicaragua, and Venezuela? If he fully identifies with Leo XIII, we should expect just that.

AETERNI PATRIS (1879)

In August 1879, Leo XIII released his encyclical letter *Aeterni Patris* (1879), on the matter of what he called "the restoration of Christian philosophy." It has been credited with nothing short of initiating a Thomistic revival—that is, of Scholastic philosophy—and a renewed appreciation of the complete compatibility between faith and reason in the modern world.[3]

That seamlessness between faith and reason is something that modernists have strived to deny. Of course, Leo XIII was widely known for taking on modernism. He saw a revival of Scholastic philosophy as key to confronting modernism. *Aeterni Patris* is a brilliant statement in the battle against modernism and secular relativism, with the Church arming itself with the heavy artillery of Thomistic teaching.

In the immediate days of Leo XIV's papacy, this encyclical was pointed out in much of the commentary on Robert Francis Prevost choosing the name of Leo XIII, and rightly so. Thus far in the Leo XIV papacy, at the time of this writing, the new pope has not yet invoked *Aeterni Patris*. Yet, if that document and its underlying framework has influenced his thought, then such speaks well of the mind of Leo XIV.

RERUM NOVARUM (1891)

What has been mentioned by Robert Francis Prevost in light of his invoking the name of Leo XIII is *Rerum Novarum*, which was Leo XIII's signature encyclical and one of the most influential writings of any religious figure in the last two centuries.

Issued May 15, 1891, *Rerum Novarum* is considered the classic, foundational text of Catholic social teaching, with a wide impact inside and outside the Catholic Church, including among Protestant communities. The encyclical focused on capital and labor, on the dignity of the human person, and particularly on the worker's rights and duties, including to both a fair wage and private property. Beyond that, in a more general sense, the encyclical dealt with the "new things" of the world, launched by "the spirit of revolutionary change" in economics, politics, and ideologies.

The direct translation of *Rerum Novarum* from the Latin is "Of New Things."

These new revolutionary changes afoot in the late 19th century, stated *Rerum Novarum*, brought with them a "vast expansion of industrial pursuits and the marvelous discoveries of science." They were dramatically impacting "the changed relations between masters and workmen," the "enormous fortunes of some few individuals," the "utter poverty" of others, and even "the prevailing moral degeneracy." There was suddenly a "momentous gravity" in the sudden change of the state of things, causing widespread confusion and "painful apprehension."

"Social justice" Catholics like to claim that *Rerum Novarum* supports some form of soft socialism, and instead only condemns communism. In truth, the words "communism" and "Marxism" never once appear in the encyclical. Neither do words like "collectivism," "redistribution," "central planning," and "command economy." The reality is that the word "socialism" appears in *Rerum Novarum* multiple times and is always condemned.

For instance, *Rerum Novarum* says (paragraphs 4–5) that rather than seeking legitimate means to remedy societal wrongs, "the socialists, working on the poor man's envy of the rich, are striving to do away with private property, and contend that individual possessions should become the common property of all, to be administered by the State or by municipal bodies." These socialists claim "that by thus transferring property from private individuals to the community, the present mischievous state of things will be set to rights, inasmuch as each citizen will then get his fair share of whatever there is to enjoy." And yet, states the encyclical, these socialist "contentions are so clearly powerless to end the controversy that were they carried into effect the working man himself would be among the first to suffer." In other words, said Leo XIII, socialism is bad for workers. The goals of socialists are "emphatically unjust, for they would rob the lawful possessor, distort the functions of the State, and create utter confusion in the community."

In stating this, *Rerum Novarum* defended the rights of the worker to his wage and his private property—the private property that socialism undermines. "It is surely undeniable," wrote Leo XIII, "that when a man engages in remunerative labor, the impelling reason and motive of his work is to obtain property, and thereafter to hold it as his very own." The worker has a right "not only to the remuneration, but also to the disposal of such remuneration, just as he pleases." If that worker lives wisely, "sparingly," and saves money, he and his family can have "greater security, invests his savings in land," and the "power of disposal that ownership obtains." Socialists, however, seek to change this. The socialists "by endeavoring to transfer the possessions of individuals to the community at large, strike at the interests of every wage-earner, since they would deprive him of the liberty of disposing of his wages, and thereby of all hope and possibility of increasing his resources and of bettering his condition in life."

Moreover, engaging in a "great and pernicious error" (paragraphs 14–15), socialists seek to supplant the family and even fatherhood with the state: "The socialists, therefore, in setting aside the parent and setting up a State supervision, act against natural justice, and destroy the structure of the home." *Rerum Novarum* continued: "Hence, it is clear that the main tenet of socialism, community of goods, must be utterly rejected, since it only injures those whom it would seem meant to benefit, is directly contrary to the natural rights of mankind, and would introduce confusion and disorder into the commonweal. The first and most fundamental principle, therefore, if one would undertake to alleviate the condition of the masses, must be the inviolability of private property."

Private property is inviolable and must be protected.

And yet, when socialists call for common ownership of the means of production, or when Marx and Engels in the *Communist Manifesto* demanded the "abolition of private property," they violate the inviolability of private property that the Catholic Church upholds. That right is as sacred and old as the Old Testament. By taking away the private property of people, socialists and communists violate God's commandment that inherently recognizes every individual's property rights, namely: thou shalt not steal.

Rerum Novarum says still more about socialists, including how their "striving against nature is in vain" in so many ways. The encyclical there gets to the heart of the socialist/Marxist problem, often underscored by popes John Paul II and Benedict XVI: socialism is an anthropological failure as well as an economic failure.

Socialism goes against human nature and dignity.

THE PAPAL LEGACY OF *RERUM NOVARUM*

Today's Leo, Leo XIV, is aiming for continuity from previous popes. That includes not just Leo XIII, obviously, but also Pope John Paul II. And it was Leo XIII's *Rerum Novarum* that inspired important successor documents by pontiffs such as Pius X and John Paul II.

In 1931, on the 40th anniversary of *Rerum Novarum*, Pope Pius XI released *Quadragesimo Anno*. That encyclical famously stated: "Religious socialism, Christian socialism, are contradictory terms; no one can be at the same time a good Catholic and a true socialist."

This was consistent not only with Church statements but of statements from various communists and Marxists who said the same. "Religion and communism are incompatible, both theoretically and practically," stated Nikolai Bukharin. "Communism is incompatible with religious faith." He urged communists everywhere: "A fight to the death must be declared upon religion, take on religion at the tip of the bayonet."[4]

In *Quadragesimo Anno*, Pius X urged "social justice" Christians who were sympathetic to socialism to simply follow the Christian Gospel. There was no reason to engage in the error of following the likes of the militantly atheist Karl Marx's *Manifesto* when Christians had the Gospel of Jesus Christ. He advised that if one is seeking "demands and desires" consistent with Christian truth, there is "no reason to become socialists." The Holy Father advised:

> Those who want to be apostles among socialists ought to profess Christian truth whole and entire, openly and sincerely, and not connive at error in any way. If they truly wish to be heralds of the Gospel, let them above all strive to show to socialists that socialist claims, so far as they are just, are far more strongly supported by the principles of Christian faith and much more effectively promoted through the power of Christian charity.

In other words, they should do what Jesus would do, not what Marx and fellow atheist communists or socialists would do. If desiring dignity for the worker and the human person and economic justice, then listen to Jesus. Pick up your Bible and follow what it advises, not what some atheist socialist philosopher prescribes. Because socialism, as Pius X affirmed, is inconsistent with Christianity and Catholicism.

All popes supported this—not merely "conservative" ones. The Vatican II pope, John XXIII, embraced by liberal Catholics, wrote in his *Encyclical on Christianity and Social Progress* (issued May 15, 1961): "No Catholic could subscribe even to moderate Socialism." John XXIII said that "Socialism . . . takes no account of any objective other than that of material well-being . . . . It places too severe a restraint on human liberty."

Especially notable in regard to Leo XIII's *Rerum Novarum* was Pope John Paul II's May 1991 encyclical *Centesimus Annus.* It was published for the centenary of *Rerum Novarum.* Its title refers to the "hundredth year" of *Rerum Novarum.* It is a stirring statement against socialism, Marxism, and collectivism that also speaks eloquently to the weaknesses and strengths of capitalism and free markets. It is a beautiful critique of not only socialism but of Western materialism. It is a statement remarkable for its balance and informed insights. It states:

> [T]he fundamental error of socialism is anthropological in nature. Socialism considers the individual person simply as an element, a molecule within the social organism, so that the good of the individual is completely subordinated to the functioning of the socio-economic mechanism. . . . Man is thus reduced to a series of social relationships, and the concept of the person as the autonomous subject of moral decision disappears, the very subject whose decisions build the social order. From this mistaken conception of the person there arise both a distortion of law, which defines the sphere of the exercise of freedom, and an opposition to private property. A person who is deprived of something he can call "his own," and of the possibility of earning a living through his own initiative, comes to depend on the social machine and on those who control

> it. This makes it much more difficult for him to recognize his dignity as a person, and hinders progress toward the building up of an authentic human community.

John Paul II contrasted this to the Christian vision of the human person. Referring to Leo XIII's 1891 encyclical, he stated in *Centesimus Annus*: "According to *Rerum novarum* and the whole social doctrine of the Church, the social nature of man is not completely fulfilled in the State, but is realized in various intermediary groups, beginning with the family and including economic, social, political and cultural groups which stem from human nature itself and have their own autonomy, always with a view to the common good." Socialism might claim what is best for the "common," but in truth it undermines the common good—and dignity of the human person.

In all, these statements, from *Rerum Novarum* to *Quadragesimo Anno* to *Centesimus Annus*, and many before, after, and in between,[5] dealt not merely with communism and socialism but more to the underlying issue at heart, with anthropology, human nature, human rights, and the dignity of the person.

THE CURRENT LEO SPEAKS TO THE CENTESIMUS ANNUS PRO PONTIFICE FOUNDATION

All of this is important background to the new pope. It does not seem lost upon Leo XIV.

It is very revealing, if not profoundly so, that one of Leo XIV's first public speeches after the conclave and even before his formal installation on May 18 was a May 17 address he gave at the Vatican to a group called the Centesimus Annus Pro Pontifice Foundation.[6]

There, he quoted Pope Leo XIII and spoke of the unifying importance of the Church's social doctrine. "You have the opportunity to show that the Church's social doctrine, with its specific anthropological approach, seeks to encourage genuine engagement with social issues," Leo XIV told the group. He made a distinction between the necessity of maintaining Church doctrine and of resisting cultural indoctrination.

To repeat: doctrine versus indoctrination.

"Indoctrination," said Leo XIV, "is immoral. It stifles critical judgement and undermines the sacred freedom of respect for conscience, even if erroneous. It resists new notions and rejects movement, change or the evolution of ideas in the face of new problems."

Though Leo XIV did not pause to say this, it is worth pausing here to note that indoctrination is what socialists and Marxists do. They indoctrinate. As Pius IX put it in *Qui Pluribus*, they "spread pestilential doctrines everywhere and deprave the minds especially of the imprudent, occasioning great losses for religion." Their doctrines are false ones that thus indoctrinate.

Here, Leo XIV did pause to make a distinction between indoctrination and good doctrine. "Doctrine," he said, is based on "serious, serene, and rigorous discourse," and "aims to teach us primarily how to approach problems and, even more importantly, how to approach people."

The Catholic Church needs doctrine; it is based on doctrine. There exists in the Church a long line of doctrinal clarity and consistency from the time of St. Peter and the Apostles to the modern popes and the Magisterium. According to Leo XIV, that positive doctrine "helps us to make prudential judgements when confronted with challenges. Seriousness, rigor and serenity are what we must learn from every doctrine, including the Church's social doctrine."

That would include positive doctrine such as the vital Church social and economic teaching provided by encyclicals like *Rerum Novarum* and *Centesimus Annus*.

LEO XIII ON THE INDIGNITY AND INHUMANITY OF SLAVERY

Not mentioned in current commentary on Leo XIV and his Leonine predecessor was Leo XIII's powerful stance against slavery. Whether this is familiar to Leo XIV is unclear at this moment, but it is worth mentioning because of the fact that Pope Francis—quite unappreciated—was excellent on the topic of slavery and human trafficking, as were recent popes like John Paul II. Leo XIII needs to be remembered for several crucial statements, which unfortunately are often neglected by fans and scholars of the great pontiff. Thousands of words could be said about these here, but I will share just a few paragraphs.[7]

The most powerful of these Leo XIII statements was *In Plurimis*, "On the Abolition of Slavery," released May 5, 1888. It was a forceful, eloquent defense of the dignity of the human person, issued at a crucial time when slavery continued to fester in countries like Brazil (which had been the largest slave nation in the entire Western hemisphere), well after slavery had been abolished in most to all Western/European nations, including the United States. Distraught by Brazil's failure to end slavery, the Leo XIII encyclical was directed to the Brazilian bishops, encouraging and urging them to hold strong in pushing the Brazilian government to stop this terrible indignity against the children of God. He also urged Church officials in Africa to remain steadfast, given that slavery was still thriving among certain African cultures. Yes, Western whites had ended the slavery of black Africans, but black Africans had not ended the enslavement of their fellow black Africans.

Leo XIII's *In Plurimis* was one of the longest (if not the longest) Church statements on the subject to date if not ever, nearly 7,000 words in English.[8] The Holy Father quoted Scripture, the Church fathers, and also appealed to the heroic witness of St. Peter Claver, an extraordinary 17th-century Jesuit whose personal motto of sacrificial service to the enslaved was "Peter Claver, slave of the Negroes for ever." Leo XIII had canonized Claver five months earlier, and had said, "No life, except the life of Christ, has so moved me as that of St. Peter Claver."[9]

Leo described slavery as a "wicked" violation of the natural law. It went against nature because God, the Creator of nature, did not intend for man to be the master of other men. Man was given dominion over the beasts, not over human beings. Here, Leo XIII quoted Saint Augustine, the inspiration of today's Pope Leo XIV:

> [S]lavery . . . is deeply to be deplored; for the system is one which is wholly opposed to that which was originally ordained by God and by nature. The Supreme Author of all things so decreed that man should exercise a sort of royal dominion over beasts and cattle and fish and fowl, but never that men should exercise a like dominion over their fellow men. As St. Augustine puts it: "Having created man a reasonable being, and after His own likeness, God wished that he should rule only over the brute creation; that he should be the master, not of men, but of beasts."

Slavery plainly was not what God had intended for His human creation. Leo XIII contended that slavery, which he repeatedly denounced as "evil," had come into the world not via the hand of God but through Satan and the fall of man. He provided a historical treatment of slavery and a moral examination of this "inhuman and wicked" practice. As a better way, he pointed to Jesus Christ, quoting St. Paul: “For you are all the children of God by faith in Jesus Christ. For as many of you as have been baptized in Christ, have put on Christ. There is neither Jew, nor Greek; there is neither bond, nor free; there is neither male nor female. For you are all one in Christ Jesus” (Galatians 3:28).

Leo XIII hailed the lengthy leadership provided in the Chair of St. Peter by his predecessors. He went back to an October 1462 letter from Pope Pius II, who had condemned the “great crime” of slavery against black people in the Canary Islands. Leo gave other examples from the likes of Paul III, Urban VIII, Benedict XIV, Pius VII, and Gregory XVI. But alas, Leo XIII regretted, slavery was still thriving in parts of the world, especially among Muslim slavers in Africa. This must be stopped, declared the Holy Father. Slavery “must be banished and blotted out.”

Other statements from Leo XIII would follow, including his poignant November 1890 encyclical *Catholicae Ecclesiae* on “Slavery in the Missions,” which was directed to the Catholic missionaries fighting to halt black enslavement of fellow blacks in Africa—their capture, sale, and ownership.[10] Leo XIII reaffirmed the Church’s goal of global emancipation, once again insisting in the strongest terms that “slavery opposes religion and human dignity.” He expressed his outrage at “How horrible it is . . . that almost four hundred thousand Africans of every age and sex are forcefully taken away each year from their villages! Bound and beaten, they are transported to a foreign land, put on display, and sold like cattle.” The pope issued a worldwide “call to common action,” including his fellow Europeans outside of Africa, to end this travesty of Africans peddling Africans and “to defend the Negro cause.” Those are just a few words from Leo XIII’s bold leadership against slavery at the end of the 19th century.

What does all this mean for Pope Leo XIV in the 21st century? The reality is that Leo XIV’s Church has been the world’s single most consistent institution in fighting the scourge of slavery for centuries. Statements like the aforementioned from Leo XIII could be cited by popes like Eugene IV and his January 1435, *Sicut Dudum*, subtitled, "Against the Enslaving of Black Natives from the Canary Islands" (which came some 400 years before Britain abolished slavery), or from Pope Paul III and his June 1537 *Sublimis Deus*, which denounced slaveowners as "instruments of Satan," or moving beyond Leo XIII to successors such as Pope Pius X, who in June 1912 excoriated "the slavery of Satan and of wicked men." These denunciations continued up through modern popes like John Paul II.

Like other modern popes, John Paul II called out the "new forms of slavery, often insidious, such as organized prostitution, which profits shamefully from the misery of the population of the Third World."[11] And as for Pope Francis, no world leader in the 21st century took a more high-profile public lead against modern slavery and human trafficking than Francis.

Thus, what this means for Leo XIV, a man committed to the Leonine legacy and unity and continuity from his recent papal predecessors, is that human trafficking and modern slavery are issues on which he is well situated to take the lead in the Chair of St. Peter. This point will be revisited in the final chapter of this book as we look to future goals of the Leo XIV papacy.

ST. MICHAEL THE ARCHANGEL

Finally, it must be noted that it was Pope Leo XIII who gave the world the St. Michael the Archangel Prayer, which he composed after a dramatic vision of hell.[12] The prayer was thereafter recited at the end of Mass in parishes all over the world. It desperately implores the mighty angel to "defend us in battle" and "be our protection against the wickedness and snares of the devil. May God rebuke him." It urges the archangel to "cast into Hell Satan and all the evil spirits who prowl about the world seeking the ruin of souls."

That powerful prayer had been used for decades until post-Vatican II parishes began dropping it. Fortunately, it has had a resurgence in recent years, especially among more traditional parishes. Very likely, Rob Prevost's parish in Dolton, Illinois, would have recited the prayer during his youth.

This Leo XIII gesture from the 1880s remains one of his most lasting.

Quite intriguingly, there is a fascinating connection between Michael the Archangel and the new pope named Leo. Leo XIV was chosen by the conclave on May 8, which happens to be the Feast of the Apparition of St. Michael the Archangel at Monte Gargano. That special, designated day commemorates the reported apparitions of the Archangel Michael on a mountain in southern Italy beginning in the late fifth century.

An ironic juxtaposition: Leo XIII had the entire universal Church invoke and call upon St. Michael the Archangel, and his Leonine successor, Leo XIV, was chosen pope on a feast day of St. Michael the Archangel. That seems quite a meaningful coincidence—if not perhaps the role of Providence.

WHY LEO XIV CHOSE THE NAME LEO

Much of this should provide clues and insights as to why Cardinal Robert Francis Prevost chose the name Leo XIV. More information will come in the years ahead as the new Leo tells us more. That said, the taciturn Leo did give us some explanation in the first days of his pontificate.

"I chose to take the name Leo XIV," he explained to the College of Cardinals the day after his election. "There are different reasons for this, but mainly because Pope Leo XIII in his historic encyclical *Rerum Novarum* addressed the social question in the context of the first great industrial revolution. In our own day, the Church offers to everyone the treasury of her social teaching in response to another industrial revolution and to developments in the field of artificial intelligence that pose new challenges for the defense of human dignity, justice and labor."

The new pope offered a compelling comparison. Just as Leo XIII had dealt with revolutionary upheaval and the momentous social changes of the "New Things" of the Industrial Revolution and the then-modern world of the late 19th century, Leo XIV is dealing with major upheaval in today's post-modern world, including the tech-information revolution and especially the new threats posed by artificial intelligence. Both revolutions, in the day of Leo XIII and Leo XIV, displaced workers and had a direct, dramatic impact on human dignity. Leo XIV, like Leo XIII, is cognizant of this major change afoot. By invoking the name of Leo XIII and *Rerum Novarum*, today's Pope Leo has thoughtfully told us much about how he sees today's world.

A week later, on May 16, Leo XIV again returned to *Rerum Novarum* and further talked about his name choice in formal remarks to the Vatican Diplomatic Corps. And there, he went further, remarking upon the nature of the human family as well, which, as this chapter has shown, was very much part of the 1891 encyclical and Leo XIII's thinking. Back then, the issue was how the new economic revolution and socialism could undercut the family and threaten even fatherhood; today, the issue is how the mass media and tech-information revolution undermine the family, male-female marriage, and threaten to redefine both. Leo XIV stated:

> I chose my name thinking first of all of Leo XIII, the pope of the first great social Encyclical, *Rerum Novarum*.

> In this time of epochal change, the Holy See cannot fail to make its voice heard in the face of the many imbalances and injustices that lead, not least, to unworthy working conditions and increasingly fragmented and conflict-ridden societies. Every effort should be made to overcome the global inequalities—between opulence and destitution—that are carving deep divides between continents, countries and even within individual societies.
>
> It is the responsibility of government leaders to work to build harmonious and peaceful civil societies. This can be achieved above all by investing in the family, founded upon the stable union between a man and a woman, "a small but genuine society, and prior to all civil society." In addition, no one is exempted from striving to ensure respect for the dignity of every person, especially the most frail and vulnerable, from the unborn to the elderly, from the sick to the unemployed, citizens and immigrants alike.
>
> My own story is that of a citizen, the descendant of immigrants, who in turn chose to emigrate. All of us, in the course of our lives, can find ourselves healthy or sick, employed or unemployed, living in our native land or in a foreign country, yet our dignity always remains unchanged: it is the dignity of a creature willed and loved by God.[13]

In this statement, Leo XIV applied *Rerum Novarum* well beyond economics and industrial and tech revolutions. Like Leo XIII, he was keenly attentive to how families were affected. The family was founded upon and thus needed to be based on the stable union between a man and a woman. Not only should the dignity of the family be protected but so should the dignity of every person, from the unborn to the elderly, from the sick to the unemployed, whether citizens and immigrants alike. He even recalled his own family's story as immigrants to America.

We can see here once again, in the words of Leo XIV, how the teachings of Leo XIII truly constitute Catholic "social" teaching. Documents like *Rerum Novarum*, not unlike antithetical documents like the *Communist Manifesto*, go well beyond economics and issues like socialism and communism, touching everything from the family to immigrants.[14]

WHAT OTHERS SAID

The choice of the name "Leo" by Robert Francis Prevost immediately struck everyone. Those with any knowledge of Church history, or familiarity with *Rerum Novarum*—again, a document known to so many inside and outside Roman Catholicism—were immediately taken by Prevost's choice of name. Upon hearing the name, millions worldwide no doubt smiled and said, "Wow, '*Leo*'!"

Among those taken by the choice was Bishop Robert Barron, the most influential and well known of all American churchmen today. Barron had been in Rome covering the conclave for EWTN television. He called the announcement of Prevost and the whole scene, "One of the more extraordinary days of my life. No one expected a choice on the fourth ballot. . . . When the white smoke occurred much earlier than any of us expected, I assumed that the frontrunner, Cardinal Pietro Parolin, had been chosen." And when he heard that it was an American, and one from no less than Barron's shared hometown of Chicago, he was shocked. "I was one of the army of commentators who confidently asserted that no American would be elected pope," said Barron. "Relying on the common wisdom, I told numerous journalists and broadcasters that until the United States was no longer a superpower, the cardinals would never hand governance of the universal Church to a citizen of the USA. Well, the electors and the Holy Spirit proved all of us rather dramatically wrong. . . . All of it seemed surreal, impossible."

And then there was the name: the choice of Leo XIV.

"It was really the name that stayed with me," said Barron. "He could have been Francis II, and we would have said, 'Oh, there he is clearly in the line of Francis.' He could have been John Paul III, then we would have thought, 'Oh, he's very much in that more conservative line.' He could have been John XXIV, and we say, 'Oh, now he's a real revolutionary liberal, et cetera.'" But instead, said Barron, "the fact that he went back, well over 100 years, to this very interesting and pivotal figure . . . our new pope was saying, 'I too, want a critical engagement with the modern world.'"[15]

Bishop Barron went directly to *Rerum Novarum* to further his point. He noted how that document had shown Leo XIII to be "a fierce opponent of Marxism, a fierce opponent of socialism and communism, a great defender of private property and of the market economy." Thus, from Leo, "there's that great 'no' to the left-wing economic revolutions. At the same time, in that same letter, [Leo XIII] comes out strongly in favor of the right to form unions. He comes out very strongly in favor of what we call the universal destination of goods."

Rerum Novarum was a statement that navigated the two extremes.

Barron underscored the encyclical's powerful support for not just property but for the poor. "In fact, Pope Leo says in that letter, once the requirements of necessity and propriety have been met in your life, the rest of what you own belongs to the poor," added Barron. "That's not a just a standard, boring, mainstream point of view. That's a pretty revolutionary statement. But notice the lovely balance in that letter between 'yes' to private property, the great 'no' to socialism and Marxism, but the great 'yes' to the universal destination of goods." Barron noted that Leo "thereby sets the tone for much of the rest of Catholic social teaching that followed him."

Barron added another critical point about Leo XIII, namely, how he has been the rare spiritual leader embraced by both the left and the right.

"[Leo XIII] doesn't fit . . . into our categories of left and right," affirmed Barron. He does not "fit into Democrat-Republican. . . . I think that's what's perhaps most interesting about him. To this day, conservative Catholics and liberal Catholics find a lot to like in Pope Leo XIII."

They do indeed. It was fascinating to see that conservative Catholic commentator Michael Knowles quite prophetically had posted a call on his X account hoping for the name "Leo XIV" when he saw the white smoke go up that May 8. Yes, to repeat: Knowles just before Prevost announced himself as Leo XIV had called for the new pope to name himself after Leo XIII. What a call![16]

Thus, Knowles said he was "elated" with the name Leo XIV. He noted that both liberals and conservatives like Leo XIII.

Knowles's and Barron's focus was mainly (and rightly) on Leo XIII, but of course, there was a long line of Leos prior to Leo XIII, and quite a line of popes that was. As noted, the Leonine line includes some of the Church's greatest defenders of Western civilization, of Rome, of the papacy, and of Church doctrine itself.

Indeed, German Cardinal Gerhard Müller, in congratulating Leo XIV just shortly after his election, called attention to the other Leos.

"[Pope Leo XIV's] predecessor in the name, Leo I, the Great, wrote a famous letter to the Council of Chalcedon [451]," observed Cardinal Müller, "in which he underlined the inseparable unity and the unconfused distinction of divine and human nature in the person of the Son of God. This is the basis and foundation of the Catholic faith." Müller next pointed to Pope Leo XIII and *Rerum Novarum*, which he credited for laying the "foundations of the

Social Doctrine of the Church" and for having "formed the foundation of a just and free modern society."[17]

A message of Cardinal Müller was Church unity in the line of Leos, and for that, he pointed to Pope Leo X, who served from 1513–1521, smack at the height of Martin Luther and his nailing the *95 Theses* to the church door at Wittenberg in October 1517, thus launching the Protestant Reformation that forever splintered Christianity. Leo X responded with one of the most important documents in the history of the Church, *Exsurge Domine*, his June 1520 papal bull condemning the errors of Martin Luther. Luther, incidentally, had been an Augustinian, just like Leo XIV.

"We hope that the new Pope," wrote Cardinal Müller, "who bears the same name and is also an Augustinian monk like Luther, 500 years later, will collaborate—in the wake of the good and holy popes for 250 years—in overcoming the divisions in Christendom and tensions in the world." Once again, Müller couched his hopes in a call for the unity the Church so badly needed after Pope Francis's disruption: "So that all Christians are united in Christ, the Son of the living God, and that, with the help of the moral authority of the papacy, the peace of God dwells in the hearts of men and hatred and war are overcome in the world."

Müller concluded with a wish that "all Christians and people of good will accompany Pope Leo XIV with his prayer, so that his pontificate may be a blessing for the Church and the world," in the name of unity and the Leonine line.

It was a wish shared by millions. We shall see if that plays out under the papacy of Leo XIV.

TWELVE

Son of Augustine

The first glimpse the world got of Pope Leo XIV came on the Loggia overlooking St. Peter's Square. He was bedecked in ceremonial white and red—the white cassock and zucchetto, the red mozzetta and red-and-gold stole—and that shiny, gleaming pectoral cross. Not one of these accoutrements was for mere fashion. Every item spoke of spiritual significance, particularly that cross.

Onlookers, from the thousands in the square to the millions watching via video, would learn only later of the composition of the pectoral cross. A gift given to Robert Francis Prevost from his grateful Augustinian order when he officially became a cardinal on September 30, 2023, it was not just some piece of handsome jewelry. It included on the inside—pressed always against his chest—five relics. They were relics from five extraordinary individuals: Saint Augustine himself; the saint's canonized mother, Monica, the pious woman who had prayed her wayward son into the faith and bosom of the Church; St. Thomas of Villanova, archbishop of Valencia in the 15th and 16th centuries; Venerable Giuseppe Bartolomeo Menochio, a heroic Italian bishop of the 18th and 19th centuries who suffered under the rule of Napoleon; and Blessed Anselmo Polanco, a martyred bishop executed by communists during the 1936–39 Spanish Civil War.

Among them, the relic of Augustine was the cornerstone: a 1,600-year-old fragment of the venerable saint's bones.

Of course, the throng below in St. Peter's Square and the millions watching worldwide knew none of that, at least not at that moment. But a small few did, and they were deeply touched by the sight of the cross. "The day before the Conclave," shared Fr. Josef Sciberras of Cardinal Prevost's Augustinian order, "I sent him [Prevost] a message, encouraging him to wear the cross we had given him, for the protection of Saints Augustine and Monica. I don't know whether it was because of my message or not, but when I saw he was wearing it when taking the oath—and again when he stepped out onto the balcony of the basilica—I was deeply moved."[1]

Sciberras, postulator general of the Augustinian Order, had chosen the relics in 2023 as he helped design this special gift to Cardinal Robert Prevost. "This cross isn't just a decorative object," Fr. Sciberras explained. "It's a visible sign of faith and a clear reflection of pastoral commitment. The relics it contains are all linked to the Augustinian tradition, and each one represents fidelity, reform, service, or martyrdom—virtues that now guide and sustain the ministry of the new Pope."

For Catholics praying that the new pope would be a man committed to fidelity, service, and tradition, that cross was a profound symbol in ways that they could not yet know. A profoundly Augustinian symbol.

And yet, right off, Catholics watching the scene at the Loggia learned of that distinctly Augustinian impact on Robert Francis Prevost. He let them know in his greeting. It was fitting that in his opening statement from the Loggia, Robert Francis Prevost identified more directly with Augustine than with anyone named Leo.[2] "I am a son of Saint Augustine," he said of himself, "an Augustinian."

That he certainly is.

PREVOST OF CHICAGO AND AUGUSTINE OF HIPPO

This book has aptly detailed the many Augustinian moments in the life of Robert Francis Prevost of Chicago: For his education, he attended high school at St. Augustine Seminary, a minor seminary in Holland, Michigan. For college, he chose Villanova University outside of Philadelphia, founded by the Augustinians. Later, at the Pontifical University of St. Thomas Aquinas in Rome, Prevost chose to study less Aquinas than Augustine, writing his doctoral thesis on "The Role of the Local Prior in the Order of Saint Augustine." It was in 1977 that he joined the Order of Saint Augustine as a novice, taking solemn vows four years later on August 29, 1981. Twenty years later, in 2001, he was elected prior general of the entire Order of Saint Augustine, where he served two six-year terms.

This book also noted the extended extemporaneous statement on Augustine made by Prevost in his October 2012 post-synod interview with the Catholic News Service, in which he spoke at length and with eloquence of how the thoughts of the fourth/fifth-century saint apply acutely to today's post-modern world.

Those are just a few of the numerous examples in this book and from Prevost's nearly seven decades of life. Overall, looking at the exceedingly Augustinian profile of Prevost, from high school to his episcopal and now papal motto, Catholic writer Matthew Becklo aptly ponders, "With Prevost, the question is less where Augustine has shown up in his journey and more where he *hasn't*."[3] Indeed.

Becklo dug deeper on this point. He sketched out a portion of the new pope's long walk with Augustine from Prevost's personal Twitter feed. Becklo shared examples of Prevost posting not only about the Order of Saint Augustine but also quoting the esteemed saint in three languages. He documented a dozen such examples.

Here are a few of the Augustine quotes that had been posted by Cardinal Prevost:

> "The measure of love is to love without measure." (Posted three times in Spanish/Italian.)
>
> "Late have I loved you, O Beauty ever ancient and ever new!" (English)
>
> "The grace of God will not take you where the grace of God will not sustain you." (English)
>
> "See what you believe in and become what you receive!" (English, a reference to the Real Presence of Christ in the Eucharist)
>
> "He who has God has everything, and he who has not God has nothing." (English)
>
> "You have made us for yourself and our hearts are restless till they rest in you." (Spanish)
>
> "No one reaches the Kingdom of Heaven except by humility." (English)
>
> "Don't let your life give evidence against your tongue." (Spanish)

Becklo gave further examples from Prevost's posts in 2023 and 2024, including material from a revealing 2024 presentation that the future Holy Father gave at St. Jude Catholic Church in Illinois, in which Prevost proudly declared (in words he would echo at the Loggia a year later), "I'm an Augustinian." He thence explained, "I have personally a great debt to the Order of Saint Augustine, to St. Augustine himself, [his] philosophy, theology, thought, humanity;

that great love of Augustine for God's Word, that infinite searching for truth, for himself, and for God in himself; and for everything that Augustine taught in terms of communion and community that marked my life."[4]

No other Church figure, other than Jesus Christ Himself, has so marked the life of Robert Francis Prevost.

POPE LEO XIV ON AUGUSTINE

Given that prodigious track record, it was no surprise that once ensconced in the Chair of St. Peter, Leo XIV began immediately telling us more about his dedication to Augustine. He wasted no time pulling the revered saint into the heart of his papacy, commencing with his opening remarks at the Loggia and beyond.

As noted earlier, his papal motto, announced shortly after he left the Loggia—and carried forth from his episcopal motto when he was first consecrated a bishop—is Augustine's statement "*In Illo uno unum*," which means "In the one Christ we are one." Augustine himself had explained in his *Exposition on Psalm 127*: "When I speak of Christians in the plural, I understand one in the One Christ. You are therefore many, and you are one; we are many, and we are one."[5] Thus, "In the One, we are one."

Two years earlier, in a 2023 interview with Vatican News, then-Cardinal Robert Francis Prevost spoke about this motto: "As can be seen from my episcopal motto, unity and communion are truly part of the charism of the Order of Saint Augustine, and also of my way of acting and thinking," he said. "I believe it is very important to promote communion in the Church, and we know well that communion, participation, and mission are the three key words of the Synod. So, as an Augustinian, for me promoting unity and communion is fundamental."[6]

There was that message again: unity.

That Augustinian motto was also stamped upon Leo XIV's coat of arms. The image takes the form of a shield divided diagonally into two sections: The upper half shows a white lily in front of a blue backdrop, whereas the lower half has a light background with an image iconic to the Order of Saint Augustine: a closed book with a heart pierced by an arrow. The pierced heart bespeaks Saint Augustine's conversion experience, captured by the Latin motto: "*Vulnerasti cor meum verbo tuo*" ("You have pierced my heart with your Word").[7] The image relates to a line from *The Confessions*: "Thou hadst pierced our heart with thy love, and we carried thy words, as it were, thrust through our vitals."[8]

Those words soon became vital to the papacy of Leo XIV.

With the start of his papacy, Leo XIV was off and quoting Augustine frequently, even more than he invoked Leo XIII or any of the previous line of Leos. By the end of his first week in office, the new pope had quoted Augustine more than any other Church figure or saint. This was captured by Courtney Mares in a compelling piece for Catholic News Agency on May 15, 2025. Mares went through the many saints and prominent Church figures quoted by Leo XIV in his first week alone. It was an eclectic, far-reaching list, from Augustine (354–430) to St. Ignatius of Antioch (death circa AD 110), St. Gregory the Great (540–604), St. Ephrem the Syrian (306–373), St. Isaac of Nineveh (613–700), St. Symeon the New Theologian (949–1022), St. John Paul II (1920–2005), St. Paul VI (1897–1978), and of course, St. Peter and the Blessed Virgin Mary.[9]

The range of saints showed Leo's knowledge of Church history and its venerable figures. But again, none were invoked quite like Augustine. Mares quoted statements ranging from the new pontiff's opening remarks at the Loggia to the line he used from Augustine's *Discourse* when speaking to journalists on May 12: "Let us live well and the times will be good. We are the times."

Leo would frequently call upon Augustine in his first days and weeks in the Petrine office, demonstrating a knowledge well beyond a typical aficionado of the saint. As of the time of this writing, he continues to go to Augustine again and again.

WHO WAS AUGUSTINE?

All of that tells us much about Leo XIV. But to know more, we need to know who Augustine was.

Known simply as "Augustine," or "Augustine of Hippo," the great saint was born with the Latin name Aurelius Augustinus, after two Roman emperors. He was born in the year 354 AD in North Africa, specifically in what today would be present-day Algeria. In *The Confessions*, a memoir that is more a religious testimony than a conventional autobiography, he begins with the words, "Great art thou, O Lord, and greatly to be praised," before detailing his roots and upbringing: "I was Roman-born, in Tagaste, North Africa, in 354." He described his parents as "not well-off, small-town North Africans." He was the son of a pagan father and a devoutly Christian mother, Monica (331–387), who never gave up on her wayward son, offering up her prayers to heaven pleading for his conversion to the faith. He eventually found that faith, thanks to his mother's efforts and those of the brilliant Bishop of Milan, Ambrose (339–397). Amid her distress, Ambrose counseled Monica to "speak less to Augustine about God and more to God about Augustine."

Today, all three are saints: Ambrose, Monica, and Augustine.

Interestingly, particularly given the widely mixed-race background of Pope Leo XIV, with some even claiming that he is a "black pope," Augustine himself came from a mixed-race background that included African birth roots, and some have claimed that Augustine himself was black, or at least partly black or somewhat dark skinned.[10] That debate will not be resolved here, but the parallel to Augustine's modern "son," one Pope Leo XIV, is intriguing.

Augustine would tell us much about himself—and even more about God—in his voluminous writings. Surviving from his vast output are some 113 books and "treatises," over 200 letters, and more than 500 sermons prior to his death in the year 430.[11] His two most lasting works were his splendid *The Confessions* and *City of God*. He became one of the first and most impactful of the Roman Catholic Church's 38 so-called "Doctors of the Church" (along with his contemporaries Saint Jerome and his mentor Saint Ambrose).

It would be impossible and unnecessary to try to sum up Augustine in this chapter, but here are a few quotations from the towering saint that capture his thoughts:

> "Our hearts are restless until they find their rest in you." *Confessions*

> "Here we shall rest and see, see and love, love and praise. This is what shall be in the end without end. For what other end do we propose to ourselves than to attain to the kingdom of which there is no end?" *The City of God*

> "Faith then is to believe what you see not; truth, to see what you have believed." *Tractates on the Gospel of John*

> "The mind commands the body, and it obeys instantly; the mind commands itself, and is resisted." *Confessions*

> "Narrow is the mansion of my soul; enlarge Thou it, that Thou mayest enter in." *Confessions*

> "Even as a boy I had heard of eternal life promised to us through the humility of the Lord our God, who came down to visit us in our pride, and I was signed with the

> sign of his cross, and was seasoned with his salt even from the womb of my mother, who greatly trusted in thee." *Confessions*
>
> "Suddenly every vain hope became worthless to me, and with an incredible warmth of heart I yearned for an immortality of wisdom and began now to arise that I might return to thee." *Confessions*
>
> "Grant me chastity and continence, but not yet." *Confessions*
>
> "I wanted to read no further, nor did I need to. For instantly, as the sentence ended, there was infused in my heart something like the light of full certainty and all the gloom of doubt vanished away." *Confessions*

There are many added phrases attributable to Augustine that sometimes are dismissed as apocryphal but more often have been crunched in a more pithy, catchy manner in varying translations. These range from "Our hearts are restless until they rest in thee" to lines like "There is a God-shaped vacuum in each of us." Another phrase often attributed to him is, "Whoever is happy has God," which is more likely pulled from Book 10, Chapter 23 of *The Confessions*, namely: "For a happy life is joy in the truth. For this is joy in You, who art 'the truth.'" There is also his famous refrain in Book 10, Chapter 27 of *The Confessions*: "Too late loved I Thee, O Thou Beauty of ancient days, yet ever new! Too late I loved Thee!" That line is often rendered simply, "Late have I loved you."

Augustine is also known, of course, as the author of "just war" doctrine, which has been a go-to guide for theologians and many politicians and diplomats for centuries. For public officials, whether prime ministers or presidents or kings, who seek to determine whether a decision to go to war is morally just, Augustine's guidelines have been the standard for 1,600 years.

Augustine is also known for stirring statements on natural law theory, a concept that was affirmed from the likes of Aristotle and Cicero (both pre-Christ) through Saint Thomas Aquinas in the 13th century and more. Augustine referred to natural law as "the law written in the human heart . . . the light we call the truth."

One of the best quotes on natural law is from Cicero, and thus it was most refreshing when the new pope invoked both natural law and that very quote from Cicero in a June 21 speech to Italian parliamentarians. Pope Leo's full application of the quote and the context in which he used it is worth quoting at length, including the references he cited in his text:

> In order to have a unitary point of reference in political action, rather than excluding a priori, in decision-making processes, the consideration of the transcendent, it will be useful to seek in it what unites us all. To this end, an essential reference is that of *natural law*, not written by human hands, but recognized as universally valid and in all times, which finds its most plausible and convincing form in nature itself. Cicero was already an authoritative interpreter of it in antiquity, who wrote in *De re publica*: "The natural law is the right reason, in conformity with nature, universal, constant and eternal, which with its orders invites us to duty, with its prohibitions diverts from evil [. . .] . It is not lawful to make any modification to this law or to subtract any part, nor is it possible to abolish it altogether; neither through the Senate or the people can we free ourselves from it, nor do we need to seek its annotator or interpreter. And there will not be a law in Rome, one in Athens, one now, one later; but one

> eternal and immutable law will govern all peoples at all times" (Cicero, *De re publica*, III, 22).
>
> The natural law, universally valid beyond and above other convictions of a more questionable nature, constitutes the compass with which to orient oneself in legislating and acting, in particular on delicate ethical questions that today arise in a much more cogent way than in the past, touching the sphere of personal intimacy.[12]

The pope's message is one that every Western politician needs to hear. He commended natural law as a point of reference if not basis for politicians crafting legislation on ethical issues, from unborn human life to gender, sexuality, and marriage between one man and one woman. Leo XIV in this speech applied natural law to religious freedom, interreligious dialogue, and the United Nation's *Universal Declaration of Human Rights*.

From Cicero to Aristotle and Aquinas to Augustine, natural law is a bedrock of Catholic teaching. It was a word not frequently heard from the previous pontiff.[13] Within just the first weeks of his papacy, Leo was initiating quite a shift. As one Italian publication put it, "With Leo XIV, natural law finally returns." Reporter Stefano Fontana noted: "These are not new ideas, but, as we said, a return to what has always been taught by the Magisterium of the Church. If these observations seem new, it is because we have not heard them for some time. . . . This is an important and necessary return to the teachings of the Church after years of neglect."[14]

It has indeed been neglected by too many in the Church of late.

Whether natural law or just war or another fundamental of Catholic-Christian thought and philosophy, in all of history, few religious figures have been as quoted as Saint Augustine. That tradition will increase under Pope Leo XIV, son of Augustine.

AUGUSTINE'S INFLUENCE

Much more could be said about Augustine in this book. Here are a few closing thoughts.

Pope Leo XIV's words on Augustine from the Loggia on May 8, 2025, drew immediate applause: "*Io sono un figlio di San Agostino.*" The mostly Italian crowd cheered, as did the audience of onlookers worldwide. Much like the name "Francesco" invoked by Cardinal Jorge Mario Bergoglio in 2013, everyone smiled. Everyone likes Saint Francis. And everyone likes Saint Augustine.

Saint Pope John Paul II called Augustine "a man for all times."[15] He called him a "towering" figure among Fathers of the Church.[16] Pope Benedict XVI called Augustine "the greatest Father of the Latin Church . . . a man of passion and faith, of high intelligence and untiring pastoral zeal." Pope Paul VI said of Augustine's *Confessions*: "All of antiquity's philosophy converges in his work."[17]

Professor Regis Martin calls Augustine "one of only a handful of truly foundational figures of the Christian West."[18] Professor Scott Hahn says that Augustine's life and work "serve as a capstone of late antiquity" and that his conversion marked not only a "personal milestone" but a "turning point in the history of ideas."[19]

Protestants, too, appreciate Augustine, who has long been widely read and admired in those circles as well. Most lists of "Top 100" or even "Top 10" books of the West in the last two millennia list *The Confessions*.[20] In 2015, *Christianity Today* surveyed its editors and contributors for a compilation of the 25 most influential Christian writings in history (exempting the Bible). No one ranked higher than Augustine, whose *Confessions* were number one on the list (*City of God* ranked fourth, and two other Augustine writings, *On Christian Teaching* and *On the Trinity*, ranked 18 and 19). That survey of leading Protestant theologians ranked *The Confessions* even above Luther's *95 Theses* and John Calvin's *Institutes*.[21]

Augustine himself influenced Luther and Calvin. As noted, Martin Luther himself had been an Augustinian friar. The founder of the Reformation claimed Augustine, as did the founder of Reformed Presbyterianism, John Calvin, who famously asserted, "*Augustinus . . . totus noster est*" ("Augustine is totally ours"). One of Calvin's noted successors, Reformed theologian B. B. Warfield, insisted, "It is Augustine who gave us the Reformation. For the Reformation, inwardly considered, was just the ultimate triumph of Augustine's doctrine of grace over Augustine's doctrine of the Church."[22]

Countless examples could be cited of influential Protestants invoking this founding father and Doctor of the Church, but here is one more who stands out in our day: in his historic letter from the Birmingham Jail, an imprisoned Martin Luther King Jr. invoked Augustine. King wrote with eloquence:

> You express a great deal of anxiety over our willingness to break laws. This is certainly a legitimate concern. Since we so diligently urge people to obey the Supreme Court's decision of 1954 outlawing segregation in the public schools, it is rather strange and paradoxical to find us consciously breaking laws. One may well ask, "how can you advocate breaking some laws and obeying others?" The answer is found in the fact that there are two types of laws: There are *just* and there are *unjust* laws. I would agree with Saint Augustine that "An unjust law is no law at all."
>
> Now what is the difference between the two? How does one determine when a law is just or unjust? A just law is a man-made code that squares with the moral law or the law of God. An unjust law is a code that is out of harmony with the moral law. To put it in the terms of Saint Thomas Aquinas, an unjust law is a human law that is not rooted in eternal law and natural law. Any law that

> uplifts human personality is just. Any law that degrades human personality is unjust. All segregation statutes are unjust because segregation distort the soul and damages the personality.[23]

Note the Rev. King's unflinching assertion that a person has a literal moral responsibility to disobey unjust laws, openly agreeing with Augustine that "an unjust law is no law at all." King then asked a crucial question regarding the difference between the two and how one determines whether a law is just or unjust. His answer was based on the natural law: "A just law is a man-made code that squares with the moral law or the law of God. An unjust law is a code that is out of harmony with the moral law." King then directly quoted Thomas Aquinas: "An unjust law is a human law that is not rooted in eternal law and natural law."

Martin Luther King Jr., a civil rights icon, went to Saint Augustine for inspiration in his single most important written statement.

We see throughout this chapter both the historically and spiritually unifying elements of the great Saint Augustine—his life, his writings, his message, his thought. Seeking to be a pope of unity, one wonders why perhaps Robert Francis Prevost did not choose the name Augustine for his papal name, in keeping with his papal words, motto, and coat of arms.

Perhaps Prevost would have seen such a choice as lacking humility. After all, there was only one Augustine. There has never been a Pope Augustine. For any cardinal-elected-pontiff to leave the conclave and invoke that name and be known as the second Augustine might be deemed too much—enormous shoes to fill.

Of course, the previous occupant of the Chair of St. Peter, Jorge Mario Bergoglio, had boldly appropriated the name of the legendary Saint Francis. That was not some minor appropriation. It was a rather extraordinary gesture. More so because for 1,100 years, every newly elected pope had picked a name that had been used by some other previous pope.[24]

Some might have deemed Bergoglio's taking of the name of St. Francis as a choice lacking humility. For Prevost to have followed in a similar vein, with two consecutive popes daring to take the names of two of the most beloved names in Christendom, whom no other pontiff prior deigned to adopt, might have been considered a bridge too far for the thoughtful Prevost, particularly as he seeks to build bridges of unity. Pope Francis might have gone there—only to bring division rather than unity—but Prevost must have known better.

Prevost knows that knowing Augustine means to know humility. In one of his Twitter posts, he posted the Church doctor admonishing, "No one reaches the Kingdom of Heaven except by humility."[25]

Surely, humility compelled Prevost to not dare take the name of Augustine for himself.

And besides, if looking for a papal name that inspires unity—the preeminent goal of his papacy from day one—then the Augustinian Robert Francis Prevost could not go wrong picking up from the line of Leo. And so, the Church now has arguably the best of two worlds: a pope inspired by both Leo XIII and Saint Augustine.

The world has an Augustinian pope, a son of Augustine committed to the Leonine legacy of unity—a double unity badly needed in the post-Francis Church.

THIRTEEN

Pope Leo XIV's First 40 Days

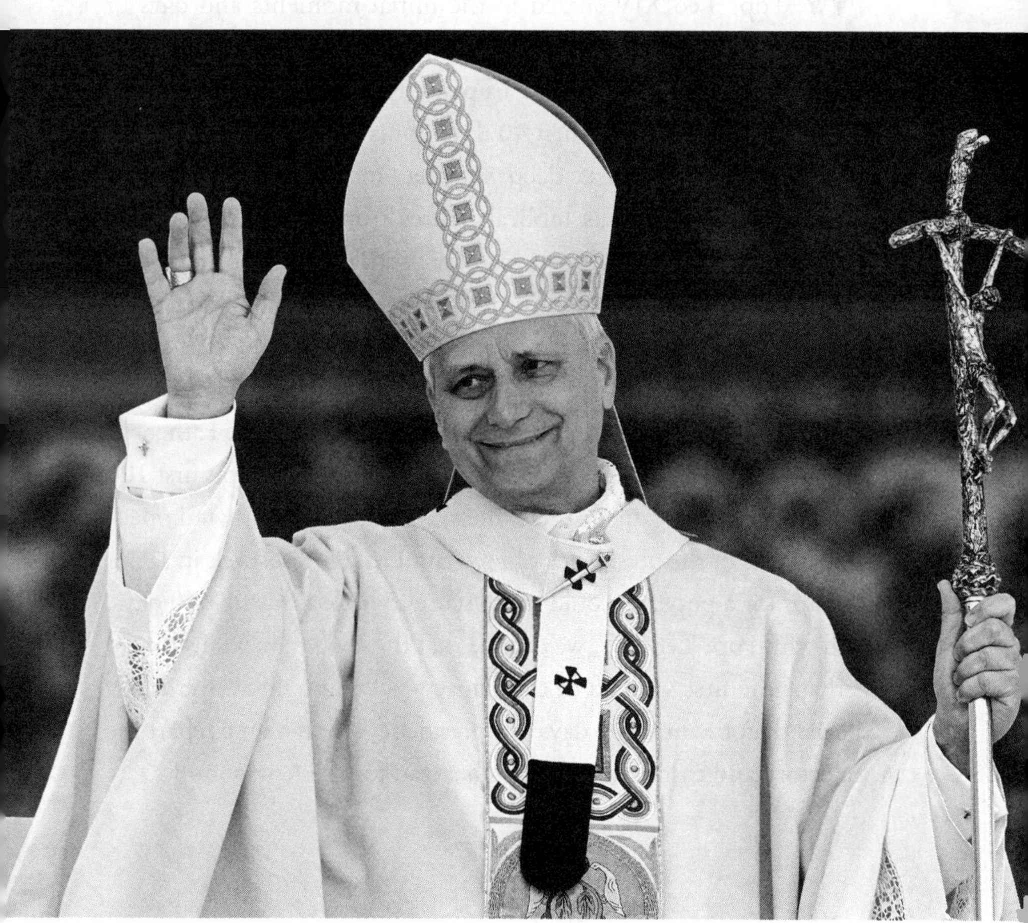

We have already seen in these pages many of the messages that Pope Leo XIV shared in the initial moments and days of his papacy, as well as the saints and popes who influenced him and the very name he took. But let us pause to take a more systematic, chronological look at the first 40 days of his papacy.

The number 40 has deep spiritual meaning in the life of Jesus Christ and various biblical figures from the Old and New Testaments. The number represents a sacrificial time of penance, trial, testing, preparation, of uniting oneself with God in a more intimate way. We saw it in the 40 days of Jesus's fast and temptation in the desert, and then later in His time with the apostles after the crucifixion and resurrection before returning to God the Father.

Americans mark a new president's start by analyzing his first 100 days. That period gained special meaning after the whirlwind opening months of the presidency of Franklin Delano Roosevelt in 1933. Perhaps for a pope, it would make sense to look at his first 40 days. And with Pope Leo XIV, we can see that those 40 days tell us much. Perhaps the first 40 days of this papacy—certainly more spiritually special than the first 100 days of a presidency—can help us chart the trajectory and cast light on the path ahead for the new pontiff.

MAY 9: THE FIRST MORNING

When 69-year-old Robert Francis Prevost awoke the morning of May 9, 2025, he was a very different individual. He was head of the global Roman Catholic Church. He was the pope.

Of course, a pope steps out of bed like everyone else, beginning with his two feet planted on the ground. But surely, Rob from Dolton, Illinois, must have felt like he was somewhere in the clouds. He must have stopped to pinch himself at what had transpired over the previous 12 to 24 hours. Was that a dream? Did it really happen?

Leo XIV dressed himself that morning in an altogether different way than he was accustomed to. Covered in all white, he headed back to the Sistine Chapel to deliver his first homily as the 267th successor of St. Peter. It was addressed to the cardinal electors who had chosen him.

Most notable, especially to the world that heard audio of the new pope's words that morning, was the fact that he opened by briefly speaking in English for the first time publicly as pontiff. For Americans and all English-speaking peoples, it was a striking thing to hear. Here was the Holy Father holding forth naturally, fluently, fluidly, in their shared native tongue, with no accent. Yes, other popes knew English, including the three previous, who had given homilies in English upon visiting America, but none spoke it quite like this, so perfectly, as a first language. Hearing the new pope, Americans thought to themselves: this guy really is one of us.

Americans had heard no English from their suddenly famous countryman at the Loggia on May 8. But he made sure they did now. He started his homily that morning with this:

> I will begin with a word in English, and the rest is in Italian.
>
> But I want to repeat the words from the Responsorial Psalm: "I will sing a new song to the Lord, because he has done marvels."
>
> And indeed, not just with me but with all of us. My brother Cardinals, as we celebrate this morning, I invite you to recognize the marvels that the Lord has done, the blessings that the Lord continues to pour out on all of us through the Ministry of Peter.
>
> You have called me to carry that cross, and to be blessed with that mission, and I know I can rely on each and every one of you to walk with me, as we continue as a Church, as a community of friends of Jesus, as believers to announce the Good News, to announce the Gospel.[1]

Thereafter, the Bishop of Rome switched to the native tongue of his fellow Romans, first by quoting (in Italian) the words of Peter to Jesus Christ: "You are the Christ, the Son of the living God" (Matthew 16:16).

For his homily, the new pope took the flock not back to his native Chicago in the 1970s, but 2,000 years to Rome. He invoked what he called "the patrimony that for two thousand years the Church, through apostolic succession, has preserved, deepened and transmitted." He then gave a powerful homily that included some harrowing words from not only the martyred St. Peter but the martyred St. Ignatius of Antioch.

It was in the city of Antioch that Christians were first called Christians. The bishop of Antioch was the great Ignatius. The first-century bishop knew the early disciples and apostles, including no less than St. John himself (the Beloved Disciple). Circa AD 107/110, Ignatius was captured and transported across the Mediterranean to be martyred in Rome—to be publicly devoured by lions in the amphitheater. And yet, he was carried to his death with a sense not of foreboding but of joy. He jubilantly awaited the crown of martyrdom and his glorious opportunity to be united in paradise with his God in Heaven.

Ignatius's epistle to the Romans as he was being shipped toward his death is an extraordinary statement in which he prays that no one will intervene to spare him, wanting to become "a meal for the beasts, for it is they who can provide my way to God. I am His wheat, ground fine by the lions' teeth to be made purest bread for Christ." He hoped: "let them not leave the smallest scrap of my flesh, so that I need not be a burden to anyone after I fall asleep. When there is no trace of my body left for the world to see, then I shall truly be Jesus Christ's disciple." Ignatius welcomed martyrdom: "Fire, cross, beast-fighting, hacking and quartering, splintering of bone and mangling of limb, even the pulverizing of my entire body—let every horrid and diabolical torment come upon me, provided only that I can win my way to Christ!"

These words are not to be taken lightly 2,000 years later, made safer by the distant passage of time. The fact is that every pope is asked to be willing to become a martyr—to die for Christ. And thus it was fitting that the new pope invoked the martyrdom of St. Ignatius of Antioch in his first homily. Leo XIV said:

> I say this first of all for myself, as the Successor of Peter, as I begin my mission as Bishop of the Church in Rome, called to preside in charity over the universal Church, according to the famous expression of Saint Ignatius of Antioch (cf. *Letter to the Romans*, Greeting). Led in chains to this city, the place of his imminent sacrifice, he wrote to the Christians who were there: "Then I shall truly be a disciple of Jesus Christ, when the world does not see my body" (*Letter to the Romans*, IV, 1). He was referring

> to being devoured by wild beasts in the circus—and so it happened—but his words recall in a more general sense an indispensable commitment for anyone in the Church exercising a ministry of authority: to disappear so that Christ remains, to make himself small so that he may be known and glorified (cf. *Jn* 3:30), to expend oneself to the end so that no one lacks the opportunity to know and love him.
>
> May God give me this grace, today and always, with the help of the most tender intercession of Mary, Mother of the Church.

That was quite an opening statement for the new pope. To repeat: he, too, must be willing to die for the faith as St. Ignatius of Antioch had. The gravity of what the Holy Father is called to is nothing short of immense. The shepherd must be willing to die for his flock.

MAY 11: FIRST SUNDAY MESSAGE, REGINA CAELI ADDRESS

The new pope spoke of martyrdom—of being devoured alive by lions—with remarkable aplomb. That demeanor was being noticed immediately. Already, the press was commenting upon and appreciating his reserve, his sense of serenity, his calm but confident style. In a headline, the Italian newspaper *Corriere della Sera* declared him "*Un Papa Calmo*"—a calm pope.[2]

He also calmly spoke of peace, despite a world on fire.

That May 11, Good Shepherd Sunday, Pope Leo XIV once again spoke of peace, this time in his first Easter season Regina Caeli address. He approached the microphone that splendidly sunny day with a cheery, "*Cari fratelli e sorelle, buon Domenica!*" ("Dear brothers and sisters, happy Sunday!") But the topic that day was deadly serious.[3]

Leo followed a prepared text. That text several times gave particular emphasis to a specific exhortation given by five of his predecessors, starting famously with Pope Paul VI, who was a survivor of two world wars. Their shared phrase continues to resonate: "Never again war!"[4]

Over 70 million people had died in those two world wars experienced by Paul VI. As Leo noted on this day, 60 million souls were lost in World War II alone. And no country in World War II had lost as high a percentage of its population as Karol Wojtyla's Poland (particularly its Jewish population). Wojtyla's country also suffered a terrible proportion of the 100 million deaths caused by communist ideology in the 20th century. Fittingly, Leo XIV in his formal remarks on May 11 echoed the exhortation of John Paul II, "Do not be afraid!"[5]

These were the famous words of John Paul II spoken during his inaugural Mass and repeated frequently throughout his papacy: "Do not be afraid," said the pope during his inaugural Mass in October 1978 and also upon his first return to Poland in June 1979, as Marxism-Leninism continued to occupy his native land and generate mayhem, murder, and martyrdom. "Open wide the doors for Christ," said Karol Wojtyla. "To his saving power open the boundaries of states, economic and political systems, the vast fields of culture, civilization and development. Do not be afraid. Christ knows 'what is in man.' He alone knows it."

In this Regina Caeli address, Leo did not invoke John Paul II by name, perhaps because those words, "Be not afraid," are so common in Scripture, but in accompanying remarks after his Regina Caeli, Leo immediately picked up by talking about the scourge that had terrified so many of John Paul II's fellow Poles: World War II.[6]

Like the pope who preceded him, Leo feared another world war. Francis had movingly and repeatedly pleaded to leaders like Vladimir Putin not to launch a "third world war." This was very much on Leo's mind the opening days of his papacy. "Never again war!"

MAY 12: THE FIRST MEETING WITH THE PRESS

On day five of his pontificate, Monday, May 12, Pope Leo XIV had his first meeting with the Vatican Press Corps in the Paul VI Audience Hall.

Speaking to the journalists at 11:00 a.m., he offered an olive branch by graciously commending them for their commitment to seeking the truth via their reporting and thanking them for their service as reporters. He also spoke to them of peace. Peace had been his first word from the Loggia on Thursday, May 8. He repeated that message on Sunday, May 11, and now he echoed it again. He surely shook up the journalists when he quoted to them Jesus's exhortation from the Sermon on the Mount: "Blessed are the peacemakers" (Matthew 5:9). This must have unsettled the journalists a bit, as if the new pope was telling them that they, too, ought to endeavor to be peacemakers, which is something that the mass media in today's world plainly is not.

Do journalists ever think of themselves as peacemakers? This was quite the challenge.

"This is a Beatitude that challenges all of us," said Leo XIV to the journalists, "but it is particularly relevant to you, calling each one of you to strive for a different kind of communication, one that does not seek consensus at all costs, does not use aggressive words, does not follow the culture of competition and never separates the search for truth from the love with which we must humbly seek it." He added: "Peace begins with each one of us: in the way we look at others, listen to others and speak about others." He urged journalists to say "no" to the "war of words and images." War was not restricted to, say, Russia's war on Ukraine or Hamas attacking Israel, or missiles and tanks, but a broader lack of peace generated by people (including journalists) attacking one another generally. "We must," said Leo, "reject the paradigm of war."

One might say, to borrow from a frequent exhortation of Pope Francis, that this was a call to the media not to engage in "calumny," character assassination, and sensationalism. Journalists, like popes, like Christians and all peoples, are called to something higher in their work.

Leo concluded with a pithy formulation: "Let us disarm words and we will help to disarm the world." The Holy Father said that "Disarmed and disarming communication allows us to share a different view of the world and to act in a manner consistent with our human dignity." He noted journalists are "at the forefront of reporting on conflicts and aspirations for peace, on situations of injustice and poverty, and on the silent work of so many people striving to create a better world." It was for this reason, he told them, "I ask you to choose consciously and courageously the path of communication in favor of peace."[7]

Editor and founder of *Inside the Vatican*, Robert Moynihan, was present at the talk, and he felt the call to higher aspirations acutely. "The new Pope said this to the thousands of journalists who have been in Rome for weeks to cover the death of Pope Francis (on April 21), his funeral (on April 26), and the Conclave that elected Leo (on May 8)," reported Moynihan. "So the central word since the beginning of Leo's pontificate, his central message, has been . . . *peace*."[8] (emphasis original)

Moynihan broke down the new Holy Father's pervasive peace message. He said that Leo had spent his first days as pope speaking of two types of peace, distinct yet deeply interrelated: (1) the spiritual peace of Christ's resurrection and the coming of the Holy Spirit; and (2) the physical peace in this world that is so sorely lacking and needed in our present time. Thus, observed Moynihan, "In this sense, Pope Leo may be seen, thus far, as the Pope of peace, of reconciliation, of the ending of war, of the coming of the great blessings of both spiritual (eternal, other-worldly) and physical (temporal, this-worldly) peace."

It was a promising message for the opening days of this new pontificate, a message for a divided world aching for reconciliation.

MAY 18: THE FORMAL PAPAL INSTALLATION

In the days ahead, Leo XIV began speaking out on the threatening issues and "isms" of the day. In a May 14 message, he lamented that today's youth must deal with "emotional instability," "superficiality," and "relativism," a common target of Pope Benedict XVI.[9] Two days later, on May 16, he gave a statement (previously mentioned) defining marriage as a "union between a man and a woman," as well as defending the dignity of unborn human beings.

The world was learning—to the regret of many—that the Catholic pope was, well, Catholic. He proclaimed Catholic truths and teachings on matters like marriage, abortion, and the scourge of relativism.

Even then, not everything for the new pope was fully formal yet.

To that end, Sunday, May 18, 2025, brought the most significant day of Leo XIV's young papacy since being announced at St. Peter's Square a week and a half earlier. This was the official Sunday Mass for the "Initiation of the Petrine Ministry of the Bishop of

Rome, Leo XIV." It was the new pope's inauguration, his formal installation to the Chair of St. Peter.

Behold, this was it. The big day for "Rob" from Dolton, Illinois.

To be clear, Robert Francis Prevost had become pope the moment that he consented inside the Sistine Chapel on the afternoon of May 8. But on this day, May 18, it became official, as he ventured through the Church's sacred rite and received the two key physical emblems of the papacy: the Pallium and the Fisherman's Ring.

The Pallium is a crucial part of the pope's vestments. It is a narrow band woven in white wool, unique to the pontiff of the Roman Catholic Church. The color and form of the material are meant to symbolize the lost sheep that Jesus Christ, both Lamb of God and Good Shepherd, carries on His shoulders. The wool that is used is actually procured from lambs raised by Trappist monks. The Pallium is looped around the neck of the pope, resting upon his shoulders over the chasuble, with two black flaps hanging in front and behind, so that the vestment resembles the letter "Y." It bears images of six black crosses and is also marked by three pins (*acicula*) that represent the nails of the cross of Christ during the crucifixion.[10]

No less ornate but more widely recognized than the Pallium donned by the pope is the Fisherman's Ring, the constant, visible symbol of his papacy, worn always, never removed, until his death. Whereas the Pallium comes off and on through the normal routine of dressing, the ring remains on the pope's finger at all times.

The ring's name directly invokes St. Peter, who was a fisherman by trade before he, too, was called to what became the papacy, the first in a long line of 267 pontiffs spanning two millennia. Jesus had told the Galilean fisherman to push out into the deep and lower his nets. He had also told Peter and the Apostles when to leave their nets to catch not fish but men. He called on them to become "fishers of men." They would set out upon a Great Commission to gather the faithful under the name of Christ, with Peter himself being the "rock" upon which Christ would build His Church. The fisherman would also become a shepherd of Christ's flock. The pope is just that: the chief shepherd of Christ's universal Church.

Beyond those nets that Jesus asked Peter to cast, He also gave the Galilean fisherman the keys to His Kingdom. "I will give you the keys to the kingdom of heaven," Jesus said to Peter. "Whatever you bind on earth shall be bound in heaven; and whatever you loose on earth shall be loosed in heaven." (Matthew 16:19)

Thus, the bestowal of the Fisherman's Ring upon a new pope is a profound gesture. It designates him officially as Peter's successor, as chief shepherd of the Christian flock holding nothing less than the keys to the kingdom.

The ring is placed upon the ring finger of the pontiff's right hand. It is so distinctly his own—a new one is cast for each new pope—that at his death the ring is destroyed. Yes, destroyed. That is because only one man at a time can wear the ring of St. Peter, just as only one man at a time can occupy the Chair of St. Peter. It is the prevailing symbol of papal authority. There are never two rings simultaneously. Only one.

Typically, the image on the ring is a design of Peter as the first pope with fishing nets or with the keys to the Kingdom of Heaven, or sometimes with both nets and the keys. The reigning pontiff's name is inscribed on the ring.

Upon the death of Pope Francis on April 21, 2025, his ring was destroyed in the presence of the other cardinals, thus designating the end of Francis's earthly authority. And now, on the morning of May 18, 2025, Pope Leo XIV would receive the Fisherman's Ring, until his death. This new pontiff's particular ring carried images of St. Peter as well the keys to the Kingdom and the net of Peter.

Leo would be reminded always of both the keys and the nets.

PETER MEETS PETER

Both the Pallium and the Fisherman's Ring are essential to the Petrine ministry that the new pope assumes that day of his installation—as are the two primary sites for the ceremony, one of them more private, witnessed by only a few, and the other very public, witnessed by millions in person and via video. And the whole thing is about Peter, that is, the first Peter and his latest successor. As the Holy See itself describes the ritual, "The connection with the Apostle Peter and his martyrdom, which fertilized the nascent Church of Rome, are further emphasized by the places where the celebrations take place, first of all the Confession of Saint Peter in the Vatican Basilica."

The rite of installation takes place inside Saint Peter's Basilica—in the crypt near the bones of St. Peter—and in the square in front.[11] But before the heir to the Chair of Peter journeys to the square for Mass, he visits Peter himself. He descends the stairs under the main altar at St. Peter's Basilica, downward to the crypt, where Peter's bones have laid for 2,000 years.

All of that was set to unfold on a perfectly picturesque, beautiful day in Rome on May 18, Year of Lord 2025. Mid-May in Rome is frequently an optimal weather day, before the beating heat of the doldrums of summer and well past the chilly days of winter. This day did not disappoint, as if the Heavens shined down their approval. If Vatican planners had sought to schedule an ideal temperature for the installation of a pope, they could not have done better than this.

Perhaps the Good Lord really was in control.

The estimated crowd of about 200,000 began lining up at St. Peter's Square early in the morning.[12] Well before the scheduled Mass time, Leo XIV thrilled the pilgrims by riding through the square for the first time in the white fiat Popemobile waving at the enthusiastic throng. He was surrounded by over a dozen security men in black suits trotting alongside the vehicle. He did this prior to the Mass rather than after, as a welcome to the faithful. In a surprise turn, his vehicle went off St. Peter's Square, cruising slowly along the Via della Conciliazione, the popular route that connects Saint Peter's Square to the Castel Sant'Angelo on the western bank of the Tiber River.

The crowd was most pleased. Leo XIV waved and smiled. He greeted and held babies thrust at him by excited mothers. The papal ride went on for about 30 minutes.

Only after this did the pope make the first of the two special visits that were part of his formal rite of installation. He first went inside St. Peter's Basilica. In a powerful private moment, with no television cameras, he descended below the main altar to pray at the tomb of St. Peter. The Church calls this moment, *Il Confessio*, "The Confession of Saint Peter." Here were Peter and Peter meeting one on one for the first time, like a long laying down of hands across two millennia from the first pope to the current.

Present in the crypt area with the pope were the Patriarchs of the Eastern Churches. This gesture is done to maintain the long bond between the Eastern Churches and the Bishop of Rome and his Latin rite. With these patriarchs, the new Roman Pontiff descends to the Sepulchre of Saint Peter to pray in silence. As he both prayed and then incensed the Apostolic Trophaeum, two deacons assumed other key roles: they picked up the Pastoral Pallium, the Fisherman's Ring, and the Book of the Gospels and carried them together in procession to be placed on the altar at St. Peter's Square for the ceremony and Mass to follow.[13]

After this moment with the first Peter, the new heir to Peter left the basilica to go back outside to St. Peter's Square for the public installation. As he sojourned, the bishops and cardinals invoked a long Litany of the Saints as they processed out of the basilica. For this walk, they intoned the solemn hymn of "Laudes Regiae," which is a special form of the Litany of the Saints in which their intercession for the pope's holiness is implored.

About an hour and 20 minutes since he had ridden through St. Peter's Square in the Popemobile, the white-hatted Bishop of Rome now sat in a chair in the square under a white tent. He faced thousands of fellow clergy in addition to the 100,000-to-200,000-throng of pilgrims. In attendance were some 200 cardinals who had remained in Rome since the conclave, plus another 750 bishops and archbishops.[14]

Also present were dignitaries representing approximately 200 foreign delegations and over 150 countries. They included the likes of Italian Prime Minister Giorgia Meloni, Canadian Prime Minister Mark Carney, Argentinian President Javier Milei, Polish President Andrzej Duda, Israeli President Isaac Herzog, and Ukrainian President Volodymyr Zelensky and his wife, Olena.[15] Officially representing Leo XIV's native land of the United States of America were the two highest-ranking officials and Catholics in the Trump administration, Vice President JD Vance and Secretary of State Marco Rubio, along with their wives, Usha and Jeanette. They sat with one of Leo's brothers.

No one could cease to be moved by the atmosphere of history and holiness. Surveying the extraordinary scene, Archbishop Andrew Nkea Fuanya of Bamenda, Cameroon, captured the feeling of many when he said simply, "I feel proud to be Catholic."[16]

The official ceremony/Mass in the square started at 10:00 a.m. Rome time. Beautiful hymns were sung in Latin. The new pope then commenced the ceremony by conveying the sign of the cross in Latin: "*In nomine Patris, et Filii, et Spiritus Sancti*. Amen." He then sprinkled holy water in various directions aimed at the vast assembly.

Then came the Old and New Testament readings, expressed in different languages: the Acts of the Apostles, sections 4 and 8–12, spoken in Spanish; Psalm 117, in Italian; 1 Peter 5, sections 1–5 and 10–11, rendered in the pope's native English; the Gospel of John 21, sections 3 and 15–19, sung twice, in Latin and Greek.

The proclamation of the Gospel in Latin and Greek is intended to underscore the unity of the Church and that the successor of Peter is the pope of both Latin Catholics and Eastern Catholics. Greek is the language of the New Testament and also of the Christian East and thus the tradition of the Eastern Churches, whereas Latin is the language of the Roman rite and thus the Western Church. The Holy Father employs both languages in that instance to convey that Christ's message is for all peoples and that the pope's ministry is genuinely universal for a worldwide Church of all.[17]

The assembly stood as the verses were invoked from Peter, "I am going fishing," and from Jesus, "I will make you fishers of men." Particularly meaningful, the gathering contemplated Jesus thrice-repeated question to Peter, "Do you love me?" and the Messiah's dramatic, prophetic warning to the fisherman that he would ultimately be led "arms outstretched" to places he would not desire to go. Those verses were given added special reverence as they were chanted by an American, Deacon Nicholas Monnin, a seminarian at the Pontifical North American College in Rome and from St. Matthew's Cathedral at the Diocese of Fort Wayne-South Bend, Indiana, not far from the hometown of Rob Prevost.

The meaning was obviously significant. The Vatican's Office of Liturgical Celebrations explained the exchanges this way: "Jesus' triple question and triple answer are accompanied in crescendo by the invitation to feed 'his lambs' and 'his sheep.' The triple question and triple answer recall and repair the triple betrayal. Despite his fragility, or rather precisely starting from it, Peter 'repented' and can 'confirm in the faith' his brothers (cf. Lk 22:31–32)."[18]

It is the task of the pope, the new Peter, to confirm in the faith his brothers and sisters.

All of which set the table for the presentation of the Pallium and the Fisherman's Ring. Three cardinals of the three Orders (deacons, presbyters, and bishops), and from different continents, approached the Holy Father to impose the Pallium and bestow the Fisherman's Ring. As Leo sat ready, the magnificent Vatican choir chanted the five-century-old hymn set to the sacred sounds of the founder of classical music, the ingenious Giovanni Pierluigi da Palestrina. Here were the Latin words pervading the square as Leo XIV prepared to receive the ring:

> *Tu es Petrus* (You are Peter)
>
> *et super hanc petram aedificabo ecclesiam meam* (and upon this rock I will build my church)
> *et portae inferi non praevalebunt adversus eam.* (and the gates of hell shall not prevail against it.)
>
> *Et tibi dabo claves regni caelorum.* (And I will give you the keys of the kingdom of heaven.)
>
> *Quodcumque ligaveris super terram, erit ligatum et in caelis,* (Whatever you bind on earth will be bound in heaven,)
>
> *et quodcumque solveris super terram, erit solutum et in caelis.* (and whatever you loose on earth will be loosed in heaven.)[19]

The atmosphere was otherworldly, as Palestrina and his Church would have wanted and in fact intended. Leo XIV was clearly deeply affected by the ceremony, by the sounds, by the placing of the Pallium around his neck, and especially by the placement of the Fisherman's Ring on his finger.

The ring was presented by Filipino Cardinal Luis Antonio Tagle, prefect of the Dicastery for Evangelization. This was fitting, given that Cardinal Tagle had sat next to Cardinal Robert Francis Prevost during the conclave. Though Prevost was a new cardinal and new face to many of the cardinal electors, he had been no stranger to Cardinal Tagle. They had first met years earlier in Manila and also in Rome when Prevost was prior general of the Order of St. Augustine. Once Prevost was named a cardinal, he and Tagle started working together in the Roman Curia starting in late 2023 as heads of their respective dicasteries on bishops (Prevost) and evangelization (Tagle).[20]

Of course, Cardinal Tagle had been considered one of the top two odds-on favorites to be the man receiving that ring at that moment. Instead, the long-shot cardinal from Chicago got the votes and was now the recipient of the ring presented by the cardinal from the Philippines.

Tagle certainly absorbed all the ironies. He wistfully recalled Prevost's reaction during the conclave when he had learned he had just been elected pope: "His reaction alternated between smiling and breathing deeply," said Tagle. "It was holy resignation and holy fear combined. I silently prayed for him." Tagle said that at the announcement that Prevost got the required number of votes, "a thunderous applause erupted," with the cardinals expressing joy and gratitude for their brother: "But it was also an intimate moment between Jesus and him, which we could not enter nor disturb. I said to myself, 'Let holy silence envelope Jesus and Peter.'"[21]

Now, at his formal installation as "Peter," Pope Leo XIV received the fisherman's ring from none other than his conclave partner, Cardinal Tagle. One wonders if Leo's mind momentarily raced back to a funny exchange at the conclave, when his friend from the Philippines had given Prevost a caramel candy to relieve his anxiety at the instant he had received the votes. "I always have a bag of sweets," said Tagle. "When he was sighing deeply, I said, 'Do you want a sweet?' He said, 'Okay, give me one.'"[22]

A caramel candy could not hold a candle to the ring of St. Peter. And now, Tagle presented Prevost with that special item at the formal installation. A smiling, visibly kind Tagle put the ring on the right-hand ring finger of the new pontiff. Leo XIV thanked him in English, saying, "Thank you very much. Thank you. Thank you."

As Tagle again left him in silence, Leo folded his hands in prayer under his chin, in much the same posture as he had at the Loggia upon being announced to the world as the next Holy Father. Leo then paused to hold his right hand downward, gazing at the ring for only a few precious seconds before once again returning his hands to a folded, prayerful position. There would be much more time later to behold the ring. Every hour of every day. Until his final breaths.

The new pope was holding back tears. Leo XIV, surely feeling more like young Bob from Chicago, was moved and visibly emotional. Video of the moment went viral on the internet.[23]

After having some time to try to compose himself, Leo XIV took a deep breath, perhaps not unlike his prolonged sigh inside the conclave on May 8. And fittingly, it was once again Cardinal Tagle who helped refocus him, not with a piece of candy this time but the large book of the Gospels. This, too, was part of the formal rite. Leo snapped into action. The new pope stood and hoisted the book in the air to bless the assembly with the words of the Lord, acclaiming: "*Ad multos annos!*" Translation: "For many more years!"

With that, the new pontiff sat again, as the choir reciprocated by singing in Latin, "Many years to you." He thanked the assemblage by nodding his head and holding his hand to his heart. Then more words were sung in Latin to the new pope. Once again came words directed at Peter by Jesus, as recorded in Matthew's Gospel, "You are Peter, and on this rock I will build my Church."

At this point in the ceremony, a dozen churchmen and laity came toward the new pope, congratulating him and kissing his ring. This is the symbolic rite of "obedience" given to the pontiff by 12 representatives of all categories of the people of God drawn from various ends of the earth.[24]

Then, at last, the new pope proceeded to give his homily, which, not surprisingly, focused on Jesus Christ and Peter the Rock. Also not surprisingly, this "son of Augustine" twice quoted the great saint from the fourth and fifth centuries, invoking his famous line from *The Confessions*, "Lord, you have made us for yourself, and our heart is restless until it rests in you." The homily elegantly tied together all the Petrine references that had crisscrossed throughout the installation ceremony, from "fishers of men" to "do you love me?" to "feed my lambs." Leo XIV then stated:

> Peter is thus entrusted with the task of "loving more" and giving his life for the flock. The ministry of Peter is distinguished precisely by this self-sacrificing love, because the Church of Rome presides in charity, and its true authority is the charity of Christ. It is never a question of capturing others by force, by religious propaganda, or by means of power. Instead, it is always and only a question of loving as Jesus did.[25]

Describing Peter as the "rock" and a "cornerstone of unity," Leo hoped: "Brothers and sisters, I would like that our first great desire be for a united Church, a sign of unity and communion, which becomes a leaven for a reconciled world. In our time, we still see too much discord, too many wounds caused by hatred." He finished with this wish:

> With the light and the strength of the Holy Spirit, let us build a Church founded on God's love, a sign of unity, a missionary Church that opens its arms to the world, proclaims the word, allows itself to be made "restless" by history, and becomes a leaven of harmony for humanity.

Together, as one people, as brothers and sisters, let us walk towards God and love one another.

It was a message both Petrine and Augustine. And befitting the firm message of this new papacy, it was about unity.

The formal installation next moved to the Eucharistic liturgy, with the new pope consecrating the bread and wine. He voiced to the faithful the very first words he had said from the Loggia: "Peace be with all of you" (in Latin). With the bread and wine consecrated to become the Body and Blood of Christ through the process of what the Church calls "transubstantiation," the multitude queued up to receive the host from the pope himself or from one of the many additional bishops and clergy present to provide the Eucharist—to feed the sheep.

In the prayer after communion, the new Holy Father asked the Father Almighty to "confirm the Church in unity and charity" and for himself to be protected along with the flock that has been entrusted to him.

Finally, in the concluding rite, Leo XIV offered his blessing by invoking the biblical image of the vine and the vineyard applied to the Church, beseeching the Lord to "guard" and "protect" the vine that He has planted, and asking that the Lord's face of salvation "shine" on all.

With that, it was official. Robert Francis Prevost was now formally Pope Leo XIV, Pallium, Ring, and more, installed once and for all, forever, until death.

MAY 19: THREE AMERICAN CATHOLICS

The next morning, Monday, May 19, Pope Leo XIV got down to papal business. Not every minute of a papacy can be as special as receiving the Pallium and the Fisherman's Ring, nor consecrating and celebrating Holy Communion. There were matters of state to deal with, too.

On his first official business day as pope, the American pontiff happened to meet with two prominent American visitors, Vice President JD Vance and Secretary of State Marco Rubio, who were both in town for his installation ceremony as well as for high-level talks in the preceding days with Vatican officials on matters of foreign policy. Rubio on Saturday had met with his fellow secretary of state, Pietro Parolin. Vance lately had been a frequent flier to Rome, going back to several weeks earlier when he was the last known American to meet with Pope Francis before he died.

Typically for visits between a pontiff and two high-ranking dignitaries, one would expect the discussion to focus almost solely on matters of state. But in this case, the situation was utterly atypical; it was historically unique. That was because for the first time ever, the three were all Americans. More so, all were Catholic. And all three (not just the pope) were serious about their faith.

Both Vance and Rubio are Catholic converts who have written in depth about their conversions. JD Vance's memoirs, *Hillbilly Elegy*, was a major bestseller before he entered politics and embarked upon a meteoric rise to the vice presidency. Marco Rubio's less-known memoirs, *An American Son*, published in 2013, addressed his conversion at length, with sophisticated theological details not expected from the memoirs of a politician. Neither man is a cradle Catholic nor an apathetic Catholic. In fact, what had earned JD Vance an X post from Cardinal Prevost back in February had been not a political remark by Vance but a theological statement about loving one's neighbor (discussed earlier). The American pope surely appreciated that Vance and Rubio are too rare politicians in that both had highly intellectual adult conversions into the Catholic faith.

There was still more to bond these three men. It cannot be understated how none of them came from wealth, privilege, or aristocracy. Vance grew up in a self-described "hillbilly" environment that many Americans would condescendingly refer to as "white trash." Rubio is the son of poor Cuban immigrants who started American life penniless. And Prevost, as we know, also came from the humblest origins.

Not one of these three men—vice president, secretary of state, or pope—could scarcely begin to imagine or wrap their heads around the possibility that they would be sitting there at the Vatican in May 2025 in those positions. No wonder that cameras captured the three of them with big smiles.

There was even a political bond among the three. As noted, voting records from Illinois show that Robert Francis Prevost's most recent votes as an American citizen had all been for Republicans. Prevost had pulled the GOP lever in the 2012, 2014, and 2016 elections. Interestingly, he did not vote in the 2016 general election, which means it is plausible that he could have voted for Marco Rubio in the 2016 Republican Primary while sitting out the general election.[26] If he did, he could have informed Rubio at that moment in the Vatican. And no doubt, the pope's partisan Republican brother, Lou, who sat with Rubio and Jeanette at the installation ceremony the day before, would have voted for Rubio as his repeatedly reelected Florida senator.

Another political point here is worth underscoring: both JD Vance and Marco Rubio are young, rising stars in the Republican Party. As they sat with Pope Leo, they also stood as the two leading contenders for the GOP presidential nomination in 2028. Ultimately, odds are good that the two could comprise the next Republican ticket together in 2028.

All of that should be helpful background to the deeper meaning of the meeting that Monday morning. Vance met with Leo first, as the higher-ranking American. The vice president strived to convey that although he was personally a committed Roman Catholic, he was serving the United States officially. For that reason, Vance chose not to kiss the pope's ring—a decision criticized by some back home. (Critics probably would have zinged Vance if he *had* kissed the ring.)[27]

Vance later explained his decision in an interview with *New York Times* columnist Ross Douthat: "I'm not there as JD Vance, a Catholic parishioner. I'm there as the vice president of the United States and the leader of the president's delegation to the pope's inaugural Mass. So, some of the protocols about how I respond to the Holy Father were much different than how I might respond to the Holy Father . . . as a citizen." He said that kissing the ring of a foreign leader would go against protocol for an American vice president. "So, no sign of disrespect," said Vance, "but it's important to observe the protocols of the country that I love and that I'm representing and that I serve as vice president of, the United States."[28]

After the veep and pope met one on one, Marco Rubio joined the meeting. In all, the two high-ranking Americans and their American pope held a 45-minute private discussion in the papal library. There was serious talk of international relations, including Russia and Ukraine, but it was also a get-acquainted period of pleasantries among three rising Americans probably struggling to absorb the moment—again, utterly unthinkable to any of them a year prior. Usha Vance and Jeanette Rubio joined for the final part of the visit, shaking hands with the pope and sharing laughs over a gift from the Americans to Leo: a Chicago Bears jersey with "Pope Leo XIV" printed on the back.[29]

Details of the discussion among the three men were not disclosed, though a photo of the three was widely published in accompanying press coverage. The photo captured Rubio and Vance seated across from the papal desk laughing with the new American pope.

The picture was more meaningful than most observers realized. It surely captured merely the first of many encounters in the years ahead among the three prominent Americans.

MAY 19: A MAJOR CHANGE FOR LIFE AT THE JOHN PAUL II INSTITUTE

Monday, May 19, also turned out to be a big day for Leo XIV because of the symbolic importance of his first major official appointment.

Day one after his installation Mass, Leo XIV made a key personnel change, naming Cardinal Baldassare Reina as grand chancellor of the Pontifical John Paul II Institute for Marriage and the Family. He thereby replaced the controversial Archbishop Vincenzo Paglia, handpicked by Pope Francis in August 2016.

Paglia had turned 80 on April 20, and was long overdue to be replaced in that position, in accordance with Vatican guidelines. At age 75, cardinals are required to formally submit their resignation to the pope, who has the option of accepting or refusing the resignation. Francis had never hesitated to quickly accept the resignations of prelates he did not like—like his so-called "right-wing archbishop of Philadelphia," Charles Chaput.

Paglia himself would explain: "It's ordinary practice in the Roman Curia. Once you reach 80, all assignments expire. I turned 80 on the very day Pope Francis died, which delayed the notification." He said that he had submitted his resignation to Francis upon turning 75, "as everyone does," but "the pope told me to continue until I was 80."[30]

Unlike Archbishop Chaput, Archbishop Paglia at the John Paul II Institute was not vulnerable to being "fired." That was because Paglia was doing Francis's work in revolutionizing, reversing, and upending the organization so close to the heart of John Paul II.

Francis continued to leave him in place. Leo XIV, however, did not hesitate to act—on day one.

Paglia's appointment by Francis was a controversy heaped upon a controversy by Francis, who had outraged Catholics worldwide when he oddly and inexplicably in the year 2017 attempted to re-establish the pontifical institute founded by John Paul II in 1982, changing its focus and releasing key longtime faculty who had faithfully served and defined the institute and its work.

What cleared the way for Francis to change the institute was the death of one of his detractors, Cardinal Carlo Caffarra, the founding president of the institute. Caffarra was a prophetic voice in the Church. Invoking the words of Fatima seer Sister Lucia dos Santos (1907–2005), Caffarra in a May 2017 speech honoring the 100th anniversary of Mary's first appearance at Fatima spoke of what he dramatically called an "anti-creation" that Satan was seeking to establish and was flagrantly "hurling" at God the Creator in our time. This anti-creation included an attempted redefining of marriage, family, and life itself. He shared a letter written by Sister Lucia, whom he knew personally, and in which she had warned that "there will come a time when the decisive confrontation between the Kingdom of God and Satan will take place over marriage and the family."[31] John Paul II himself had issued similar warnings.[32]

By the time of the Francis papacy, Cardinal Caffarra had long continued his faithful service at the John Paul II Institute, though because of his age that long tenure was nearing the end. When Caffarra offered his resignation as archbishop of Bologna on October 27, 2015, Pope Francis accepted it. Soon, Caffarra butted heads with Francis on a major matter three years into Francis's pontificate: In the spirit of the "dialogue" that Pope Francis claimed to want, Caffarra expressed serious concerns with Francis's March 2016 *Amoris Laetitia,* which he feared was at odds with John Paul II's teachings and the Church's Magisterium. He thus became one of the five *dubia* cardinals (along with Cardinal Burke) who sought clarification of the document, and who Francis proceeded to ignore, never once responding to their requested clarification.

Caffarra died on September 6, 2017. With his death, Francis just days later reconstituted the John Paul II Institute. It was said that Francis could be vindictive toward his perceived "enemies." Was he taking retribution at Caffarra's institute? Whatever the impetus, a mass revamping proceeded under Francis and Paglia.

Now in control of the institute, Archbishop Paglia and his allies quickly implemented what they hailed as a "new pastoral theology" that was anchored more in conventional sociology and secular social sciences than on the moral theology that was a specialty and hallmark of Pope John Paul II. This "new" approach was certainly something novel coming from this institute renowned for its moral clarity. From Paglia and his new faculty came confusing statements that seemed to contradict or call into question Church teachings on subjects from abortion and contraception to euthanasia and assisted suicide. Symptomatic of Francis's own leadership, confusion now issued from this institute long respected for its precision and lucidity.

The world certainly noticed these changes.

In short order, by July 2019, students and alumni of the John Paul II Institute published an open letter expressing their "immense concern about the sudden publication of the new statutes and the new ordinance of studies of our Institute." That statement was followed by an open letter signed by more than 200 professors, including prominent Catholic scholar Scott Hahn and Princeton professor Robert George, expressing their "great concern" with the dismissals of the institute's top scholars, urging that they be reinstated. Among those dismissed as a lecturer was Pr. Stanisław Grygiel, a close friend of Pope St. John Paul II, who said that the Francis–Paglia changes were not about renewal and reform but rather about the institute's "dissolution and destruction."[33]

The institute that attracted so many young scholars now seemed to repel them. Reportedly, enrollment at John Paul II's blessed institute "flatlined" after the "restructuring."[34] What was once a thriving body under John Paul II and Pope Benedict XVI for over 40 years was suddenly suffering.

John Paul II biographer George Weigel stated unequivocally that under Archbishop Paglia's leadership, the Pontifical Academy had "betray[ed] the intention of the saint and scholar who founded it."[35] One particularly tragic loss with the "new" institute was the sudden disappearance of John Paul II's profound work on his Theology of the Body. Weigel himself had referred to the Polish pontiff's Theology of the Body as a "theological timebomb set to go off" in the 21st century. However, the timer on that bomb suddenly seemed to be on hold, and the delay could not have come at a worse time. The world in these years of rapid legalization of same-sex "marriage," a proliferation of new "gender options," and a radical redefinition of family—unlike any period in the history of humanity—ached for moral instruction from John Paul II's theological teachings. Instead, his institute seemed to go either silent or unclear.

John Paul II had fearlessly implored the world to "be not afraid." His institute now seemed afraid to confront the *zeitgeist* sweeping and haunting the Western world. As Pope Benedict had warned at the death of John Paul II, a "dictatorship of relativism" was prevailing. Under Francis and Paglia, the institute seemed fearful of taking on that dictatorship, or perhaps simply lacked the depth or the desire.

The institute's decline was a direct result of not only the organization's work and staff shakeup but also of Paglia's personal statements as well as financial mismanagement. Most of the blame was directed at Paglia's leadership, which seemed a fair assessment. He was widely criticized for the institute's perceived new moral ambiguity and perceived moral rationalizations.

Veteran Catholic writer John Grondelski referred to Paglia as "Rome's Mario Cuomo," a reference to the late liberal Catholic governor of New York who was infamous for trying to reconcile and justify his "pro-choice" views on abortion with his Catholicism. Grondelski described Paglia as "the Pope Francis sycophant who presided over the demolition of the original John Paul II Institute for Studies on Marriage and Family." He said that "Francis's apparent goal was to align the institute's work with his larger deconstruction of theology into 'pastoral theology,' more preoccupied with 'accompanying' the twists of the *Zeitgeist* than with clear theoretical foundations, rooted in unchanging human nature, to guide people's moral choices." Grondelski said that Paglia replaced many of the original faculty with individuals willing to waffle on the Church's teachings on sexual ethics in the name of "pluralism" and "dialogue."[36]

Alas, the ship needed to be set back on course.

One person who apparently noticed was Cardinal Robert Francis Prevost. Thus, on day one after his formal installation at St. Peter's Square, Leo XIV replaced Paglia with Reina at the John Paul II Institute.

At 54 years old, Baldassare Reina is much younger than Paglia. He is a Sicilian, known affectionately as "Don Baldo." ("Don" is an honorific term in Italy, used for priests, among others.) Reports described him as "hardworking" and "very active" and say that those who know him like him. The only controversy attached to his name was an accusation by a former seminarian turned LGBTQ activist that Reina had asked him to seek out conversion therapy for his homosexual desires.[37]

Though not much has been printed on Reina, from early accounts, he seems unlike Paglia. The shift at the John Paul II Institute is thus expected to be palpable. It should be felt by the mere replacement of Paglia and with Francis no longer pope.

The Catholic publication *The Pillar* immediately called it "one of the most significant personnel changes in the opening weeks of Pope Leo XIV's pontificate." *The Pillar* said that Leo's selection of Reina "effectively restores the earlier structure" of the institute prior to Francis's revolutionary changes.

As for Reina's background, *The Pillar* noted that, akin to Cardinal Robert Francis Prevost in Peru, he "has rarely given interviews and has kept himself out of the spotlight . . . but Reina is widely thought to be a less theologically controversial pick than Paglia." Nonetheless, and again akin to Prevost, Reina has made statements suggestive of a serious individual committed to doctrinal clarity. In a 2024 interview with *The Pillar*, Reina had said that the antidote to secularization is "a new evangelization, as John Paul II already called for more than two decades ago now." When asked if the Church should adapt its teaching to the times, Reina replied: "the Church always listens to what man lives today. Yet, the moral teachings have a solid foundation: the teachings of Holy Scripture and what God has always revealed. So, the Church does not need to adapt to the times but must act in such a way that the times adapt to the logic of the Gospel."

As with the background of Robert Francis Prevost, one could look deeper into the background of Baldassare Reina's actions as a bishop and there find examples of his support for the "culture of life" that John Paul II so eloquently spoke of. For instance, Reina steadfastly supported the canonization process of Servant of God Chiara Corbella Petrillo, an Italian mother of three who had sacrificed her life for her baby rather than abort her baby.[38]

Chiara's story here deserves pause, because it could be a hopeful sign of the change for life at the John Paul II Institute under Reina and Leo XIV.

CHIARA CORBELLA AND BALDASSARE REINA

Chiara Corbella was born in Rome on January 9, 1984. She grew into a remarkable woman of faith. She made frequent spiritual pilgrimages outside the Eternal City, particularly to Assisi. She also made a pilgrimage to Medjugorje, the popular Marian destination in the former Yugoslavia, where she met her husband, Enrico Petrillo.[39]

The two married and were eager to have a family. They conceived on their honeymoon. Their excitement, however, was soon tempered when the ultrasound revealed that their unborn child had anencephaly. But Chiara and Enrico were undeterred. They were asked if they would like to abort. They said no. The child was born on June 10, 2009, but tiny Maria Grazia Letizia died only a half hour later.

Chiara's next pregnancy was even more problematic. The ultrasound revealed that the baby had severe malformations, including no kidneys and no lower limbs. Asked again if they wanted to abort, Chiara and Enrico said no. The child was born Davide Giovanni on June 24, 2010. Like the sister who preceded him, Davide lived only about 30 minutes.

Unafraid, Chiara and Enrico did not give up on life. And in fact, the news for their third pregnancy was much better: the ultrasound revealed a healthy baby boy. But then, major health complications struck again—this time to the mother.

Chiara was diagnosed with cancer on her tongue and face. She refused treatment because she feared the chemotherapy and other drugs would harm her unborn child. To save her own life, she could accept the cancer treatment and could abort her child. Chiara refused.

"Humanly we can do nothing except to pray and to ask God for the strength to live this trial in sanctity," said Chiara. She went to Mass every day and offered up her suffering.

On May 30, 2011, Chiara gave birth to a perfectly healthy boy, who she and Enrico named Francesco, after Saint Francis.

Immediately after Francesco's birth, Chiara started receiving intense cancer treatments, but it was too late. The cancer had metastasized throughout her body. She had trouble speaking and seeing, and wore an eyepatch. There was no saving her.

Chiara died at home on June 13, 2012. She was dressed in her wedding gown, with her beloved husband at her side. She was only 28 years old.

Chiara Corbella Petrillo lived a saintly life, so much so that not long after her death many began calling for her canonization. In fact, she has been called "the second Gianna," in reference to the extraordinary Saint Gianna Beretta Molla, an Italian woman and physician who in April 1962 likewise gave up her own life for the child in her womb. Gianna was beatified by Pope John Paul II in April 1994, the Year of the Family, and canonized by him in May 2004.[40]

Though Chiara has been referred to as "the second Gianna," her situation was even more acute than St. Gianna's. Consider again: Chiara had been advised to abort her two previous children in the womb. Both were born, albeit with serious, ultimately fatal abnormalities. Each died within an hour of birth. For her third pregnancy, she was urged again to abort. She again refused. This time, with her third pregnancy, Chiara was diagnosed with cancer, but refused treatment until after his birth, not wanting to harm her unborn child. She died from that cancer a year later.

And so how does this inspiring story relate to Baldassare Reina, Pope Leo XIV's new head at the John Paul II Institute?

It was Monsignor Bishop Baldassare Reina who served as the presiding priest for the closing session of the so-called "Diocesan Inquiry into the Life, Virtues, Reputation for Sanctity and Signs of the Servant of God Chiara Corbella." That deeply moving ceremony took place in June 2024 at St. John Lateran Basilica in Rome, the official home parish of the Diocese of Rome and the Bishop of Rome. The ceremony was the first step toward sainthood for Chiara.

There, in front of the family of the late Chiara, including her husband and her healthy surviving son, Francesco, Reina testified beautifully on her behalf:

> It is a day of joy and celebration for our diocese, for the whole Church, for the Church of Rome in particular. We thank the Lord both for the gift of Chiara's life, and for the gift of holiness, this seed that God planted in the heart of each one of us on the day of our baptism.
>
> We are here to contemplate a shoot, a seed of holiness that the good Lord placed in Chiara's heart and that we contemplate today. We thank the Lord for this sister of ours. We commit ourselves to imitating Chiara, because we are all called to holiness in our daily lives, in difficulties, in problems, in illnesses. Chiara teaches us, together with an infinite host of men and women, that holiness is a possible path. It is the only path that makes us happy.[41]

Reina continued: "We strongly trust that the Church, after a careful and accurate discernment of her life and virtues, will want to soon celebrate also on earth this daughter of our Church of Rome and propose her as an example of Christian life to contemporary Christian generations."[42]

Reina's assessment of the life and choice of Chiara Corbella Petrillo suffered no moral ambiguity. She had chosen heroically for life. A wishy-washy, week-kneed Catholic theologian might have advised Chiara to take birth-control pills or to sacrifice her unborn children's lives for her own, or at the least might have waffled on her situation. But that was not Chiara's witness nor position, nor that of

John Paul II and his institute. Both she and the institute projected moral strength. They stood against the *zeitgeist* and winds of the dictatorship of relativism. They were unafraid.

And now, a decade later under a new pope, Reina has been tasked to pick up the torch at that institute.

Here was a major personnel change by Leo XIV at a key post on day one of his pontificate. As the world had learned under Pope Francis, "personnel is policy." Under Francis, the personnel led to policies of chaos and confusion. Under Leo XIV, there was hope that Reina, unlike Paglia, could bring policies of clarity.

Many Catholics were immediately hopeful of just that. The Catholic news source Zenit stated, "With Cardinal Reina, the Vatican seems intent on restoring both trust and tradition [and] reinforcing a sense of theological and institutional unity."[43]

Veteran Catholic commentator and former publisher and editor of *Crisis Magazine* Deal Hudson was especially optimistic about the switch from Paglia to Reina, seeing it as a promising symbol that Leo was bringing back Pope John Paul II's moral teachings on the family and life after nearly a decade of seeming "dissolution" under Pope Francis and Vincenzo Paglia. "One of the very first things that Pope Leo XIV has done is to fire the man [whom] Pope Francis appointed," said Hudson, "and to put in a man whose reputation is that of being very orthodox, very evangelical, Cardinal Reina." Hudson called it "symbolic at the most important level. It's a level of saying, 'I'm going to reverse in this particular instance something that Pope Francis did, because it represents a rejection of John Paul II. I'm embracing John Paul II in this pontificate.'"[44]

The extent to which that is true remains to be seen. But it is undeniable that such a change on the first day after Pope Leo XIV's official installation is symbolically significant.

THE PEGORARO APPOINTMENT

Alas, as a coda to this story, several days after the appointment of Cardinal Reina, Leo XIV made a related appointment that drew concern, criticism, and even apprehension from some of the same voices who had been encouraged by his appointment of Cardinal Reina. That initial optimism soured somewhat when Leo named Msgr. Renzo Pegoraro as president of the Pontifical Academy of Life.

Few could doubt Pegoraro's credentials. A native of Padua in northern Italy, the 65-year-old Renzo Pegoraro has degrees in medicine and surgery from the University of Padua, in addition to degrees in theology. The ordained priest and trained bioethicist received a licentiate in moral theology from the Pontifical Gregorian University in Rome as well as a postgraduate diploma in bioethics from the Catholic University of the Sacred Heart. He served as a professor of bioethics at the Theological Faculty of Triveneto and more recently, in the early 2000s, was a professor of nursing ethics at the Bambino Gesù Pediatric Hospital in Rome. He also served as president of the European Association of Centres for Medical Ethics.[45]

What concerned some was not Pegoraro's credentials but his association with Archbishop Vincenzo Paglia. Indeed, his appointment by Leo was greeted with this headline the next day at the *National Catholic Register*: "Pope Appoints Archbishop Paglia's Right-Hand Man as President of Pontifical Academy for Life." Edward Pentin's opening paragraph framed the selection this way: "Pope Leo XIV has appointed as head of the Vatican's bioethics think tank Msgr. Renzo Pegoraro, the longtime deputy of its outgoing president, Archbishop Vincenzo Paglia, signaling a desire to continue the course set under Pope Francis."[46]

Whether this truly signaled such a desire could not be known at that moment, especially in light of the Reina appointment. Besides, the first pope to elevate Pegoraro was not Francis but Benedict XVI. As the next line in Pentin's piece noted, Pegoraro since 2011 had served as chancellor of the Pontifical Academy for Life, appointed to that position by Pope Benedict XVI. He was a Benedict choice, not a Francis choice. And yet, as Pentin also noted, the monsignor had continued in that position throughout Archbishop Paglia's "turbulent term as president, which was marked by the appointments of pro-abortion members and problematic statements regarding assisted suicide and contraception." During that term, he reportedly had not publicly spoken out against his boss (which certainly is not uncommon for any subordinate, particularly in the hierarchy of the Church). Pentin quoted Dr. Thomas Ward, founder of Britain's National Association of Catholic Families, who said that he never recalled Msgr. Pegoraro "disassociating himself from any of the egregious positions and comments of Archbishop Paglia."

Pentin put it this way on Pegoraro: "From 2016 until the present, he was Archbishop Paglia's key collaborator at a time when the pontifical academy was accused of drifting from John Paul II's original mission to defend the sanctity of life and instead accommodating heterodox and secular ethical arguments, changing its statutes, and undermining its credibility as a pro-life institution." Pentin cited two occasions in which Pegoraro as chancellor "added his voice to this perceived drift away from the academy's mission by publicly supporting dissenting positions that had won sympathy during Pope Francis' pontificate."

The degree to which that can be asserted seems a stretch.

One of these two statements—pointed to not only by Pentin but others quickly critical of the Pegoraro appointment[47]—was a December 2022 interview with Francis X. Rocca of the *Wall Street Journal*, where the monsignor had said that contraception might be permissible "in the case of a conflict between the need to avoid pregnancy for medical reasons and the preservation of a couple's sex life." In that interview, Pegoraro did not elaborate, nor did the article expound on his specific position; it offered only that single-sentence remark. Nonetheless, the title of that article, "Is the Catholic Church Rethinking Contraception?" rattled longtime supporters of John Paul II's teachings on life and sexuality, as did the scary subtitle, "In the climate of openness under Pope Francis, theologians are revisiting the morality of birth control for the first time in decades."[48]

To be fair to Pegoraro, at that point, the "revisiting" seemed not because of him but because of the overall drift of the Pontifical Academy for Life under Archbishop Paglia and Pope Francis. How much of that drift could be pegged on Pegoraro?

The other statement from Pegoraro that concerned Edward Pentin (and others) was a February 2022 remark in which the monsignor (in Pentin's words), "appeared to support two members of the academy who publicly favored assisted suicide as a tactic to prevent the legalization of voluntary euthanasia in Italy." In this situation, Pegoraro had told the French Catholic newspaper *Le Croix*: "We are in a specific context, with a choice to be made between two options, neither of which—assisted suicide or euthanasia—represents the Catholic position."[49]

Pegoraro understood that the law was a foregone conclusion, and thus said of the two possibilities, "assisted suicide is the one that most restricts abuses because it would be accompanied by four strict conditions: the person asking for help must be conscious and able to express it freely, have an irreversible illness, experience unbearable suffering and depend on life-sustaining treatment such as a respirator."

A close look at that statement, however, raises questions about the questions raised against Pegoraro. In the scenario that he posed, such a person, apparently, would be facing a natural death, being kept alive artificially. Such a situation is very different from what most Western liberals advocate when speaking of assisted suicide or euthanasia.

In that interview with *Le Croix*, Pegoraro called both choices "evil," and discussed how to deal with the practical choice of choosing between two evils. He emphatically made clear: "The Church always condemns assisted suicide, as it does with euthanasia." The question was not one of questioning morality but of deciding what to do with a political situation involving two laws that both go against Church teaching. Here was a prudential question in which (in the words of Pegoraro) "In any case, there will be a law." How does the Church then respond to those laws?

Together, the two Pegoraro statements from 2022—made to *Le Croix* and to the *Wall Street Journal*—do not seem to constitute a cut-and-dry case and crystal-clear indictment of Pegoraro's lifelong record on matters of life. But what does seem a legitimate concern, raised by Edward Pentin and others, is that Pegoraro was reportedly second in command to Paglia during the chaos under Paglia and Francis. But what was his personal attitude and role? Did he reluctantly albeit obediently serve Paglia with doubts kept close to the vest? Or was he enthusiastic and fully supportive of the new direction under Paglia and Francis? It was not clear.

Interestingly, in his statement thanking Paglia at the time of his appointment by Leo XIV, Pegoraro said only that "The work done over these years alongside Archbishop Vincenzo Paglia, and previously with Bishop Ignacio Carrasco de Paul, has been both fascinating and stimulating, in line with the operational and thematic directions of the late Pope Francis."[50]

Well, that work was indeed done in line with the operational and thematic directions of Francis. The task of Pegoraro was to follow that line.

Would that line now change under Leo XIV? The replacement of Paglia with Reina suggested so. Presumably, Leo XIV wants Pegoraro to follow his line.

Nonetheless, just days after the Reina appointment, which had inspired optimism among John Paul II fans, the promotion of Pegoraro suddenly made them less enthusiastic, legitimately or not. Time will tell.

And yet, there were soon signs for optimism. Immediately after the appointments of Reina and Pegoraro, the French bishops on May 27 stepped forward with a bold condemnation of the passage of a new euthanasia bill by France's National Assembly.[51] And in the United States, New York Archbishop Cardinal Timothy Dolan published a May 29 column in the *Wall Street Journal* urging New York lawmakers to "prevent, don't assist, suicide."[52]

Whether actions like these had the urging or involvement of the likes of Reina, Pegoraro, and Leo XIV was not reported, but it was obvious that none of the three in any way had hindered these defenses of life by bishops in France and the United States. In the new era under Leo, Catholic prelates were stepping forward for life. They clearly had a sense of assurance that they would be backed by Rome.

MAY 25—TAKING POSSESSION AT ST. JOHN LATERAN

On Sunday, May 25, two and a half weeks after his election by the conclave, Leo XIV took another (if not final) formal step in officially assuming the papal throne. That afternoon, in the language of the Church, he "took possession" of his so-called *cathedra*—that is, papal throne. This occurred at the Bishop of Rome's diocesan church, St. John Lateran Church.

That process unfolded both inside the church and also on the way to the church. Given his new status as Bishop of Rome, the Holy Father on his way to the basilica stops to officially meet with the mayor of Rome. Mayor Roberto Gualtieri greeted the pontiff at the foot of the staircase of the Capitoline Hill that serves as the main entrance to the Palazzo Senatorio, the administrative "city hall" that serves as the seat of the civic government of Rome. Here were the spiritual and civic leaders of the city meeting together.[53]

"Rome will always be distinguished by those values of humanity and civilization that draw their lifeblood from the Gospel," stated Leo XIV. "For two millennia, the Church has carried out her apostolate in Rome, proclaiming the Gospel of Christ and dedicating herself to works of charity." The pontiff's remarks were brief, but he finished by borrowing from St. Augustine in telling the mayor and citizens of Rome, "Today I can say that for you and with you I am Roman!"

Leo XIV then made his way to the basilica.

It is crucial to understand what St. John Lateran Basilica is. It is the mother church of the universal Roman Catholic Church. St. John Lateran bears the honorary title of "mother and head of all the Churches in the city of Rome and the whole world." This visible symbol of the universal Church was originally erected by the Emperor Constantine, dedicated in the year 324. It houses the bones of numerous deceased popes and even the skulls of Saints Peter and Paul, which are elevated high above the basilica's main altar. It stands without peer, even compared to St. Peter's Basilica, which, contrary to public perception, is not the pope's or diocese's official church.

Inside that venerable edifice on May 25, 2025, Leo XIV addressed the cardinals that serve in the Roman Curia, as well as bishops, priests, deacons, religious, and laity of the Diocese of Rome. Among the cardinals present was Cardinal Vicar Baldassare Reina, the newly appointed head of the John Paul II Institute. But above all, represented at the ceremony were laypeople who are members of the flock of the Bishop of Rome. Their recognition is done formally during the liturgy of the Mass, namely, in the Rite of Obedience, when the pope receives a pledge of fidelity from a representative group of people in the diocese. That group included two young people and a local family to represent the laity, as well as a parish priest, a deacon, a canon, a parochial vicar, an auxiliary bishop, a nun, a monk, an educator, and a catechist.[54]

All of this is done to accentuate the reality that although the new Holy Father is chief shepherd to the world, he is also a local bishop—to the people of Rome.

Inside the basilica, Leo XIV gave his homily, with this "son of Augustine" yet again quoting the great saint, as well as invoking saints Peter and Paul (physically present high above that altar), Saint Leo the Great, and even Blessed John Paul I, the immediate predecessor to Saint John Paul II, who had served only 33 days in the papacy before his unexpected death, but in that short time was loved and known as "the smiling pope."

Referring to the Apostles listening to the words of Jesus, Leo emphasized the importance of Christians "listening to God's voice. . . . For only in this way can each of us hear within the voice of the Spirit crying out 'Abba! Father!' and then, as a result, listen to and understand others as our brothers and sisters." He stressed listening to the voice of the Holy Spirit to find not only individual peace with God but unity in the universal Church.

This process, said Leo, "assures us that we are not alone in making our decisions in life. The Spirit sustains us and shows us the way to follow, 'teaching' us and 'reminding' us of all that Jesus said." He stated: "The more we let ourselves be convinced and transformed by the Gospel—allowing the power of the Spirit to purify our heart, to make our words straightforward, our desires honest and clear, and our actions generous—the more capable we are of proclaiming its message."

Leo brought this message to his new diocesan church and what he called "our great diocesan family." Here they were, at their home church, this historic St. John Lateran Basilica. According to Leo XIV, this made all of them together "heir to a great history, grounded in the witness of Peter, Paul, and countless martyrs." These families shared in the mission of the basilica "to be 'Omnium Ecclesiarum Mater,' mother of all the Churches."

With this shared mission, Pope Leo XIV, the former Robert Francis Prevost of Chicago now turned Bishop of Rome, was ready to lead his spiritual family.

MAY 31—FIRST MASS OF ORDINATION

On Saturday morning, May 31, the new pope carried out his first ordination of new priests in his diocese as Bishop of Rome. In a reverent, poignant Mass at St. Peter's Basilica, teeming with 5,500 congregants, Pope Leo XIV ordained 11 seminarians from the Pontifical Roman Major Seminary and the Redemptoris Mater Seminary.

Leo XIV called it a moment of "great joy for the Church."

In his homily, the pontiff echoed the words of St. Paul to the early Christian community in Ephesus: "You know how I lived the whole time I was with you." His message was one of priestly service and leadership through fidelity. Only by living the priestly life faithfully and virtuously could these men expect to inspire their flock and their Church—an embattled, wounded Church badly in need of healing. "We live among the people of God so that we may stand before them with a credible witness," said the new Bishop of Rome. "Together, we rebuild the credibility of a wounded Church, sent to a wounded humanity, within a wounded creation."[55]

But more stirring than the words of the Holy Father were the visible, physical actions of the 11 men and their pope.

With the homily and its words of encouragement finished, the seminarians then presented themselves for the formal process of ordination. The 11 men adorned in white stood and then took their positions in front of the altar. Each of them lay prostrate on the marble floor of the giant basilica, five in a front row, followed by six behind them. The young men lay there, arms stretched out.

One by one, each of the 11 stood and walked up to the Holy Father and knelt in front of him, as he one by one placed his hands on their heads and prayed over them. As this new pope did this for the first time, he was visibly emotional. Leo XIV was shaking slightly as he lifted his arms, tangibly feeling the weight of the moment. By the fourth ordinate, he was holding back tears, eyes misty, and took a few hard swallows.

Then after that process, as each newly ordained man went back to his station, though this time not prostrate but kneeling in devotion with hands folded, Leo prayed, calling on God, the "Author of Human Dignity," and his Son, the Lord Jesus, to be with each man and "to assist them in their task" ahead as priestly servants. "We ask you Lord, in our weakness," requested the pontiff, to give "these your servants" the "spirit of holiness." He called on them to be "worthy coworkers with the order of bishops," striving "to the ends of the earth," to be "faithful stewards of Your mysteries . . . so that sinners may be reconciled and the sick raised up. Through one God, your Son, in the Holy Spirit, forever."

Each was then vested with the stole to begin his priestly ministry.

After that, each of the 11 went up to the altar as the Holy Father sanctified their hands with chrism oil, said a few words, sometimes shook hands, and exchanged smiles. Leo, now more composed, did this with joy, making the sign of the cross on each man's hands: the hands that would consecrate the Eucharist many thousands of times in the days ahead. Some of the young men clearly savored the occasion, staring into the Holy Father's eyes, knowing that this singular moment would never happen again. Each was now a priest, forever, but this moment was now, in the present, and would never be repeated. Their hands were now consecrated for sacred service.

The 11 filed out of the basilica imbued with the spirit and inspired as new priests, as was the feeling of their new pope.

JUNE 1: ON MARRIAGE AND FAMILIES

On Sunday, June 1, Pope Leo XIV gave a special "Mass for the Jubilee of Families, Children, Grandparents, and the Elderly" at St. Peter's Square. There he gave a homily that stands as his first major papal pronouncement on family and marriage. What he said was significant.

In a 1,200-word-plus homily (translated in English) he started with the Gospel reading on Jesus at the Last Supper, with the Lord "praying on our behalf" and exhorting that "all be one." Leo referred to this unitive ambition as "the greatest good that we can desire, for this universal union brings about among his creatures the eternal communion of love that is God himself: the Father who gives life, the Son who receives it and the Spirit who shares it." This was a call from the Lord for "unity," said Leo, underscoring once again that central message of his young pontificate.[56]

The Holy Father applied Jesus's words of unity and "infinite love" to the Jubilee of Families, Children, Grandparents, and the Elderly. Here, the new pope coined a memorable statement about families, exhorting: "Let us not forget: families are the cradle of the future of humanity."

The family itself serves as the cradle of the human person.

Leo gave examples of several Christian spouses in recent decades and centuries who had been beatified and canonized by the Roman Catholic Church, such as Louis and Zélie Martin, the French parents of Saint Therese of the Child Jesus (1873–97). He pointed to such parents as "exemplary witnesses of married life." And herein, he gave a definition of marriage: "I would remind all married couples that marriage is not an ideal but the measure of true love between a man and a woman: a love that is total, faithful and fruitful. This love makes you one flesh and enables you, in the image of God, to bestow the gift of life."

On fruitfulness, Leo's formal text of his homily here included a reference to Saint Pope Paul VI's *Humanae Vitae,* section 9, on the subject of "married love," which contains this affirmation of fruitful marriage: "love is fecund. It is not confined wholly to the loving interchange of husband and wife; it also contrives to go beyond this to bring new life into being." *Humanae Vitae* there states that, "Marriage and conjugal love are by their nature ordained toward the procreation and education of children. Children are really the supreme gift of marriage."[57]

In all, here was Leo XIV's expressed desire for exemplary marriage: it was based on a faithful, loving man and woman who together become one flesh in the fruitful, supreme gift of life to their children. To the parents present that day and throughout the world, the Holy Father said that they had a responsibility "to be examples of integrity to your children, acting as you want them to act, educating them in freedom through obedience, always seeing the good in them and finding ways to nurture it." In turn, he said to the children of these parents: "And you, dear children, show gratitude to your parents. To say 'thank you' each day for the gift of life and for all that comes with it is the first way to honor your father and your mother."

The pope also had a word here for "dear grandparents and elderly people," asking them to "watch over your loved ones with wisdom and compassion, and with the humility and patience that come with age."

Leo finished: "In the family, faith is handed on together with life, generation after generation. It is shared like food at the family table and like the love in our hearts. In this way, families become privileged places in which to encounter Jesus, who loves us and desires our good, always."

This was Pope Leo XIV's first major statement on the family. Providentially, it was given on June 1, which throughout the West was kickoff day for Pride Month, the month when LGBTQ activists most aggressively seek to enshrine their attempted redefinition of marriage and family. Those nature-redefiners would have angrily rejected Pope Leo XIV's definition of marriage and family as one man and one woman committed lovingly to the goal of reproducing human life. In their eyes, such a definition would be noninclusive, bigoted, and "hateful."

No doubt, what Leo said that Sunday at the Vatican stood fully contrary to the culture and prevailing *zeitgeist*. What he said was consistent with Church teaching on marriage, repeatedly affirmed over previous centuries and throughout the prior pontificate of Pope Francis. What he said was really nothing new for the Roman Catholic Church, but the need to declare it anew, once again, in this new pontificate, was as vital as ever.

Here, the new Holy Father did just that.

JUNE 4: POPE LEO'S PHONE CALL WITH VLADIMIR PUTIN

On Wednesday afternoon, June 4, Pope Leo XIV made a special phone call, his first to Russian President Vladimir Putin. They focused, of course, on Russia's war on Ukraine.

Few details were released. Matteo Bruni, director of the Holy See Press Office, told reporters that the pontiff made an appeal to the Russian dictator "to take a gesture that would favor peace, emphasizing the importance of dialogue to create positive contacts between the parties and seek solutions to the conflict." They also discussed ongoing efforts for prisoner exchanges, specifically such efforts by Cardinal Matteo Maria Zuppi, Archbishop of Bologna, who in 2023 was designated as a peace envoy to Ukraine and Russia.[58]

The American pope also brought up Patriarch Kirill, head of the Russian Orthodox Church, conveying to Putin his gratitude to Kirill for congratulating him for his selection of pope at the beginning of his pontificate. He told Putin that the "shared Christian values" of the Roman Catholic Church and Russian Orthodox Church could be (in Bruni's words) "a light that helps to seek peace, defend life, and pursue genuine religious freedom."[59]

The pope's call with Putin came three weeks after his first call with Ukrainian President Volodymyr Zelensky on May 12. Zelensky had said of that call: "It was our first conversation, but already a very warm and truly substantive one. I invited His Holiness to make an apostolic visit to Ukraine. Such a visit would bring real hope to all believers and to all our people." Zelensky had said that he "thanked His Holiness for his support of Ukraine and all our people. We deeply value his words about the need to achieve a just and lasting peace for our country and the release of prisoners. We also discussed the thousands of Ukrainian children deported by Russia. Ukraine counts on the Vatican's assistance in bringing them home to their families."[60]

Six days after that call, Zelensky and his wife, Olena, attended the pope's installation ceremony at St. Peter's Square. Zelensky and Leo met privately later that afternoon after the ceremony.[61] Now, the new pope hoped to talk to Putin as well.

The Leo–Putin call on June 4 was a surprise and big news, with reporters scurrying for more information. The Kremlin released a brief statement, saying only that Putin told the Holy Father that "the Kyiv regime is banking on escalating the conflict and is carrying out sabotage against civilian infrastructure sites on Russian territory."[62]

Though information on the phone call was sparse, a news item outside the walls of the Vatican sheds added light on the importance of Leo XIV's gesture that day. Back in Leo's native land, the American president, Donald Trump, also had a call with Vladimir Putin that day. It was not clear which phone call to Putin came first, from the pope or the president, but the fact that both talked to the Russian dictator the same day was surely no coincidence and seemed to suggest some coordination, especially given the recent diplomatic efforts of Secretary of State Marco Rubio, Vatican Secretary of State Parolin, and Cardinal Zuppi.

The significance of Leo's call to Putin—a breakthrough—is illustrated by the notable lack of papal communication with Putin in the months and years prior. Repeated diplomatic olive branches offered to Russia by Pope Francis's Vatican had not been firmly embraced. When Cardinal Zuppi was first sent to Moscow as a special envoy to address "humanitarian issues" between Russia and Ukraine, he was not received directly by Putin. The closest he could get to Putin was through one of the Russian authoritarian's advisors. As for Pope Leo, early in his pontificate he had renewed an offer by Pope Francis to Russia to use the offices of the Holy See as a neutral meeting ground for the two sides to negotiate. That peace offering was rejected as "inappropriate" by Putin hardline Russian Foreign Minister Sergey Lavrov. In keeping with the strident Russian-Orthodox nationalism of both President Putin and Patriarch Kirill, Lavrov reportedly said that such an offer was "not fitting"—that "two Orthodox states" (Russia and Ukraine) should not and would not meet to discuss their problems in a Catholic state.[63]

All of which makes the Leo–Putin call so remarkable. In fact, here is a further such sign:

The June 4 call from Leo was the first papal communication with Putin since Pope Francis had talked to the Russian tyrant four years prior. The last time President Putin spoke with the head of the Catholic Church had been on December 17, 2021, when he phoned Pope Francis to wish him a happy birthday.[64] The relationship soured when Putin two months later, on February 24, 2022, sent his Russian Army storming into Kiev. Reportedly, Putin thereafter refused to take any calls from the pope, firmly unreceptive to any pleas for peace from the pontiff.[65] Putin also did not attend Pope Francis's funeral (Zelensky did), but that was surely because he could have been arrested for war crimes by international authorities—a key reason that Putin has not left "mother Russia" since he began slaughtering Ukraine. For similar reasons, Putin did not attend Leo XIV's May 18 installation ceremony. Russia was represented by its ambassador to the Holy See, Ivan Soltanovsky.

In all, Pope Leo XIV's June 4 phone conversation with President Vladimir Putin was significant, and somewhat of a diplomatic breakthrough just weeks into his papacy. For a new pontiff whose first words from the Loggia on May 8 had been "Peace be with all of you," a message he was reinforcing almost daily, his successful outreach to Russia's presidential warlord was a positive achievement. Since the opening days of his papacy, Leo had consistently called for a "just and lasting" peace in Ukraine.[66]

Whether peace will prevail seems a long shot yet to be determined. Leo, however, was not hesitating to reach out, including directly to Vladimir Putin. Previous Leos had major success dealing with invaders, even with the likes of Attila the Hun. How Leo XIV will ultimately fare with Vladimir Putin remains to be seen.

JUNE 4: LEO NAMES HIS FIRST GROUP OF SAINTS

In other positive news that same Wednesday afternoon, June 4, this time dealing not with despots but saints, the Vatican's Office of Liturgical Celebrations released a list of blesseds whose cause for canonization would be approved by Pope Leo XIV in coming weeks—the first canonizations of his young pontificate.

The group was a diverse lot of holy men and women, featuring some particularly interesting characters who had led complicated, sometimes checkered, but ultimately redeeming lives. That would certainly apply to the first name listed by the Vatican, Blessed Bartolo Longo (1841–1926), an Italian layman, attorney, and founder of the Shrine of Our Lady of the Rosary in Pompeii, Italy, to which Cardinal Robert Francis Prevost himself had a special devotion. Longo had once been a Satanist and spiritualist before embracing Catholicism in one of the turn-of-the-century's most impressive conversions. He credited the Blessed Mary with changing his life forever. His final words were: "My only desire is to see Mary who saved me and who will save me from the clutches of Satan."[67]

Also named to be canonized was the Venezuelan so-called "doctor of the poor," Dr. José Gregorio Hernández (1864–1919); Peter To Rot (1912–45), the first blessed from Papua New Guinea, who was martyred during World War II for defending marriage; Ignazio Choukrallah Maloyan (1869–1915), an Armenian martyr brutally killed in the 1915 genocide; Vincenza Maria Poloni (1802–55), founder of the Sisters of Mercy of Verona (Italy); María del Monte Carmelo Rendiles Martínez (1903–77), known as "Mother Carmen," founder of the Congregation of the Servants of Jesus, who would become Venezuela's first female saint; Italian nun Maria Troncatti (1883–1969), who spent much of her life as a missionary in Ecuador; and Pier Giorgio Frassati (1901–25).[68]

Notable among the group is Frassati, an Italian skier, mountain climber, and adventurer who died at the young age of 24 on July 4, 1925. Frassati was the son of the founder of the Italian newspaper *La Stampa*. He hailed from an upper-class family but dedicated his life to serving the poor, the homeless, and wounded and maimed demobilized servicemen returning from World War I. Frassati is a popular figure among young Catholics worldwide, somewhat of a rock-star saint. He is frequently invoked as a confirmation name for youth around the globe.

For the new pope, this was quite the freshmen class of saints. What stood out about them was their diversity of story and place. And yet, at the same time, this eclectic list was also unusually modern, with all of them hailing from the 19th and 20th centuries. Here were tales of heroic Christian service from holy men and women who ultimately fought against the winds of the dictatorship of relativism.

JUNE 8: REMOVING FR. RUPNIK'S ALLEGED "RAPE ART"

On Sunday, June 8, came another early indicator of Pope Leo's emergent style of quiet but firm leadership. That day brought the removal of the artwork of a Slovenian priest who had become notorious, as had Pope Francis's protection of him. The priest is Fr. Marko Rupnik.[69]

Rupnik was accused of abuse by roughly two dozen women, mostly former nuns. They charged him with spiritual, psychological, and sexual abuse over the course of three decades. Rupnik's alleged behavior was so bad that the Jesuits expelled him in June 2023 for his "stubborn refusal to observe the vow of obedience."[70]

Nonetheless, Rupnik was reportedly being protected by the world's top Jesuit, Pope Francis. Enraged Catholics called for Rupnik to be put on trial, removed from the priesthood altogether, and for his artwork to be taken down—at the very least removed from Vatican websites, where it was often featured. Digital images of Rupnik's work were frequently used by the website *Vatican News* to illustrate descriptions of the Church's liturgical feast days. Likewise, the Dicastery for Communication website featured images of the priest's work.[71]

The priest's artwork was displayed not only at official Vatican sites but at shrines and chapels around the world, including the National Shrine of St. John Paul II in Washington, DC, the basilica at Our Lady of Lourdes in France, and the Redemptoris Mater Chapel in the Vatican's Apostolic Palace, where the work had been commissioned by Pope John Paul II in 1996.[72] Many of these sacred places (with the exception of Francis's Holy See) had removed or covered up Rupnik's art as allegations surfaced about him.[73]

Part of the debate over Rupnik's art was about the nature of art itself. Some voices argued that it was wrong to punish the art. The artist might be guilty of terrible misconduct, but should his art be canceled based on his misdeeds? If Rupnik's art must be removed because of the sins of the man, then which work of other artists is fair game for removal? Was Caravaggio without sin?

That comparison was made by Fr. Raymond de Souza, who noted that Caravaggio was "guilty of slander and vandalism, a hot temper, and eventually convicted of murder during a duel in Rome, after which he became a fugitive." And yet, "Caravaggio's splendid works adorn Italy to this day, and are often used for spiritual reflections." De Souza added, "An immediate response might be that Father Rupnik is not Caravaggio; the world can suffer the loss of Father Rupnik's art but not the work of one of the greatest painters ever to live."[74]

Perhaps. But here was where the controversy with Rupnik's art got particularly ugly. As de Souza noted, "While the Vatican courts have not yet managed to hold a trial for Father Rupnik, there is a widespread consensus—based on the claims of dozens of women—that he sexually coerced women in his religious community as part of the process of creating his paintings and mosaics. The term 'rape art' has thus been used to characterize Father Rupnik's work."

That is an extraordinary, alarming charge. If such claims are accurate, then they surely merit the removal of such grotesquely inspired work, certainly from Vatican websites. Removing a work of "art" affixed to the side of a stone wall takes considerable physical effort, but deleting it from a website does not.

The "rape" element was at the core of the indictment of Rupnik's work. Christopher Altieri stated at *Crux*:

> Rupnik allegedly abused his victims as part of his "creative process"—a fact survivors, victim-advocates, and observers from across the spectrum of opinion in the Church say makes Rupnik's abuse inseparable from his "art" works. . . . Some victims and advocates have called Rupnik's work "rape art" and many have called for its removal from sacred space.[75]

To repeat: this linking of Rupnik's "creative process" to "rape" is a startling claim. It seems hard to imagine that when the disgraced Jesuit priest was doing conventional representations of the face of Jesus or the Blessed Mother, he was inspired by rape. If put on trial, facts could emerge, with the priest defending himself and his accusers making their case. However, such a legal process did not commence because Rupnik was reportedly being shielded by the previous pope.

That brings us back to the principal focus here: the pope.

Popes are not artists. They are moral leaders. They are shepherds of the flock. And that flock was badly wounded and still suffers scars—some of them fresh, anew, and ongoing—of sexual abuse by clergy. It must not be tolerated, and the perpetrator not protected.

Under Pope Francis, Rupnik was reportedly protected, despite public outcry both inside and outside the Church. These voices urged the removal of his images, if not him.

Among the most influential voices was American Cardinal Sean O'Malley, the founding president of Pope Francis's own Commission for the Protection of Minors. O'Malley said that "pastoral prudence would prevent displaying artwork in a way that could imply either exoneration or a subtle defense of or indicate indifference to the pain and suffering of so many victims of abuse."[76] O'Malley had pushed for the removal of the images, with no action taken by Francis and his allies.[77]

But that resistance suddenly changed, under the new pope.

This was poignantly captured by veteran Catholic writer John Grondelski, who thoughtfully linked the new pope's action to the important feast day at hand:

"Yesterday [Monday, June 9] was the Memorial of Mary, Mother of the Church, a relatively new feast for a very old theological reality," wrote Grondelski of this new feast day created by Pope Francis. "Until last Saturday, the Vatican News website was still featuring [for the feast day] the work of Marko Rupnik, the notorious abuser of nearly thirty religious women, who still somehow functions as a priest, seemingly protected by someone high up in Rome."[78]

The "someone high up" was assumed to be the previous pope. As Grondelski put it, "the biggest cover-up of Rupnik was in Francis's Vatican."

But at last, the protection of Rupnik and the prominent featuring of his artwork finally, suddenly, quietly came to an end, after over a year of uproar under Francis.

"Sometime between Saturday night and Sunday morning, his work disappeared," noted Grondelski, "replaced by a mosaic similar to the '*Mater Ecclesiae*' mosaic looking down on St. Peter's Square, erected by Pope St. John Paul II in gratitude to Our Lady for saving his life from an assassin's bullet."

Such a replacement was long overdue. And Leo was reportedly responsible for the shift.

Crux put it this way: "Images of artwork created by a disgraced celebrity cleric accused of serial sexual and other abuse have disappeared from official Vatican Media websites without explanation, almost a year after the head of the Vatican's communications outfit strongly defended his department's continued use of the images even in the face of sustained public outcry."

Crux asked Matteo Bruni, the Vatican's press office director, who had ordered this "complete policy reversal." Crux did not get an answer, but did speculate: "Observers have already noted, however, that the removal of the Rupnik images came hot on the heels of Pope Leo's meeting with O'Malley and officials of the Commission for the Protection of Minors, which took place on Thursday of last week."[79]

Indeed it had. Just two or three days before the change.

This was a marked shift, noted *Crux*, as officials "had no indication the change would be taking place" under Francis or even prior to the Leo meeting with Cardinal O'Malley. One Vatican official told *Crux* that Rupnik "was protected by Pope Francis," and added that "things are changing" under Pope Leo.[80]

The Italian publication, *La Nuova Bussola Quotidiana* (*The New Daily Compass*), was even clearer about the immediate Leo effect, with journalist Nico Spuntoni reporting: "just hours after Leo XIV granted an audience to the Pontifical Commission for the Protection of Minors, *Vatican News* hastily 'cleaned up' its websites of images of the works of the accused priest. This marks a clear U-turn from the stance taken by the head of the communications department at a conference in the US last year." Spuntoni concluded: "It is hard not to attribute this turnaround to the election of Leo XIV and the persistence of O'Malley, who has also publicly reprimanded Francis on several occasions in recent years."[81]

No question. The timing does not seem a coincidence.

Given the pains of the Church's scandalous sex-abuse crisis, the Holy Father ought to be more concerned about moral crimes against humanity than nuances of "artistic expression." Pope Leo seemed to be willing to draw the line where Francis did not, and mere weeks into his pontificate. And befitting his quieter style, he seemed to have made a significant change silently but firmly.

Here was yet another early sign of a different Chief Shepherd in the Chair of St. Peter.

JUNE 14: POPE LEO'S FIRST AMERICAN MASS

On Saturday, June 14, came an important first for the new American pontiff, though nothing like what the *real* first will be like *in person* someday. That afternoon, in his native Chicago, from the home field of his beloved Chicago White Sox baseball team, Leo participated in his first American Mass—via video.

The event organized by the Archdiocese of Chicago was billed "Chicago Celebrates Pope Leo XIV." An estimated 30,000 Catholics attended, though the stadium was not at the max capacity as when Robert Francis Prevost had taken a seat to join a full house to watch the Chicago White Sox in the 2005 World Series.[82] The new pope had more recently bonded with his native Chicagoans when a few days earlier he donned the Sox's black hat for a smiling photo op outside of St. Peter's Basilica.[83]

On this Saturday, Leo provided an eight-minute-long video, seated and clad in white at the Vatican, for his first direct message to the people of his hometown and home nation since becoming the first American pontiff. Leo did not provide a homily; rather, he offered a welcoming address that served as the highlight of pre-Mass programming at the afternoon celebration. The event featured musical performances by a local Catholic school and an original song for Leo called *One of Us*, written and performed by Augustinian brother David Marshall. Popular shirts at the event included White Sox jerseys with "Pope Leo" and "Da Pope" (popular Chicago vernacular) emblazoned in block letters.[84]

Leo's message was aimed at youth and focused on the virtue of hope.

"I'd like to send a special word of greeting to all the young people," said Leo, including any youth watching online. "As you grow up together, you may realize, especially having lived through the time of the pandemic—times of isolation, great difficulty, sometimes even difficulties in your families, or in our world today—sometimes it may be that the context of your life has not given you the opportunity to live the faith, to live as participants in a faith community." Speaking to this generation that had been isolated unwittingly by COVID and wittingly by their phones and computers, he urged them to step out, get out, reach out, and to connect to "a friend or a relative, a grandparent," and find ways to serve others. "And in that service to others," said Leo, "we may find that coming together in friendship, building up community, we too can find true meaning in our lives." Leo added that, "So many people who suffer from different experiences of depression or sadness—they can discover that the love of God is truly healing, that it brings hope." This "love of God can truly heal us, can give us the strength that we need, can be the source of that hope that we all need in our lives." He urged young people "to share that message of hope" with one another and the whole world.[85]

Not surprisingly, this Church scholar and son of Augustine twice quoted the great saint (and cited his sources):

> We have to look beyond our own—if you will— egotistical ways. We have to look for ways of coming together and promoting a message of hope. Saint Augustine says to us that if we want the world to be a better place, we have

> to begin with ourselves, we have to begin with our own lives, our own hearts (cf *Speech* 311; *Comment on St John's Gospel, Homily* 77). . . .
>
> We all live with many questions in our hearts. Saint Augustine speaks so often of our "restless" hearts and says: "Our hearts are restless until they rest in you, O God" (*Confessions* 1,1,1). That restlessness is not a bad thing, and we shouldn't look for ways to put out the fire, to eliminate or even numb ourselves to the tensions that we feel, the difficulties that we experience. We should rather get in touch with our own hearts and recognize that God can work in our lives, through our lives, and through us reach out to other people.

Pope Leo XIV concluded with a message of hope. He quoted Saint Paul from his Letter to the Romans (5:5): "Hope does not disappoint." In turn, Leo told the youth: "When I see each and every one of you, when I see how people gather together to celebrate their faith, I discover myself how much hope there is in the world."

Such concluded his first direct message to his fellow Chicagoans, who expressed the hope that they might soon meet Leo in person back in their shared hometown.

DAY 40: A MESSAGE OF PEACE

It was troubling but also fitting that day 40 of Leo's papacy, June 17, 2025, was marked by an explosion of war in the Middle East, with Israel and Iran trading blows unlike any time before in the history of the two nations. Hundreds if not thousands of missiles had been fired, killing many people on both sides. The day included a most ominous threat from the Supreme Religious

Leader of Iran, Ali Khamenei, the violent, repressive successor to the Ayatollah Ruhollah Khomeini who had launched the Iranian revolution in 1979.

Posting a disturbing image that showed balls of fire raining down upon an ancient city as a sword-wielding man storms the gate, the Supreme Leader vowed that "the battle has just begun," and "We will show the Zionists no mercy." State-controlled Iranian television ominously reported that "a great surprise will occur—one that the world will remember for centuries."[86]

Pope Leo XIV's first word from the Loggia as the new pope had been "peace," and his first diplomatic overtures in that regard had been directed toward Volodymyr Zelensky and Vladimir Putin to try to quell Russia's war on Ukraine. But suddenly, with Iran and Israel, he seemed to be facing something more dreadful. He spoke out.

"The heart of the Church is rent asunder," said Pope Leo in his general audience, lamenting the "cry of pain rising from places devastated by war, especially Ukraine, Iran, Israel and Gaza." He urged: "We must never get used to war" and "the temptation to have recourse to powerful and sophisticated weapons needs to be rejected."[87]

Pope Leo XIV declared that "War is always a defeat" for humanity. He finished by quoting the words of the World War II pontiff, Pius XII, who faced the Nazis inside the gates of Rome: "Nothing is lost with peace," said Pius XII. "Everything may be lost with war."

The 69-year-old Holy Father, just weeks earlier a mere humble cardinal from Chicago who had served in the peripheries of Peru, could hardly imagine the world exploding as it was at that moment. But in the long history of evil, popes have scarcely been surprised. As stated in the *Catechism of the Catholic Church*, re-issued under the papacy of John Paul II (section 409): "The whole of man's history has been the story of dour combat with the powers of evil, stretching, so our Lord tells us, from the very dawn of history until the last day. Finding himself in the midst of the battlefield man has to struggle to do what is right, and often at great cost to himself."

What sort of dour combat with the powers of evil Leo XIV might face in the future beyond his first 40 days would remain to be seen. It was something only his Lord could know, even as he knew that the battle stretched from the dawn of history until the final days. Leo would pray for peace and repeat his first words from the Loggia: "Peace be with all of you."

From Ukraine and Russia to Israel and Iran and more.

FOURTEEN

The Future of Leo XIV and the Church

These pages have aimed to provide some helpful information on the new pope, on the Roman Catholic Church he now leads, and on where Leo XIV might guide the Barque of St. Peter in the future. This biographical treatment was careful to address not only the person Robert Francis Prevost but also his Church, his predecessors in the papacy, and the issues and challenges facing the faithful, the culture, and the world.

The closest witness to Leo accepting that immense responsibility was the man who had been the front-runner for the papacy, Cardinal Pietro Parolin. Recall that it was Parolin, as the conclave's senior-most cardinal inside the Sistine Chapel, who had the task of asking the newly elected pontiff for his consent to the position on May 8, 2025. When Cardinal Robert Francis Prevost said, "*Accepto*," Parolin looked into his eyes and was struck with this thought: "What struck me most about him was the serenity . . . even though I imagine he was very aware of the many and not-so-simple problems facing the Church today."[1]

Surely, he was very aware. The problems are many and not simple. The head of the Roman Catholic Church has a job like no other individual.

There truly is no other leader like the pope. Protestantism has no such figure nor rival. Neither does the secular world. The most powerful president or prime minister cannot match the unique influence of the Holy Father. No matter how humble the pope might be as an individual, he cannot avoid the heavy reality that no earthly figure has his impact. It is an impact that rises well beyond the confines of the Roman Catholic Church, whether his desire or not.

His influence is unavoidable.

To that end, this concluding chapter could be ambitious in underscoring potential roles for the Bishop of Rome in resolving various global conflicts, in mediating between countries like Russia and Ukraine, or Israel, Iran, and Gaza. It could delve into the ability of the Holy Father to affect everything and anything from poverty to the climate. But staying focused on matters raised in this book, this chapter will finish with an analysis of several areas where we might expect the new pope to make an impact based on the recent history of the papacy, the Church, and the thinking of Robert Francis Prevost.

Here are some closing observations and expectations. These are just a few things to watch for in the years ahead with Pope Leo XIV.

REVERSING THE DECLINE IN CATHOLICISM AND CHRISTIANITY

Pope Francis presided over a period of dismal growth in Catholics practicing their faith and new people entering the Church outside of Africa and Asia.[2] The deterioration has been especially pronounced in Europe and the Americas, including Latin America, where it had been expected that the first Latin American pope—Jorge Mario Bergoglio—would spark a resurgence. There were predictions and hopes of a "Francis effect." To the contrary, Francis's papacy did not pick up the sagging numbers. In many places, they shot in the opposite direction.[3]

It was particularly shocking that Francis never once went to his home country of Argentina as pope. One would have expected a dramatic hero's welcome in Buenos Aires, akin to the incredible receptions for Pope John Paul II in his native Poland. Instead, there was not a single trip to Argentina by Francis. Not one. No triumphant return. That highly conspicuous absence was terribly revealing.[4] Bergoglio was picked by the March 2013 conclave surely in part because he was a non-European and the cardinal electors figured he would reverse the Church's sagging numbers in its onetime stronghold of the Western hemisphere.

Assessing the tasks facing the next Holy Father prior to the May 2025 conclave, Fr. Raymond J. de Souza wrote a piece titled, "New Pope Must Correct the Declining Course of Catholicism in Latin America." De Souza could not have known that the new pope—Leo XIV—would be a man with a foot on each side of the Americas, both north and south, America and Peru. And yet, that is the pope that the universal Church now has. And Latin America needs him. The faith was once thriving in Latin America, but not anymore. As in North America and Western Europe, Catholicism even in richly Catholic Latin America has been in a steep decline, especially through rapidly declining rates of Mass attendance.

Not unrelatedly, the crash in Mass attendance has been attended by a crash in vocations among men to the priesthood and women seeking religious life as nuns. Such has been the sad state of the faith in much of the world. The trajectory is a downward arrow. And to be fair to Pope Francis, such has been the direction for decades, especially since Vatican II (1962–65), which marked the start of a long decline for the faith and especially for vocations.

Robert Francis Prevost has observed this dire situation most acutely in his own life. The lovely little parish of his youth, where he served as an altar boy and first found Jesus, is today abandoned, shuttered, marred by broken windows and holes in the walls, and is filled inside not with people and pews (even the pews have been removed) but with graffiti and spray-painted walls.

When "Rob" left that thriving parish for minor seminary in Holland, Michigan, in the late 1960s, he arrived at a place teeming with young men seeking to be priests. Alas, no more. That seminary likewise has long since been closed. Even more alarming, the entire Grand Rapids Diocese that contains Holland produced not a single new priest in all of 2025. In 2024, it produced merely one. Parishes in the diocese are merging because there are not enough priests. "In 2024, we had one priestly ordination," the diocese lamented in a June 29, 2025, statement. "In 2025, seven pastors were either granted senior priest status or reassigned outside the Diocese of Grand Rapids, and there were no priestly ordinations."[5]

At that rate of replacement, the situation with priests is unsustainable.

Unfortunately, the "crippling priest shortage" in the Grand Rapids diocese that once produced the first American pope is hardly unusual. Quite the contrary, it is actually more reflective of the norm in many if not most American dioceses. And Robert Francis Prevost, who once held the position of vocations director as one of his first jobs as a priest, knows this intimately, painfully well.

In Western Europe, the situation with Catholic dioceses and parishes is even grimmer. There, the decline in Mass attendance has been nothing short of astonishing. The Catholic Church in America is thriving in comparison to its doldrums in Europe, where the de-Christianization has been calamitous.

Slowing if not reversing this disaster will be one of Pope Leo XIV's greatest, gravest challenges. It is certainly unfair to lay this enormous if not insurmountable task at his feet. Nonetheless, he is the inheritor of this calamity. Whether he can stop the hemorrhage remains to be seen.

The same can be said for Christianity in general. In some cases, the freefall in Protestantism—especially the mainline denominations—is worse than in Roman Catholicism. Here again, this is especially true in the West, in Western Europe and the United States (the Protestant faiths likewise continue to do better in Africa and Asia). Membership in many of the mainlines is shrinking if not collapsing at an astounding rate.

Obviously, the pope is not a Protestant, but he is the undeniable global leader of Christianity. To the extent that Pope Leo XIV heeds the call and expands the mission of the Great Commission, he will help Christianity *en masse*. The pope is a Catholic, which means the pope is a Christian. All Christians, Catholic and non-Catholic, stand to benefit from his leadership in spreading the faith.

GUARDING TRADITION

One area where church attendance in America has been increasing, if not booming, is the more traditional churches, particularly the Traditional Latin Mass parishes. Ironically, that was the one area of Catholicism where Pope Francis drew a bull's-eye.

Francis's July 2021 papal document *Traditionis custodes* was one of the most divisive actions of his papacy. This official *motu proprio*, purportedly aimed at "guarding tradition," actually targeted Church traditionalists, sparking feelings of persecution among the victims and causing much confrontation and controversy throughout the Church. It wrecked the touted unity it supposedly sought to create. It became a weapon for Church liberals to use against Church traditionalists, the people Francis framed as "rigid" "fundamentalists" akin to modern Pharisees. Or as Francis harshly described them, "whitened sepulchres," shiny and clean on the outside but "evil" on the inside, "full of rottenness . . . wickedness."[6]

For Francis enthusiasts of the leftist bent, *Traditionis custodes* gave them their papers to suppress the traditionalists that they, too, did not like. Many such examples could be cited, but of special interest was an outrageous case that exploded in the opening weeks of Pope Leo's pontificate in the Diocese of Charlotte, North Carolina. The perpetrator was Bishop Michael Martin of Charlotte, whose proposed restrictions in his diocese were so flabbergasting that they were leaked to the Catholic press and (prior to that) apparently to the Vatican as well. In fact, they seemed to have caught the attention of none other than Cardinal Robert Francis Prevost, head of the Vatican's Dicastery for Bishops, mere weeks before he became pope.

The story erupted in the national press in late May 2025, when Bishop Martin's letter to priests in his diocese was leaked first to the traditionalist blog *Rorate Caeli* and then to the *National Catholic Register*. The *Register* told readers that the bishop's numerous changes included "barring *ad orientem* worship and traditional prayers at the foot of the altar, including the St. Michael Prayer," as well as restricting, if not banning, altar rails, kneeling, chants, the wearing of veils, and limiting if not terminating altogether the Latin language in ways that surely violated Vatican II as well as subsequent guidelines under every pope since (including Francis). Oppressive as that sounded, the actual text of the lengthy document, ironically titled, "Go in Peace," was breathtaking in its long list of stupefying restrictions.[7] Many seemed so capricious and downright erroneous that they would clash with the US Catholic Conference of Bishops and even liberal cardinals like Blase Cupich in Chicago.

And yet, much like Pope Francis, Bishop Martin's list of sweeping dictates was done with the stated intention of "purifying and unifying the celebration of the Mass." Citing Francis, Martin said that his actions were consistent with the *Traditionis custodes*' goal of promoting "concord and unity."

Predictably, of course, Martin's "Go in Peace" mandate promptly spawned not concord and unity but anger and division. "I think you all know that I am heartbroken by this," said Fr. Timothy Reid to his St. Ann's Catholic Church congregation in Charlotte upon announcing the news of Martin's crackdown. "And I know that you are too. Bitterness and despair must find no despair in our hearts." As for his traditionalist worshippers, the type who Pope Francis had said were filled with "greed" and "present themselves as so 'perfect,'"[8] Reid urged them: "Don't allow whatever anger you're feeling to be sinful. . . . Let's not focus on what's being taken away, but focus on what we're being given: an opportunity to suffer a deprivation for Christ."[9]

One of the hundreds of young people in Reid's parish, 20-year-old college student Patrick Gallagher, said: "Fr. Reid was choked up and tearing up a little bit from the pulpit because he knew that his parishioners were going to be torn between choosing their preferred form of liturgy and their fellow parishioners and the pastor. It was powerful to see."[10]

Twenty-four-year-old Augusta Westhoff said of Fr. Reid's homily: "It really helped encapsulate the right way to order our response as Catholics: to not let your anger become sinful, to recognize this deprivation as a cross, and to pray and fast."[11]

Ironically, St. Ann's was a shining example of what was positive and growing in the declining American Catholic Church. In most American parishes, the congregation is old and vanishing, with a lot of white hair among the pews but few families, few babies, few First Communions each year, and often an exhausted elderly priest well beyond retirement age but tasked to the Mass because younger priests are not being ordained in the local diocese. But like most TLM churches, St. Ann's is teeming with youth and vitality: more than 1,100 families registered, with 29 years old the average age of a parishioner. Another traditional parish in the Charlotte diocese is St. Thomas Aquinas, where the Sunday Latin Mass draws upward of 425 attendees from its huge number of 3,000 parish families. St. Thomas Aquinas draws hundreds of attendees even to non-Sunday

Masses. Its monthly First Saturday and weekly Thursday Latin Masses draw around 250 attendees.[12]

The TLM families have been drawn to the reverence of these parishes. They have escaped the clown shows that many nontraditional parishes have become in the West.

"Mass is not a show here," says Patrick Gallagher. "We've taken down the TV screens [in the church]."[13]

They prefer not big TV screens but candles, altar rails, kneelers, veils. And for their dedication to guarding these traditions, liberal Bishop Michael Martin, hoisting Pope Francis's "Guardians of Tradition," has targeted them. All in the name of "peace" and "unity."

The Charlotte diocese was thriving under the previous bishop, who responded to the desires of his faithful flock. Everything changed under Bishop Michael Martin.

In response to Bishop Martin's iron fist, the people in the Charlotte diocese of 565,000 Catholics (plus many Catholics nationwide) were distraught, trying to hold back anger. That includes non-TLM attendees. One parishioner in the diocese, who neither prefers nor attends the Traditional Latin Mass, said of Martin: "He is a boomer tyrannical '70s liberal priest in the style of Francis. Absolutely awful." Another said: "Bishop Martin is not a leader but a manipulator. He is unqualified but promoted by the Bishop of Atlanta. Charlotte had an excellent Bishop, who became ill. Francis has poisoned the well with Martin. Terrible outcome, folks are outraged."[14]

With all of that said, here is where the story becomes particularly interesting.

Bishop Martin's "Go in Peace" edict was written while Pope Francis was alive. But even before that, his heavy-handed approach had so divided the diocese that he had come to the attention of Rome. An influential letter within his diocese had accused him of "arbitrary micromanagement" and an "autocratic approach," including unilaterally rushing ahead with aggressive plans for a new cathedral. And so, in early April 2025, shortly before the death of Pope Francis, Bishop Martin was called to Rome for a one-on-one hourlong meeting with the prefect of the Vatican's Dicastery for Bishops.[15]

That prefect was Cardinal Robert Francis Prevost, that is, the future Pope Leo XIV.

According to the *Charlotte Observer*, Bishop Martin had been summoned to Rome to discuss what the newspaper called "administrative matters." Asked about the meeting, Martin told the *Observer* that Cardinal Prevost was "very, very relaxed" and "calm" as they discussed "a few things that needed to be addressed." He said that the future pope was "interested in me and what was happening in Charlotte."[16] Befitting his more taciturn style, Prevost did not publicly comment on the meeting, though it was reported by *The Pillar* that, "Prevost—now Pope Leo XIV—encouraged Martin to make change more slowly."[17]

Notably, Martin's meeting with Prevost occurred before his confrontational "Go in Peace" missive was leaked and published by *Rorate Caeli* and the *National Catholic Register*. Now, with Prevost no longer a cardinal but pope, things were escalating. Martin's actions had exploded onto the front pages in America and abroad. The bishop's actions were being reported as a direct challenge to the new pope to see how Leo XIV would respond.

"The controversy in Charlotte is rising to international attention, as it represents the first major liturgical dispute during the reign of Pope Leo XIV, who has pledged to bring unity to a divided Church," stated the *National Catholic Register*. "The North Carolina diocese is now considered a test case to see what, if any, indication Leo gives about not only the future of the TLM but also Vatican II's authoritative teaching on the liturgy more broadly."

The response of Pope Leo XIV would say much about the new leader of the universal Catholic Church and the future of *Traditionis custodes*. Pope Francis's document had cruelly and almost mockingly given the illusion that he was committed to guarding tradition. The hope is that Francis's successor, Leo XIV, will actually do just that.

In the interim, there was soon an update to this unfolding story: once Bishop Martin's actions exploded, going practically viral on the internet, they just as quickly met the pause button. On June 3, the *Catholic News Herald*, the official diocesan newspaper of Charlotte, reported that Bishop Martin had suddenly delayed his plan to restrict the TLM. He said that he would shift a decision date from July 8 (the original date for when his plan would go into effect) to October 2. Martin suddenly seemed much more interested in genuine dialogue. "I want to listen to the concerns of these parishioners and their priests, and I am willing to give them more time to absorb these changes," said Bishop Martin. He added that if the Holy See decided to make changes to the restrictions on the TLM (or how he perceived those restrictions), he was willing to "abide by those instructions."[18]

It was a very interesting reversal. Had Pope Leo and the Vatican intervened to effect this change of heart from Bishop Michael Martin? He did not say.

The story would continue to develop.

DEALING WITH *TRADITIONIS CUSTODES*

Even before the Bishop Michael Martin blowup in Charlotte, major Church figures were already openly questioning the future of *Traditionis custodes* and hoping that the new pope would do something to heal this Francis wound and bring unity back to the Catholic faithful. The wound had become an oozing sore.

At the start of the year, in January 2025, the highly respected Cardinal Robert Sarah had decried "the plan to definitively abolish the traditional Tridentine Mass, a rite that dates back to St Gregory the Great, a liturgy that is 1,600 years old, a Mass celebrated by so many saints: St Padre Pio, St Philip Neri, St John Mary Vianney: the Curé of Ars, St Francis de Sales, St Josemaria Escrivá, etc. And all the way back to Pope Gregory the Great (590–604) and even to Pope Damasus (366–384). This project, if it is true, seems to me to be an insult to the history of the Church and to Sacred Tradition, a diabolical project that seeks to break with the Church of Christ, the Apostles and the Saints."[19]

And yet, some forces in the Church seemed hell-bent on just that. They targeted the traditional Mass and those who preferred it, escalating their attack through that winter and spring.

Mere days after Leo's election, German Cardinal Gerhard Ludwig Müller said of the divisions caused by Pope Francis in targeting traditionalists: "We cannot absolutely condemn or forbid the legitimate right and form of the Latin liturgy." Saying he was optimistic about Pope Leo's very different temperament and character, he said of the new pope: "I think he is able to speak with people and to find a very good solution that is good with everybody."[20]

Cardinal Müller said of Pope Leo: "I am convinced that he will overcome these superfluous tensions [that were] damaging for the Church. We cannot avoid all the conflicts, but we have to avoid the not necessary conflicts, the superfluous conflicts."

The Francis conflict with traditionalists and the TLM was not only unjust but unnecessary. In fact, what had made it so unjust was precisely that it had been so unnecessary. The Argentinian pontiff had targeted one of the most worshipful blocks of Catholic faithful, certainly in the West and the United States. They and even many who did not prefer the TLM scratched their heads at the conflict that Francis desired with them. Why was this self-proclaimed pope of "mercy" and "Who am I to judge?" pursuing them so mercilessly and judgmentally?

The likes of Cardinal Müller hoped that with Leo this sort of unnecessary acrimony launched from the Chair of St. Peter would now stop.

Also hopeful was Singapore Cardinal William Goh, who had said after Pope Leo's election that he had seen "no reason" for Pope Francis to have tried to "stop people who prefer the Tridentine Mass." These people "are not doing anything wrong or sinful," contrary to Francis's judgment of them. Like many defenders of those who prefer the TLM, Goh said, "I do not personally celebrate the Tridentine Mass, but I am not opposed to those who do."[21]

Goh pointed to a small group of around 300 people in his country, mostly professionals, who celebrate such a Mass. Unlike Francis, Goh sought genuine dialogue and understanding with these people, meeting with them and asking them why they prefer the traditional Mass. They told him that they find the Tridentine Mass "more reflective and contemplative" and said that it brings them "closer to God." Thus, figured Goh, "Why should I stop them?" He found that they were not rejecting the teachings of Vatican II or doing anything else that required disciplinary action and therefore felt: "I do not think we should discriminate against them." "After all," continued Goh, "this is the Mass that has been celebrated for hundreds of years."[22]

Goh insisted that "the unity of the Church must be preserved," understanding that Francis had been generating anything but his claimed call for unity by instead creating discord and disunity with traditionalists. Goh was hopeful that Leo, a man with "a solid foundation in the tradition and spirituality of St. Augustine," would be more respectful of people who respect tradition.

Agreeing with Goh is San Francisco Archbishop Salvatore Cordileone, who said that "lifting restrictions" on the traditional Mass would be "grand, healing, and unifying."[23]

In a piece aptly titled, "Pope Leo Faces an Early Challenge: How to Deal with Pope Francis' Restrictions on the Latin Mass," Edward

Pentin surveyed a number of Church officials and Catholic writers and theologians exploring the options of what might be done in the wake (or earthquake) of *Traditionis custodes*. He quoted Peter Kwasniewski, who lamented that the chaos under Francis, particularly the lack of continuity on the traditional Mass from the prior pontificates, had left no other option than to "openly reverse" the Francis *motu proprio*. Both Kwasniewski and Catholic writer Amy Wellborn said that Leo could also simply say that he was restoring the prior policy of Pope Benedict XVI's *Summorum Pontificum*.[24]

Still others were less optimistic. They fear that Francis's "war of annihilation against traditionalism" was so deep that "peace" will not return anytime soon.

Kwasniewski is skeptical that unity can be achieved, given the "depth of hatred for tradition" thriving among "a certain generation and a certain type of progressive."[25]

Francis had fed that hatred and fanned the flames. The hatred had been consigned to mere ashes, and at most smoldering embers, when Cardinal Jorge Mario Bergoglio was elected in March 2013. The liberal Catholics were growing old with their parishes, which, like them, were dying out. But even as they faded, their dislike for conservative Catholics remained alive. Francis invigorated their worst impulses, giving them a weapon with *Traditionis custodes* to use against the younger Catholic families that they had driven out of their parishes with their liturgical abuses; bad music; irreverence toward the Eucharist; rejection of natural family planning, embrace of birth control and same-sex marriage, and desire for female priests and deacons; removal of altar rails and incense; and steady annihilation of tradition. When those families (often veiled) fled for more traditional churches, the Catholic progressives blamed anyone but themselves. They directed their anger at these "rigid" "fundamentalists." *Traditionis custodes* gave them a cudgel to chase after their foes who peacefully sought safe haven elsewhere.

For those 1970s Catholics, the desire to discriminate against these opponents remains strong. Whether *Traditionis custodes* will survive them remains to be seen. Again, much will depend on Pope Leo XIV, a reality emerging ever more clearly day by day.

DETROIT'S DESTROYER OF TRADITION

Indeed, the stark reality is that the Catholic Church's anti-traditionalist ideologues were forcing Pope Leo's hand almost immediately into his pontificate.

Shortly after the Bishop Martin blowup in Charlotte, another liberal bishop took extreme steps to limit the TLM in the Diocese of Detroit, where the traditional rite was being practiced in thriving parishes of packed pews and large families. Invoking phrases like "unity," "diversity," "spiritual richness"—and the spirit of Francis's *Traditionis custodes*—Detroit Archbishop Edward Weisenburger sent out a June 13 letter ordering a crackdown on TLM celebrations in his diocese.[26]

The archbishop's letter began with a tease, as if he was not restricting the TLM: "As there are a number of the faithful in our local Church who have found spiritual richness in this form of the Mass," said the archbishop, "I am permitting it to continue in accord with the Holy See's parameters." He thus said that beginning July 1, 2025, the Traditional Latin Mass would be offered at St. Joseph Shrine in Detroit in the Central Region and three nonparish churches in each additional region of the Archdiocese of Detroit. But that would be it. As TLM worshippers knew, this was a restriction, not an expansion or protection. Weisenburger put the hammer down: "Permission for this celebration at all other sites will expire on June 30, 2025."

The archbishop framed his decision as an act of benevolence for "unity" among his flock, insisting: "I take seriously my charge to care for all the faithful and am confident that this new arrangement is faithful to the Church's law while expressing my concern for your spiritual welfare."

As for those whose spiritual welfare was thriving at the TLM sites to be closed by the archbishop in two and a half weeks, they could go back to a parish in their neighborhood where the reverence had been so lacking that the pews had gone empty.

Since the death of Francis, Weisenburger had become increasingly strident in his ideological colonization of his diocese. A few weeks after his TLM decree, Weisenburger fired three of the most popular, respected, veteran faculty members of the Sacred Heart Seminary in Detroit. The suspicion was that he fired them because he disagrees with their theological views and because they had criticized Pope Francis.

"Archbishop Weisenburger told me that he was terminating my position at the seminary effective immediately," said one of the fired professors, Ralph Martin. "When I asked him for an explanation, he said he didn't think it would be helpful to give any specifics but mentioned something about having concerns about my theological perspectives."[27]

When asked to explain the firings, Weisenburger, Francis-like, gave no response. When asked for an explanation by a reporter from *Our Sunday Visitor*, the diocese's communications director said only that "the Archdiocese of Detroit does not comment on archdiocesan or seminary personnel matters."[28]

No doubt, the progressive bishop took this action, too, in the name of "unity" and "diversity."

One of the fired faculty members told the press that he was seeking legal counsel over the dismissal. The actions of Detroit's bishop had now resulted in a very public lawsuit in his diocese. In the name of "unity."

With their decrees, bishops like Weisenburger in Detroit and Martin in Charlotte seemed to be almost taunting the new pope, challenging him, getting more aggressive in their implementation of Francis's crackdown on traditionalists in the weeks after the pope's death. Weisenburger had concluded his letter to his flock by saying (with no irony intended) that he was "impressed by the rich expressions of the Catholic faith in southeast Michigan," even as he was restricting it for traditional expressions that had been practiced by Catholic believers for centuries. He called upon his flock to show its "fidelity to Christ, [which] is only possible if we remain faithful to the Church, under the leadership of our Pope and the local bishop."

Well, the pope was no longer Francis but Leo. What would he do?

FRANCIS'S LEGACY OF FISSURES, BATTLE LINES, AND LEAKS

This chaos was a predictable legacy of Pope Francis's actions. Well after his death, the mess was not over. Far from it. Like an undetonated hand grenade left on the battlefield, the *motu proprio* was set to explode even at a time when everyone wanted peace again. The groundwork had been laid for further detonations to come. Liberal bishops were ready for combat. Battle lines that formed under Pope Francis were now facing off under Pope Leo.

One person springing into action was Cardinal Raymond Leo Burke, long an advocate for traditionalists. He could see what was happening. And he spoke to the new pope about it.

On June 14, Burke addressed a London conference organized by The Latin Mass Society of England and Wales. Speaking via streaming video from Rome, Burke shared with attendees his hope that the new pontiff will "put an end to the persecution" of faithful Catholics who prefer to celebrate Mass using the "more ancient usage" of the Roman liturgy. "I certainly have already had occasion to express that to the Holy Father," said the prefect emeritus of the

Apostolic Signatura. "It is my hope that he will, as soon as is reasonably possible, take up the study of this question." He added: "It is my hope [Leo will] even continue to develop what Pope Benedict XVI had so wisely and lovingly legislated for the Church."[29]

Burke did not elaborate on details, including what Leo XIV said in response to his request. But it was clear that Leo would soon face a decision on *Traditionis custodes*. Church progressives were ensuring it.

Burke himself began to organize traditional Masses. He announced in late July that his Shrine of Our Lady of Guadalupe in La Crosse, Wisconsin, would mark its coming 17th anniversary with a special "Mass of the Americas." This would be a solemn pontifical Mass in the traditional Latin rite, which Burke would concelebrate with Archbishop Salvatore Cordileone of San Francisco. Joining them as homilist for the Mass would be Cardinal Willem Jacobus Eijk, archbishop of Utrecht in the Netherlands.

Further, in a particularly remarkable move, Burke announced that he would be celebrating a special Solemn Pontifical Mass at St. Peter's Basilica in Rome on October 25, 2025. This would constitute a return to the prior custom—an annual Summorum Pontificum pilgrimage of Catholics devoted to the high Latin Mass—that had been axed by Pope Francis since 2022. The presiding bishop does the special Mass from the Altar of the Chair of St. Peter. In 2023 and 2024, the Summorum Pontificum group followed Francis's guidelines in making a request to the Vatican to receive authorization to continue celebrating the Mass. The request was rejected.[30] Under the new pontiff, however, it was not rejected. Pope Leo gave permission for the Pontifical Mass.[31] Pope Leo issued no statement, but quietly approved of Burke's action.

Clearly, traditionalists like Cardinal Burke are hoping to hold their ground against destroyers of traditions such as Weisenburger and Martin, and with the new pope's blessing.

Amid these fissures, something extraordinary happened, a striking indictment of Francis.

Adding to the drama, on June 30, a day after Pope Leo XIV celebrated a beautiful and highly traditional Mass on the Solemnity of Saints Peter and Paul at St. Peter's Basilica, replete with Latin and rich with the traditional trappings of the Church, journalist Diane Montagna dropped a bombshell, releasing an exclusive report quickly picked up by media worldwide, including secular sources from ABC News to the Associated Press, who could smell a foul cover-up.[32]

Leaked to Montagna were Vatican documents that suggested Pope Francis had not been truthful (or was somehow misled) about the results of a strange 2020 Vatican survey of bishops that he had felt compelled to commission on the Latin Mass. Francis had claimed that the subsequent 224-page report showed widespread disunity and dissatisfaction caused by the TLM, thus demanding and requiring him to intervene and provide restrictions. This led Francis to insist that he reluctantly needed to suddenly reverse one of the signature liturgical legacies and successes of his predecessor's (Pope Benedict XVI's) papacy. "The responses reveal a situation that preoccupies and saddens me, and persuades me of the need to intervene," Francis contended.[33]

But in truth, as Montagna reported, the majority of bishops surveyed in the report were fine with the TLM and in fact had warned Francis that restricting it would "do more harm than good." Montagna's posts leaked from the Vatican included a five-page "overall assessment" of the survey findings, which had been put together by Francis's own Congregation for the Doctrine of the Faith, plus a seven-page compilation of quotes from both individual bishops and bishops' conferences.

Those reading Montagna's posts agreed that what Francis had claimed was not accurate.

As the Associated Press reported, "The documents posted online, however, paint a different picture. They suggest the majority of bishops who responded to the Vatican survey had a generally favorable view of Benedict's reform and warned that suppressing or weakening it would lead traditionalist Catholics to leave the church and join schismatic groups." The bishops warned that any changes "would seriously damage the life of the church, as it would recreate the tensions that the document had helped to resolve."[34]

The reality was that the Church's bishops shared the widespread view that the TLM parishes were doing plenty of good. They were producing vocations among their young families and were drawing young Catholics to the "sacredness, seriousness and solemnity of the liturgy."

But that was not how Francis portrayed his survey, which, revealingly, he did not share publicly. He painted a grim, dour picture and expressed the need to intervene immediately and issue a crackdown on traditional communities. He hence did so with *Traditionis custodes*.

Diane Montagna's bombshell disclosure revealed how disingenuous if not dishonest the entire Francis effort had been. The pope of dialogue and synodality had taken an action that went contrary to the views of his bishops.

For the record, Montagna's unsettling revelation was unfortunately not unthinkable in what it suggested about Francis. It had been widely suspected that Pope Francis had manipulated the 2014 synod on marriage and family, to the point that whole books were written on the suspected rigging.[35] Cardinal George Pell was so incensed by what he was witnessing that he reportedly slammed his fist on the table and exclaimed, "You must stop manipulating this Synod!"[36]

Accurately or not, the pope had been accused of manipulating his synod reports in 2014. Might he have done so again with his 2020 survey on traditionalists?

Francis aside, by the summer of 2025, there was a new pope in town—Leo XIV. How would he react to Montagna's revelation? Would he seek to resolve this injustice that was done under his predecessor?

Much is yet to come. This is an ugly mess that Leo must deal with.

RESCINDING OR REFINING FIDUCIA SUPPLICANS

Traditionis custodes was not the only Francis document to create chaos among the faithful worldwide. Pope Leo is also forced to deal with Pope Francis's mess with *Fiducia supplicans*, the Christmas 2023 "declaration" allowing blessings of same-sex couples.

At first, the LGBTQ lobby and sympathetic Church officials were ecstatic with the document created by Francis and his right-hand man, Cardinal Tucho Fernández. The likes of Fr. James Martin jumped right into the water by immediately blessing legally married homosexual men in Manhattan the very day the document was issued.[37]

But wait—did *Fiducia supplicans* permit that? Did it bless and, thereby, perhaps condone and even approve of "gay marriages" or at least "same-sex couples?" What did it mean to "bless?" Could the Vatican's new "dicastery" clarify? Would it? It made muddled attempts that only seemed to make things messier.[38]

In short order, no one, from the most progressive, pro-gay-marriage German prelates to the most theologically orthodox conservative African clergy, had a clear understanding of what Francis and Fernández were trying to do with *Fiducia supplicans*, especially as their document boasted "a broadening and enrichment of the classical understanding of blessings." Every Fernández follow-up semi-clarification merely served to muddy the waters more. The

African hierarchy flat out said publicly that it was going to ignore the same-sex blessings edict, and Francis seemed to oblige them, contradicting whether the blessings were now universal Church teaching or policy. As for Fr. Martin's actions, the Vatican made no public rebuke. It did not say no to what Martin did. Were his actions valid?

More and more questions were raised, and answers yet again seemed unclear and unsatisfying to all. No one was happy. Everyone, whether "pro" or "anti" or indifferent, was confused.

Few people inside and outside the Church, including advocates in the LGBTQ community and among gay activist priests, fully understood *Fiducia supplicans*. To this day, even the German bishops are divided and battling each other over the blessings.[39] The document stands as a perfect testimony to the mess Francis desired. And as such, the new pope is now compelled to deal with it.

Some conservatives would surely like the new pope to declare the document anathema. But even if Leo XIV wanted to do that, he could not do so without an eruption among liberals, secularists, and the homosexual community. Instead, he is boxed into a position of trying to refine or clarify the document in a way that Francis and his chief handmaiden could not do. If that is possible.

Fr. Gerald Murray calls on Pope Leo XIV to rescind *Fiducia supplicans*. "He needs to roll back *Fiducia supplicans*," says Fr. Murray, a canon lawyer. "The main and principal job of the Roman pontiff is to confirm the brethren in the faith, which means to strengthen them in professing what is true Catholic teaching, not error or innovations that are erroneous and undermine Catholic teaching." Murray adds: "The notion that Pope Francis put forward is that homosexuals who become a 'couple,' which means that they enter into a sexual relationship, that they as 'couples' are blessable by a priest. This is a notion repugnant to Catholic doctrine."[40]

Murray furthered: "We do not bless sin. And the odd thing is, of course, Pope Francis, before *Fiducia supplicans*, a year and a half previously, had authorized a publication of a document from the Congregation of the Doctrine of the Faith saying, 'We do not bless sin,' rejecting pressure for 'blessing' same-sex or homosexual 'couples.' So, you don't have to go too far back to say, 'We're going to return to what the doctrine of the faith said, and we're going to abolish *Fiducia supplicans*.'"

Fr. Murray said that doing this would constitute "an act of real charity, because it's telling people who are in homosexual relationships: 'The Church loves you so much that we're going to rebuke the sin you've entered into to call you to repentance because what's at stake here is your eternal salvation.'"

Of course, advocates of the blessings would never view striking down the document as an act of charity. They would implode at the news. Thus, one would think that Murray's call to rescind *Fiducia supplicans* likely will not happen. Of course, the job of the new pope is to be a pope, not a politician. If the previous pontiff produced error, his successor should fix it. Still, a mess is a mess, and Leo XIV was here handed another hot mess.

And yet, even liberal prelates know that the document at least needs to be clarified by the new pope.

For instance, consider the words of Cardinal Jean-Claude Hollerich, the Jesuit archbishop of Luxembourg who was elevated to cardinal by Francis in 2019, and a leading Church liberal on homosexual issues. He told the Italian press on May 12, shortly after the election of Pope Leo: "About *Fiducia supplicans*, I hypothesize that the new pope could reinterpret but not abolish it. By the way, the Church does not intend to equate same sex unions with marriage. In fact, the declaration places the emphasis on the fact that every person is blessed by God."[41]

One might say that such is indeed the proper interpretation of the document, but the confusion created by Francis and Fernández left that unclear to many throughout the Church (and especially to the media) and opened wide the door for homosexual activists inside the Church to seemingly equate same-sex unions with marriage and to bless the unions/marriages themselves.

Hollerich added: "It is very difficult for the teaching to be removed. It could be readapted, but not annulled."

Perhaps. Hollerich is right that at the least the new pope faces major difficulties should he try to reinterpret and readapt the document and tidy up the mess.

Those difficulties were made manifest when a coalition of 25 Catholic associations on September 15, the feast day of Our Lady of Sorrows, delivered to the Holy Father by courier a "filial appeal" calling on him to "confirm and reaffirm" the Church's perennial teaching on sexuality and to revoke *Fiducia supplicans*.[42] The urgency of the coalition's request was prompted by the mass chaos and confusion sparked by a "Jubilee pilgrimage" to Rome by "LGBTQ+ Catholics" the previous week, which included an official Mass at the Jesuit mother church in Rome on September 6.[43] The resulting media maelstrom had heads spinning everywhere trying to figure out Pope Leo's pre-knowledge of and role in the controversy. Misinformation and manipulation abounded.[44]

The besieged new pontiff found himself in a mess that had started long before he was chosen pope, one neither of his doing nor desiring.[45] It was just one of many yet to come.

REFORMING THE CURIA

An issue of importance to the Holy See, albeit considerably less titillating to the world than matters of faith and morals or culture and sex, is the nonetheless significant bureaucratic matter of reforming the Roman Curia. That is, the Curia that serves as the often inefficient, wasteful, and chronically debt-ridden governing body of the

Holy See. The Vatican financial deficit for 2024, the last full year of Francis's papacy, was $93.3 million. No recent pope, or Vatican official of any stripe, has been able to get a handle on the waste and important task of reforming the Church's central governing body. But here is why Pope Leo XIV might offer some hope.

As noted earlier with the impressive analysis of the Curia by Prof. Giovanni Sadewo, Robert Francis Prevost had a meteoric rise up the ranks of the Roman Curia, with a depth of experience that rapidly surpassed the most seasoned Vatican officials and diplomats, including leading *papabile* candidates such as cardinals Tagle and Secretary of State Parolin. By the end of 2023, this new American cardinal, given the red hat from Pope Francis only as recently as September 2023, already had more shared experience on curial bodies than any other bishop or cardinal in the Holy See.[46]

As for what that experience means for the next pope, Prof. Sadewo concluded his extensive analysis with this assessment of Leo XIV: "Serving in multiple curial bodies also gave him significant influence over Church policies beginning in 2023. He became familiar with the inner workings, dynamics, and politics of the Roman Curia." Sadewo notes that Prevost's institutional knowledge may not run as deep as that of "more entrenched figures" like Cardinal Parolin or Tagle, but surely that is partly a good thing. Indeed, observes Sadewo, Prevost's "relatively brief tenure may have spared him from becoming overly enmeshed in the system." That is no doubt true. And yet, "his wide network provides him with considerable social capital, enhancing his ability to influence and collaborate with other cardinals."

As for what this could perhaps mean for Leo XIV's papacy, Sadewo rightly speculates that Prevost's quickly acquired and broad curial connections could enable him to reform the Curia more effectively than his predecessors. "He possesses enough insider knowledge to understand the system's mechanics," writes Sadewo, "but his recent arrival allows for a level of objectivity that longer-serving members might lack. His relationships with fellow cardinals—developed through shared service—could also make it easier to build consensus and implement necessary changes."

Sadewo notes how this contrasts from popes Francis and John Paul II, who came to the Curia as outsiders. As the newly appointed CEOs of the Curia, so to speak, they attempted to enact curial reforms but did not have good success. Sadewo hopes: "Pope Leo XIV, by contrast, may represent a new type of reformer: one who knows the system intimately but is not bound by it."

That is indeed the case. And early talk around Rome was hopeful that this American could bring more fiscal responsibility and accountability to the Holy See's governing body, as well as moral and spiritual accountability.

To that end, less than a month after Sadewo's article appeared, Pope Leo XIV celebrated Mass for officials of the Roman Curia on the Jubilee of the Holy See, where he called for greater holiness from each and every member. "[T]he best way to serve the Holy See is to strive to be holy," the pope told Curia officials. He said each member should do so "according to his or her state of life and the task entrusted."[47]

For Leo XIV, reforming the Curia was not just some fiscal matter but spiritual, too. A Curia committed to greater holiness "bears witness to the fruitfulness of Mary and the Church." Each official should carry out the work of his Holy See office as best he can "with love and faith."

Reforming the Curia meant also reforming thyself.

Finally, Leo might be a good fit for financially reforming the Curia not only spiritually but mathematically. Remember that Robert Francis Prevost is a mathematician as well as a theologian. He is a numbers person, with an analytical mind. That sort of mindset and ability further distinguishes him and might add to a unique skill set that could perhaps at long last bring some measure of fiscal sanity back to the Curia.

HUMAN DIGNITY, HUMAN TRAFFICKING, AND MODERN FORMS OF SLAVERY

As noted in the chapter on Pope Leo XIII, the current pontiff's namesake was an eloquent voice of conscience on the matter of 19th-century slavery, particularly through encyclicals such as his powerful, poignant May 1888 *In Plurimis*. That Leonine leadership on slavery was picked up by successor popes, such as Pius X, who denounced this "worst of indignities," which fills "our heart with horror" and "great compassion" at something "so cruel and so barbarous as to scourge men and brand them." In February 1992, Pope John Paul II picked up that long line of moral continuity by going to Goree Island, once the epicenter of the source of the West African slave trade, to denounce this "shameful commerce" and "this sin of man against man, this sin of man against God."[48]

Such papal leadership continued under Francis, who sought to rally the world in the early 21st century by calling out human trafficking, child labor, forced prostitution, and modern forms of slavery. His statements on the issue were numerous, including formal papal documents such as *Laudato Si*, *Evangelii Gaudium*, and *Fratelli Tutti*.[49] Francis was superb in this area. It was difficult to find any other leader who had taken a firmer lead on the issue on the global stage.

For Leo XIV, this is a major opportunity, as these evils persist—shown vividly in influential modern films such as the unexpected 2023 blockbuster *The Sound of Freedom*. As Leo XIV seeks continuity from Francis and other predecessors, and certainly from Leo XIII as well, he could hoist this torch to shed light on this ongoing scourge against humanity. Among matters of basic human dignity and respect for the human person, here is an old one that sadly resonates into the 21st century.

Similarly, Leo XIV can pick up from his namesake (as well as John Paul II) the commitment to opposing socialism and communism, an area where Pope Francis failed or seemed largely unconcerned, most saliently in regard to China and also nations like Nicaragua and Venezuela. No ideology in history has killed as many people as communism. Like slavery and human trafficking, this a major matter of human dignity.

UNDERSTANDING THE REAL PRESENCE

At the time of the writing of this book, Leo XIV has not acknowledged the dismal, tragic reality of substantial majorities of Roman Catholics who do not understand nor even accept and believe one of the central tenets of their faith: the Real Presence of Jesus Christ in the Eucharist.

The data on this is grotesque, revealing a decades-long failure of rudimentary catechesis resulting in an appallingly ignorant laity. An August 2019 Pew Research Center study found that less than one-third of American Catholics (31 percent) believe that "during Catholic Mass, the bread and wine actually become the body and blood of Jesus."[50] Subsequent surveys have found similar abysmal numbers.[51]

The data show that the vast majority of these Catholics reject a core tenet of their faith—one of the Church's seven sacraments. They do not believe what they were taught from the time of their first Holy Communion.

Again, Pope Leo has not (yet) acknowledged this, but one might suspect that his heavily Augustinian focus could well lead him in that direction. Saint Augustine, after all, had some inspiring insights into the Real Presence, certainly known to a son of Augustine and onetime head of the Augustinian order.[52]

"The Lord Jesus wanted those whose eyes were held lest they should recognize Him, to recognize Him in the breaking of the bread," wrote Augustine. "The faithful know what I am saying. They know Christ in the breaking of the bread. For not all bread, but only that which receives the blessing of Christ, becomes Christ's body."[53]

Unfortunately, an embarrassingly high number of self-identified Catholics would be perplexed by what Augustine was saying. They do not recognize Christ in the breaking of the bread. Two thousand years ago, the disciples on the Road to Emmaus recognized Him in the breaking of the bread, and so did their Church henceforth.

One of Saint Augustine's most moving discourses on the Real Presence of Christ in the Eucharist was his analysis of the *Explanations of the Psalms* (ca. 400) 33,1,10. There, Augustine commented on Psalm 119:109.[54]

> "And he was carried in his own hands." But, brethren, how is it possible for a man to do this? Who can understand it? Who is it that is carried in his own hands? A man can be carried in the hands of another; but no one can be carried in his own hands. How this should be understood literally of David, we cannot discover; but we can discover how it is meant of Christ. For Christ was carried in His own hands, when, referring to His own Body, He said: "This is My Body." For He carried that Body in His hands.

According to Augustine, when Jesus held up the bread at the Last Supper, He was holding Himself in His hands. It was a miracle atop a miracle.

And yet, large swaths of Catholic do not believe that such a miracle takes place today in their parishes when their priest, *in persona*

Christi (in the person of Christ), consecrates the host. Of course, their pope most certainly believes it. And perhaps their new pope, Leo XIV—student, scholar, and son of Augustine—can help teach them otherwise and return them to this core doctrine of their Catholic faith.

In that respect, the faithful got an encouraging sign in the opening weeks of Leo XIV's pontificate. In a powerful display, the new pope led the faithful in a Eucharistic procession through the streets of Rome during Corpus Christi Sunday on June 22, 2025. This is the special annual day on the Church liturgical calendar set aside specifically for focused attention on the Real Presence of Christ in the Eucharist. The priest after Mass leads the congregation outside of the parish and through the streets elevating the exposed Eucharist in the monstrance for all to see.

It is an uplifting gesture that rouses the faithful wherever and whenever it is done, dating back to the 13th century. Unfortunately, it is not done in a majority of parishes around the world. Moreover, it has not been consistently done by the Bishop of Rome himself.[55] But Pope Leo XIV quietly did just that. He made no grand announcement, called no press conference, and did not have the Vatican Press office quote him afterward. He simply, silently did it.

Leo led a 45-minute-long procession nearly a mile in 90-degree heat between the basilicas of St. Mary Major and St. John Lateran, the official home diocese of the Bishop of Rome. The pontiff led a massive gathering of 20,000 pilgrims through the streets of Rome, hoisting high a golden monstrance encircled by precious stones. In his homily at St. John Lateran, the pope said that "the procession we are about to take" would be a "sign" to the world that "we will feed on the Blessed Sacrament, adore Him, and carry Him through the streets. In doing so, we will present Him before the eyes, the consciences, and the hearts of the people." They would do this both for "those who do not believe" and for those who believe "that they may believe more firmly."[56]

On that, the son of Augustine quoted Augustine saying that "Christ is truly present" in the bread that the faithful see and consume: the Eucharist "in fact, is the true, real, and substantial presence of the Savior, who transforms bread into Himself in order to transform us into Himself."[57]

This was a meaningful portent of greater emphasis, respect, and reverence for the Real Presence from the new pope. More signs will hopefully come. And hopefully it will rub off on the faithful who are supposed to have faith in the Real Presence of Jesus Christ in the Eucharist.

DOCTRINE UNITES; INDOCTRINATION DIVIDES

It is sometimes asserted in certain Christian circles that "doctrine divides." Doctrine is viewed by some as rigid, narrow. Instead, it is said, churches need more diversity and inclusion in order to be more welcoming to everyone.

As the most diverse institution in the world, the Catholic Church is certainly not against including and welcoming people; the very word "catholic" means "universal." The Catholic Church is present on every continent. Jesus Christ welcomed everyone. But both Christ and the Church understand that the Church has teachings; it has doctrines. These teachings and doctrines provide rules and rails within which human freedom can flourish. Christian freedom is a freedom that acts within the boundaries of the teachings of Christ. Doctrine, in that sense, brings Christians together under Christ, rather than separating them. A Church without doctrine is not really a Church, or at least not a house likely to continue to stand. A house divided against itself eventually falls.

To that end, one of the more telling Leo XIV moments in the first days of his pontificate, even before his formal installation at St. Peter's Square on Sunday, May 18, was a May 17 address he gave at the Vatican to the Centesimus Annus Pro Pontifice Foundation.[58]

As noted earlier, the foundation is named for the 1991 John Paul II encyclical *Centesimus Annus*, released for the centenary of Leo XIII's *Rerum Novarum*. Expectedly, Leo XIV in that address spoke of his predecessor's classic 1891 encyclical, but he more specifically spoke to the matter of doctrine and its vital importance—including its *unifying* importance. He told the group to uphold the Church's social doctrine for the purpose of building bridges to other communities and bringing everyone together. He said: "Let us help one another, as I said on the evening of my election, 'to build bridges through dialogue and encounter, joining together as one people, always at peace.'"

Doctrine unites, said Leo, whereas *indoctrination* divides. "Indoctrination is immoral," said the Holy Father. "It stifles critical judgement and undermines the sacred freedom of respect for conscience, even if erroneous." Doctrine has the opposite effect, when done properly and thoughtfully with care and rigor. Said Leo: "Doctrine, on the other hand, as a serious, serene and rigorous discourse, aims to teach us primarily how to approach problems and, even more importantly, how to approach people."

Leo said that he understands that for many people in the contemporary world, the words "dialogue" and "doctrine" seem incompatible. When they hear the word "doctrine," they think of a restrictive set of ideas "belonging to a religion." And yet, said, Leo, "In the case of the Church's social doctrine, we need to make clear that the word 'doctrine' has another, more positive meaning, without which dialogue itself would be meaningless."

For two opposing sides to sit down together to dialogue and build bridges toward one another, they must first acknowledge their differences. Doctrine clarifies those differences. You do not build bridges by falsely claiming with fake, feel-good language that two opposite sides are the same, knowing that they are not. You build bridges by accepting differences and sometimes simply agreeing to disagree. But without doctrine, there is no definition nor knowledge of the differences.

Doctrine thus allows for genuine dialogue. Today's world is rife with an impoverished dialogue that instead turns into shouting. Leo stated: "There is so little dialogue around us; shouting often replaces it, not infrequently in the form of fake news and irrational arguments proposed by a few loud voices. Deeper reflection and study are essential, as well as a commitment to encounter and listen to the poor, who are a treasure for the Church and for humanity."

Here was Leo XIV, very much in the footsteps of his Leonine predecessor, as well as previous popes and the Magisterium of the Church, emphasizing that the Catholic Church needs doctrine. This student of canon law knows well the importance of careful thought and discernment, for which doctrine provides the rules and rails.

The new pope concluded his talk to the Centesimus Annus Pro Pontifice Foundation by quoting the Vatican II document *Gaudium et Spes*: "in every age, the Church carries the responsibility of reading the signs of the times and of interpreting them in the light of the Gospel, if she is to carry out her task. In language intelligible to every generation, she should be able to answer the ever-recurring questions which people ask about the meaning of this present life and of the life to come, and how one is related to the other."

Again, Church doctrine helps that process and task. It unifies rather than divides. It allows for true dialogue.

"In our day," Leo finished, "there is a widespread thirst for justice, a desire for authentic fatherhood and motherhood, a profound longing for spirituality, especially among young people and the marginalized, who do not always find effective means of making their needs known. There is a growing demand for the Church's social doctrine, to which we need to respond."

Leo's recognition of this is something that the cardinals of the Catholic Church themselves recognized, and wanted in the next pope, badly so. An example is Singapore Cardinal William Goh, who went so far as to say that he believed that Leo "is exactly the pope the world needs right now." Specifically, he believes that Leo will be able to resolve the doctrinal disputes that had become so "ambiguous" under Francis. That includes the divisions inside and outside the Church on "certain issues, such as marriage, LGBTQ+ rights, and transgender rights. These issues have divided the Church because, at a certain point, it became unclear what the right thing to do was." Goh noted that "people came to the Church and said, 'But the pope said this.'" Goh hoped that Leo (unlike Francis) "will not be ambiguous and will not leave the interpretation of his words open to individual interpretation."[59]

Cardinal Goh affirmed that the Church cannot proceed "without unity in doctrines."[60] Goh is hopeful that Leo "will clarify doctrine." In that way and more, Goh concluded: "I believe Leo XIV is the right man for the job."[61]

Echoing Cardinal Goh is the distinguished Catholic historian and Pope John Paul II biographer George Weigel. When asked the day after Leo's selection what his hopes were for the new papacy, Weigel went to several of the items noted in this chapter, from doctrinal clarity to reforming Church governance in the Curia. He called for "Clarity of doctrinal and moral teaching, good governance, thoughtful appointments to the episcopacy and the College of Cardinals, encouragement of missionary discipleship, and defense of persecuted Christians."

All these things, said Weigel, would "flow from a bold witness to Christ." Pointing to the sainted Polish pope—his papal subject, John Paul II—who had urged the world to "be not afraid," Weigel added: "the best thing this pope, or any pope, can do is follow the example of John Paul II and summon people to a fearlessness that transcends partisanship and narrow nationalism and that calls aggression and evil for what they are."[62]

John Paul II was not afraid to call evil just that. Leo likewise has not shirked from that call. In his first statement from the Loggia, after wishing everyone peace, Leo XIV exhorted the faithful: "God loves us, God loves you all, and evil will not prevail." On May 11, his first Sunday as pope, Leo offered an extemporaneous homily at the Mass he celebrated at the tomb of St. Peter, where he urged the flock: "Take courage! Without fear! Many times in the Gospel Jesus says: 'Do not be afraid.'"

The doctrines of the Church tell us that evil exists and that the faithful must resist it. It is a truth of the faith.

This desire for truth in clarity as well as charity also seems very Augustinian of Leo. Robert Royal of *The Catholic Thing* says that, "among the many encouraging signs that he's already given as pope," Leo's Augustinian commitment to finding "order, meaning, truth, and peace as individuals and in our common lives together, no merely human scheme—no science, psychology, self-help regime, politics, economics, diplomacy, or cultural renewal—will give us what only God Himself can give. That's exactly what our sad and confused times most need to hear."[63]

Finally, another early sign of this commitment to doctrinal clarity came with the unexpected but highly welcomed announcement by Leo on July 31 that he would be declaring St. John Henry Newman a doctor of the Church. There have only been 37 doctors, and now Newman is the 38th.

Newman is hailed for works such his *Apologia Pro Vita Sua* and *The Idea of a University*. It was Pope Leo XIII who had made Newman a cardinal in 1879, early in his papacy, in recognition of his contributions to the Church. Among them were his crucial if not brilliant insights into the development of doctrine, particularly amid the turmoil and travails of the modern world.

Perhaps it is a good sign for doctrinal clarity that the first doctor of the Church named by Pope Leo XIV is a Church figure extolled for his thinking on doctrine.

BRINGING UNITY, BRINGING HEALING

A theme throughout this book has been the need for the new pope to bring unity to a Catholic Church scarred by Pope Francis, the most divisive pope in modern times. This is something that weighed heavily on the cardinals as they headed into the conclave and was a major reason for their quick and overwhelming pick of Cardinal Robert Francis Prevost. The new pope got the message. In fact, he need not be told. He knew intuitively, by nature and attitude, why he was selected. The desire for peace was and remains high on the new pope's mind. Little else needs to be said beyond this: the first word from the mouth of Leo XIV on the Loggia on May 8 was "peace."

That salient message has been noted many times in this book, and it bears repeating in its final pages.

"Peace be with all of you," Leo had wished. The crowd, theretofore silent at the spectacle of this largely unknown man perched above them, cheered. After 12 years of a pope who had sown discord and division, peace is what everyone wanted. And within the first minutes and hours if not days and weeks of Leo's papacy, there was widespread optimism that this pope would be an improvement. At the least, it appeared that he was making it a priority to bring unity and healing.

"How much can we glean about the young pontificate of Pope Leo XIV?" asked Fr. Brian A. Graebe on Pentecost Sunday, June 8,

2025, a month after Leo stepped onto the Loggia. "Early signs may not be definitive, but they can be suggestive. . . . In his first remarks from the balcony of St. Peter's Basilica on the day of his election, Pope Leo spoke of walking together 'as a united Church.'"[64]

In an article title, "A Time to Heal," Fr. Graebe further noted that in Leo's inaugural Mass on May 18, he had exhorted: "Brothers and sisters, I would like that our first great desire be for a united Church, a sign of unity and communion, which becomes a leaven for a reconciled world." Resonating from that inaugural Mass was the message that the pope, like the St. Peter he succeeds, is tasked by Jesus to "strengthen the brethren" in the faith. Thus, noted Fr. Graebe, "Catholics rightly look to the pope as a voice of creedal clarity and a bulwark against confusion and distortion." And yet, "The preceding pontificate was marked by unprecedented doctrinal confusion. Certainly, there has been confusion and error since the earliest days of the Church; what was different was that the confusion came from the pope himself."

What was worse, as Fr. Graebe noted, "Pope Francis seemed to revel in studied ambiguity: not explicitly changing Church teaching (which he had no authority to do anyway) but winking at those who would like him to."

Fr. Graebe gave this example: "Can a priest bless a same-sex couple, or simply bless individuals who happen to form a same-sex couple? Can something that touches so closely on the Church's understanding of marriage and human sexuality be permitted in Germany but forbidden in Nigeria?"

Pope Francis, as well as his doctrinal chief, fellow Argentinian Jesuit Victor Manuel "Tucho" Fernández, seemed to not want to give an answer. In the end, both sides, if not all sides, suffered from the ambiguity, from the pontiff's desire to "make a mess of things." And when Francis said that he wanted a mess, he said so with a laugh. But the chaos was not funny, and the faithful were not amused. The lost sheep wanted answers from their shepherd who, above all, was supposed to lead them rather than lose them.

As Fr. Graebe lamented, "Pope Francis had little regard for such questions, and his biggest fans were always those most eager to see the Church capitulate to the secular *zeitgeist*. Combined with a certain harshness, especially against those drawn to the Church's most ancient forms of worship, Pope Francis left behind a deeply divided and wounded Church."

The only people benefitting from these rifts were the Church's enemies, committed not to the abiding beliefs of Roman Catholicism but to the blowing winds of the prevailing *zeitgeist*. Francis's biggest fans were often the very people who would never darken a parish pew, no matter how much the Church changed to their shifting whims and fancies. Their desire was not to build it up but to tear it down. Radical secularists relished the mess.

Early indications are that Pope Leo XIV desires to be different. As Fr. Graebe notes, Francis's successor from the start has displayed a "more subtle savviness, and his calls for unity are not lost on those who have felt left out in the cold," particularly traditionalists. Leo's "serene and confident demeanor, unafraid to embrace the external signs of an office larger than himself, suggests to many Catholics that he is aware of their suffering and wishes to heal the family rift."

A remedy to the rifts is not some arbitrary collection of dogmas, but doctrine expressed with clarity and charity. Doctrine, done right and in truth itself—in Truth Himself—unites rather than divides, brings harmony rather than discord, enlightens rather than excludes.

Pope Benedict XVI frequently spoke of what he called the "hermeneutic of continuity." Fr. Graebe cleverly observes that *unity* (grounded in proper continuity) may prove to be the "hermeneutic key" to understanding Leo XIV. Remember Leo XIV's episcopal/papal motto from his mentor, St. Augustine: *In illo Uno unum* ("We are one in the One").

As Fr. Graebe notes, it was "nothing short of remarkable" that the largest and most diverse conclave in history—bitterly divided going in—needed only four ballots to elect Robert Francis Prevost as the 267th pope. Cardinals from every corner of the world, and across the spectrum of a divided Church, albeit guided by the Holy Spirit, "took less than 24 hours to elect this man as the visible source of unity in the one Church." And thus is Leo's challenge, and our hope: "To unify the Catholic Church as quickly as he unified the Cardinals in the Sistine Chapel."

Now is the time. It is, says Fr. Graebe, a time to heal.

BRING REAL PEACE

For the Holy Father, this means above all bringing real peace to the Church and truly, genuinely listening—not just empty talk about listening. Pope Francis claimed to want to listen, to desire diversity, and yet often refused to answer critics or merely those who legitimately raised questions seeking clarification of unclear statements that puzzled the faithful. Instead, he sometimes vilified individuals in harsh terms as "Pharisees," as "wicked," "rigid fundamentalists," as "whitened sepulchers." His response to the likes of Cardinal Raymond Leo Burke was to punish them. The Bergoglian persecution of persons like Burke surely alarmed nearly every reasonable person at the Holy See for its apparent vituperation, utterly unbecoming of a pope. Popes should exude kindness, love, and mercy—faith, hope, and charity.

A pontiff who genuinely wants peace and unity will reach out to and break bread with such individuals with a real desire to listen.

So far under Pope Leo XIV, this appears to be happening. It was telling that about six weeks into his papacy, Leo quietly paused to do something unexpected in the case of Cardinal Burke. He wrote a June 17 letter—in Latin—thanking Burke for 50 years of priestly ministry, "for the prompt service" that he had "zealously carried out and the earnest care" he had "demonstrated most especially for the law, which has also been of good service to the dicasteries of the Apostolic See." He commended Burke for having "preached the precepts of the Gospel according to the heart of Christ" and for "diligently offering devoted service to the Church universal."

That 50th anniversary for Burke was June 29, but Leo's note of appreciation was sent well ahead of that. The new pope evidently learned about the upcoming anniversary and moved early. Burke was pleased by the gesture, stating emphatically: "Praised be Jesus Christ! I am very humbled to have received this letter from His Holiness, Pope Leo XIV. . . . Please join me in thanking Our Lord for the election of Pope Leo XIV, Successor of Saint Peter, as the Shepherd of the Church throughout the world." Burke asked the flock to "please pray" for Pope Leo XIV "that Our Lord . . . will grant him abundant wisdom, strength, and courage to do all that Our Lord is asking of Him in these tumultuous times. May God bless Pope Leo and grant him many years. *Viva il Papa!*"[65]

The whole exchange was emblematic of the marked shift in the Chair of St. Peter. The letter only became known when Burke several weeks letter (on July 8) posted it on his official X account. Several reports then followed in Catholic media.[66] The discreet, workmanlike way in which Leo XIV went about doing this was very much in keeping with his demeanor. His olive branch to Burke was a sign of a new tone and sincere peace seeking.

AVOIDING POLARIZATION AMID THE MINEFIELDS

Leo himself soon made clear that this new tone and attitude were very intentional. In one of his first major interviews, the new pontiff underscored his desire to avoid polarization. Speaking to Elise Ann Allen of *Crux*, Leo XIV described himself as "someone who has a deep appreciation for humanity" and who also has an "ability to sit with other people and recognize the goodness in them." The pontiff said: "I know how to listen, I believe, quite well. When I am with people, I respect everyone's point of view, but then I also reach a point with them, when it is possible, to say, 'We have to make a decision here, friends. Somehow, let's try to unite everyone's ideas.' It's not only about compromise. . . . It's about looking ahead and bringing the people with you as you do it." Leo stated: "I'm not a lone ranger, I never have been. It's the way to build this sense of 'we're in this together,' and, again, respect for every member of the group, of the Church, of the community."[67]

When asked about the sexually divisive issues facing the Church, Leo told Allen that in the "back of my mind" was a comment from a cardinal from the East who lamented that the Western world is "fixated, obsessed with sexuality." On such issues, said the pontiff, "I'm trying to not continue to polarize." He does not want to "promote polarization in the Church."

No doubt, the protracted period of polarization must end. To that end, a prediction: Leo's desire to bring harmony in the post-Francis era, often through compromise, will at times be messy, sometimes for better but sometimes for worse. Francis dropped minefields everywhere. He also poisoned the well with much of the laity. Huge numbers of Catholics (especially in America) are conditioned to now assume the worst from their pope. Their period of patience and goodwill is over, thoroughly exhausted by Francis, to the detriment of his successor; they have a short fuse, with a hair-trigger reaction ready to launch on the new pontiff. We always knew that whoever followed Francis would be assuming an enormous challenge, particularly in trying to restore unity. Many examples of this will emerge, and some have already reared their ugly head. Here are just two examples as this book goes to press:

Pope Leo had two bad weeks in late September and early October 2025 directly resulting from residual effects of Francis. First, he faced a debacle created by Francis ally Cardinal Blase Cupich, who outrageously offered a lifetime achievement award to pro-abortion U.S. Senator Dick Durbin (D-IL), whose anti-life actions have been so egregious that he has long been denied the Eucharist in his own diocese by Bishop Thomas Paprocki. The American bishops have long adhered to a policy of not granting awards to pro-life politicians. The liberal Cupich flatly ignored that policy in awarding his fellow liberal, Sen. Durbin. Cupich did not consult his brother bishops. They quickly protested his action, as did the laity. A petition rapidly gained tens of thousands of signatures. When Pope Leo was asked about this by a reporter (on the run), he conceded that he was not "terribly familiar with the particular case." He subsequently showed just that by providing a response that caused an uproar in the American Church that he was hoping to heal.[68] Durbin ultimately responded by declining the award, but the damage to the new pope was done.

The next week, Pope Leo released his first apostolic exhortation, *Dilexi te*, which was on a Francis-like topic: poverty. In fact, the document had been drafted by Francis and sounded like him from start to finish. Like other new popes, Leo honored his predecessor by releasing his final document. Leo reportedly made some edits. Once again, critics erupted, claiming that Leo was no different than Francis and, in fact, "Francis II."

In truth, of course, Leo is different from Francis. Nonetheless, in his attempts to reach compromise and unity post-Francis, bringing all sides together, Leo inevitably will not make everyone happy as he navigates the minefields. He will continue to step on more than a few. Each time he does, the Church will erupt again. Ending polarization post-Francis will be exceedingly difficult.

Every day and every hour at every Mass in every parish around the world, the presiding priest—operating *in persona Christi*, in accordance with the Holy Father and one, holy, catholic, and apostolic Church—offers the Communion Rite. There, he invokes Jesus Christ, who said to His Apostles, "Peace I leave you, my peace I give you." (John 14:27) He asks that "peace and unity" be granted to Christ's Church. He then says to the faithful, "The peace of the Lord be with you always." They reply: "And with your spirit." The priest then says: "Let us offer each other the sign of peace."

Such was Pope Leo XIV's first wish from the Loggia.

In the opening months of Leo's papacy, there was a palpable feeling of hope among the faithful that they can once again reasonably expect their Holy Father to provide unity. They were exasperated and exhausted by the mess of things. They hope that Leo XIV will bring clarity and charity to a Church that for 12 years suffered chaos and confusion. The cardinals who elected Leo believe they have chosen a Holy Father who is serene, pensive, firm, listens, will steadily do his job, will not spout off sloppy opinions, and will engage critics rather than ignore or punish them or denounce those he does not like with judgmental invectives.

At long last, it is time to clean up the mess. The hope and prayer is that the first American pontiff, Robert Francis Prevost, is the right man for the job.

To that end, the new pope has a request to the faithful worldwide. It is a wish that Pope Francis had shared. The prior pontiff constantly exhorted the faithful to pray for him, as he would for them. Leo XIV has asked the same. "I ask you to sustain me with your prayer and closeness," requested the pope from the central balcony of St. Peter's Basilica on May 25. Thousands had gathered in St. Peter's Square that Sunday, waving flags from their various home countries and hoisting signs that read "Long live Pope Leo XIV!"[69]

The new pope admitted his own fragility, and that he, too, needed prayer. The shepherd, like his flock, needs to be lifted up.

Let us pray that the first American pontiff, Leo XIV, brings the peace and unity that he and all of us desire.

EPILOGUE

An *American* Postscript

Though this book's title underscores that the new pope is an American pontiff, I have tried to make this biography accessible to readers worldwide. Of course, they surely expected that an American writing on the first American pope would naturally accentuate that element. And no doubt, the biggest surprise about Leo XIV was and remains that he is the first American pontiff. Still, the goal was to make this book first and foremost about the new head of the universal Roman Catholic Church.

The pope is pope to the world.

Nonetheless, I would like to share a few closing thoughts on some quintessentially American aspects of the new pope—some very American insights.

The most famous American Catholic has been Bishop Fulton Sheen (1895–1979), rightly called by one of his biographers "America's Bishop."[1] Sheen was widely beloved. I have written on him at length in articles and books and have been intimately close to his home parish, his museum, and his distinctly American town of Peoria, Illinois. It almost pains those of us who admire Sheen to concede that with the election of Leo XIV, Sheen no longer bears the crown of most influential American Catholic. But alas, such is now the case. Fulton John Sheen passes the torch to Robert Francis Prevost. And Sheen, who Pope John Paul II called a "loyal son of the Church," would have been happy to do so.

It is interesting that both Sheen and Prevost—America's bishop and the American pontiff—come from Illinois. In my 2017 book *A Pope and a President*, which was about John Paul II and Ronald Reagan but had much material on Fulton Sheen, I noted the irony that the two greatest communicators of the 20th century (Reagan was dubbed "the Great Communicator") hailed from small farm towns merely miles apart in northwestern Illinois, the American Midwest, the Heartland. Add Leo to that distinction, growing up in little Dolton, Illinois.

To be sure, Leo does not have Sheen's communications skills (no one does), but he will have a platform far larger than Bishop Sheen ever had. Sheen was incredibly influential on radio and television, but his microphone pales to the megaphone that Leo XIV now possesses. Hopefully, the American pope shall use it well.

Here it should be noted that Leo XIV a few weeks after his installation told a young newly married couple in Rome that Fulton Sheen "had an influence" on him, and that he grew up watching Sheen on television. That young couple, Kristen and Austin Savage, first met at a Sheen-themed event at the Cathedral of St. Mary of the Immaculate Conception in Peoria, the very parish where Sheen had been ordained a priest and that today holds his remains. Kristen and Austin asked the new Holy Father and fellow Illinois native to consider picking up Sheen's cause for canonization that was so oddly and suddenly dropped during the Francis years.

"Venerable Fulton Sheen played a major role in our relationship," said Kristen. "And during our marriage preparation, we always asked for his intercession. So he's always been someone who we wanted to see canonized." And thus, "when I saw the Holy Father, I said, 'We'd really like to see his canonization'—and what better person to plead our cause to than the Holy Father himself?"[2]

What was Pope Leo's response? "The Holy Father did specifically say he would remember what we said," said Kristen. "So that definitely did give us hope for Fulton Sheen's canonization. Maybe we will see it during Pope Leo's pontificate."

Maybe so.

The Sheen period represented a golden era of American Catholicism. It reminds of a remarkable statement by another influential American bishop, John Lancaster Spalding (1840–1916). A cofounder of the Catholic University of America in Washington, DC, Spalding was the first bishop of Peoria (1877–1908), where he encountered a precocious altar boy named Fulton Sheen.

There at that same St. Mary's Cathedral in Peoria, Spalding stunned the boy with a prophetic prediction forecasting big things ahead for him. The eight-year-old altar boy was shaken up after dropping a wine cruet on the floor, which loudly shattered. Rather than scold or further embarrass the child, Bishop Spalding pulled him aside after Mass and predicted that he would one day study at the esteemed Louvain University in Belgium (as Spalding had) and that the boy would one day become a bishop: "someday you will be just as I am."[3]

That was quite the prophecy. But beyond the person of Fulton Sheen, Bishop Spalding also predicted big things for the future of American Catholicism. In 1880, Spalding had forecast: "there are many reasons for thinking that no other religion is so sure of a future here [in America] as the Catholic."[4]

That Spalding prediction might at long last be consummated in this election of the first American pontiff.

Perhaps.

Of course, that depends on what type of pontiff Leo XIV turns out to be. Some on the traditional side might hope that this extraordinary surprise of an American pontiff is a gift to the American Church for its suffering under Francis. Traditional Catholics had been so strong, flourishing, and faithful, and yet Francis targeted them. Could the election of Prevost turn out to be a reward for their suffering? Truly only the Lord knows.

Overall, the tone of this biography has been hopeful, but the author most certainly has no idea how the pontificate of Leo XIV will turn out. Personally, I was very positive about the Francis papacy in its opening months and years and spent the vast majority of his pontificate defending him and not criticizing him in public. Even when I finally decided and agreed (with Cardinal Pell) that his papacy had been a catastrophe, I bit my tongue until after he passed out of respect for the position of the papacy.[5]

Will my same positive feelings about Leo be dashed as they were under Francis? That remains to be seen. Overall, however, Francis surely was an anomaly. Most popes were not like Francis. Most popes bring order and stability, not chaos and confusion. Most pontiffs do not desire to make a mess of things.

Returning to my point: Will Americans find this new American moment with the American pontiff to be a grand one for them and the Church in their country? Will it bring another Sheen-like golden era? Will they witness the realization of Bishop Spalding's prophetic vision?

Let us hope and pray so. And of course, those Americans must pray not only for the American Catholic Church but for the worldwide universal Roman Catholic Church. The pope—Leo XIV, American—is pontiff and shepherd to us all.

SOX
47

Acknowledgments

It was April 23, 2025, two days after the death of Pope Francis, that I received an email from Keith Pfeffer, the excellent deputy publisher of Humanix Books, asking if I might be interested in writing a short biography of the next pope. Keith was envisioning a book of about 40,000 to 50,000 words and a very quick turnaround. How quick? I shall quote from Mr. Pfeffer's email: "1–3 months for a quick publication after the announcement. VERY FAST."

My first thought was that the dear Keith was insane. Of course, I knew—and they did, too—that I write crazy fast, perhaps to the level of insanity myself. And summer was approaching, meaning that I as a professor had three full months to focus on a book. And I knew that I would be really into the subject of the next pope—carefully following the conclave, the various *papabili*, and wanting to know everything about the new man selected as the next heir to the Chair of St. Peter. I would be writing about it a lot, least of all as a columnist and the editor of *The American Spectator*, not to mention a papal biographer and Church historian.

I did have two other books that I was working on. However, both of those manuscripts had been long finished and were awaiting the input of editors and publishers. They were in limbo for the foreseeable weeks if not months. I wouldn't be doing much at all on those two books during the summer ahead. They were out of my hands for the time being.

I had more encouraging news for Keith and Humanix Books: I know Italian—I read it and speak it (somewhat). I was figuring the next pope would likely be an Italian. Possibly Parolin or Pizzaballa. This was an added advantage for me and the publisher.

So I took some time to think and pray about it. Keith and I went back and forth on the details. Wondering if even the good Lord Himself could produce a book on the new pope in a mere month or two, I told Keith that I needed three months. We set a deadline of August 18, the Monday before classes would start for the fall semester at Grove City College. It all came together on April 29, the Feast Day of St. Catherine of Siena—one of my favorite saints and the literal cover girl for my most recent book on stigmatists. We had a deal.

I eagerly began laying out the structure of the book and scribbling down thoughts for the opening chapters on the history of the papacy, the Francis mess, and collecting material on the various *papabili* (especially the front-runners), but otherwise, I waited, along with the world, for the conclave to render its decision. When the news first broke on Thursday, May 8, that the conclave had made its choice, I was very surprised and absolutely not ready. I was at our offices of *The American Spectator* in Old Town Alexandria when my colleagues Leonora Cravotta and Stephan Kapustka alerted me of the breaking news. We were preparing for an event in Washington, DC, that evening, and I knew this news would derail the remainder of my plans for the day. But I was about to be even more surprised—downright astounded. When the protodeacon announced Robert Francis Prevost—an American—as the next pope, I was literally speechless. I genuinely did not know what to say (unusual for me).

Perhaps that was just as well, given that I was committed to emceeing an event that evening as interview requests started pouring in from sources as diverse as CNN and Newsmax wanting me for their evening shows. I told them that I had to decline, mainly because I did not know a thing about Robert Francis Prevost. In my wildest imagination, I would have never predicted him (or any American) as the next pope.

I was flabbergasted. I texted and emailed knowledgeable friends in the Catholic world, only to learn that they likewise were at a loss for words. "I know absolutely nothing about this guy," was a typical response.

On the plus side, these giant unknowns about the new pope made my biographical project all the more interesting, albeit harder to get information—at least initially, though I knew that would change quickly enough. In time, I found a lot of information and was really intrigued by what I was digging up.

In the end, Keith's request for a manuscript of "not less than 40–50K words" became no problem at all. The book became my summer obsession and labor of love. I turned in a manuscript on August 18 of roughly 112,000 words and enjoyed every moment writing the book. As I said, I know that I write crazy fast, but the amount of words I cranked out surprised even me. Then again, a writer writes, and I love to write, especially about the subject dear to me: the Catholic faith. (Incidentally, I had 40–50K words written within a month.)

I was so glad that I said yes to Keith back on April 29, Feast Day of St. Catherine of Siena.

I must add one funny lament: As my wife and I together considered whether I should take on this project, I told her: "Hey, I think the next pope will be an Italian. Let's plan on a two-week trip to Italy this summer with the kids for this project. Rome, maybe Tuscany, Milan, Verona, Venice, Siena, Florence—my family's native land of Calabria." Well, as soon as Susan and I learned of the choice of Prevost as pope, she texted me: "I guess we're going to Chicago instead of Tuscany?"

Big-time bummer there. No offense, Chicagoans. I'm sure you understand.

Two closing thoughts, beginning with words of thanks:

My thanks to my wife and eight kids for once again encouraging and supporting me in this work (I knew they would be into this project) and for always happily allowing me the time to write while also reminding me that as a dad I need to keep time for them, too. I tried to make sure that when the boys wanted to play catch, go to the creek, shoot hoops, or toss the football, I walked away from the laptop. Amid the writing, we found time for several family trips and a vacation to the beach (Virginia, not the Mediterranean).

I'm often asked how I juggle this stuff. Well, I learned years ago how to successfully (I hope) manage family and personal life with professional life. I've done at least two dozen books. I understand the process, the management, and the discipline. And regardless, to repeat, I love to write (I also like the reading and research). It is a joy to me, not onerous at all.

I also want to thank two excellent student assistants at Grove City College, Scott Cross and Johnathan Idoni, who were splendid in grabbing information for me, especially related to the conclave and the announcement of Prevost, his installation ceremony, and his life and background. They were terrific.

I should also add that in the course of my rapidly writing this book, others were quicker. I'm referring to the wonderful Matthew Bunson of EWTN, who somehow had a biography printed by late May. I'm told that there were also AI-generated "biographies." I never did a search to see who else was writing books on Pope Leo XIV. I did not read or consult any of these books. I felt I should do my own research and investigation fully independent of them, plowing ahead in full gear. Once my book is printed, I will look at those other biographies. Like me, those authors also had a limited universe of material on the very new pope and the sparse background of Robert Francis Prevost. Thus, I expect some overlap among our books. I do hope that our presentations are not too similar. If they are, well, my apologies for something I could not help. We shall assume that great minds think alike!

Again, my gratitude to all involved. And my thanks to Keith and Humanix Books for asking me (a fellow crazy man) to write this biography in a timeframe that seemed impossible but turned out to be doable and great fun.

Oh, and to our new pope: I do hope I did okay.

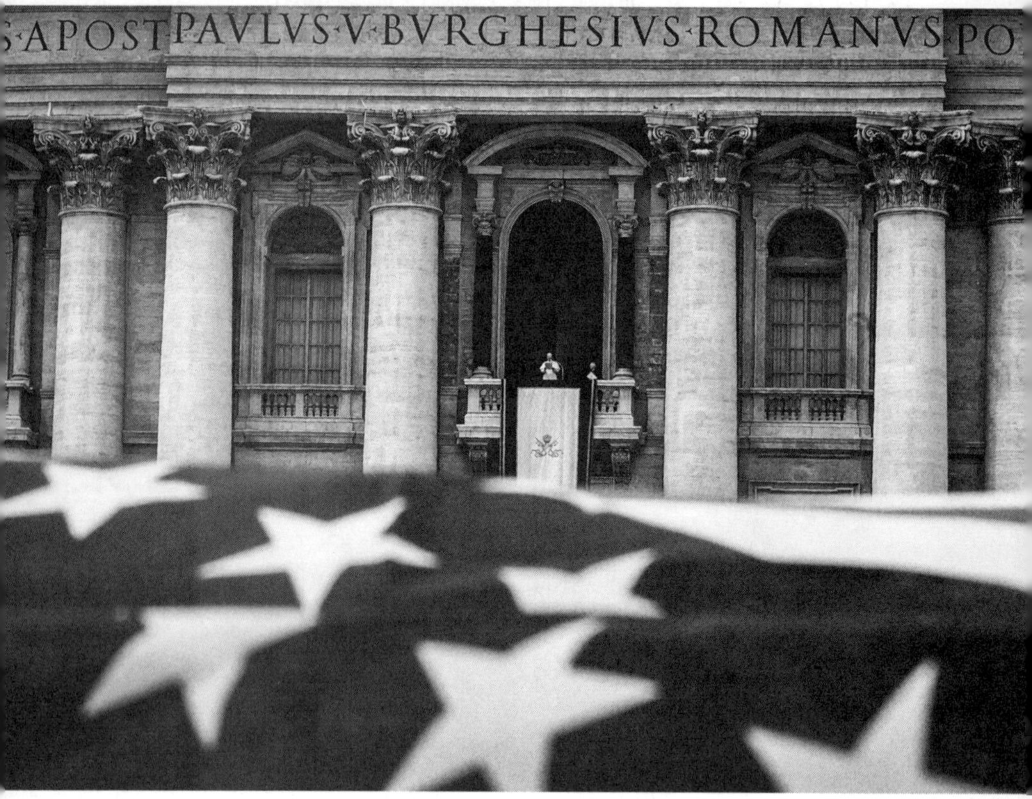
S·APOST·PAVLVS·V·BVRGHESIVS·ROMANVS·PO

Photograph Credits

Page a: Getty Images/Dimitar Dilkoff/Contributor

Page v: Getty Images/Xinhua News Agency/Contributor

Page 1: iStock/Photo Beto

Page 13: Getty Images/Alessandra Benedetti-Corbis/Contributor

Page 39: Getty Images/Vatican Pool/Contributor

Page 57: Getty Images/Vatican Pool/Contributor

Page 67: Getty Images/Tiziana Fabi/Contributor

Page 87: Getty Images/Vatican Pool/Contributor

Page 105: Getty Images/Vatican Pool/Contributor

Page 129: Alamy/Archivio GBB

Page 155: Public domain

Page 181: Getty Images/Vatican Pool/Contributor

Page 195: Getty Images/Print Collector/Contributor and iStock/Nastasic

Page 221: Getty Images/Alessandra Benedetti-Corbis/Contributor

Page 237: Getty Images/Alberto Pizzolia/Contributor

Page 297: Getty Images/Alberto Pizzolia/Contributor

Page 341: Getty Images/Vatican Pool/Contributor

Page 346: Getty Images/SOPA Images/Contributor

Page 352: Getty Images/Jeff Pachoud/Contributor

Photograph Credits

Notes

Preface

1. "Leo XIV is the new Pope," *Vatican News*, May 8, 2025.
2. The *Vatican News* summary of the announcement of Leo XIV and his greeting can be found here: https://www.vaticannews.va/en/pope/news/2025-05/pope-leo-xvi-peace-be-with-you-first-words.html.
3. "First Urbi et Orbi Blessing of the Holy Father Leo XIV," Central Loggia of St. Peter's Basilica, Thursday, 8 May 2025, posted at https://press.vatican.va/content/salastampa/en/bollettino/pubblico/2025/05/08/250508a.html.

Chapter One

1. Cornelius Tacitus, *The Annals*, Book XV, Chapter 44.
2. The phrase, "*Quo vadis*?" is well known. A dramatic 1951 Hollywood epic by that name envisions that moment and what the persecutions under Nero looked like.
3. Thomas Craughwell, *St. Peter's Bones* (NY: Image Books, 2013), p. 6.
4. As with the "*Quo vadis*?" account, these reports come from the Apocrypha's *Acts of Peter*, thus from outside the New Testament, though they have more established roots in Christian tradition, including from major Church fathers such as Origen, Jerome, and Tertullian.
5. Saint Paul said in Romans 12:1–2: "I urge you, brothers and sisters, by the mercies of God, to offer your bodies as a living sacrifice." Paul added in Colossians 1:24: "I rejoice in what I am suffering for you, and I fill up in my flesh what is still lacking in regard to Christ's afflictions, for the sake of his body, which is the church."
6. Some accounts end the period in the year 1376. Indeed, the pope by the end of 1376 had decided to leave Avignon, though he did not arrive back in Rome until January 1377.
7. Quoted by Thomas McDermott, OP, "St. Catherine of Siena and leaving the Church," *Catholic World Report*, April 28, 2023.
8. Steve Weidenkopf, "How St. Catherine Brought the Pope Back to Rome," *Catholic Answers Magazine*, April 29, 2014. Also see the extended discussion in the biography of Catherine's spiritual director, Blessed Raymond of Capua, *The Life of St. Catherine of Siena: The Classic on Her Life and Accomplishments as Recorded by Her Spiritual Director* (Charlotte, NC: TAN Books, 2011).
9. Craughwell, *St. Peter's Bones*, pp. 1–3

10. Craughwell, *St. Peter's Bones*, pp. 1–3, 56–60, 79, and 101.
11. Craughwell, *St. Peter's Bones*, p. 58.
12. See, among others: Bishop Robert Barron, "We've Been Here Before: Marriage and the Room of Tears," Word on Fire website, June 29, 2015.
13. Gerald Korson, "How Pius XII was an 'active conspirator' in three anti-Hitler plots," *Crux*, June 17, 2016.
14. Among others, see the books by Dan Kurzman, *A Special Mission* (on Hitler's plot to seize the Vatican and kidnap Pius XII), and Mark Reibling's *Church of Spies: The Pope's Secret War Against Hitler*. For a short article, see: Edward Pentin, "The Plot to Kidnap Pius," *National Catholic Register*, July 12–25, 2009.
15. Quoted in Camille M. Cianfarra, *The Vatican and the Kremlin* (NY: E. P. Dutton & Co., 1950), p. 28.
16. Among the various works on Pope Pius XII and the Nazis and the Soviets, including the Soviet-communist smear of the pontiff as "Hitler's Pope," see the works by Rabbi David Dalin, *The Myth of Hitler's Pope: How Pope Pius XII Rescued Jews from the Nazis*; Ronald Rychlak's *Hitler, the War, and the Pope* and *Righteous Gentiles: How Pius XII and the Catholic Church Saved a Half Million Jews from the Nazis*; Gordon Thomas, *The Pope's Jews: The Vatican's Secret Plan to Save Jews from the Nazis*; and Sister Margherita Marchione's numerous writings; and still others.
17. That topic is the subject of my lengthy 2017 work, *A Pope and a President: John Paul II, Ronald Reagan, and the Extraordinary Untold Story of the 20th Century* (Wilmington, Delaware: ISI Books, 2017).

Chapter Two

1. This is not an exaggeration. It is a fact that lightning struck the Vatican twice that day, February 11, 2013, shortly after Benedict announced his resignation. This is instantly confirmable by any online search. Photos captured the two strikes. (See, among others: "Lightning really does strike twice," BBC News, February 12, 2013.) As for Benedict's resignation, it was the first by a pope since 1415.
2. See among others the Vigano public letters/statements from December 20, 2023, and June 20, 2024.
3. Archbishop Carlo Maria Vigano, "The Church, the Papacy, and the Conclave: My Interview with Francesco Borgonovo," April 29, 2025, posted at https://exsurgedomine.it/250429-borgonovo-eng/.
4. Even the mild-mannered, veteran Catholic Church reporter John Allen's antennae were raised early in the Francis pontificate. See: John L. Allen Jr., "Does Pope Francis have an enemies list?" *Crux*, November 4, 2014. Allen concluded that column by asserting: "Francis might need to find an occasion to explain in his own voice why he's going after the people and groups that find themselves in his sights. Otherwise, the risk is that a good chunk of the Church may conclude that if the pope sees them as the enemy, there's no good reason they shouldn't see him the same way."
5. Charles Collins, "Pope Francis reportedly uses offensive term for homosexuality a second time," *Crux*, June 12, 2024.
6. Elise Harris, "Pope warns against dangers of 'adolescent progressivism,'" Catholic News Agency, November 18, 2013.

7. Paul Kengor, "The politically incorrect francis—14 shocking statements," *Crisis Magazine*, March 22, 2019.
8. See: Joel Baden, "Pope's shocking Hitler youth comparison," *The Daily Beast*, February 20, 2015.
9. "Pope Francis on celibacy, child abusers, same-sex unions, secularism, and traditionalists," *Aleteia*, September 1, 2017.
10. See my piece on this: Paul Kengor, "Pope Francis," *Crisis Magazine*, July 17, 2019.
11. See: Salvatore Cernuzio, "The Pope: 'If there is a doubt of homosexuality, it is better not to let him enter the seminary,'" *La Stampa*, May 25, 2018.
12. See, among others: "Pope Francis 'worried' about homosexuality in the priesthood," BBC News, December 2, 2018; and Fr. Roger Landry, "Pope Francis on the 'gay mentality' that has 'influenced the Church,'" *National Catholic Register*, December 12, 2018.
13. See my various articles on this at the time, including: Paul Kengor, "Cherry-picking Pope Francis," *The Hill*, September 23, 2015; Paul Kengor, "Pope Francis: poster boy for gay marriage," *The American Spectator*, November 15, 2013; and Paul Kengor, "Is Pope Francis duping liberals on marriage?" *The American Spectator*, November 21, 2014.
14. See: Edward Pentin, "Cardinal Bergoglio hits out at same-sex marriage," *National Catholic Register*, July 8, 2010. Here again, I wrote on these early in the Francis papacy: Paul Kengor, "Pope Francis: 'Children have a 'Right' to a mother and father,'" *Crisis Magazine*, June 8, 2015; and Paul Kengor, "Pope Francis shocks liberals on same-sex 'marriage,'" *Crisis Magazine*, January 23, 2015.
15. See, among others: Eric J. Lyman, "Pope: Abortion is 'white glove' equivalent to Nazi crimes," *USA Today*, June 16, 2018; Francis X. Rocca, "Pope Francis likens abortion to Nazi eugenics," *Wall Street Journal*, June 16, 2018; and "Pope Francis on abortion: it's what the Nazis did, only with 'white gloves,'" Associated Press, June 17, 2018.
16. See my article on this: Paul Kengor, "Never forget: Pope Francis on COVID," *Crisis Magazine*, April 25, 2025.
17. Michael Sean Winters, "Pope: 'I want a mess!'" *National Catholic Reporter*, July 26, 2013.
18. Among other examples, a potentially disturbing case was reported in May 2016 involving an especially substantive (indeed, Sacramental) matter: the proposal by radical German Cardinal Walter Kasper on Communion for divorced and remarried couples. Apparently quoting Francis, Archbishop Bruno Forte reportedly said that Francis had said as a "joke": "If we speak explicitly about Communion for the divorced and remarried, you do not know what a terrible mess we will make. So we won't speak plainly; do it in a way that the premises are there, then I will draw out the conclusions." Forte allegedly seemed to approve of this, in turn "joking" of Francis: "Typical of a Jesuit." This exchange was reported in English (from the original Italian source) by Steve Skojec, "Forte: Pope did not to speak 'plainly' of communion for remarried," OnePeterFive, May 7, 2016. To read in full (including the original Italian), go to: https://onepeterfive.com/pope-speaking-plainly-communion-divorced-messy/. I am relegating this exchange to an endnote because it is not entirely clear.

19. Betsy Reed, "Pope: God loves even those who make 'a complete mess of things,'" *The Guardian*, December 24, 2019.
20. Elise Ann Allen, "Pope in Dili calls for end to bullying, tells youth to 'make a mess,'" *Crux*, September 11, 2024.
21. "Late Cardinal George Pell called Pope a 'catastrophe' in anonymous memo," BBC News, January 12, 2023.
22. I wrote on this at the time: Paul Kengor, "Pope Francis and the Cardinal Mindszenty Treatment in China," *Crisis Magazine*, February 12, 2018.
23. See, among others: "Vatican Official Praises China for Witness to Catholic Social Teaching," *National Catholic Register*, February 7, 2018.
24. "Vatican Official Praises China for Witness to Catholic Social Teaching."
25. See, among others: Edward Pentin, "Full text and explanatory notes of cardinals' questions on 'amoris laetitia,'" *National Catholic Register*, November 14, 2016.
26. For the record, I personally do not prefer the TLM and I am not a member of a TLM parish.
27. Wikipedia definition retrieved May 30, 2025.
28. Larry Chapp, "'Traditionis Custodes' 3 years on: Pope Francis' Latin mass 'motu proprio' has generated division, not unity," *National Catholic Register*, July 8, 2024.
29. Peter Stravinskas, "Good Pharisees, bad Catholics, and the humble of heart," *Catholic World Report*, August 1, 2021
30. Adriana Masotti, "Pope at mass: be careful around rigid Christians," *Vatican News*, October 16, 2018.
31. Joshua McElwee, "Francis criticizes traditionalist Catholics who 'safeguard the ashes' of the past," *National Catholic Reporter*, June 2, 2019.
32. One particular sacrilegious performance occurred at a parish in (predictably) Germany, where the congregants received Holy Communion to the echoing sounds of the "Chicken Dance." See: "A Vatican II Moment: The Chicken Dance Mass," *Rorate Caeli*, February 20, 2024, posted at https://rorate-caeli.blogspot.com/2024/02/a-vatican-ii-moment-chicken-dance-mass.html.
33. As someone who writes and lectures on conservatism, I must note that some of the foundational voices in modern conservatism, such as Russell Kirk (1918–94), argued against describing conservatism as an ideology. Kirk characterized conservatism as an attitude, a temperament, and asserted that ideology is for ideologues, with the political left being the home of ideologues.
34. On how Francis did not deny the Vigano claims about Chaput, see: Jeremy Roebuck, "Memo: Pope says Philadelphia Archbishop Chaput 'too right-wing,'" *Philadelphia Inquirer*, December 13, 2018.
35. See: Jason Horowitz, "Pope Francis long knew of cardinal's abuse and must resign, archbishop says," *New York Times*, August 26, 2018.
36. See: "Pope Francis replaces conservative archbishop of Philadelphia," *New York Times*, January 23, 2020; and Peter Feuerherd, "Archbishop Chaput gives notice after tenure of culture war and consolidation," *National Catholic Reporter*, September 25, 2019.
37. Trudy Ring, "Anti-LGBTQ Archbishop Charles Chaput fired in Philadelphia," *The Advocate*, January 23, 2020.

38. To cite just one source who acknowledged these rumors in print, see: Robert Royal, "Cardinal McElroy and the God of surprises," *The Catholic Thing*, January 8, 2025. Royal is a highly knowledgeable source from inside Washington, DC, who would have good information on these rumors.
39. Gerard O'Connell, "Pope Francis received Father James Martin in private audience for the second time," *America Magazine*, November 11, 2022.
40. "Pope Francis: free women from the slavery of prostitution," *Vatican News*, July 29, 2019.

Chapter Three

1. John Gizzi, "Vatican preps for conclave as 'Pope is dying,'" *Newsmax*, December 7, 2021.
2. See: Christopher White, "Conclave roundup: Parolin's star falls, spotlight on synodality," *National Catholic Reporter*, April 30, 2025; and Ellie Gardey Holmes, "Some progressive cardinals express displeasure with pre-conclave meetings," *American Spectator*, May 1, 2025.
3. Gerard O' Connell, "Backer of Cardinal Parolin attacks Francis' push for lay involvement in church governance," *America Magazine*, April 30, 2025.
4. See: Francesco A. Grana, "Conclave, the tear of the Bergoglian: 'Too many turncoats have been seen,'" *Il Fatto Quotidiano*, May 4, 2025; and Camillo Barone, "Conclave roundup: Conclave to begin in less than 48 hours," *National Catholic Reporter*, May 5, 2025.
5. Pope John Paul II, Apostolic Constitution, *Universi Dominici Gregis*, "On the vacancy of the Apostolic See and the election of the roman pontiff," February 22, 1996, posted at https://www.vatican.va/content/john-paul-ii/en/apost_constitutions/documents/hf_jp-ii_apc_22021996_universi-dominici-gregis.html.
6. See: Marcantonio Colonna, *The Dictator Pope: The Inside Story of the Francis Papacy* (Washington, DC: Regnery, 2017).
7. "Francis' legacy: the good, the bad, and the ugly," Bill Donohue interviewed by Conor Gallagher of TAN Books on podcast, "The Conor Gallagher Show," posted May 1, 2025.
8. Iacopo Scaramuzzi, "Cardinal Müller: 'An era is ending, there have been ambiguities about women, gays and Islam,'" *la Repubblica*, April 24, 2025.
9. Sources for this include CNBC.com, the *Las Vegas Review-Journal*, BetUS.com, *Sportsbook Review*, and (among others) *USA Today*. Catholic News Agency also did a piece on May 7, 2025, titled, "Gamblers are betting millions of dollars on who will be the next pope."
10. Ibid.
11. See statement on Pentin's website, posted December 12, 2024: https://edwardpentin.co.uk/a-groundbreaking-interactive-website-on-the-college-of-cardinals-is-launched/.
12. Edward Pentin, "Edward Pentin's list of 10 papal contenders you should know," *National Catholic Register*, May 4, 2025.
13. Eric Sammons, "Have you no decency, Holy Father?" *Crisis Magazine*, March 20, 2024.

14. See, among others: "On COVID vaccinations, Pope says health care is a 'moral obligation,'" NPR.org, January 10, 2022; and Kengor, "Never forget: Pope Francis on COVID."
15. Philip Pullella, "Conservative Cardinal Burke says he is 'still alive' after rare pope meeting," *Reuters*, December 29, 2023.
16. Pullella, "Conservative Cardinal Burke says he is 'still alive' after rare pope meeting."
17. See: College of Cardinals Report: https://collegeofcardinalsreport.com/.
18. College of Cardinals Report: https://collegeofcardinalsreport.com/cardinals/?_papabili=1.
19. Riccardo Cascioli, "Parolin, the great manipulator who wants to be the Pope," *La Nuova Bussola Quotidiana*, May 3, 2025.
20. Ellie Gardey Holmes, "*Papabile* stresses need for a holy pope," *American Spectator*, May 1, 2025; and John L. Allen Jr., "'Papabile' of the day: Cardinal Péter Erdő," *Crux*, April 26, 2025.
21. Ellie Gardey Holmes, "All the cardinals are talking about Pizzaballa," *American Spectator*, May 2, 2025; and Ellie Gardey Holmes, "Cardinal Pizzaballa calls for ceasefire in Gaza put him on *papabili* shortlist," *American Spectator*, March 29, 2024.
22. "New favorite emerges to replace Francis," *Newsweek*, May 2, 2025.
23. See Tobin remarks: "How Cardinal Joseph Tobin found his calling in the Catholic Church," *NBC Today Show*, April 17, 2019. Posted at https://www.today.com/video/how-cardinal-joseph-tobin-found-his-calling-in-the-catholic-church-1496688707952.
24. See the aforementioned puff piece by the *Today Show*: "How Cardinal Joseph Tobin found his calling in the Catholic Church." The *Today* reporter hailed Tobin as "in the mold of Pope Francis." Also see: Sharon Otterman, "As Church shifts, a cardinal welcomes gays," *New York Times*, June 13, 2017.
25. Christopher White, "Once on the outs, American Cardinal Tobin now a contender," *National Catholic Reporter*, April 28, 2025.
26. Heidi Schlumpf, "AOC is the future of the Catholic church," *National Catholic Reporter*, July 27, 2020.
27. "Cardinal Burke launches novena for the universal church as conclave approaches," *National Catholic Register*, April 26, 2025.

Chapter Four

1. See, among others: "Who chooses the next pope?" *Time Magazine*, April 23, 2025; Solene Tadie, "Why the upcoming conclave will be a decisive step for Europe," *National Catholic Register*, April 29, 2025; Jonathan Liedl, "Meet the 10 US cardinals preparing to elect the next pope," *National Catholic Register*, May 1, 2025; and "Who are the cardinals selecting the pope?" *Time Magazine*, May 7, 2025.
2. "Conclave: How a pope is elected," *Vatican News*, May 6, 2025.
3. Bishop Robert Barron, EWTN Television, May 7, 2025.

Chapter Five

1. See among others: Pope Francis, "God of surprises," Morning Meditation in the Chapel of the Domus Sanctae Marthae, May 8, 2017, posted at the Vatican

website: https://www.vatican.va/content/francesco/en/cotidie/2017/documents/papa-francesco-cotidie_20170508_god-of-surprises.html.

2. I personally published a short article saying just this on April 24, 2025, in my biweekly column in the *Pittsburgh Tribune-Review*, titled, "The pope of surprises." Portions of what I have written here (coming after the selection of Leo XIV) are partly cut and paste from that column in the hopes of preserving the authenticity of what I had conjectured.
3. "Who chooses the next pope," *Time Magazine*, April 23, 2025.
4. See: Julia Meloni, *The St. Gallen Mafia* (TAN Books: Gastonia, NC: 2021).
5. I was told this in early May 2025 by one source close to one such cardinal.
6. "Parolin on Robert Prevost's election as Pope Leo XIV," *Aleteia*, May 20, 2025.
7. "The election of a pope: From white smoke to 'Habemus Papam,'" *Vatican News*, May 7, 2025.
8. "Leo XIV is the new pope," *Vatican News*, May 8, 2025.
9. Apostolic Blessing, "Urbi et Orbi," First Greeting of the Holy Father Pope Francis, Central Loggia of St. Peter's Basilica, Wednesday, 13 March 2013, posted at https://www.vatican.va/content/francesco/en/speeches/2013/march/documents/papa-francesco_20130313_benedizione-urbi-et-orbi.html.
10. John C. Rao, "Francis and Leo: starkly different from the Loggia," *OnePeterFive*, May 9, 2025.
11. Philip Kosloski, "Pope Leo chose his motto from this sermon by St. Augustine," *Aleteia*, May 9, 2025.
12. The first Catholic call-in radio talk show that I heard after the pope's announcement included a call from a New Jersey woman who said she was "angry and offended" that this first American pope had spoken not a word of English from the Loggia. I personally did not hear many such complaints from American Catholics, though I imagine there were other such objections.
13. The following is a video of the remarks. The Latin blessing begins at 12:15: https://news.sky.com/video/watch-new-pope-gives-first-speech-after-eruption-of-applause-from-vatican-13364016.

Chapter Six

1. Within 30 minutes of Prevost's opening papal statement, my email box was dinging with interview requests from sources as diverse as CNN and Newsmax. I had to confess what so many other knowledgeable Catholics had to confess, namely, that little to nearly nothing was known about this man. This was so evidently so that one of my first thoughts was that the College of Cardinals quickly selected this consensus pick precisely because he did not have a lengthy track record of statements.
2. Some of the original X posts on this issue have been taken down. Did Vance first use the phrase, or did some other source use it to describe Vance's thinking, prompting Vance to then use the phrase? Again, the paper trail is not clear.
3. Kat Armas, "JD Vance is wrong: Jesus doesn't ask us to rank our love for others," *National Catholic Reporter*, February 1, 2025.
4. See: Jonah McKeown, "Pope Francis, Vance clash over 'Ordo Amoris,'" *National Catholic Register*, February 13, 2025.

5. Source on the 674 number: "Holy smokes: we have a pope!" Sirius XM Catholic Channel live coverage of the conclave, May 8, 2025.
6. Kit Maher, "New pope appears to have reposted critical social media posts about Trump and Vance," CNN.com, May 8, 2025.
7. See: David Gardner, "New Pope Leo XIV bashed Trump and JD Vance on Twitter just weeks ago," *The Daily Beast*, May 8, 2025. Examples of these are so numerous that citations here are not necessary.
8. Vance post at 2:45 p.m. on May 8, 2025. See: https://x.com/JDVance/status/1920550545061810261.
9. Trump post at 1:25 p.m. on May 8, 2025. See: https://truthsocial.com/@realDonaldTrump/posts/114473380014194441.
10. In his first major media interview, with *Newsmax*, Lou said: "I've had to modify my activities and what I do, what I say, what I write in public spaces or say in public spaces. I've seen a couple already, 'the pope's brother said this.' I don't want to get him in trouble or raise any grief or cause problems." (See: Sandy Fitzgerald, "Pope's Brother: I was watching Newsmax when announcement came," *Newsmax*, May 11, 2025.) Soon thereafter, Lou did a May 12 interview with reporter Piers Morgan that was both entertaining and illuminating. Asked by Morgan about some of the derogatory posts about liberal Democrat politicians, Lou was apologetic, conciliatory, and tried to dial back any heated rhetoric. He said of one post he had done about former Speaker of the House Nancy Pelosi, a liberal Catholic known for her radical support of abortion, "I posted it and I wouldn't have posted it if I didn't kind of believe it. However, I had no idea that what was coming [Leo becoming pope] and I can tell you, since then, I've been very quiet, biting my tongue." He told Piers Morgan: "I don't want to create waves that don't need to be there because I'm a MAGA type and I have my beliefs. I don't need to create heat for [the new pope]. He's going to have enough to handle as it is without the press going 'the pope's brother says this.' He doesn't need that." (See: David Propper, "Pope Leo XIV's oldest brother doubles down on awful 'drunk' Nancy Pelosi post, reveals how new pontiff may lead Catholic Church," *New York Post*, May 12, 2025; and Tyler Arnold, "President Trump extols Pope Leo XIV, meets brother Louis Prevost," Catholic News Agency, May 21, 2025.)
11. Tyler Arnold, "President Trump extols Pope Leo XIV, meets brother Louis Prevost," Catholic News Agency, May 21, 2025.
12. The very first texts that showed up on my phone regarding the new pope were from two conservative friends related to an alleged sex-abuse cover-up in Peru by Prevost.
13. "Report: a chance encounter with Fr Martin and Austen Ivereigh reveals their papal candidate," Edward Pentin's Newsletter, May 5, 2025, posted at https://edwardpentin.substack.com/p/report-a-chance-encounter-with-fr.
14. Here is the link to the original article: https://infovaticana.com/2025/05/05/cronica-romana-un-encuentro-con-james-martin-y-austin-ivereigh-que-delata-su-candidato-a-papa/.
15. See: "Report: critics of Pope favorite Prevost received $150K to remain silent," *Globe Banner*, May 4, 2025; and Riccardo Cascioli, "Handicap start for Pope Prevost," *New Daily Compass*, May 6, 2025. The latter was originally posted on May 6, but the most recent/updated post of the article is dated May 9.

16. Bob Ortega and Rob Kuznia, "Victims' group alleges Pope Leo XIV mishandled sexual abuse cases involving priests in Chicago and Peru," CNN.com, posted at 11:55 a.m. EDT, Friday, May 9, 2025.
17. See: Walter Sanchez Silva, "Peruvian Bishop defends Pope Leo XIV against accusations of cover-up," *National Catholic Register*, May 14, 2025.
18. "Smear merchants attack Pope Leo XIV," Catholic League e-newsletter, May 14 and July 2, 2025.
19. See: Bill Donohue, "Pope Leo XIV is not Francis II," Catholic League, May 9, 2025. The e-newsletter reported: "Is Pope Leo XIV a Republican, a Democrat or an independent? He's a Republican. A registered Republican in Illinois, he pulled the GOP lever in the 2012 . . ."
20. Robert Mackey, "Unearthed comments from new pope alarm LGBTQ+ Catholics," *The Guardian*, May 9, 2025.
21. Fr. James Martin post on X: https://x.com/JamesMartinSJ/status/1920536623176982839.
22. Fr. James Martin video from Rome posted on X, 4:56 a.m. EST, May 9: https://x.com/JamesMartinSJ/status/1920764838411649226.
23. "Report: A chance encounter with Fr Martin and Austen Ivereigh reveals their papal candidate," Edward Pentin's newsletter, May 5, 2025, posted at https://edwardpentin.substack.com/p/report-a-chance-encounter-with-fr.
24. The Burke statement was posted on his X account at 5:51 p.m. on May 8, within just hours of Pope Leo XIV appearing on the Loggia. See: https://x.com/cardinalrlburke/status/1920597510059389096.
25. Cardinal Sarah did his post at 2:52 a.m. on May 9, 2025. See: https://x.com/Card_R_Sarah/status/1920733574908506323.
26. See: Kristina Millare, "Cardinal Goh: Pope Leo XIV is the 'right person' to bring unity, balance to the Church," Catholic News Agency, May 20, 2025.
27. Nico Spuntoni, "Cardinal Goh: Leo will clarify doctrine," *New Daily Compass*, May 22, 2025.
28. "Cardinal Müller says Pope Leo XIV's election was the work of the Holy Spirit," LifeSiteNews.com, May 21, 2025.
29. "Swedish Cardinal reflects on conclave, says he's 'grateful' for Pope Leo XIV," Catholic News Agency, June 10, 2025.

Chapter Seven

1. This is source that had personally texted me. I have left him anonymous.
2. Stefano Zurlo, "The Italian disappointment. The favorite Parolin remained without the votes from Africa and Asia. Decisive pre-Conclave and Dolan's 'direction," *Il Giornale*, May 9, 2025.
3. Fulton Sheen had dubbed Mindszenty the "dry martyr of Hungary." A dry martyr is someone brutally persecuted but not killed. See: Paul Kengor, "Pope Francis and the Cardinal Mindszenty treatment in China," *Crisis Magazine*, February 12, 2018.
4. Cascioli, "Parolin, the great manipulator who wants to be the Pope."
5. Alberto Melloni, "Parolin's advantage, then the votes shifted (in a few hours): this is how Robert Francis Prevost was elected," *Corriere Della Sera*, May 9, 2025.

6. Nico Spuntoni, "Conclave's three-way race: Prevost was favored from the start," *La Nuova Bussola Quotidiana* (*New Catholic Compass*), June 5, 2025.
7. Edward Pentin, "Cardinals' voting patterns emerge as Leo XIV Is welcomed as a pope of peace," *National Catholic Register*, May 12, 2025; and Robert Moynihan, "The Moynihan Letters," May 12, 2025.
8. Nicole Winfield, "Conservatives are cautiously hopeful that Pope Leo XIV will restore rigor to the papacy," AP News, May 13, 2025.
9. Winfield, "Conservatives are cautiously hopeful that Pope Leo XIV will restore rigor to the papacy."
10. Diana Montagna with Raymond Arroyo on EWTN's "The world over with Raymond Arroyo," EWTN Television, May 19, 2025.
11. "US cardinals hold a press conference after Robert Prevost is named Pope Leo XIV," *Associated Press*, May 9, 2025. See press conference posted at https://www.youtube.com/watch?v=sMhAmJGGV-w.
12. Giovanna Dell'Orto, "As 'born in the U.S.A.' plays, American cardinals in Rome celebrate Pope Leo XIV," *AP News*, May 9, 2025.
13. See my analysis, quotes, and sources in Paul Kengor, "Never Forget: Pope Francis on COVID," *Crisis Magazine*, April 25, 2025.
14. Timothy Cardinal Dolan, "Cardinal Dolan reveals how Pope Leo XIV 'impressed' him at the Conclave—and predicts what kind of pontiff he will be," *New York Post*, May 10, 2025.

Chapter Eight

1. Sandy Fitzgerald, "Pope's brother: I was watching Newsmax when announcement came," *Newsmax*, May 11, 2025.
2. Bradford Betz, "Pope Leo XIV's brother reacts to his historic election: 'There are no words,'" *FoxNews.com*, May 9, 2025.
3. For one of the first video interviews with John Prevost after the papal announcement, watch: https://www.msn.com/en-us/video/peopleandplaces/full-interview-a-proud-brother-talks-about-the-new-pope-leo-xiv/vi-AA1Er7zz.
4. "Destined to be pope: brother says Leo XIV always wanted to be a priest," ABCNews.com, May 11, 2025.
5. I mean this in an endearing, thoroughly noninsulting way. I am a mutt, as are my kids and my wife.
6. For an outstanding genealogical analysis, see: "Pope Leo XIV's family tree shows Black roots in New Orleans," ABC News, May 9, 2025, posted at https://abcnews.go.com/US/pope-leo-xivs-family-tree-shows-black-roots/story?id=121644537.
7. Sunny Hostin of the women's TV show *The View* was among others to say just that, asserting flatly, "We have a black pope." See: "Sunny Hostin changes tune on Pope Leo XIV after learning of Haitian roots, declares 'we have a black pope,'" *New York Post*, May 12, 2025.
8. "DEI" is diversity, equity, and inclusion. "CRT" refers to the toxic critical race theory taught in American schools and tearing apart Americans on matters of race.
9. For instance, to cite just one example, in certain parts of India, there are very dark-skinned groups of people, darker skinned than many Americans who are identified as black.

10. The ABC News analysis quoted one genealogist: "To be, you know, Creole in Louisiana, to be a free person of color in New Orleans in that time really indicates that there was at some point an enslaved person that had to fight for their freedom." The ABC News reporters noted, however, that "genealogists have yet to find direct evidence linking the pope's ancestry to any enslaved individual." That may only be a matter of time.
11. Many prominent Catholic men and women had been slaves. Here are a mere handful of popes and saints of varying races and backgrounds: Pope Callixtus I (third century), Saint Frumentius of Ethiopia (fourth century), Saint Nino of Georgia (fourth century), Saint Patrick of Ireland (fourth to fifth century), Saint Brigid of Ireland (sixth century), Saint Bathildis of England (seventh century), Blessed Francisco de Paula Victor of Brazil (19th century), and Saint Josephine Bakhita in the 20th century, a modern slave with a truly extraordinary story both heartbreaking and inspiring. Others were children of slaves, such as St. Martin de Porres, born in Lima, Peru, in December 1579, the son of a freed slave of African and native descent. Himself of mixed race, St. Martin is considered the first black saint in the Americas and Patron of the Negroes. I wrote a full book on this subject. See: Paul Kengor, *The Worst of Indignities: The Catholic Church on Slavery* (Steubenville, OH: Emmaus Road Publishing, 2023).
12. It also has been reported that Pope Leo's paternal grandfather was Jean Lanti Prevost, from Settimo Rottaro, a village in Turin, Italy. Turin is in northern Italy, and has very rich religious roots, including as the home of the iconic Shroud of Turin. Much of the early reporting on the paternal grandfather seems to be inaccurate. More information continues to emerge. There is a lot of contradictory material. The information on the various Wikipedia pages related to Pope Leo's family background also continues to evolve. I have attempted to do my best with changing and evolving material.
13. It seems that Giovanni and Suzanne might not have been formally or legally married. See, among others: Julie Bosman, "A century-old romance that gave the pope his family name," *New York Times*, May 16, 2025.
14. At the time of this writing, it is reported (including at Wikipedia) that the couple—Giovanni and Suzanne—gave their boys the surname "Prevost" at birth and adopted it themselves. The name had been the surname of Fontaine's mother.
15. Pope Leo XIV, "Greeting to the delegation of the National Italian American Foundation," Rome, June 4, 2025.
16. See: Henry Louis Gates Jr., "Five key discoveries in the family tree of Pope Leo XIV," *New York Times Magazine*, June 12, 2025; and Matthew McDonald, "Pope Leo's family tree has it all," *National Catholic Register*, June 24, 2025.
17. Differing sources online list the square footage anywhere from 750 to 1,200 square feet.
18. Lauren FitzPatrick, "From the south suburbs to helping choose the next pope," *Chicago Sun-Times*, May 3, 2025.
19. Kori Rumore, "Pope Leo XIV's family: What to know about his parents and their deep Chicago ties," *Chicago Tribune*, May 9, 2025.
20. Rumore, "Pope Leo XIV's family: What to know about his parents and their deep Chicago ties."

21. FitzPatrick, "From the south suburbs to helping choose the next pope."
22. For further details on the pope's father's military service and time at Normandy, see: Claire Barrett, "Pope Leo XIV is the son of a D-Day veteran," *Military Times*, July 15, 2025.
23. Barrett, "Pope Leo XIV is the son of a D-Day veteran."
24. Other reports say that Louis graduated from the old Central YMCA College in the Hyde Park section. (See: FitzPatrick, "From the south suburbs to helping choose the next pope.") For the record, that college was a remarkably ethnically diverse college, truly reflective of the Chicago melting pot, with large numbers of black students, Jewish students, and (among others) Catholic. The percentage of black students at the time far exceeded black enrollment at other colleges around America. It was eventually renamed Roosevelt University in 1945. Much like the information being reported on Louis Marius's father, there are contradictions and some inaccurate information.
25. Rumore, "Pope Leo XIV's family: what to know about his parents and their deep Chicago ties."
26. FitzPatrick, "From the south suburbs to helping choose the next pope."
27. FitzPatrick, "From the south suburbs to helping choose the next pope."
28. Nicole Winfield, "Pope speaks about childhood and early mornings as an altar boy in unscripted visit with campers," Associated Press, July 5, 2025.
29. FitzPatrick, "From the south suburbs to helping choose the next pope."
30. FitzPatrick, "From the south suburbs to helping choose the next pope."
31. FitzPatrick, "From the south suburbs to helping choose the next pope."
32. Sandy Fitzgerald, "Pope's brother: I was watching Newsmax when announcement came," *Newsmax*, May 11, 2025. Leo himself said that his parents prayed the rosary together every day. See: "Pope Leo's first 100 days," *National Catholic Register*, August 16, 2025.
33. Fitzgerald, "Pope's brother: I was watching Newsmax when announcement came."
34. FitzPatrick, "From the south suburbs to helping choose the next pope."
35. Angel Saunders and Wendy Grossman Kantor, "Pope Leo's childhood friend reveals the fitting name everybody at school used to call him (exclusive)," *People Magazine*, May 9, 2025.
36. Saunders and Kantor, "Pope Leo's Childhood Friend Reveals . . ."
37. Saunders and Kantor, "Pope Leo's Childhood Friend Reveals . . ."
38. Saunders and Kantor, "Pope Leo's Childhood Friend Reveals . . ."
39. FitzPatrick, "From the south suburbs to helping choose the next pope."
40. Jonathan Liedl, "Visiting Pope Leo XIV's Chicago: how the South Side shaped America's first pontiff," *National Catholic Register*, May 12, 2025.
41. Belinda Luscombe, "The making of an American pope," *Time*, July 2, 2025.
42. Luscombe, "The making of an American pope."
43. Luscombe, "The making of an American pope."
44. See: "Rev. L. Dudley Day, O.S.A. (1927–2010)," Midwest Augustinians website, posted at https://www.midwestaugustinians.org/l-dudley-day-osa.
45. Luscombe, "The making of an American pope."
46. Solene Tadie, "From Chicago to the Chair of Peter: the journey of Pope Leo XIV," *National Catholic Register*, May 11, 2025.

47. Mike Lowe, "Seminary schoolmate reflects on Pope Leo's humble beginnings at St. Augustine Seminary High School," WGNTV.com, June 6, 2025; and Luscombe, "The making of an American pope."
48. Lowe, "Seminary schoolmate reflects on Pope Leo's humble beginnings at St. Augustine Seminary High School."
49. Luscombe, "The making of an American pope."
50. Lowe, "Seminary schoolmate reflects on Pope Leo's humble beginnings at St. Augustine Seminary High School."
51. Luscombe, "The making of an American pope."
52. Bradford Betz, "Pope Leo XIV's brother reacts to his historic election: 'There are no words,'" *FoxNews.com*, May 9, 2025.
53. The website of Villanova University claims that it is "the only Augustinian Catholic university in the nation": https://www1.villanova.edu/university.html. There is, however, another college that claims Augustinian roots, even as that college—Merrimack in North Andover, Massachusetts—is not particularly faithfully Catholic let alone very Augustinian. Perhaps Villanova was making a statement about Merrimack's commitment to Augustinian principles, which would not be undue. And such is not to argue that Villanova is particularly faithfully Catholic or Augustinian nowadays either.
54. Matthew McDonald, "Pope Leo, mathematician: math-minded Catholics claim pope as one of their own," *National Catholic Register*, June 5, 2025.
55. My oldest daughter Amanda immediately remarked upon it and brought it up several items as something significant about the new pope, which "non-math" people might not appreciate.
56. McDonald, "Pope Leo, mathematician."
57. Anne Hendershott, "Pope Leo XIV is a gift to US Catholic colleges and universities," *Crisis Magazine*, May 14, 2025.
58. Shawnette Wilson, "Pope Leo XIV previously worked as groundskeeper at cemetery in Havertown," Fox29.com (Philadelphia Fox affiliate), May 8, 2025.
59. "Biography of Pope Leo XIV, born Robert Francis Prevost," *Vatican News*, May 8, 2025. Also see timeline for Robert Francis Prevost/Pope Leo XIV posted at Catholic-Hierarchy.org: https://www.catholic-hierarchy.org/bishop/bprevost.html. Hereafter referred to as "Prevost/Leo at Catholic-Hierarchy.org."
60. Luscombe, "The making of an American pope."

Chapter Nine

1. Andrea Tornielli, "Father Robert became a priest 43 years ago, just steps from the Vatican," *Vatican News*, June 19, 2025.
2. See Augustine's *Expositions on the Psalms* (Psalm 103, III, 9).
3. Andrea Tornielli, "Father Robert became a priest 43 years ago, just steps from the Vatican," *Vatican News*, June 19, 2025.
4. "Biography of Pope Leo XIV, born Robert Francis Prevost," *Vatican News*, May 8, 2025; and "Prevost/Leo at Catholic-Hierarchy.org."
5. Diego López Marina, "Pope Leo XIV's Peruvian goddaughter shares testimony," Catholic News Agency, May 26, 2025.
6. Marina, "Pope Leo XIV's Peruvian goddaughter shares testimony."

7. Alexander Villegas and Marco Aquino, "As a young priest in Peru, Pope Leo XIV survived a bomb threat and charmed locals," *Reuters*, May 14, 2025.
8. Villegas and Aquino, "As a young priest in Peru, Pope Leo XIV survived a bomb threat and charmed locals."
9. At the time of the writing of this book, Pope Leo has just announced a 38th doctor to be named: Cardinal John Henry Newman.
10. Hannah Brockhaus, "Future Pope Leo XIV's doctoral thesis offers clues to his pontificate," Catholic News Agency, May 15, 2025.
11. Brockhaus, "Future Pope Leo XIV's doctoral thesis offers clues to his pontificate." Catholic News Agency, May 15, 2025. Also see: Brendan Towell, "How Leo XIV's rarely-seen thesis sheds light on his vision for the Church," *National Catholic Register*, May 17, 2025.
12. Brockhaus, "Future Pope Leo XIV's doctoral thesis offers clues to his pontificate."
13. Brockhaus, "Future Pope Leo XIV's doctoral thesis offers clues to his pontificate."
14. "Biography of Pope Leo XIV, born Robert Francis Prevost," *Vatican News*, May 8, 2025; and "Prevost/Leo at Catholic-Hierarchy.org."
15. Ibid.
16. Ibid.
17. Ibid.
18. See the coming book by John Bachman, *Turning Point: How Reagan Liberated Grenada and Won the Cold War* (NY: Humanix Books, 2026).
19. For a detailed examination of this, see: Paul Kengor and Patricia Clark Doerner, *The Judge: William P. Clark, Ronald Reagan's Top Hand* (San Francisco, CA: Ignatius Press, 2006), pp. 203–20.
20. For a particularly good, balanced, recent historical analysis on Bishop Oscar Romero, see: Shiv Parihar, "Marxists have no claim to Archbishop Oscar Romero," *The American Spectator*, July 26, 2025.
21. Mario Vargas Llosa, "Breviare d'un massacre," *Esprit*, October 1983.
22. Pol Pot competes for that title because of the astounding percentage of his population that was killed during the 1975–78 reign of terror of his Khmer Rouge in Cambodia. Upward of 1.7 to 3 million died out of a total population of 5 to 7 million, in only four years.
23. The author of this axiom was Peruvian writer-philosopher Jose Carlos Mariategui.
24. See: Pascal Fontaine's chapter, "Communism in Latin America," in Stephane Courtois et al., *The Black Book of Communism* (Cambridge: Harvard University Press, 1999), pp. 675–81.
25. Fontaine, in Courtois et al., *The Black Book of Communism*, pp. 679–81.
26. See my long presentation on this in Paul Kengor, *The Devil and Karl Marx* (Gastonia, NC: TAN Books, 2020), and especially the Catholic Church's March 1937 encyclical on atheistic communism, *Divini Redemptoris*.
27. "Former Soviet spy: we created Liberation Theology," Catholic News Agency, May 1, 2015, posted at https://www.catholicnewsagency.com/news/former-soviet-spy-we-created-liberation-theology-83634.
28. Ion Mihai Pacepa and Ronald Rychlak, *Disinformation* (Washington, DC: WND Books), 2013.
29. "Former Soviet spy: we created Liberation Theology."

30. Peru's Truth and Reconciliation Commission (TRC), which was tasked with trying to calculate the number of deaths, estimated that the Shining Path was responsible for 54 percent of the nearly 70,000 deaths and disappearances during the violence that raged from 1980 into the 1990s.
31. Fontaine, in Courtois et al., *The Black Book of Communism*, pp. 680–81.
32. "Three murdered European priests beatified in Peru," *Catholic Herald*, December 7, 2015; and "Killed by terrorists, named a martyr: the life of Fr. Alessandro Dordi," Catholic News Agency, February 6, 2015.
33. Villegas and Aquino, "As a young priest in Peru, Pope Leo XIV survived a bomb threat and charmed locals."
34. I was forwarded from a reputable source at a credible Catholic organization a list of several anti-communist quotes attributed to Robert Francis Prevost between 1995 and 2010, along with precise dates and locations. This individual received the alleged quotes from what he said was a highly reliable source (a Catholic attorney) in Rome who proceeded to share them in the media when speaking on the new pope in May 2025. Unfortunately, I have not been able to verify these quotes, even as the specificity on date/place are noteworthy and would suggest credibility. They are: (1) "Marxist theology seeks to replace grace with revolution, and ends up worshipping the State above God." (April 12, 1995, seminar at Villanova University); (2) "Communism is the error of the 20th century that still threatens our most vulnerable communities. Its atheism is its first poison." (March 15, 2001, to a "Congregation in Lima, Peru"); (3) "Christians must resist the ideological temptations of extreme collectivism that enslaves the soul in the name of social justice." (June 23, 2003, "Spiritual retreat in Cusco"); (4) "The moral relativism promoted by certain Marxist currents denies the truth of Christ and corrupts the consciences of young people." (December 8, 2007, Pastoral Letter in the Diocese of Chiclayo); and (5) "Communism has penetrated even Christian circles disguised as solidarity. It is our pastoral duty to unmask it." (May 14, 2010, "Conference before Latin American Bishops").
35. See: "Pope Leo XIV approves decrees for more than 170 martyrs," *Vatican News*, June 20, 2025; and "Pope recognizes 154 martyrs, and various laity and religious," *Aleteia*, June 21, 2025.
36. Rumore, "Pope Leo XIV's family: what to know about his parents and their deep Chicago ties."
37. Villegas and Aquino, "As a young priest in Peru, Pope Leo XIV survived a bomb threat and charmed locals."
38. Diego López Marina, "Pope Leo XIV's Peruvian goddaughter shares testimony," Catholic News Agency, May 26, 2025.
39. Villegas and Aquino, "As a young priest in Peru, Pope Leo XIV survived a bomb threat and charmed locals."
40. Marina, "Pope Leo XIV's Peruvian goddaughter shares testimony."
41. To watch a funny example of this in action, live and shortly after Prevost became pope, watch the online Associated Press interview with brother John Prevost as the new pope calls him while John is being interviewed by the AP. The pope tells his brother that he has been calling for the last two hours and asks why he has not picked up his phone. See: "Pope Leo XIV answers his

brother's call during AP interview," Associated Press, May 9, 2025, posted at https://www.youtube.com/watch?v=mIjlmLYWMSM.

42. "Biography of Pope Leo XIV, born Robert Francis Prevost," *Vatican News*, May 8, 2025; and "Prevost/Leo at Catholic-Hierarchy.org."
43. Summaries of these texts, beginning with the Prevost's "intervention," are posted by the Holy See Press Office at https://www.vatican.va/news_services/press/sinodo/documents/bollettino_25_xiii-ordinaria-2012/02_inglese/b11_02.html#-_Rev._F._Robert_Francis_PREVOST,_O.S.A.lain_,_Prior_General_of_the_Order_of_St._Augustine_(Augustinians).
44. Francis X. Rocca, "Pope Leo XIV's countercultural past and clues for the future," *National Catholic Register*, May 10, 2025.
45. "Pope Leo on media and evangelization," Catholic News Service, posted at https://www.youtube.com/watch?v=QXVkJ5TQi1s.
46. "Pope Leo XIV on the counterculture of the new evangelization (Part 1 of 2)," Catholic News Service, posted at https://www.youtube.com/watch?v=WttXvZt3m6k.
47. "Pope Leo on inclusion in the church," Catholic News Service, posted at https://www.youtube.com/watch?v=qsS5R6HHS-g.
48. Lou Prevost said this to Piers Morgan. For an analysis, see: "Pope Leo's brother: the pope is not woke—he will 'be down the middle,'" Breitbart.com, May 13, 2025.
49. See among others: "Pope Leo XIV voted in 4 general elections and 3 Republican primaries, voting records show," CNN.com, May 8, 2025; and "Pope Leo XIV has voted often in Illinois, public records show," *New York Times*, May 8, 2025.
50. Unlike some states with "closed primaries," Illinois allows voters to vote for whichever candidate they would like, Republican or Democrat or another party, regardless of their voter registration. Thus, a Democrat could vote for a Republican in the Republican primary, or vice versa. But most likely, Prevost consistently voting in the Republican primary in those years would certainly suggest he is a Republican.
51. A number of sources have reported conclusively that Prevost is a Republican. A Catholic League piece on the new pope stated: "Is Pope Leo XIV a Republican, a Democrat or an independent? He's a Republican. A registered Republican in Illinois . . . ." See: Bill Donohue, "Pope Leo XIV is not Francis II," Catholic League, May 9, 2025.
52. "Biography of Pope Leo XIV, born Robert Francis Prevost," *Vatican News*, May 8, 2025; and "Prevost/Leo at Catholic-Hierarchy.org."
53. "Pope Leo XIV in his own words: The pontiff on abortion, climate change, homosexuality, and capital punishment," *New York Post*, May 8, 2025.
54. Steven Ertelt, "Cardinal Prevost, now Pope Leo XIV, condemned abortion: 'God's mercy calls us to protect every life,'" *LifeNews.com*, May 8, 2025.
55. Among others, see: "Pope Francis: gender ideology is the ugliest danger of our time," *Vatican News*, March 1, 2024.
56. Joshua McElwee, "Prevost, first US pope, supported Francis and shunned spotlight," *Reuters*, May 8, 2025.
57. "Biography of Pope Leo XIV, born Robert Francis Prevost," *Vatican News*, May 8, 2025; and "Prevost/Leo at Catholic-Hierarchy.org."

58. For an insightful piece on this, see Matthew McDonald, "Pope Leo XIV is first missionary to become pope in a long, long time," *National Catholic Register*, May 14, 2025.

Chapter 10

1. "Prevost/Leo at Catholic-Hierarchy.org."
2. Walter Sánchez Silva, "Leo XIV, in 2023, acknowledged previous meetings with Pope Francis in which they disagreed," Catholic News Agency, May 12, 2025, reprinted and translated from *ACI Prensa*, CNA's Spanish-language news partner, where the article first appeared.
3. For a thoughtful, balanced appraisal of Prevost's short time at the Dicastery for Bishops, see: Serre Verweij, "Leo XIV: the man, the priest, and the bishop—who is he?" *Rorate Caeli*, May 11, 2025. In that piece, the author also briefly considers the largely unknown role of Prevost in the handling and removal of Bishop Joseph Strickland from the diocese of Tyler, Texas. Notably, Strickland himself said after the election of Leo that he did not know if Prevost was involved in his removal as bishop. He was optimistic about Prevost. See: "Will Pope Leo XIV offer the Church a chance for renewal? Bishop Strickland weighs in," *LifeSiteNews.com*, May 14, 2025.
4. Ricardo Morales Jiménez, "Interview with Cardinal Robert Prevost OSA: 'Above all, a bishop must proclaim Jesus Christ,'" May 8, 2025, posted at the official website of the Augustinian order: https://www.augustinianorder.org/post/interview-with-cardinal-robert-prevost-osa-above-all-a-bishop-must-proclaim-jesus-christ.
5. Jiménez, "Interview with Cardinal Robert Prevost OSA."
6. Felipe Salvosa II, "Same-sex blessings issue highlights need for bishops' conferences' doctrinal authority," *CBCP News*, October 24, 2023.
7. Courtney Mares, "Cardinal at synod on synodality: 'clericalizing women' will not solve problems," Catholic News Agency, October 26, 2023.
8. Mares, "Cardinal at synod on synodality."
9. Ertelt, "Cardinal Prevost, now Pope Leo XIV, condemned abortion."
10. Giovanni Sadewo, "The network that led to Pope Leo XIV's election," *Crisis Magazine*, May 13, 2025.
11. Colleen Dulle, "Explainer: How Cardinal Fernández is changing the Vatican doctrine office," *America Magazine*, January 23, 2024.
12. "Tucho Fernández, the perfect prefect for the demolition of the faith," *La Esperanza*, July 11, 2023.

Chapter Eleven

1. According to Marx and Engels, communism would progress through stages, from feudalism to capitalism to socialism to communism. During this process, institutions such as property, democracy, the family, religion, the state, and money, would "wither away." Vladimir Lenin, co-namesake of Marxism-Leninism, would write in his classic *The State and Revolution*: "And this brings us to the question of the scientific distinction between socialism and communism. . . . What is usually called socialism was termed by Marx the 'first,' or lower, phase of communist society."

2. I provide a lengthy discussion of Church and papal statements against communism (as well as Pope Francis's limited statements) in my book *The Devil and Karl Marx*, particularly in Chapter 6. I have also written many articles on this subject for *Crisis Magazine* and the *National Catholic Register*. Among them, including a piece that led with a Francis statement on communism, see: Paul Kengor, "The Book of Acts Does Not Support Communism," *Crisis Magazine*, April 20, 2023.
3. Among others, see: James Hennesey, "Leo XIII's Thomistic Revival: A Political and Philosophical Event," *The Journal of Religion*, 1978, Vol. 58, pp. 185–97; and Michael L. Brock, "Pope Leo XIII: A Critique of the Modern World," Christendom Press, Winter 1975–76, pp. 13–29, posted at CatholicCulture.org, https://www.catholicculture.org/culture/library/view.cfm?recnum=905.
4. Bukharin wrote this in Chapter 11 of his 1920 classic, *The ABC of Communism*, posted at https://www.marxists.org/archive/bukharin/works/1920/abc/11.htm. For that and other similar statements from Marxists on the incompatibility of communism and Christianity—and also from Pope Francis saying the same—see: Kengor, "The Book of Acts Does Not Support Communism."
5. Again, see my lengthy analysis of these in Chapter 6 of my book, *The Devil and Karl Marx*.
6. "Pope Leo XIV addresses Centesimus Annus Foundation on Catholic social teaching," Catholic News Agency, May 17, 2025.
7. I happen to know about these statements because I did a book on the Church and slavery. See my lengthy analysis of those statements in Kengor, *The Worst of Indignities: The Catholic Church on Slavery*.
8. See text at Vatican website, posted at https://www.vatican.va/content/leo-xiii/en/encyclicals/documents/hf_l-xiii_enc_05051888_in-plurimis.html.
9. See my lengthy discussion of St. Peter Claver in my book, *The Worst of Indignities: The Catholic Church on Slavery*, or for a shorter summary, see: Paul Kengor, "Since Before the Witness of St. Peter Claver to Today, the Catholic Church Has a Long, and Often Overlooked, History Opposing Slavery," *National Catholic Register*, August 25, 2023.
10. See text posted at the Vatican website at https://www.vatican.va/content/leo-xiii/en/encyclicals/documents/hf_l-xiii_enc_20111890_catholicae-ecclesiae.html.
11. "Pope asks forgiveness for slave trade," UPI, February 22, 1992.
12. For a detailed analysis of the origins of the prayer, which attempts to separate fact from fiction, see: Kevin Symonds, *Pope Leo XIII and the Prayer to St. Michael: An Historical and Theological Examination* (Boonville, NY: Preserving Christian Publications, 2018). The vision occurred during Mass sometime between 1884 and 1886. It was a vision of demons, if not of Satan himself.
13. "Audience to Members of the Diplomatic Corps Accredited to the Holy See," Clementine Hall, Vatican, May 16, 2025.
14. In the *Communist Manifesto*, Marx and Engels wrote: "Abolition of the family! Even the most radical flare up at this infamous proposal of the communists."
15. See: "Bishop Robert Barron: What Leo's choice of name tells us about the new pope," FoxNews.com, May 14, 2025; and Alec Schemmel, "Pope Leo XIV's

name gives clue to how he'll handle social, political divides, bishop says," FoxNews.com, May 9, 2025.

16. Michael Knowles interviewed on "Trace Gallagher Show," Fox News Channel, May 8, 2025.
17. Cardinal Müller's letter was published on May 9 on the website InfoVaticana: https://infovaticana.com/2025/05/09/cardenal-muller-esperamos-que-el-nuevo-papa-colabore-en-la-superacion-de-las-divisiones-en-la-cristiandad-y-de-las-tensiones-en-el-mundo/.

Chapter Twelve

1. Tiziana Campisi, "Pope Leo XIV's pectoral cross holds relics of Saints Augustine and Monica," *Vatican News*, May 10, 2025.
2. Immediately upon the announcement of Robert Francis Prevost as Pope Leo XIV, a Roman group called *Circolo San Pietro* that day created and donated to the new pope a silver pectoral cross that contained relics of Saint Leo the Great as well as St. Augustine, St. Thomas of Villanova, and Blessed Anselmo Polanco. See: Campisi, "Pope Leo XIV's pectoral cross contains a relic of St. Leo the Great."
3. Matthew Becklo, "Pope Leo XIV: 'A Son of St. Augustine,'" *National Catholic Register*, May 12, 2025.
4. Becklo, "Pope Leo XIV: 'A Son of St. Augustine.'"
5. See: "Pope Leo XIV's motto and coat of arms," *Vatican News*, May 10, 2025; and Philip Kosloski, "Pope Leo chose his motto from this sermon by St. Augustine," *Aleteia*, May 9, 2025.
6. "Pope Leo XIV's motto and coat of arms."
7. "Pope Leo XIV's motto and coat of arms."
8. "What Pope Leo XIV's coat of arms and motto reveal about his dedication to the ideals of St. Augustine—an art historian explains," *Religion News Service*, May 16, 2025.
9. Courtney Mares, "All the saints and Church Fathers Pope Leo XIV quoted in his first week," Catholic News Agency, May 15, 2025,
10. Numerous articles could here be cited. As just one example, see: Fr. Alexander Lucie-Smith, "Was St Augustine black?" *Catholic Herald*, August 7, 2027.
11. See "advisory editor" note by Betty Radice in R. S. Pine-Coffin's translated 1961 edition of *The Confessions* by Penguin Classics Books.
12. Pope Leo XIV, "Address of His Holiness Leo XIV to Parliamentarians on the Occasion of the Jubilee of Government Leaders," June 21, 2025.
13. This is not (necessarily) to say that it was totally neglected by Pope Francis. A search of Vatican online documents reveals that Francis (or his writer/ghostwriter) mentioned natural law in statements/messages on October 31, 2019; November 29, 2019; March 7–8, 2024; and in *Amoris Laetitia* (March 2016). Also see: Samuel Gregg, "Pope Francis and the return of natural law," *National Review*, March 22, 2013.
14. Stefano Fontana, "With Leo XIV, natural law finally returns," *La Nuova Bussola Quotidiana* (*New Catholic Compass*), June 23, 2025.
15. Pope John Paul II Apostolic Letter, *Augustinum Hipponensem*, August 28, 1986, letter written to the Augustinian Order on the 1,600th anniversary of Augustine's conversion.

16. John Paul II General Audience, October 25, 2000.
17. Quotes from Rex Warner, translator, *The Confessions of Saint Augustine* (NY: Penguin Signet Classics, 2009); and Pope Benedict XVI, General Audience, January 9, 2008.
18. Regis Martin, "The impact of Saint Augustine," *Crisis Magazine*, September 28, 2024.
19. Scott Hahn, "How St. Augustine lost—then found—his faith," *Letter and Spirit*, July 23, 2024.
20. See foreword by Elizabeth Block in Warner, translator, *The Confessions*, p. xxi.
21. The survey was done by the Christian History Institute, which published the results in a special edition of *Christian History* magazine, titled, "25 Writings that changed the Church and the world" (issue #116, 2015). To read the list online, see: https://christianhistoryinstitute.org/magazine/article/did-you-know-great-writings/.
22. Fr. Bonaventure Chapman, O. P., "Saint Augustine: ever ancient and yet ever new," *Word on Fire*, August 28, 2019.
23. To view a PDF of King's original letter, see: https://fee.org/articles/letter-from-a-birmingham-jail/.
24. See: Philip F. Lawler, *Lost Shepherd: How Pope Francis Is Misleading His Flock* (Washington, DC: Regnery Gateway, 2018), pp. 8–9.
25. Becklo, "Pope Leo XIV: 'a son of St. Augustine.'"

Chapter Thirteen

1. "Homily of the Holy Father Leo XIV," Sistine Chapel, May 9, 2025, posted at https://www.vatican.va/content/leo-xiv/it/homilies/2025/documents/20250509-messa-cardinali.html.
2. Fr. Raymond de Souza, "Pope Leo XIV: initial impressions on a papal first," *National Catholic Register*, May 9, 2025.
3. Earlier that same day, Leo visited the Vatican Grottoes to celebrate Holy Mass at the altar near the tomb of Saint Peter.
4. "Pope sings Regina Caeli, pleads 'never again war,'" *Aleteia*, May 11, 2025.
5. Pope Leo XIV, "Regina Caeli, Loggia of the blessings of St. Peter's Basilica," Sunday, May 11, 2025
6. Pope Leo XIV, "Regina Caeli."
7. Pope Leo XIV, "Address to journalists," Paul VI Audience Hall, Vatican City, Monday, May 12, 2025.
8. Robert Moynihan, "The Moynihan letters," May 12, 2025.
9. "Pope Leo XIV laments that today's youth have to deal with 'relativism' and 'superficiality,'" Catholic News Agency, May 15, 2025.
10. "Eucharistic celebration for the beginning of the ministry of the Bishop of Rome," Ritual for the Beginning of the Petrine Ministry, Office of Liturgical Celebrations, Holy See, St. Peter's Square, May 18, 2025.
11. "Eucharistic celebration for the beginning of the ministry of the Bishop of Rome."
12. Edward Pentin, "Pope Leo XIV's pontificate officially begins with a resounding call for unity and peace," *National Catholic Register*, May 19, 2025.
13. "Eucharistic celebration for the beginning of the ministry of the Bishop of Rome."

14. Data provided by EWTN commentators during live EWTN television coverage of the installation, May 18, 2025.
15. "World leaders, delegates set to attend Pope Leo XIV's inaugural mass," Catholic News Agency, May 17, 2025.
16. Edward Pentin, "Pope Leo XIV's pontificate officially begins with a resounding call for unity and peace."
17. "What to watch for: key moments taking place in Pope Leo XIV's inaugural mass," Catholic News Agency, May 18, 2025.
18. "Eucharistic celebration for the beginning of the ministry of the Bishop of Rome."
19. Robert Moynihan, "The Moynihan letters," May 17, 2025.
20. Alessandro Gisotti, "Cardinal Tagle reflects on Pope Leo XIV as a missionary shepherd," *Vatican News*, May 16, 2025.
21. Gisotti, "Cardinal Tagle reflects on Pope Leo XIV as a missionary shepherd."
22. Victoria Arruda, "Cardinal Tagle hilariously recalls offering Pope Leo XIV candy moments before his election," *Church Pop*, May 21, 2025.
23. Alyssa Murphy, "WATCH: Pope Leo XIV's emotional moment receiving the fisherman's ring goes viral," *National Catholic Register*, May 19, 2025.
24. "Eucharistic celebration for the beginning of the ministry of the Bishop of Rome."
25. "Full text of Pope Leo XIV's homily from inauguration mass: 'this is the hour for love,'" *National Catholic Register*, May 18, 2025.
26. My speculation here is easy because I personally voted that way in the 2016 Republican Primary and general election.
27. For fair, calm, and balanced analysis of this debate and Vance's decision, see: Eric Sammons, "Should Vance have kissed the ring?" *Crisis Magazine*, May 27, 2025.
28. Tyler Arnold, "In new interview, JD Vance explains how his Catholic faith informs his political views," Catholic News Agency, May 21, 2025.
29. Hannah Brockhaus, "Pope Leo XIV meets U.S. Vice President JD Vance, Secretary of State Marco Rubio," *National Catholic Register*, May 19, 2025.
30. "Archbishop Paglia concludes mandate as President of Pontifical Academy for Life," *Vatican News*, May 26, 2025.
31. See: Edward Pentin, "Cardinal Caffarra: Satan is hurling at God the 'ultimate and terrible challenge,'" *National Catholic Register*, May 20, 2017.
32. See: Paul Kengor, "John Paul II's warning on 'final confrontation' with the 'anti-church,'" *National Catholic Register*, October 5, 2018.
33. Edward Pentin, "Departure of Archbishop Paglia marks end of turbulent chapter at John Paul II Institute," *National Catholic Register*, May 22, 2025.
34. "Paglia replaced at JPII institute," *The Pillar*, May 19, 2025.
35. "Pope Leo XIV appoints new grand chancellor of Pontifical Academy for Life," CatholicVote.org, May 19, 2025.
36. John Grondelski, "Rome's Mario Cuomo is gone," *First Things*, May 20, 2025.
37. "'Don Baldo' Reina, Francis' choice to lead his Diocese of Rome," *Aleteia*, October 22, 2024.
38. "Pope Leo XIV appoints new grand chancellor of Pontifical Academy for Life," CatholicVote.org.
39. See my extended piece on this: Paul Kengor, "A hopeful Pope Leo change for life," *American Spectator*, May 21, 2025.

40. Saint Gianna Beretta Molla was born October 4, 1922, the tenth of 13 children. Highly intelligent, she pursued educational opportunities and decided to pursue a career in a medicine at a time when few women went to medical school. Her career took off, but she longed for a family. Her prayers were answered when in December 1954 she met 42-year-old engineer Pietro Molla. They married in September 1955. Gianna happily balanced roles as wife, mother, and physician. Everything changed, however, with Gianna's pregnancy with her fourth child. She had cancer of the uterus. Her fellow doctors advised that she have an abortion in order to save her life, but Gianna refused. She vowed to God: "If you must decide between me and the child, do not hesitate to choose the child. I insist." Gianna stayed true to her word, giving her life for that child.
41. "Rome, diocesan phase of the cause of beatification of Chiara Corbella closed. Mons. Reina, 'let us commit ourselves to imitating Chiara. Holiness is the only way that makes us happy,'" SIR Information Agency (Italian language), June 21, 2024.
42. Hannah Brockhaus, "Diocese of Rome Closes First Step Toward Sainthood for Chiara Corbella Petrillo," *National Catholic Register*, June 21, 2024.
43. "Pope Leo XIV removes controversial Italian bishop as head of John Paul II Institute for the family," Zenit, May 19, 2025.
44. "Will Pope Leo XIV restore clarity to the Church?" LifeSiteNews.com, May 21, 2025.
45. "Msgr. Renzo Pegoraro appointed President of Pontifical Academy for life," *Vatican News*, May 27, 2025.
46. Edward Pentin, "Pope appoints Archbishop Paglia's right-hand man as president of Pontifical Academy for life," *National Catholic Register*, May 28, 2025.
47. See among others: Michael Haynes, "Archbishop Paglia replaced as head of Pontifical Academy for life," LifeSiteNews.com, May 27, 2025.
48. Francis X. Rocca, "Is the Catholic Church rethinking contraception?" *Wall Street Journal*, December 30, 2022.
49. "Assisted suicide: the Vatican's strategic turn on bioethics," *Le Croix*, February 8, 2022.
50. "Msgr. Renzo Pegoraro appointed president of Pontifical Academy for life," *Vatican News*, May 27, 2025.
51. Solene Tadie, "French bishops condemn passage of euthanasia bill," Catholic News Agency, May 31, 2025.
52. Timothy Dolan, "Prevent, don't assist, suicide," *Wall Street Journal*, May 29, 2025.
53. "Pope to Rome's mayor: 'For you and with you I am Roman,'" *Vatican News*, May 25, 2025.
54. Victoria Cardiel, "Pope Leo delivers first homily as bishop of Rome at Basilica of St. John Lateran," Catholic News Agency, May 25, 2025.
55. Pope Leo XIV, "Holy mass with presbyteral ordinations," St. Peter's Basilica, May 31, 2025. For video, see: https://www.vatican.va/content/leo-xiv/en/events/event.dir.html/content/vaticanevents/en/2025/5/31/ordinazioni-presbiterali.html. Also see: AC Wimmer, "Pope Leo XIV ordains 11 new priests for Rome, urges transparent priesthood," Catholic News Agency, May 31, 2025; and EWTN broadcast of the mass, May 31, 2025.

56. "FULL TEXT: Homily of Pope Leo XIV on Jubilee for Families, Children, Grandparents, and the Elderly," Catholic News Agency, June 1, 2025.
57. See: Pope Paul VI, *Humanae Vitae*, July 25, 1968, section 9.
58. "Pope Leo XIV speaks by phone with Russian President Putin," *Vatican News*, June 4, 2025.
59. "Pope Leo XIV speaks by phone with Russian President Putin."
60. Carol Glatz, "Ukrainian president speaks with Pope Leo and invites him to Ukraine," Catholic News Service, May 13, 2025.
61. "Elise Ann Allen, "Pope has phone call with Putin same day Trump does," *Crux*, June 5, 2025.
62. "Pope Leo XIV has phone call with Russian President Vladimir Putin," Catholic News Agency, June 4, 2025.
63. Gerard O'Connell, "Pope Leo XIV and Russia's Vladimir Putin have first phone call," *America Magazine*, June 4, 2025.
64. "Putin gives Pope birthday call, praises his global role," Associated Press, December 17, 2021.
65. O'Connell, "Pope Leo XIV and Russia's Vladimir Putin have first phone call."
66. "Cardinal Parolin: 'No war is inevitable, no peace is impossible,'" *Vatican News*, June 4, 2025.
67. See the post on Bartolo Longo by the Catholic News Agency: https://www.catholicnewsagency.com/saint/blessed-bartholomew-longo-615.
68. "8 blesseds scheduled to be elevated to the altars," Catholic News Agency, June 4, 2025.
69. Much of the material in this section is taken from my June 15, 2025, article for the *American Spectator*, titled, "Pope Leo removes alleged 'rape art.'"
70. "Vatican News removes Rupnik art from website," *Catholic World Report*, June 9, 2025.
71. "Vatican News removes Rupnik art from website."
72. See: "Spirituality and brief history of the Redemptoris Mater Chapel," posted at https://www.vatican.va/content/dam/vatican/virtualtour/redemptorismater/index-en.html.
73. Hannah Brockhaus, "Lourdes bishop covers Rupnik mosaics on doors to Basilica of the Rosary," Catholic News Agency, March 31, 2025.
74. Fr. Raymond J. de Souza, "When It comes to comparisons with Father Rupnik, think Cosby, not Caravaggio," *National Catholic Register*, June 11, 2025.
75. Christopher Altieri, "Vatican website removes pictures of artwork created by priest accused of abuse," Crux, June 9, 2025.
76. Altieri, "Vatican website removes pictures of artwork created by priest accused of abuse."
77. Nico Spuntoni, "Zanchetta and Rupnik: signs of change under new pontificate," *New Daily Compass*, June 11, 2025.
78. John M. Grondelski, "Movement (Finally) on the most notorious sex-abuser?" *The Catholic Thing*, June 10, 2025.
79. Altieri, "Vatican website removes pictures of artwork created by priest accused of abuse."
80. Altieri, "Vatican website removes pictures of artwork created by priest accused of abuse."

81. Spuntoni, "Zanchetta and Rupnik: signs of change under new pontificate."
82. The 30,000 estimate was provided by the Chicago-based Catholic radio network Relevant Radio, which sent representatives to cover the event and to participate. See: John Hanretty, "From the basilica to the ballpark: a holy moment in White Sox stadium," Relevant Radio newsletter, June 17, 2025.
83. "Pope Leo breaks from papal dress codes—with a White Sox baseball cap," CNN.com, June 12, 2025.
84. Jonathan Liedl, "Pope Leo XIV encourages young people to be 'beacons of hope' at Chicago event," *National Catholic Register*, June 14, 2025.
85. "Full text of Pope Leo XIV's address to Catholics in Chicago," Catholic News Agency, June 14, 2025.
86. "Iranian Supreme Leader declares 'the battle begins' and warns Israel about 'great surprise . . . that the world will remember for centuries,'" *Daily Mail*, June 18, 2025.
87. Pope Leo XIV, "Transcript of general audience," Vatican website, June 18, 2025.

Chapter Fourteen

1. "Parolin on Robert Prevost's election as Pope Leo XIV," *Aleteia*, May 20, 2025.
2. See, among others: "By the numbers: How the Catholic Church has changed during Pope Francis' pontificate," Catholic News Agency, March 13, 2023; and "New Church statistics reveal growing Catholic population, fewer pastoral workers," *Vatican News*, March 20, 2025. The first article (measuring the 10th anniversary of Francis as pope) noted that the "total number of Catholics worldwide grew from 1.253 billion in 2013 to 1.378 billion in 2021, an increase of nearly 10%." The second more recent article notes that "The global Catholic population increased by 1.15% between 2022 and 2023, rising from approximately 1.39 billion to 1.406 billion." Both articles, however, show that the growth has been mainly in Africa and Asia. Moreover, the growth in vocations has been very poor in Europe and North America, as have rates of Mass attendance. Particularly disappointing are the huge numbers of cradle Catholics in America and the West who no longer practice their faith. Among the latest analyses of that dismal picture, see: "Study: 9 in 10 Cradle Catholics Are Leaving the Church," Catholic News Agency, August 13, 2025.
3. Many times during the Francis papacy I thought of the warnings of my late colleague at *The American Spectator*, the fearless Catholic journalist, George Neumayr, who died very unexpectedly in January 2023. In 2017, George wrote the aptly titled book, *The Political Pope: How Pope Francis Is Delighting the Liberal Left and Abandoning Conservatives*. He predicted that rather than leading a reinvigorated Catholic Church, with exploding numbers, the first Jesuit pope would preside over a shrinking Church, as he had in Argentina. George assured that the "Francis effect" would be just the opposite of what liberal media advocates were predicting. The number of Catholics, especially conservative ones, who left the Church under Francis is no doubt astonishingly high. I had to talk many into hanging in there and staying. Moreover, I could name various prominent non-Catholics who would have converted during those 12 years if not for Francis. But did Francis not bring liberals into the Church and grow it that way? No. Secular liberals want to remake the Catholic Church in

their own image, only for the purpose of taking it down, not joining it. Francis endeavored to please them, but there was no pleasing them.

4. Several times over the years I had marveled to George Neumayr at the mystery of why Francis had not visited his home country of Argentina. George was not surprised. In fact, George spent a lot of time in Argentina researching Bergoglio's background. He was soon convinced that Francis was not welcome in Argentina, and that he embarrassingly would be booed rather than cheered if he returned. I found that difficult to believe. But alas, Francis never once set foot back home.
5. "Crippling priest shortage leads to restructuring of Grand Rapids Diocese," Catholic News Agency, July 10, 2025.
6. Adriana Masotti, "Pope at mass: be careful around rigid Christians," *Vatican News*, October 16, 2018.
7. The bishop's letter to his fellow priests in the diocese is titled, "Go in peace, glorifying the Lord by your life, a pastoral letter on the celebration of the liturgy, in the Diocese of Charlotte." It is posted at https://rorate-caeli.blogspot.com/2025/05/rorate-exclusive-anti-traditional-and.html.
8. Francis said this in his October 2018 homily at Casa Santa Marta. See: Adriana Masotti, "Pope at Mass: be careful around rigid Christians," *Vatican News*, October 16, 2018.
9. Jack Figge, "'Mass is not a show here'—young Charlotte Catholics respond to liturgy policy," *The Pillar*, May 31, 2025.
10. Figge, "'Mass is not a show here.'"
11. Figge, "'Mass is not a show here.'"
12. Figge, "'Mass is not a show here.'"
13. Figge, "'Mass is not a show here.'"
14. I received these emails from two members of the Charlotte diocese on May 30, 2025. I am keeping them anonymous out of fear of retribution against them.
15. "At Prevost meeting, Charlotte's Martin urged to slow down on cathedral project," *The Pillar*, May 29, 2025.
16. Joe Marusak, "Charlotte Catholic bishop met future Pope Leo XIV for one-on-one chat in Rome," *Charlotte Observer*, May 9, 2025.
17. "At Prevost meeting, Charlotte's Martin urged to slow down on cathedral project."
18. "Bishop grants request to pause restrictions on Latin Mass until Vatican's October deadline," *Catholic News Herald*, June 3, 2015.
19. Robert Sarah, "Cardinal Robert Sarah: 'A diabolical project against the Latin Mass,'" *New Daily Compass*, January 22, 2025.
20. Nicole Winfield, "Conservatives are cautiously hopeful that Pope Leo XIV will restore rigor to the papacy," AP News, May 13, 2025.
21. Nico Spuntoni, "Cardinal Goh: Leo will clarify doctrine," *New Daily Compass*, May 22, 2025.
22. Spuntoni, "Cardinal Goh: Leo will clarify doctrine."
23. Archbishop Cordileone post on X, May 23, 2025.
24. Edward Pentin, "Pope Leo faces an early challenge: how to deal with Pope Francis' restrictions on the Latin Mass," *National Catholic Register*, June 3, 2025.
25. Pentin, "Pope Leo faces an early challenge."

26. "The 'mercy' hammer comes down on Traditional Latin Masses in Detroit—10 parish masses to be closed," *Rorate Caeli*, posted June 13, 2025, posted at https://rorate-caeli.blogspot.com/2025/06/the-mercy-hammer-comes-down-on.html#more.
27. Lauretta Brown, "Detroit archbishop fires 3 Sacred Heart Seminary theologians who criticized Pope Francis," *National Catholic Reporter*, July 26, 2025.
28. Brown, "Detroit archbishop fires 3 Sacred Heart Seminary theologians who criticized Pope Francis."
29. Kristina Millare, "Cardinal Burke appeals for restoration of Traditional Latin Mass," Catholic News Agency, June 16, 2025.
30. Hannah Brockhaus, "Cardinal Burke to celebrate Traditional Latin Mass in St. Peter's Basilica," Catholic News Agency, September 9, 2025.
31. See, among others: "Pope Leo's Permission for Latin Mass in St. Peter's Gives Traditionalists Hope," *New York Times*, October 25, 2025.
32. Nicole Winfield, "Debate over Latin Mass heats up after apparent leak of Vatican documents that undermine Pope Francis," *Associated Press* (posted by ABCNews.com), July 3, 2025.
33. Montagna released the material on her Substack page. See: Diane Montagna, "EXCLUSIVE: Official Vatican report exposes major cracks in foundation of *Traditionis custodes*," Substack, July 1, 2025, posted at https://substack.com/home/post/p-167259174. Also see Montagna's important follow-up post on July 10, 2025: https://substack.com/inbox/post/167944683.
34. Winfield, "Debate over Latin Mass heats up."
35. See: Edward Pentin, *The Rigging of a Vatican Synod?* (San Francisco, CA: Ignatius Press, 2014). Pentin quoted one senior Vatican source saying of the midterm report from the Synod: "It was then that I realized. It wasn't like a jaw-dropping moment because one suspected. But this was it. This made me realize it's all about [Francis]. This is his proposal."
36. See: Lawler, *Lost Shepherd: How Pope Francis Is Misleading His Flock*, p. 84. Cardinal Pell is quoted in Chapter 4, which is titled, "Manipulating the Synod."
37. See, among others: "Making history on a Tuesday morning, with the Church's blessing," *New York Times*, December 19, 2023.
38. The third and four paragraphs of the document (released December 18, 2023) state: "As with the Holy Father's above-mentioned response to the *dubia* of two Cardinals, this Declaration remains firm on the traditional doctrine of the Church about marriage, not allowing any type of liturgical rite or blessing similar to a liturgical rite that can create confusion. The value of this document, however, is that it offers a specific and innovative contribution *to the pastoral meaning of blessings* [emphasis original], permitting a broadening and enrichment of the classical understanding of blessings, which is closely linked to a liturgical perspective. Such theological reflection, based on the pastoral vision of Pope Francis, implies a real development from what has been said about blessings in the Magisterium and the official texts of the Church. . . . It is precisely in this context that one can understand the possibility of blessing couples in irregular situations and same-sex couples without officially validating their status or changing in any way the Church's perennial teaching on marriage." See the full document posted at the Vatican website: https://

www.vatican.va/roman_curia/congregations/cfaith/documents/rc_ddf_doc_20231218_fiducia-supplicans_en.html.

39. See, among others: "German bishops divided sharply over same-sex blessing guidelines," Catholic News Agency, August 7, 2025.
40. "Fr. Murray calls on Pope Leo XIV to rescind *Fiducia Supplicans* and *Amoris Laetitia*, restore Latin Mass," *LifeSiteNews.com*, May 16, 2025.
41. Hollerich said this in a May 12 interview with the Italian publication *La Stampa*. See, among others: "The world over live with Raymond Arroyo," EWTN Television, May 12, 2025; and "Gay blessings 'will remain' under Pope Leo, Vatican doctrine chief says," *National Catholic Reporter*, July 7, 2025. The latter article quotes Tucho Fernández stating that the blessings will continue, but it also notes that he was not speaking with authority on behalf of Leo and the Vatican; he was giving an impromptu remark to a reporter. Once again, the chaos continues.
42. "A Filial and Apprehensive Supplication to His Holiness Pope Leo XIV," September 15, 2025, submitted by the American Society for the Defense of Tradition, Family, and Property, posted at https://www.tfp.org/a-filial-and-apprehensive-supplication-to-his-holiness-pope-leo-xiv/. Also see: Edward Pentin, "Catholic Coalition Asks Pope Leo XIV to Reject 'Powerful Lobby' Pushing Same-Sex Unions," *National Catholic Register*, September 18, 2025.
43. See, among others: Kristina Millare, "Italian bishop celebrates Mass for LGBT pilgrimage in Rome's Church of the Gesu," Catholic News Agency, September 6, 2025.
44. The media coverage by the *New York Times* and *Washington Post* was surprisingly accurate. For a balanced compilation and astute analysis, see: Bill Donohue, "Pope 'Disappoints' LGBTQ Catholics," Catholic League, September 8, 2025.
45. In an exclusive interview with Elise Ann Allen, Leo regretted that the West is obsessed with sexual issues (echoing a point he had made in his October 2012 interview with Francis Rocca). He told Allen: "I was asked about that already a couple of times during these first couple of months, about the LGBT issue. I recall something that a cardinal from the eastern part of the world said to me before I was pope, about 'the western world is fixated, obsessed with sexuality.'" See: "Pope Leo speaks to Crux's Elise Ann Allen about LGBTQ+ issues and the liturgy," *Crux*, September 18, 2025.
46. Giovanni Sadewo, "The network that led to Pope Leo XIV's election," *Crisis Magazine*, May 13, 2025.
47. Devin Watkins, "Pope Leo XIV: holiness of Curial officials should sustain Holy See," *Vatican News*, June 9, 2025.
48. "Pope asks forgiveness for slave trade," UPI, February 22, 1992.
49. See, among others: Pope Francis, "No longer slaves, but brothers and sisters," World Day of Peace Message, Vatican, December 8, 2014, posted at https://www.vatican.va/content/francesco/en/messages/peace/documents/papa-francesco_20141208_messaggio-xlviii-giornata-mondiale-pace-2015.html; Pope Francis, "Human trafficking is a plague on humanity," Vatican Radio, April 18, 2015; Ashley McGuire, "Pope Francis leads the charge against 21st century slavery," *Crux*, April 21, 2016; and Kengor, *The Worst of Indignities: The Church on Slavery*.

50. See: "Just one-third of U.S. Catholics agree with their church that Eucharist is body, blood of Christ," Pew Research Center, August 5, 2019, posted at https://www.pewresearch.org/short-reads/2019/08/05/transubstantiation-eucharist-u-s-catholics/.
51. A survey released in 2023 by the Center for Applied Research in the Apostolate (CARA) shows similar numbers. See, among others: "Survey finds majority of Catholics do believe in Real Presence," Aleteia.org, September 29, 2023.
52. For an informed discussion of this and other Augustine statements on the Eucharist, see: Tim Staples, "Did Tertullian and St. Augustine deny the Real Presence?," *Catholic Answers Magazine*, December 12, 2014. As Staples notes, some Protestants claim that Augustine only spoke of the Real Presence "figuratively" as akin to a "sign" or "symbol." But in fact, Augustine spoke of the Real Presence as both literal and figurative. Yes, it was a sign and symbol of Christ's sacrifice, but it also really represented the actual body and blood of Christ.
53. Ibid.
54. In this analysis, Augustine was using the Vulgate translation. Again, see: Staples, "Did Tertullian and St. Augustine deny the Real Presence?"
55. Pope Francis actually participated in the Corpus Christi procession in June 2024, though his poor health that year prohibited him from walking. He joined the celebration at the end of the procession. Even in years of better health, Francis had not usually walked in the procession. This was the first time that Francis had participated in the procession since 2017. See: "Pope Francis joins in Corpus Christi celebration in Rome for first time in years," *National Catholic Register*, June 2, 2024.
56. "Pope carries Eucharist in Roman Corpus Christi procession," Aleteia, June 22, 2025.
57. "Christ is God's answer to humanity's hunger, Pope Leo XIV affirms on Corpus Christi," Catholic News Agency, June 22, 2025.
58. "Pope Leo XIV addresses Centesimus Annus Foundation on Catholic social teaching," Catholic News Agency, May 17, 2025.
59. Nico Spuntoni, "Cardinal Goh: Leo will clarify doctrine," *New Daily Compass*, May 22, 2025.
60. See: Kristina Millare, "Cardinal Goh: Pope Leo XIV is the 'right person' to bring unity, balance to the Church," Catholic News Agency, May 20, 2025.
61. Spuntoni, "Cardinal Goh: Leo will clarify doctrine."
62. "'Doctrinal clarity, strong governance, thoughtful appointments' among Weigel's hopes for new papacy," *Our Sunday Visitor News*, May 9, 2025.
63. Robert Royal, "Augustine, Augustinianism, and the New Papal Moment," *The Catholic Thing*, May 19, 2025.
64. Fr. Brian A. Graebe, "A Time to Heal," *The Catholic Thing*, June 8, 2025.
65. Post on Cardinal Burke's X account, July 8, 2025, 7:52 p.m. See link: https://x.com/cardinalrlburke/status/1942733464245051854.
66. See among others: Courtney Mares, "Pope Leo XIV thanks Cardinal Burke, who clashed with Francis, for 50 years of priestly ministry," *National Catholic Register*, July 9, 2025.

67. "Pope Leo XVI speaks to Crux's Elise Ann Allen on relations with other churches," *Crux*, September 18, 2025.
68. Pope Leo on September 30, 2025, said of the Durbin controversy: "I am not terribly familiar with the particular case. I think it's important to look at the overall work that a senator has done during, if I'm not mistaken, in 40 years of service in the United States Senate. I understand the difficulty and the tensions. But I think as I myself have spoken in the past, it's important to look at many issues that are related to the teachings of the Church. Someone who says I'm against abortion but is in favor of the death penalty is not really pro-life. Someone who says I'm against abortion but I'm in agreement with the inhuman treatment of immigrants in the United States, I don't know if that's pro-life." The pope continued: "So they are very complex issues and I don't know if anyone has all the truth on them, but I would ask first and foremost that they would have respect for one another and that we search together both as human beings and in that case as American citizens and citizens of the state of Illinois, as well as Catholics, to say that we need to be close to all of these ethical issues. And to find the way forward as a Church. The Church teaching on each one of those issues is very clear." Clearly, Leo was trying to reach a compromise, but to many observers, he seemed to be equating abortion with immigration. And regardless, the position of the Church has long been to not give awards to pro-abortion politicians. "Pope Leo XIV Wades Into Durbin Debate," *National Catholic Register*, September 30, 2025. Leo's response on the run prompted some observers to urge him to not give interviews off the cuff, as Francis was notorious for doing. Perhaps Leo will learn from this example.
69. Victoria Cardiel, "Pope Leo XIV at the Regina Caeli: 'I ask you to sustain me with your prayer and closeness,'" Catholic News Agency, May 25, 2025.

Epilogue

1. See: Thomas C. Reeves, *America's Bishop: The Life and Times of Fulton J. Sheen* (San Francisco: Encounter Books, 2001).
2. Jonah McKeown, "Illinois newlyweds share their love of Venerable Fulton Sheen with Pope Leo XIV," *National Catholic Register*, July 13, 2025.
3. This story was often recounted by Sheen and his biographers. See, among others: Reeves, *America's Bishop*, pp. 45–46. For easy retrieval, see the short biography of Fulton Sheen posted at the website of the Catholic University of America: https://fulton-sheen.catholic.edu/bio/.
4. J. L. Spalding, *The Religious Mission of the Irish People and Catholic Colonization* (NY: The Catholic Publication Society, 1880), p. 58.
5. I said these things in my obituary on Francis published the day of his death. See: Paul Kengor, "The death of Pope Francis," *The American Spectator*, April 21, 2025.

Index

About the Author

Paul Kengor, Ph.D., is editor of *The American Spectator*, chief academic fellow at the Institute for Faith & Freedom, and professor of political science at Grove City College in Grove City, Pennsylvania.

Dr. Kengor's work has focused on Ronald Reagan, the Cold War, communism, conservatism, and Catholicism, and he is a *New York Times* bestselling author of over 20 books, including*: A Pope and a President, God and Ronald Reagan, The Divine Plan, The Stigmatists, Dupes,* and *The Devil and Karl Marx*. His classic, *The Crusader: Ronald Reagan and the Fall of Communism*, was the basis for the 2024 biopic, *Reagan*, starring Dennis Quaid. His articles have appeared in publications from the *Washington Post* and *USA Today* to the *Wall Street Journal* and *New York Times.*

Dr. Kengor is a frequent contributor and expert historian to sources from NEWSMAX to MSNBC, C-SPAN, EWTN, and FoxNews, and has been a guest on many TV shows and podcasts, including with Mark Levin, Jordan Peterson, Glenn Beck, and Prager University. A frequent public speaker, he has lectured at the Ronald Reagan Library, the Reagan Ranch Center, National Press Club, the John Paul II National Shrine, the Fulton Sheen Center, the Museum of the Bible, and at colleges from Notre Dame University to Princeton University.

Dr. Kengor received his master's degree from the American University's School of International Service in Washington, DC, and his doctorate from the University of Pittsburgh's Graduate School of Public and International Affairs. He holds an honorary doctorate from Franciscan University. He and his wife, Susan, have eight children.